THE EARLY HISTORY OF
RAILWAY
TUNNELS

Ill. 1 A railway enthusiast's dream or perhaps a nightmare for others. A view from the dining room of the tunnel cottage above the northern entrance to Clayton Tunnel in Sussex. *Author*

THE EARLY HISTORY OF RAILWAY TUNNELS

HUBERT PRAGNELL

AN IMPRINT OF PEN & SWORD BOOKS LTD.
YORKSHIRE – PHILADELPHIA

First published in Great Britain in 2024 by
Pen and Sword Transport
An imprint of
Pen & Sword Books Ltd.
Yorkshire - Philadelphia

Copyright © Hubert Pragnell, 2024

ISBN 978 1 39904 940 5

The right of Hubert Pragnell to be identified as author of this work has been asserted by him in accordance with the Copyright, Designs and Patents Act 1988.

A CIP catalogue record for this book is available from the British Library.

All rights reserved. No part of this book may be reproduced or transmitted in any form or by any means, electronic or mechanical including photocopying, recording or by any information storage and retrieval system, without permission from the Publisher in writing.

Typeset in 10/12 Palatino by SJmagic DESIGN SERVICES, India.

Printed and bound in the UK on paper from a sustainable source by CPI Group (UK) Ltd., Croydon. CR0 4YY.

Pen & Sword Books Ltd. incorporates the imprints of Pen & Sword Books: After the Battle, Archaeology, Atlas, Aviation, Battleground, Discovery, Family History, History, Maritime, Military, Politics, Select, Transport, True Crime, Fiction, Frontline Books, Leo Cooper, Praetorian Press, Seaforth Publishing, Wharncliffe and White Owl.

For a complete list of Pen & Sword titles please contact

PEN & SWORD BOOKS LIMITED
George House, Beevor Street, Off Pontefract Road, Hoyle Mill, Barnsley, South Yorkshire, England, S71 1HN.
E-mail: enquiries@pen-and-sword.co.uk
Website: www.pen-and-sword.co.uk

or

PEN AND SWORD BOOKS
1950 Lawrence Rd, Havertown, PA 19083, USA
E-mail: uspen-and-sword@casematepublishers.com
website: www.penandswordbooks.com

CONTENTS

List of Illustrations 8
Acknowledgements 11

Chapter 1   Introduction: The Fascination of the Railway Tunnel 13
                     The tunnel in railway history 14
                     Literature and landowners 17
                     Engineers 19
                     Travellers and observers 20
                     Sources 22

Chapter 2   The Need for a Railway Tunnel and the Problems
                     of Construction 26
                     Why build a Tunnel? 27
                     The criteria for tunnelling 27
                     The earliest railway tunnels 28
                     Robert Stephenson's early tunnels 29
                     The first tunnel for steam passenger haulage 31
                     Practical problems of tunnel construction on early
                     trunk routes 31
                     Bottlenecks 34
                     Environmental considerations 35
                     Collapse and abandonment 36
                     Celebration 37
                     Box Tunnel 38

Chapter 3   A Railway, a Landowner and his Estate 48
                     Proposing a railway 50
                     Definition of a landowner's domain 53
                     The nature of opposition? 54
                     Personal gain or national interest? 57
                     Eccentric and unusual objections 59
                     Brunel and landowners 63
                     Other planning interests or constraints 66
                     The impact of landowner opposition on the early railways 67
                     Shugborough and the Earl of Lichfield 69

Chapter 4	The Fascination of Early Railway Tunnels	78
	The early fascination with caves and grottoes	80
	The Castleton Cavern	82
	The attraction of early mining tunnels	83
	Joseph Williamson and his passion for tunnels	84
	The impact of a giant portal	85
	The Liverpool tunnels	86
	The earliest passenger experiences of tunnels elsewhere	90
	The role of the early railway guide	91
	The glorification of the London and Birmingham Railway	92
	The Great Western Railway	97
	Crossing the spine of England	100
	Dante's Inferno, or a modern vision of Hell	101
	A trip beneath cliffs and downs	102
	Fiction	105
	The tunnel in art	105
	The earliest railway illustrations	108
	Illustrating the London and Birmingham Railway	110
	The Romantic portal: Shugborough	119
	Bourne's Great Western Railway	121
	The tunnel portrait	127
Chapter 5	The Fear of a Railway Tunnel	135
	The fear of speed	135
	Vibration	136
	Public feelings and health	137
	How many tunnels to Brighton?	139
	The propaganda of fear and reassurance	140
	Ventilation, the views of Lardner, Herapath and Storer	141
	The fear of collapse and prolonged darkness	145
	The question of lighting	147
	The fear of collision	151
	Signalling	154
	Crime in the carriage	155
	Fear as entertainment	157
	The chance of death in a tunnel	158
	Enlightenment	160
Chapter 6	Style and Taste: Unnecessary Splendour	
	Classical or Castellated?	162
	Stephenson's tunnel portals	164
	Shugborough Tunnel drawings, the south portal	176
	The north portal	178
	Brunel's Tunnel Portals	180
	The Box Tunnel drawings	180

	The east portal	181
	The west portal	184
	The forgotten tunnel: Middle Hill	188
	Between Bath and Bristol: Twerton and Brislington tunnels	191
	The classic castellated portals: Bramhope and Red Hill	203
	The mystery of Clayton Tunnel	206
	The cost, a necessary architectural extravagance?	213
Chapter 7	Postscript	215
Glossary of Railway Companies and Abbreviations		219
Appendix 1	Architectural Terminology	220
Appendix 2	Tunnel Portals with Distinctive Architectural Character	224
Appendix 3	Accidents in Tunnels 1830–70 reported to the Board of Trade or in the Press	226
Appendix 4	Cost of Construction	230
Bibliography		231
Endnotes		246

LIST OF ILLUSTRATIONS

1. A railway enthusiast's dream where trains run beneath your sitting room, the view from Tunnel Cottage above Clayton Tunnel, Sussex. (Author)
2. Penge Tunnel from Sydenham Hill Station. (Author)
3. Tyler Hill Tunnel northern portal on the former Canterbury and Whitstable Railway opened in 1830.
4. View looking west from above the portal of Box Tunnel *c*.1840. J.C. Bourne's *Great Western Railway*, 1846.
5. Gisburn Hall Tunnel, former East Lancashire Railway. (Private photo)
6. Audley End Tunnel, Essex, south portal. (English Heritage)
7. Shugborough Tunnel north portal.
8. Clayton Tunnel north portal, Charles Harper, *The Brighton Road*, 1922.
9. Entrance to the tunnels at Edge Hill, Liverpool, T.T. Bury Ackermann, London, 1830. Science Museum Group.
10. Primrose Hill Tunnel, east portals from adjacent garden. (Railway Heritage Trust)
11. Celebrating Brunel's Birthday, *Daily Telegraph*, 12 April 1859.
12. Sevenoaks Tunnel watercolour, anon. (Science Museum Group)
13. Wapping Tunnel, Liverpool, T.T. Bury, Ackermann, 1838.
14. Tyler Hill Tunnel, Henry Lewin's *Early British Railways*, 1925.
15. Boxmoor Tunnel interior under construction, J.C. Bourne. (Science Museum Group)
16. Primrose Hill Tunnel, east portal 1836 wash, J.C. Bourne. (Science Museum Group)
17. Primrose Hill Tunnel, east portal, April 1837, J.C. Bourne. (Science Museum Group)
18. Primrose Hill Tunnel east portal, watercolour, J.C. Bourne, Elton Collection, Ironbridge Museum.
19. Primrose Hill Tunnel east portal, J.H. Nixon & J. Kleghorn, October 1837, coloured lithograph. (Science Museum Group)
20. Primrose Hill Tunnel, Edwin T. Dolby. (Science Museum Group)
21. Primrose Hill Tunnel west portal, 12 July 1848, Elton Collection, Ironbridge Museum.
22. Kilsby Tunnel working shaft, J.C. Bourne, *London & Birmingham Railway*, 1839.
23. Kilsby Tunnel giant air shaft, J.C. Bourne, *London & Birmingham Railway*, 1839.
24. Watford Tunnel, lithograph, T.T. Bury. (Science Museum Group)
25. Watford Tunnel south portal, 6 June 1837, J.C. Bourne 'Elton Collection' Ironbridge Museum.

LIST OF ILLUSTRATIONS • 9

26. Watford Tunnel south portal, J.C. Bourne, *London & Birmingham Railway*, 1839.
27. Linslade Tunnel north portal, anon. woodcut, *Drake's Road Book,* 1839.
28. Shugborough Tunnel north portal, anon, woodcut, *Illustrated London News*, 4 December 1847.
29. Shugborough Tunnel watercolour, anon. (Science Museum Group)
30. Tunnel No. 1. Frontispiece of J.C. Bourne's *Great Western Railway*, 1846.
31. Box Tunnel west portal under construction, pen & wash drawing, Bath, Royal Victoria Museum.
32. Box Tunnel West Portal, J.C. Bourne, *Great Western Railway*, 1846.
33. Box Tunnel West Portal, steel engraving, J. Shury, 1841.
34. Interior of Box Tunnel, J.C. Bourne, *Great Western Railway*, 1846.
35. Randall & Saunders, Quarrymen, letterhead, *c.*1850.
36. Eastern Portal of Shakespeare Cliff Tunnel, coloured lithograph, E.T. Dolby. (London, Science Museum)
37. Summit Tunnel on the Manchester & Leeds Railway, coloured lithograph, A.F. Tait, *Views on the Manchester & Leeds Railway*, 1845.
38. Elland Tunnel west portal, lithograph A.F. Tait, *Views on the Manchester & Leeds Railway*, 1845.
39. Milford Tunnel, watercolour, anon. (Elton Collection, Ironbridge Museum, AE 185.39)
40. Littlebury Tunnel, *Illustrated London News*, 2 August 1845.
41. Clayton Tunnel north portal, George Measom, *Guide to the London & Brighton Railway*, 1853.
42. Designs for Tunnel Fronts from S.C. Brees, *Railway Practice*, 1838.
43. Grosmont Tunnel, original north portal. (Private photo)
44. Primrose Hill Tunnel east portal, elevation signed by John Shaw, 26 June 1836. (Network Rail Archive)
45. Primrose Hill Tunnel east portal, frontispiece to S.W. Simms *Public Works*, 1838.
46. Primrose Hill original west portal. (Author)
47. Watford Tunnel south portal. (Private photo)
48. Kilsby Tunnel south portal. (Railway Heritage Trust)
49. Beechwood Tunnel east portal. (Private photo)
50. Summit or Littleborough Tunnel. (Jeff Mills)
51. Bramhope Tunnel south portal. (Science Museum Group)
52. Elland Tunnel west portal. (Science Museum Group)
53. Milford Tunnel north portal under construction, lithograph, anon. (Science Museum Group)
54. Shugborough Tunnel south portal, ink drawn elevation. (Staffordshire Records Office)
55. Shugborough Tunnel north portal, ink drawn elevation. (Staffordshire Records Office)
56. Shugborough Tunnel south portal. (Private photo)
57. Shugborough Tunnel northern portal. (Private photo)

58. Box Tunnel, elevation of east portal, watercolour elevation. (Network Rail Archive)
59. Box Tunnel east portal *c.*1920. (Private collection)
60. Box Tunnel west portal, watercolour elevation. (Network Rail Archive)
61. Box Tunnel west portal, architectural details. (Watercolour Network Rail Archive)
62. Middle Hill Tunnel, watercolour elevation. (Network Rail Archive)
63. Middle Hill Tunnel, Locomotive *King George V* posed beneath arch *c.*1935. (Railway Heritage Trust & Swindon Steam Museum)
64. Twerton Short Tunnel, watercolour elevation. (Network Rail Archive)
65. Twerton Long Tunnel east portal, watercolour elevation. (Network Rail Archive)
66. Twerton Long Tunnel west portal. (Network Rail Archive)
67. Twerton Long Tunnel east portal. (Private collection)
68. Saltford Tunnel, watercolour elevation. (Network Rail Archive)
69. Fox's Wood Tunnel, west portal. (Private collection)
70. St Anne's Park Tunnel or Tunnel No. 2, J.C. Bourne, *Great Western Railway*, 1846.
71. Tunnel No. 1, Brislington, sketch, 13 December 1835. (Brunel Archive, University Bristol)
72. Tunnel No. 1 before it was opened out in 1896. (Science Museum Group)
73. Bramhope Tunnel north portal. (Private photo)
74. Redhill Tunnel, Nottinghamshire. (Science Museum Group)
75. Clayton Tunnel north portal, watercolour in original form. (Elton Collection, Ironbridge Museum)
76. Clayton Tunnel north portal. (Author's photo)
77. Clayton Tunnel north portal showing inner arch and watchmen's cottage. (Author's photo)
78. Hipperholm Tunnel, watercolour elevation of portal design. (Network Rail Archive)
79. Hipperholm Tunnel, watercolour elevation of portal design. (Network Rail Archive)
80. Killiecrankie Tunnel. (Railway Heritage Trust)
81. Crystal Palace Tunnel sometimes known as Paxton's Tunnel. (Author's photo)

ACKNOWLEDGEMENTS

My thanks go first to Prof. Colin Divall of the University of York, who saw promise or 'light' in my initial proposal for research and encouraged me to think around the subject and broaden the aspect of my research, as well as my interest in railway history. He gave guidance and criticism and pointed me in new directions.

Also at York, Dr David Clayton, who cast a critical eye over my research and gave helpful advice.

I also owe a debt of gratitude to archivists and librarians in a number of institutions: Sophia Brothers, Keeper of the Science & Society Picture Library at the London Science Museum; Karolina Koziel, Curator, Image Library, Science Museum; Steven Brindle and John Minnis for suggesting various points of research on Brunel's works and sources in the National Archives, and early tunnels in eastern England. John in particular alerted me to documents on the north portal of Clayton Tunnel; Eleni Paparasileiou for helping me with lists of Brunel's numerous notebooks and sketchbooks in the Brunel Archive at the University of Bristol; Felicity Jones, Collections and Exhibitions Officer, Museums and Heritage, Swindon Borough Council; Tim Hedley-Jones at the Railway Heritage Trust for helping me to find pictures; Caroline Sampson, University of Leicester Special Collections Archivist.

Mike Chrimes at the Institution of Civil Engineers for helping me examine the involvement of Robert Stephenson in the tunnels on the London & Birmingham Railway; Carol Morgan in the archives of the Institution of Civil Engineers for fishing out early nineteenth-century railway books and journals, and all the library staff who have been so helpful and friendly; the staff at the Stafford & Staffordshire Record Office for making the Anson archive available, and allowing me to photograph the beautifully preserved elevations of Shugborough Tunnel; the staff of the National Railway Museum, York, for their help and advice in tracking down books and documents; Gillian Booth, Vicky Stretch & Laura Empson at Network Rail Archives, York, for allowing me to use illustrated material from the archive and answering my numerous enquiries; John Powell at the Ironbridge Gorge Museum and his successor, Joanne Smith, curator of the Elton Collection, for introducing me to several visual gems, including one that turned out to be an early watercolour of Clayton Tunnel north portal in its original state.

I must also thank David Porter of Clayton Tunnel North Portal Cottage, who allowed me to see the inside of what must be one of England's strangest residences, and Rob Kitchin-Smith, who has allowed me to see his research into the preservation and listing of historic railway structures including tunnel portals.

I am grateful to Graham Jackson for his patience in showing me how to master the formatting procedure of my computer, and for being ever ready to rescue me from the impulse to press the wrong key. Also to Charlotte Mitchell at Pen & Sword Publishing for carefully editing this into a readable work.

Finally to my wife Dorothea and daughter Charlotte who acted as footplate crew peering into the darkness for signals at red, as they checked my text for grammatical derailments.

DEDICATION

To my parents in memory of those happy days with me watching steam trains rushing into and out of tunnels. And to Dorothea who has been very patient during my many hours in archives or locked away at the computer.

Chapter 1
INTRODUCTION: THE FASCINATION OF THE RAILWAY TUNNEL

To all who have constructed a model railway layout or even just watched a miniature train rush past on a small piece of base-board, a tunnel is a basic ingredient to the effective layout. Tunnels create that air of mystery as the mind invokes the experience of rushing at speed into a cavern of smoky gloom and darkness. Those who aspire to an ambitious layout on different levels will build bridges and viaducts as well. Fascinating as they are to the model enthusiast or railway historian, they are all features passed at speed by the average traveller with hardly a nod of the head, unless distracted by the shriek of children surprised at the sudden onset of 'night time'. Perhaps the words of author John Steegman in his *Victorian Taste: A Study of the Art & Architecture from 1830 to 1870* aptly introduce the subject:

> To a far greater extent than the railway station however, tunnel mouths were from the beginning seen to provide an opportunity for the engineer-architect. Occasionally they proclaimed themselves for what they were, in classical simplicity. More often the novel and gigantic labour of piercing through a hill, the very thought of trains roaring through the dark earth to emerge safely into the light called for something more romantic to emphasise the heroic achievement. The Gothic ruin and the castellated fortress were made, over and over again, to serve this purpose. The tubular bridge at Conway, serving as an introduction to the great castle, shows how successful this marriage of the past with the present could sometimes be.[1]

These words were reinforced by Gordon Biddle in 2003, who said the 'Gothic was regarded as particularly appropriate to the awesome excitement that tunnels engendered in those incurable Romantics, the early Victorians'.[2] They often suffered one serious physical disadvantage: tunnel portals were usually hidden deep in cuttings, and so not easily visible, although some received architectural treatment that 'by their solidity, re-assured the timid traveller',[3] a point emphasised a few years earlier by Edgar Jones in his *Industrial Britain*.[4]

Although there has been a radical movement in railway studies and literature in recent years, away from technical studies to social studies, there has not been any serious study of the railway tunnel and its significance in the development of railways and its impact on travellers. The railway station has been studied, both for its architecture and for its contribution to social history; but tunnels, which were built in the same period, and which were often technically more complex to construct, have not received the same amount of attention. This book aims to fill this lacuna of social history.

It covers the period up to 1870, by which time most major trunk routes were open, and tunnels had become a familiar feature of railway travel. Of particular significance was the opening of the London Metropolitan Railway in 1863, which was used by thousands of people travelling into London on a daily basis and had a large number of tunnels, thereby conditioning people to tunnel travel.

This will not attempt to explain the science of tunnel engineering, which is the province of technical literature, but will focus instead on the social impact tunnelling made on the locality through the demands of labour and requirements for materials. The relationship between railway companies and landowners, often delicate, will be discussed as well as opposition from influential figures of the day.

I will look at how early railway tunnels made their way into art as well as into travellers' literature and diaries, and how the terror of a tunnel journey with its darkness, noise, vibration, flickering oil lamps for those lucky enough to be in a carriage, and sulphurous smells introduced a totally new dimension of human experience, and which could even inspire Victorian theatre.

The great tunnel portals, which emanate grandeur, were admired by spectators and passengers when they were first built, and they still impress today. However, behind these great edifices of stone or brick is the work of Victorian architects and engineers. A small proportion of drawings, watercolours and ink and wash elevations survive, which this book draws on, and many are works of art in their own right and allow us to glimpse this aspect of the early development of our railways.

THE TUNNEL IN RAILWAY HISTORY

In 1985 F.L.M. Thomson predicted that in a hundred years' time derelict nuclear power stations will have merged into the landscape and have acquired admirers, and notes 'certainly one does not have to look far today to find admirers of railway lines which were once denounced as raw scars on the scenery'.[5] New railway lines in the UK are still controversial, and are denounced as scars on the landscape. However, the recent restorations of St Pancras, King's Cross and Paddington demonstrate how now, in the early twenty-first century, these Victorian stations are deemed to have become part of London's cityscape, and significant sums of money are spent on preserving their original architecture. In contrast, to date Victorian tunnel portals have received comparatively little attention. Perhaps this is because the architecture of a tunnel portal is not as visible to the community as the architecture of a station: whereas people spend time in stations and on platforms, a tunnel portal is often barely visible from a moving train window, and the tunnels are often located in inaccessible areas, so few passers-by see the portals. Very few are at the end of station platforms.

The architecture of tunnels has largely been ignored by scholars, although as long ago as 1909 E.W. Twining published a paper in *Railway Magazine* on the original tunnels of the Great Western Railway. This was the first study of the architectural styles of the portals on the line between London and Bristol. Twining stated that no complete set of photographs had ever been published, 'and yet these tunnels, engineered and designed by I.K. Brunel … are in several respects remarkable and unique amongst work of their class'.[6] But for many years this was an isolated study. Christian Barman's *An Introduction to Railway Architecture* (1950) did not mention tunnels at all, although seven pages are devoted to the subject in his *Early British Railways*, published in the same year.[7] Even the Nikolaus Pevsner volumes of the *Buildings of England*, published from the 1950s, make cursory reference to tunnel portals: for example, Pevsner's *Sussex* volume, co-authored by the late Ian Nairn, dismisses Clayton Tunnel portal as 'yellow brick with a pointed arch for the trains to disappear into and castellated turrets'.[8] Even Historic England does not keep photographs of tunnel portals unless the structure is listed.

By the 1960s greater interest was being taken in our industrial heritage including that of railways, stimulated by the destruction of the Euston Arch in 1962, although the *Economist* called it a 'hobby for harmless lunatics'.[9] Three years later R.A. Buchanan's overview of industrial archaeology in Britain still largely ignored tunnels, as did Jack Simmons' first volume (1978) of his magisterial *The Railway in England and Wales 1830–1914*; Henry Holland's otherwise informative study, *Traveller's Architecture* (1971), only included a few drawings of the classical portals of Box and Shugborough tunnels, concentrating largely on station buildings.[10] Marcus Binney and David Pearce edited a fine black and white illustrated introductory volume by members and associates of Save Britain's Heritage, *Railway Architecture*, in 1979, but omit tunnels altogether although covering a wide range of buildings from stations to goods sheds.[11] In the 1980s Barrie Trinder's survey of industrial landscapes more or less ignored railway tunnels; Gordon Biddle and O.S. Nock listed a few tunnels in their official survey of Britain's railway heritage, but scarcely in proportion to the numbers still extant, let alone built.[12] But at least they mentioned tunnels: in contrast, in the 1990s John Summerson's excellent survey of Victorian architecture discussed railway termini but ignored other railway structures, while David Lloyd went as far as to exclude tunnels (along with bridges and viaducts) when he concluded that the architectural heritage of railways is impressive. At least Marilyn Palmer and Peter Neaverson argued that bridges and viaducts make a worthwhile contribution to the landscape.[13] Similarly Peter Burman and Michael Stratton's collection of essays on railway heritage scarcely mentioned tunnels.[14] As late as 2000 Stafford Linsley was suggesting that viaducts and bridges were 'under studied', but he made no mention of tunnels or their portals.[15] Some relief came with Gordon Biddle's huge survey, *Britain's Railway Buildings* (2003), which included many references to tunnels, but since this was a gazetteer Biddle could not give an extended treatment of every example.[16]

This comparative neglect of railway tunnels from the architectural point of view extends to periodical literature; a systematic search of publications such as *Industrial Archaeology Review*, *Industrial Archaeology*, *Industrial Archaeology News* and the *International Journal for the History of Engineering and Technology* (formerly the *Transactions of the Newcomen Society*) as far back as the 1960s confirms that there has been little interest in railway structures apart from stations, engine houses and warehouses.[17] Even the impact of the construction of tunnels on the local social and natural environment has been largely absent from scholarly journals such as *Southern History*, *Midland History* and *Northern History*, although the building of Balcombe Tunnel was the subject of a paper in 2000, in which Pat Milward admirably navigated the complex negotiations for the route from London to Brighton through the Sussex Weald.[18]

It would, however, be wrong to suggest that nothing has been written about railway tunnels, but the problem is that the quite extensive literature has been largely of a technical nature, and not on what we may define as the architectural, aesthetic and wider cultural aspects. This more technically orientated literature has a long lineage, and can be useful background for a cultural study. The earliest book published in Britain was Frederick Simm's *Practical Tunnelling* (1844), which discusses Bletchingley and Saltwood tunnels on which Simms worked. Subsequent editions referred to continental examples of great length, for instance the Mont Cenis, Switzerland, then 7½ miles long.[19] Another, much more recent, work with a good historical survey of European and American tunnelling is Gosta Sandstrom's *A History of Tunnelling* (1963).[20] A further book with much useful technical information is Alan Blower's *British Railway Tunnels* (1963), although the scholarly value is limited by a lack of references.[21] Other books not aimed at academic audiences nevertheless contain useful background detail – for instance Roy Anderson and Gregory Fox's *A Pictorial Record of LMS Architecture* (1981).[22] Even better is Adrian Vaughan's *Pictorial Record of Great Western Architecture* (1977), which combines a scholarly introduction with numerous photographs and sectional drawings of tunnels; Vaughan even occasionally passes judgement on aesthetic matters.[23] So too does Richard Morriss in his *The Archaeology of Railways* (1999), although once again the emphasis is largely technical.[24] Many of these predominantly technical books do at least stress the characteristics of what was a vernacular form of industrial architecture: here the fifteen volumes (excluding Ireland) of the series of regional railway histories originally published by David and Charles are invaluable when it comes to basic facts and figures.[25]

The human side of tunnelling has also received some scholarly attention: to build tunnels demanded massive labour sometimes on a scale even greater than in a dockyard. For example, David Brooke's *The Railway Navvy* (1983) takes the story of British labourers' expertise in railway construction far beyond our shores to the Crimea, and to their successors, the engineers on the Somme in the First World War. He also analyses where the labourers came from, and how many were working at specific locations. How engineers organised their work and the role of the contractors in the process is discussed in a series of papers edited by Mike Chrimes in *The Civil Engineering of Canals and Railways before 1850* (1998).[26] A rare dissertation on British railway tunnels also deals with the social consequences of the influx of labour, in this case on the small Kentish town of Sevenoaks in the 1860s.[27] Other aspects of the broader context of tunnel construction have also been studied, notably problems with landowners. For instance, a doctoral thesis by J.R. Hepple examines how landowners sometimes caused tunnels to be built in order to protect their estates, while Tim Warner demonstrates how a small area of land could become a battlefield between landowners and rival railway companies.[28] But in general the British railway tunnel as a cultural product – as a piece of infrastructure that embodies meanings beyond the railway's functional or utilitarian working – has very largely been ignored by scholars.

LITERATURE AND LANDOWNERS

Despite this neglect of the cultural aspects of railway tunnels, enough has been written elsewhere on the subject of large-scale infrastructure, and more particularly subterranean space, to demonstrate the value of a book on the subject. For example, the American historian Rosalind Williams has explored how in high and popular culture over at least two hundred years the tunnel was transformed from a physical experience, such as going into a cave or mine, into an imaginary journey through the underground world that expressed all sorts of wild hopes and fears, to the future prospect of tunnels forming access to subterranean houses as projected in Japan.[29] She starts her exploration by demonstrating through literary reference the fascination the underground, or in the literary context, the underworld, had since Virgil's Aeneas was guided by a Sybil through a cave to the subterranean Lake Avernus. In the early seventeenth century Francis Bacon saw the underground as the 'mine of natural knowledge' and therefore mining, hitherto the job of slaves, was to become the model for intellectual activity, even though some saw it as a violation of the 'earth's womb'.[30] This was to lead on one hand to the beginning of modern archaeology and geology in the eighteenth century, and on the other, to the increasing wild or imaginative literature of the Romantics in the nineteenth century. Quoting authors from Beckford's *Vathek*, to Jules Verne, H.G. Wells, Charles Kingsley and Edgar Allen Poe, Williams explores the cultural resonances of journeys into depths far beyond any earthly tunnelling. In *Vathek* (1787), Beckford creates a picture of a vast subterranean palace of fire supported by rows of columns and arcades, on one hand, a vision of Hell, and on the other, the remains of a lost civilisation.[31] She cites Kingsley's *Alton Locke* (1850), in which in a dream, the hero Alton, a tailor by trade, sees nobility in the challenge of tunnelling through a mountain, as an obstacle to be overcome, making it a metaphor for the abstract progress of civilisation. Success is seen as a victory for the civilising work of man with all hint of the brutal removed, whereas in reality hundreds may have died or fallen prey to injury.[32]

Williams goes on to introduce the age of the railway tunnel and how the accomplishments of the engineers could be romanticised through the writings of Samuel Smiles, who elevated the men featured in his *Lives of the Engineers* (1857) to great Victorian heroes. Yet, of course, as Williams points out, the real heroes were the railway navvies. Williams also examines the other great Victorian tunnel creation: the Paris sewers, where sub-surface brick tunnels expanded from under 100 miles in 1851 to 348 miles by 1870, much more than London at the time. The sewers were so impressive that Victor Hugo devotes chapters to them in *Les Miserables*, and they were so large that they could carry gas lines, steam pipes, water pipes and, later, telephone cables.[33] They have even retained the status of a visitor attraction in a way that caves and early mines had in eighteenth-century England.

Williams was writing from the American perspective where the development of the railway was across vastly greater spaces than in Britain, or at least England, where there was already a dense system of roads linking towns rarely more than 20 miles apart. In England, railways had to go as direct as possible, as land was expensive and labour relatively cheap, so enormous embankments, cuttings and tunnels were constructed. In contrast in America, where land was cheaper, tracks could circumvent natural obstacles rather than confront them, although there were tunnels such as the Hoosac in Massachusetts, under construction from 1851 and 1875, and at 4¾ miles, it was then the second longest in the world. Dug and blasted through solid rock, the Hoosac is an example of what Williams, citing Kenneth Clark, called 'heroic materialism'.[34]

Several other American scholars have looked at the American attitude to railways from the 1820s to the 1860s. David Nye argues that in the USA railways were seen as instances of the technological sublime – a term we shall shortly return to – spanning the wild landscape from coast to coast, and celebrated in enormous terminals, roundhouses, freight yards and of course tunnels such as the Hoosac.[35] Another, Leo Marx, has written at length about how the Americans saw the development of the railways as a challenge, the 'struggle between civilised man and barbarous uncultivated nature' where the railroad, animated by its powerful locomotives, appears to be the personification of America.[36] The railway was seen as unifying the States. Marx quotes the rhetorician David Webster, 'the ancients saw nothing like this till the present generation'.[37]

Over the past three or more decades the whole thrust of historical study of railways, along with that of other modes of transport, has been to emphasise the social context rather than the engineering context of railways.[38] Indeed, in 1993 Terry Gouvish had called for a greater place for the study of railway buildings in railway studies to rival what Stephan Multhesius had done for the terraced house.[39] As recently as 2007 Jack Knight observed in a paper addressed to engineers that 'railway tunnels are a superb legacy from the bygone age built by eminent Victorian engineers', although he suggested a lack of contemporary sources makes them a difficult subject for research.[40] But as already noted, historians have long been interested in the relationship between landowners and the selection of railway routes, and this offers a starting point for a much more detailed analysis of tunnels than has previously been attempted. As scholars such as Marilyn Palmer, Peter Neaverson and Ian Whyte observe, the nineteenth-century railway network caused some of the greatest visual intrusions upon the rural and urban landscape, which aroused strong feelings amongst the landed gentry.[41] Yet as J.R. Ward showed, landowners' opposition to railways was far from total, particularly once they realised the advantages that access to wider markets might offer for agricultural produce; furthermore landowners could often be bought off, either by money, or by the aesthetic enhancement of their estates, or by both means.[42] Other scholars have started to detail how the latter was realised, but the tunnel and its portals rarely feature.[43] The first part of this book analyses the power landowners had, first to force the construction of tunnels that were not necessary for practical reasons, and then to require railway companies to design portals in a way to fit their surroundings, despite additional costs.

As well as contributing to the historiography on railways and landowners, this book therefore has something to offer to the literature on the emergence of distinctive Victorian aesthetics: as J. Morduant Crook discussed back in 1987, the insistence of landowners on something more than strictly functional arguably facilitated, by the 1840s, a range of company house styles that combined utility with art.[44] Simon Heffer's recent history of early and mid-Victorian Britain notes that early railway architecture was often an attempt to combine functionality with craftsmanship and beauty, as a reaction against the great wave of factory building of the 1810s and 1820s. This happened in spite of Ruskin's plea not to waste money or effort in order to make railway stations attractive, an opinion he would no doubt have applied to tunnel portals as well.[45] In the final chapter we will examine a number of examples of tunnel portals showing the various styles of portal adapted by various railway companies where there was a delicate balance between the aesthetic, technical and financial considerations. Is it just an accident that all tunnel portals on the London and Birmingham Railway had a strong classical flavour? Why did the Great Western adopt the Gothic? What Mowl and Earnshaw wrote of lodge gates to the great estates – that they were intended to inculcate in the visitor a mood mingled of awe and anxiety – could equally be applied to some tunnel portals: this thesis demonstrates this point.[46]

ENGINEERS

The historian David Cole has argued that with regard to buildings, railway engineers had a very significant role in deciding which of the two dominant Victorian aesthetics, classicism or Gothic, to draw upon, and so engineers feature strongly in this thesis.[47] Obviously no tunnel portal ever achieved the sculptural magnificence of the Arch of Constantine, but most were of a greater dimension. Might there have been a connection, conscious or unconscious, with the work of renowned architects of the past? Did Robert Stephenson or Isambard Kingdom Brunel see their tunnels as standing alongside the masterpieces of Vanbrugh, Hawksmoor, Chambers, Rennie, or indeed Michelangelo, or the musical genius of Mozart, as Kenneth Clark suggested in his television series *Civilisation*?[48] He demonstrates the achievement of Brunel by displaying a lithograph by J.C. Bourne of a train in the Box Tunnel near Bath, where the size and grandeur of the tunnel suggested more a giant cave rather than something hewn by man. More recently Michael Freeman has traced the connection between Brunel and the romantic painter John Martin, claiming that some of the Great Western's grand tunnel porticoes are reflected in Martin's pictures of Egypt and Babylon.[49] He even cites the inclusion of a railway train in Martin's *Last Judgement* where the railway carriage carries the names of cities of the world bringing the troops to Armageddon.

Such studies might also help to resolve some of the points of dispute that have emerged in recent biographies about the balance of aesthetic and financial judgement exercised by some of the engineering giants and lesser ranks of the nineteenth century. Brunel is an excellent example, for writers such as L.T.C. Rolt, Adrian Vaughan, Angus Buchanan and Steven Brindle have variously judged him to have been a genius – including in the aesthetic realm. Yet his treatment of subordinates, and especially George Burge, the contract engineer for most of the Box Tunnel, has for the most part been overlooked, and may on the other hand portray him as a tyrannical spendthrift. Brindle has seen his weakness to be more in the field of technical matters such as locomotive design, atmospheric railway and of course the broad-gauge track, rather than working relationships.[50] Buchanan's otherwise wide-ranging study omits almost all discussion of tunnels with the notable – and well-known – exception of Box. He hints at Brunel's wish to oversee everything rather than delegate, even so his account leaves much unexplored. Would for example, any other engineer have made the western portal of Box Tunnel into such a Roman triumphal arch to proclaim conquest of the greatest natural obstruction on the line, Box Hill? And what of the other Brunel tunnels ignored by Buchanan and most other historians and contemporaries, such as Middle Hill Tunnel, just a few hundred yards west of Box, with its two portals almost the equal of Box? (It receives one line in E.T. MacDermot's classic *History of the Great Western Railway*.)[51] How much design freedom did engineers such as Brunel, Robert Stephenson and other lesser-known engineers such as Joseph Locke have; or to what extent were they acting under the instruction of the railway corporations that employed them and had to make a commercial success of the new technology of the railways within the cultural imperatives of late Georgian and early and mid-Victorian society.

TRAVELLERS AND OBSERVERS

Railways were built to be used, and so it is important to analyse how passengers – or at any rate potential passengers – understood the tunnel. Even those members of the public who were unlikely ever to use or perhaps even see a train found it hard to ignore the growing presence of the railway in the popular imagination, particularly once comparatively cheap lithographs and illustrated papers became more widely available from mid-century. Again this emphasis on the meanings inscribed into infrastructure by users and non-users is very much in tune with recent developments in the wider historiography of transport technologies.[52]

Serious scholarly interest in the experience of travelling by train is often dated to Wolfgang Schivelbusch's study, first published in the 1970s, although it has recently been criticised for largely ignoring any but the middle-class journey.[53] However there is no denying Schivelbusch's influence on the extensive literature on the cultural dimensions of travel by train and other modes. American scholar Julie Wosk's *Breaking Frame* discussed the influence of the visual arts on nineteenth-century technology including early railways in America, England and France, and how they were perceived by early travellers.[54] This perception was for many formed by the images created by artists and illustrators, especially the latter in popular journals. While Wosk mentions fear of tunnels, she cites other causes of fear beyond the initial one of speed: boiler explosions, fractured wheels, broken axles, and even sparks from the locomotive setting light to clothing, and many more causes leading to injury and possible death. She compared the way artists often depicted the railway, especially if in the service of railway companies: in England, as a triumph of engineering carefully grafted into the landscape and in America as the locomotive conquering the wide open interior, or as Leo Marx would have it, 'the machine in the garden'.[55] In contrast, illustrators often fed newspaper and journalistic reports, especially of accidents, with lurid and sometimes exaggerated woodcuts and engravings. On this theme Paul Fyfe produced a fascinating paper on their depiction in *Illustrated London News*, showing how middle-class fear of railway travel was stoked by graphic illustrations of potential disaster.[56]

Ralph Harrington, who has made a special study of the Victorian neuroses of railway travel, considered the specific fear aroused by travelling through tunnels in 'unsteady claustrophobic wooden boxes' with the doors locked.[57] As David Turnock has suggested, in the 1830s and 1840s the mere risk of crashes was enough to induce fear of death and injury on an untold scale, particularly within the confines of a tunnel.[58] Simon Bradley's recently published *The Railways, Nation, Network and People* is a masterly study of the history of the British railway system from earliest days to the present, in which the tunnel is set into the context of railway development as well as the experience of the travellers at all social levels, including their risks and anxieties, not least in unlit carriages in tunnels.[59] But these scholars are the exceptions that prove the rule: most historians have either ignored the experience, anticipated or actual, of travelling through tunnels or treated it superficially.

Much remains to be done before we have a detailed understanding of how the railway companies countered these deep-seated concerns. For example, in retrospect such worries seem out of all proportion to the real risks: so how did the railways persuade people that tunnels were not unsafe? And having conquered their initial fears, just how did passengers understand and experience the tunnel as they passed through in a dimly lit carriage or open wagon? Did some passengers really feel they were being devoured by a smoking monster, or taken into the jaws of Death? Did the prospect of getting from London to Birmingham or Bristol in under five hours by travelling at a speed through a dark and smoky cavern, as opposed to perhaps twenty hours by coach, appeal to the mass public? In a rare detailed study of working-class excursions before 1860, Susan Major has analysed the experience of travelling as part of the crowd in a packed train, but even she has not paid much attention to the specific emotions associated with tunnels.[60]

Although passengers and would-be passengers were just two groups within late Georgian and Victorian society, it is probably wrong to try to distinguish their perceptions of railway tunnels from those held by other social groups in Britain at the time. After all, Barman argued over sixty years ago that it was tunnels above all that caught the public imagination in the early days of railways; 'They represented the most adventurous aspect of engineering, the side that connected with the wildness and mystery of nature at its most untameable.'[61] Barman thus started to make intellectual connections between railways and wider cultural movements, particularly Romanticism: this was after all the age when intrepid visitors were discovering the beauty of the Lake District, Snowdonia and the Derbyshire Peaks, a beauty hinted at in the landscape paintings of Richard Wilson and Joseph Wright of Derby as early as the 1780s. Visitors could now experience Derbyshire by travelling through man-made caverns, perhaps less dangerous than wandering about the caverns in the neighbourhood of Matlock. But while these general points about railways and cultures have been made countless times by scholars, the role of the tunnel remains to be examined in detail. What for instance should we make of Brunel's treatment of tunnels on the Great Western between Bath and Bristol, where in several cases he deliberately gave portals the air of being hewn directly out of the rock in a primitive state, or the castellated entrance to a huge underworld?

Whilst viaducts have the power to uplift and were compared with the construction of Roman aqueducts, and proving that no valley, no matter its width, was beyond the task of the engineers, tunnels on the other hand might induce a feeling of horror or gloom, or surprise and awe, another dimension of the sublime. In the early days of railway construction some were adorned with portals that rival contemporary arches to dockyards, prisons and other public works in aesthetic quality. Some mixed stone and brick and elaborated the result with patterns of coloured masonry; perhaps a prime example, now sadly blackened, is the eastern portal of Primrose Hill Tunnel. The slow entry to this could surely arouse a sense of the sublime in the early traveller?

If some early passengers could write with excitement and enthusiasm for this new form of transport and its architecture, who were the detractors, and what part did they play in forming public opinion? What force did the cultural commentators such as Ruskin carry? He may have championed the painter Turner, who painted perhaps the most celebrated railway painting ever, *Rain, Steam and Speed*, however he hated railways and could not see that they were ever useful; 'but if they had to be, let nothing be spent upon them but what made for safety and speed'.[62] Another detractor was Cardinal Wiseman who, while condemning the bridge carrying the railway over Ludgate Hill, might well have appreciated the efforts of some railway companies to ornament their tunnel portals; after all as he said, 'Roman Emperors would have treated railways as they did aqueducts. They would have compelled them, whenever they came into public view, to harmonise with the architecture and to become even more monumental.'[63]

SOURCES

This book analyses the cultural shaping and reception of the Georgian and early Victorian railway tunnel by a range of historical actors, notably railway companies and their technical experts (the engineers), landowners, passengers and the 'general public'. It uses a wide range of sources, including correspondence, newspapers, journals and other periodicals. We must remember that all such accounts were written from a particular perspective, and so this section discusses some of the strengths and weaknesses of the main kinds of evidence used in this thesis.

Sources include drawings held in the National Archives, the Network Rail Archives and in local authority records offices. These allow us to examine tunnel portals as important contributions to early railway architecture, as well as admiring the drawings as masterpieces of subtle ink draughtsmanship and coloured wash in their own right. They remain for the most part little-known works of art; Kew, for example, holds a scaled drawing of the full length of Kilsby Tunnel, which is about 8ft long (not illustrated).[64] However, little is known about the drawing offices of consulting engineers and of the various railway companies. For example, Brunel's drawings of portals, discussed in Chapter 6, are arguably a fascinating insight into his fertile mind playing with various interpretations of castellated portals. Initial pencil and sometimes ink-lined sketches would have been placed in the hands of a team of draughtsmen, and without signatures or other identifying marks it is impossible to attribute the scaled colour-wash drawings to a particular person. Whoever drew these elevations such as those of Box Tunnel created minor works of art that remain as silent monuments to nineteenth-century engineering and the aesthetic imagination. The drawings certainly deserve a more prominent place in our industrial and architectural heritage, but they raise as many questions as they answer in regard to the creative process. The well-known names such as Brunel took overall responsibility and credit for the portals, but there are fleeting signs that individuals who have largely dropped out of history were the true progenitors, as discussed in Chapter 2. William H. Budden, who was appointed as an office assistant to the London and Birmingham Railway in May 1834, designed the sensational classical east portal of Primrose Hill but does not feature in contemporary dictionaries of architects and engineers.

The experience of early railway travellers can be accessed through general and railway-orientated periodicals, and in the case of the London and Birmingham and Great Western railways, substantial hardcover books intended for the library shelves rather than travellers' pockets. The earliest pocket journal, the *Railway Times*, started in the mid-1830s and reached a weekly circulation of 27,000 by 1845. Another was *Herapath's Railway Magazine and Annals of Science*, published monthly from September 1835.[65] They were joined by the *Railway Chronicle* in 1842. A series called 'Railway Rambles' appeared in the *Penny Magazine* from 1841, and in 1842 Sir Henry Cole wrote a series of 'Daily Excursions out of London' in the *Athenaeum*. Their success encouraged Cole to produce *The Railway Travellers Charts or Iron Road Books for Perusal on the Journeys* in 1864. These adopt a format like a traditional road map in which the route was in the form of a vertical strip down the centre of the page with descriptive text on either side and the marking of features such as towns, villages, churches, mansions, parks as well as those of the railway including stations, cuttings, gradients, bridges, viaducts and of course tunnels. Many railway companies were building comparatively short stretches of track, even if they were later amalgamated with a larger company, where there was little in the way of monumental architecture and sometimes even less in the way of dramatic or sublime landscape on which to comment.[66] A popular illustrated journal, especially for potential middle-class travellers, which from 1841 frequently reported on railways and included the construction of tunnels, was the *Illustrated London News*. Its tone was generally sympathetic to, even celebratory of, railways, and so it is a good source for understanding how tunnels became part of the established cultural order of the emerging Victorian middle class. Much more critical, especially in the 1840s, when the railway mania threatened the finances of significant parts of middle-class society, was *Punch*.

For the architectural profession *The Builder* was essential reading, and it introduced a special section on railway intelligence from the early 1840s. It was read beyond the confines of the architectural profession and certainly by rich landowners and the Church. Reference will therefore be made to *The Builder* as well as the other contemporary, *Civil Engineers and Architect's Journal*. Local newspapers reported on the progress of railway construction in their respective areas; often however newspapers copied each other, even *The Times* sometimes 'lifted' railway news from provincial newspapers. Some were biased depending on their editorial stance such as the Brighton papers reporting the construction of the London and Brighton Railway. It is likely that every reading member of the public would have known of the significance of Kilsby and Box tunnels.

Britton in his two volumes on the London and Birmingham Railway and Great Western Railway, illustrated by J.C. Bourne, extolled the monumentality of tunnels as well as bridges and viaducts. Another major work of this kind was Thomas Roscoe's guide to *The London and Birmingham Railway*, 1839, which includes descriptions of tunnel portals. This was after all a company whose achievements Roscoe compared with the building of the Great Wall of China. Sometimes library-bound handbooks and travel guides, like newspapers, copied passages from each other, especially those describing features on the London and Birmingham Railway. Another early publication was *Views on the Newcastle and Carlisle Railway*, 1839, consisting of a number of engravings by J.C. Carmichael and a descriptive text by John Blackmore.[67] Its aim was to open up to the traveller the wonders of what had hitherto been one of the most inhospitable areas of Britain, as well as suggesting that the careful channelling of the railway through the landscape actually enhanced it by its bridges and viaducts.

Images of the railway, particularly in the form of woodcuts and lithographs, were an early and vital ingredient in the promotion of early lines from the opening of the Stockton and Darlington Railway in 1825, and like the previously mentioned volumes, were meant for a wealthy middle-class audience. The depiction of the tunnel in these images, and its place in nineteenth-century popular art, will therefore be studied. Perhaps more with the intention of acting as reference to an actual journey were the paperback travel guides of George Measom. These took the form of a basic simple line map of the route down each page with notable sights on either side of the track and with small vignettes of objects of interest including tunnel portals. His guides for the Great Western Railway and London, Brighton and South Coast Railway are just two such examples.[68]

Tunnels and especially portals can be classed not only as part of our architectural heritage, but as a vital part of our historical heritage. The Institution of Civil Engineers has compiled a survey of historic monuments including stations, bridges, viaducts and tunnels, as well as factories and mills throughout Great Britain and Ireland. This has been published as a series of volumes, *Civil Engineering Heritage*, from 1981, which include photographs and reference to the records in the Institution's archive.[69] Whilst not complete, and relying to a certain extent on field-workers' reports, they have filled vital gaps left by the earlier editions of the *Buildings of England* edited by Pevsner. Other bodies such as Historic England and National Monuments Records have been compiling a photographic record of industrial buildings including those on the railway system. A similar collection of photographs applicable to British railways is being compiled at the National Railway Museum, York, but only a few tunnel portals are included.

To help locate these resources and other lesser-known locations of railway material historians must be grateful to the pioneering work of George Ottley's *Bibliography of British Railway History*, 1966, revised and updated most recently by the National Railway Museum in 1998. Cliff Edward's *Railway Record, a Guide to Sources*, 2001, is invaluable in listing the prefix of company documents in the National Archives, including those transferred from the Ministry of Transport. Finally a number of websites have appeared dealing with aspects of railways and tunnels and their history. Some appeal more to the eccentric enthusiast who likes walking through derelict tunnels or clambering across viaducts, but for the serious student of railway heritage perhaps the best is *Forgotten Relics of an Enterprising Age*, which lists hundreds of railway structures including tunnels, bridges and viaducts along with photographs and historic film.[70]

This book shows how the public's perception of early railway travel, and the tunnel experience in particular, was formed by newspapers, journals, popular literature and the views of public figures. However, whatever the fears, or fascination and novelty of the early railway tunnel, by the 1870s, indeed by 1863, with the opening of the first sub-surface underground railway in London, the railway tunnel largely became an accepted feature of a transport network that was essential to life in the heyday of Victorian Britain. So let the journey begin.

Ill. 2 The Southern portal of Penge Tunnel taken from the platform of Sydenham Hill Station. This took the line from Victoria to Chatham and Dover beneath Crystal Palace Hill. *Author*

Chapter 2
THE NEED FOR A RAILWAY TUNNEL AND THE PROBLEMS OF CONSTRUCTION

Before beginning our journey into the aesthetic qualities of this hitherto often neglected area of our architectural heritage, it is first necessary to give a clear definition of what we mean by a tunnel. A tunnel may be described as a passage driven through a barrier of earth or rock, although some were artificial in that they were filled-in excavations, covered with an arch. Both entrance faces would normally incorporate an arch, which usually dictated the shape of the bore throughout its length. There are numerous forms of faces, but most have the arch or portal flanked by projecting walls acting as buttresses. At their most elaborate they may be semicircular in the form of turrets with a projecting parapet, possibly crenellated or castellated at the ridge (see Appendix 1: architectural terminology). The face might be holding back a steep earthen slope that may pour water against the parapet so drainage gullies are normally inserted behind it. The parapet might be supported on a classical cornice with dentils or modillions beneath. Unless a tunnel is driven directly into an escarpment, the face will be approached through an earthen excavation or cutting. This will need to be held in place by abutments or wing walls on either side of the face. Depending on the width of the cutting, these abutments can be curved to terminate in an elegant pier, or extend as wings against the face of the hillside. If expenditure allows, tunnel faces could introduce considerable elaboration. The surface, if of stone, could be ashlar, i.e. smooth squared stones in regular courses. Perhaps less elegant, but suggesting a romantic or time-worn style, might be a rubble surface or irregular or rough undressed blocks. At its most elegant the surface might be built of rusticated surfaces with chamfered edges forming each course.

Arch shapes range from semicircular and elliptical to the pointed unique lancet Gothic at Shakespeare Cliff Tunnel, Kent. Occasionally the arch forms a horseshoe with the walls curving inwards at the base. The lip of the arch may be given characteristic features. Classical arches normally have their centre emphasised by a keystone with radiating voussoirs on either side. Brick arches may have several recessed edges that look effective when caught by a strong light. Occasionally the outer edge may be bevelled or supported by raised blocks of stone or brick like Romanesque billet moulding (see Appendix 1).

WHY BUILD A TUNNEL?
Because railway tunnels were usually on a totally different scale to those on the canals, it is worth asking the question, why build a railway tunnel? Basically, a railway contractor or constructor had less flexibility over the course of the tracks and not least the gradient. They could not be taken over hills in a series of locks nor curve or meander to the degree that a canal could and did. For example, Thackley Tunnel near Bradford was built through a spur in the Aire Valley where the meander of the river was too sharp for the railway to follow.[1] If, when completed, a canal tunnel suffered from slight water seepage it did not matter, especially from unlined rock, as it simply fell into water, but with a railway tunnel it could cause flooding. The rest of this chapter will consider the problems involved in building a tunnel and uses Box as a case study where most problems facing nineteenth-century railway tunnellers were encountered.

While the visual appeal of a tunnel is obviously in its portal and in certain cases the ventilation shafts that may be embellished, the architectural aspect and choice of style will be dealt with in Chapter 6, but in many cases the portals or entrances to such structures were relatively plain, and conforming to company policy or regional character. However, such is the appearance of the western portal of Brunel's Box Tunnel that it often finds a place in books on Victorian architecture, having secured an iconic status in Victorian England, and being known even to those who had little but the barest interest in railways or a fear of travelling through tunnels.

It is appropriate here to explain briefly the stages of constructing a railway tunnel without the expectation of hidden problems. First the land route is surveyed over the hill and fixed by means of sighting towers visible in a line from each other. A series of shafts are then cut at intervals to extract earth or rock, and eventually provide ventilation to the tunnel. When the designated depth is reached, calculated with a lead-weighted plumb line, cuttings are made in both directions to the next shaft using a nautical compass. The headings, initially no more than a working gallery, are reinforced with wooden props. Cutting is by pick and shovel through earth and clay, and gunpowder charges through rock. When the headings are linked including passages to both projected entrances, the working gallery is increased to the full height of the projected tunnel, which will be shaped into an arch using a pre-shaped matrix of wood wedged against the tunnel walls. Drainage channels or soakaways will be created to drain off groundwater. Then the tunnel will be lined by layers of brick or stone, two or more in thickness, and the shafts either filled or retained for ventilation. Finally the vertical wall of the entrance portals will be backfilled with earth so as to act as buttresses against the earth or hillside behind. Tunnelling consumed millions of bricks, and often, as at Penge Tunnel on the London, Chatham and Dover Railway, the excavated clay was taken to nearby kilns and fired into solid hard bricks for reuse in the tunnel.[2]

THE CRITERIA FOR TUNNELLING
Sir Francis Bond Head wrote in 1849 that in 'defining whether the line should proceed by tunnelling or cutting, the engineers' rule usually is to prefer the latter

for any depth less than sixty feet; after which it is generally cheaper to tunnel'.[3] This was certainly not observed as a strict rule; for example on the line to Brighton the northern approach to Merstham Tunnel is through a cutting nearly 2 miles long and over 100ft deep, one of the longest in Europe. If the decision was made in favour of a cutting rather than a tunnel, the cost could be even greater. For instance, the 2-mile long cutting at Tring cost £144,000, whereas the boring of the 1-mile long Watford Tunnel and 4 miles of track cost £138,000.[4] Edward Churton in his *The Rail Road Book of England*, published in 1851, gives a summary of the chief engineering features on each major route from London and remarks that the cuttings on the London and Birmingham Railway are hardly less impressive for their labour than the tunnels.[5] One travel guide emphasised that, had Linslade Tunnel on the London and Birmingham Railway not been built, the excavation would have been upwards of 80ft deep.[6] The greatest number occurred in the southern and western areas of England, with a few over 2 miles in length. Railway construction (whether a tunnel or cutting) in remote areas such as the Pennines required shanty towns for the construction workers, which was an additional construction cost.

THE EARLIEST RAILWAY TUNNELS

The question as to which is the oldest railway tunnel in Britain is not a straightforward one. As Trinder points out, it is not easy to establish, as the underground origins of mine wagon-ways make it difficult to distinguish between an adit that had a railway going into it, and a tunnel built for communication.[7] He cites a tunnel at East Kenton, Newcastle upon Tyne, built by Christopher Bedlington in 1796, with an entry and exit for the passage of a wagon-way, or hybrid railway. It was about 3 miles long, largely cut through solid rock from the mine at East Kenton to Scotswood, to transport coal to the Tyne.[8] In Wales there were a number of early mine and quarry tunnels for horse-drawn traffic. Perhaps the earliest was the Sirhowy, promoted in 1802 to transport iron from the Tredegar Ironworks to Newport, which involved tunnelling under a mountain to Ebbw Vale.[9] Another early tunnel is Penrhyn, on the Penrhyn quarry railway built between 1798 and 1801 for a gauge of only 2ft; it is now part of a cycle track.[10]

If one adopts as the definition of 'railway tunnel' a tunnel through which a steam locomotive passed from its first day of operation, then the Pentrebach Tunnel near Merthyr Tydfil, opened in 1804, may claim the honour. Samuel Humphrey, owner of an ironworks at Penydarren, commissioned the Cornish engineer Richard Trevithick to design a steam locomotive that ran on iron rails. The railway ran from the ironworks to the canal at Abercynon that linked the Glamorgan Canal to Cardiff. On its first run the locomotive is said to have pulled 10 tons of iron and a number of passengers, although it did not subsequently prove a success.[11] The trackbed is now a cycle track and the tunnel has been blocked.[12]

In Derbyshire, the Cromford and High Peak Railroad or Tramway may lay claim to four early tunnels in the conventional sense.[13] It was an ambitious venture passed by Parliament on 2 May 1825; it was over 33 miles long and climbed to 1,266ft, to transport stone and minerals from Whaley Bridge to High Peak Junction on the Cromford Canal, and was one of the earliest mineral railways to use iron rails. It was engineered by Josias Jessup and Benjamin Outram. The carriages were to be propelled in sections by rope from stationary engines on the nine inclines and by horse on the flat sections. Besides the tunnels there were about sixty bridges crossing highways, and many cuttings and embankments of limestone.[14]

ROBERT STEPHENSON'S EARLY TUNNELS

Technically the first public railway to open with a tunnel was the Canterbury and Whitstable Railway in May 1830 with a half mile single bore beneath Tyler Hill (Ill. 3). However, due to steep gradients it was not used throughout by steam-hauled trains until 1846. It has been claimed, but without foundation, that the directors of the Canterbury and Whitstable Railway Company insisted on a tunnel for the excitement of the journey and to attract passengers by its novelty. The Resident Engineer was John Dixon, who had been sent from the Stockton and Darlington Railway; George Stephenson only came down briefly on several occasions.[15] As a result of the route involving a tunnel, the final cost of construction was £71,000, instead of £31,000, which was the initial estimate for construction. The *Kent Herald* in 1827 reported what must be the earliest ever report of the construction of a railway tunnel:

> On Sunday morning last about half-past two o'clock the workmen employed in the tunnel of the Canterbury and Whitstable Railway effected a communication with the north and south ends by means of cutting an aperture about sixty-five yards in length. The situation of the excavators has been truly distressing for some time in consequence of the stagnated state of the air, but the great rush of the purer element has entirely cleared the tunnel. It appears so nice was the calculation of the engineer that although the line of the rail is more than 2,400 feet in length it has been preserved to within an inch.[16]

Though a public railway, the brick tunnel mouths were undistinguished, even if the tunnel could lay claim to being the oldest purpose-built railway tunnel in the world.[17]

At Liverpool there were two tunnels cut for the Liverpool and Manchester Railway, one from Edge Hill to a passenger terminus at Crown Street terminus, and another for goods only, to the docks at Wapping. Both opened in September 1830 with rope haulage for carriages and wagons (Ill. 9). The passenger station at Crown Street proved to be short-lived as it was so popular that there were calls for a new and larger terminal station. The new station, nearer to the centre of the city, was built at Lime Street, and opened in August 1836.[18] The new passenger line necessitated a tunnel over a mile long from Edge Hill, again for rope haulage.[19] One goods route from Edge Hill to the docks through the Wapping tunnel was not enough, and so in 1844 another tunnel was proposed, to lead from Edge Hill to the docks at the north end of the town.[20] This second goods line, through two tunnels, the Victoria and Waterloo, to the goods station opened on 1 August 1849.[21] It was later to take 'ocean liner' expresses direct to the quayside with rope haulage until 1890.[22]

Two other tunnels by Robert Stephenson were the short Grosmont Tunnel for the then horse-drawn Whitby and Pickering Railway, opened in 1832, and the Glenfield Tunnel, on the Leicester and Swannington Railway, also opened in 1832. At Grosmont the portals were designed by John Cass Birkinshaw. Later a large tunnel for double tracks was cut alongside, and the original tunnel has now become a passage for visitors to the preserved locomotive shed for the North York Moors Railway. The Glenfield Tunnel was for steam-hauled coal traffic. Stephenson recommended a tunnel rather than inclined planes over Glenfield Ridge. Before trial borings were sunk it was assumed that the structure was rock and would not need lining. However, it soon transpired that the workmen were boring through hundreds of yards of sand. As a result Stephenson advised that the roof and walls would have to be brick lined to a depth of up to 18in in parts to contain the sand. This meant the tunnel cost over £7,000 in excess of the estimate.[23] The line, which was never economic, closed to passenger traffic in 1930 and goods in 1952.

Ill. 3 Tyler Hill Tunnel's now blocked north portal for the Canterbury and Whitstable Railway opened in May 1830. *Author*

THE FIRST TUNNEL FOR STEAM PASSENGER HAULAGE
Marsh Lane tunnel, Leeds, just to the south of the original terminus of the Leeds and Selby Railway, was opened in September 1834 for steam-hauled trains from the start of operations. Only 700 yards long, it is said to have cost many lives in its construction. It was very smoky, and to allay public fear, the walls were at first whitewashed and copper reflectors were added to improve lighting. However, it was opened out in 1894 to be replaced by a five-track cutting. Were it to have survived it would lay claim to be the oldest tunnel for steam haulage from the start.[24] However, those tunnels on the London and Birmingham Railway opened in 1838 were used by steam from the start, and may therefore be presumed to be the oldest still used for their original purpose. While Marsh Lane may claim therefore to be the oldest tunnel for conventional-gauge steam haulage, the partial conversion of the Strood Canal Tunnel to take a single track for the South Eastern Railway between Gravesend and Rochester in 1844 may, since it was opened in 1802, allow it to claim the distinction of the oldest large-dimension tunnel to be used for a railway.[25] The canal was drained to provide space for a second track in 1850.[26]

Scotland, with its challenging terrain, has few tunnels. Engineers preferred communication along the bed of valleys rather than attempting tunnelling through high hills or mountains with obvious problems of ventilation. Among the earliest tunnels are those on the Edinburgh, Leith and Newhaven Railway, which were given the Royal Assent in August 1836.[27] Two short tunnels at Rodney Street and Trinity Street were opened with the line from Canonmills to Newhaven in August 1842. However the last part of the route, opened in 1847, was by rope haulage through the steep inclined 1,000-yard tunnel at Scotland Street beneath Edinburgh New Town. The tunnel was gas-lit, causing objection from residents living above a gas-lit tunnel.[28]

Finally, cutting or boring through hills was one thing, the challenge to tunnel beneath a river was another. The first underwater tunnel anywhere in the world to be successfully opened after construction was hindered by flooding was the Thames Tunnel between Wapping and Rotherhithe, opened as a foot tunnel in 1843. In 1869 it was converted to a tunnel for the East London Railway. The River Severn, with its wide estuary, was a barrier and a challenge to railway engineers. The first attempt was made to bore a tunnel beneath the Severn at Newnham in 1845, but this failed through lack of funds.[29] It was not until the late 1870s that the Great Western Railway set about shortening the route between Bristol and Cardiff with the opening of the Severn Tunnel in 1887, having overcome hidden springs and flooding.

PRACTICAL PROBLEMS OF TUNNEL CONSTRUCTION ON EARLY TRUNK ROUTES
Frederick Simms, in the preface to the third edition of his *Practical Tunnelling*, wrote:

> Every tunnel has its own peculiar history; in execution, difficulties are continually occurring which cannot be foreseen in the estimates.

Contingencies are met with which require all the resources of mechanical science, and all the experience and enterprise of engineers and contractors, so leading the work to a successful conclusion.[30]

He was resident engineer for the South Eastern Railway from Tonbridge to Dover and used Bletchingley and his other tunnel at Saltwood near Folkestone as exemplars for his *Practical Tunnelling – Public Works in Great Britain*, 1844. He had, of course, written this after lessons had been learned from the construction of the long tunnels at Kilsby and Box, where construction was almost abandoned due to flooding, prolonging the projects by over a year, and thus increasing the cost of construction. For the purpose of this section it is best to confine my study principally to the problems on three early railway projects: the London and Birmingham, London and Brighton, and South Eastern Railway.

The cost of construction of a tunnel was very different to almost any other type of structure. In the case of a bridge, as with a house or public building, the costing for the preliminary excavation for foundations and subsequent quantities of materials could be roughly quantified; also the construction time could be roughly predicted, as well as the size of the labour force needed. A tunnel was different. According to a contemporary *Encyclopaedia Britannica*, canal tunnels could be constructed for less than £4 per yard, while railway tunnels of much larger bore varied from about £20 per yard in sandstone rock (which is easy to excavate and able to stand up without any lining of brickwork or masonry) – to £140 per yard in very loose ground (such as quicksand, which may require a lining of brickwork 27in thick).[31] When a decision was taken to bore a tunnel through a hill, a preliminary geological survey would be made that gave a rough idea of what lay beneath the ground.[32] If it was soft clay or gravel, it might mean that contractors could assume a brick-lined tunnel throughout, and depending on the length, make a rough estimate of time needed for construction. On the London and Brighton Railway no water was expected in the tunnels, however, in fact it frequently obstructed operations especially during winter months and was one of the reasons for costs to overrun.[33] At Primrose Hill on the London and Birmingham Railway the brick lining had to be increased in thickness and using special mortar due to the dampness of the clay.

At Kilsby Tunnel estimates of construction time were made that ultimately proved to be over two years out due to hidden springs unleashing vast quantities of water. Stephenson, in evidence to the House of Lords in 1835, said he could see no objection to a tunnel 20 miles long.[34] In March 1837 Stephenson had confidently stated 'that unless very unexpected quantity of water should be found, where at present no sign of it exists, we may reckon upon this tunnel being opened from end to end in about seventy weeks'.[35] Francis Head, in Chapter 1 of his *Stokers and Pokers*, 1849, devotes eight pages to the difficulties encountered in the construction of Kilsby Tunnel, where the 'latent difficulties which occasionally evade the investigations, baffle the calculations, and which, by chastening as well as humbling, eventually elevate the mind of every man of science who had practically to contend with the hidden secrets of the crust of the earth we inhabit'.[36]

At nearly 1½ miles long, the Kilsby Tunnel was the longest proposed railway tunnel up to then, with the sinking of two large ventilation shafts as well as seven subsidiary shafts. Throughout the work, 1,300 men were constantly employed along with twelve steam pumping engines working day and night, until quicksand stopped progress. John Francis wrote of Robert Stephenson's direction:

> Mr Stephenson then undertook the task and confronted the difficulty with a most inventive spirit. Though the water rose and covered the works, though the pumping apparatus appeared insufficient, though the directors were inclined to abandon the task, the engineer, by aid of their capital and his skill … raised 1,800 gallons of water per minute night and day for eight months, from the quicksand alone, and infused into the workmen so much of his own energy, that when another of their comrades were killed by their side, they merely threw the body out of sight, and forgot his death in their exertion.[37]

Smiles, in his *Life of George Stephenson*, described it with a little more colour: 'the traveller in India could scarcely be more alarmed at the sudden sight of a crouching tiger before him than the contractor was at the unexpected appearance of this invisible enemy'.[38] According to *The Times*, the contractor subsequently 'died of fright at the responsibility he had assumed'.[39] The news of the tunnel's progress was reported in newspapers and professional journals as if all the nation was watching with keen interest, comparable to a modern horse race. One such from the *Railway Times* reported 'one hundred and fifty yards of Kilsby Tunnel were completed last month, one hundred and seventy-four the month preceding leaving only seven hundred and fifty-six yards to accomplish'.[40] By the time it was completed some 36 million bricks had been used. The lining had been intended to be 18in thick but was increased to 27in to resist the seepage of water.[41]

The construction of the London and Brighton Railway from 1838 was frequently compared with the much longer London and Birmingham Railway. It was often described as 'Herculean'. There were frequent reports of the progress of what *The Times* described as 'this great undertaking'.[42] For example, 'Clayton cutting exceeds the Tring cutting both in length and depth, with the addition of a tunnel 1,700 yards long; Balcombe cutting exceeds Tring in depth with a tunnel half a mile in length on a curve. Merstham exceeds Tring with the addition of a tunnel three quarters of a mile long.'[43] At Clayton Tunnel 'impossible impossibilities' had to be overcome.[44] The *Brighton Guardian* doubted whether the line could ever be built without diversion to avoid 'these dropsical hills'. On the other hand, the rival *Brighton Herald* saw no cause for alarm as Mr Rastrick was confident of draining the water into neighbouring brooks. Perhaps as a dig against its rival, the *Herald* claimed that those who had little faith in the project were those who were willing to attack Brighton and its prosperity.[45] At Balcombe Tunnel the water was found in greater quantity than anticipated.[46] The ground described by Rastrick 'swells and effloresces as soon as exposed to air',[47] and he frequently records in his diary for 1840 the problems of excessive water in Merstham Tunnel.[48] In spite of this the 50 mile line was opened in September 1841 'for the conveyance of passengers, parcels and private carriages', which was remarkably quick for the vast engineering involved.[49]

The South Eastern Railway's route between Folkestone and Dover involved the cutting of one short and two long tunnels through the crumbling chalk under Abbot's Cliff and Shakespeare Cliff. Such was the enormity of the task that in January 1840 there were no fewer than 10,000 men working between Dover and Folkestone.[50] At Abbot's Cliff there were frequent falls of rock from the chalk cliffs blocking the entrance to the tunnel,[51] while at Shakespeare Cliff, because the rock was so unstable, the tunnel was constructed of twin single-track bores, about 12ft apart, with pointed portals in the shape of slender Gothic arches to reduce the pressure from the chalk above (Ill. 36). These are about 30ft high set within a brick retaining wall without any other embellishment. The choice of this unique design was to reduce the pressure exerted on the crown of the arches by the treacherous shifting chalk.[52] To facilitate excavation, seven adits were sunk diagonally from the cliff face to allow the extraction of excavated chalk. They are brick-lined throughout 'except where the hardness of the chalk does not require such support'.[53] The tunnel is ventilated by seven shafts, which make a curious sight in perfect alignments across the bleak clifftop.

Between the tunnels extensive areas of cliff had to be blasted to clear a path. According to *The Builder* in April 1843, 'many people believe it would be either impossible to complete this portion of the railway according to Mr Cubitt's original plan, or that if finished, it would be liable to be overcome by the fall of the cliff above it'.[54] Those consulted included Sir John Hershall, then Astronomer Royal and General Pashley of the Ordnance Department. As a result, a substantial portion of the cliff was blown apart on 26 January 1843.[55] Naturally, the public were warned and *The Builder* commented:

> most of the lower orders of Dover watched from their houses or retired in apprehension to a safe distance in the hills, but there were many brave or foolhardy souls, including ladies, whose curiosity led them to the very edge of the nearby cliffs from which they would normally have shrunk in terror.[56]

The tracks were originally carried on a viaduct of heavy beams of timber framed and bolted together. *The Builder* described it as one of the most gigantic pieces of railway, about ¾ mile in length, up to 70ft in height, and about 25ft in thickness at the foundation.[57] It was subsequently replaced by a high stone wall or promenade for the tracks.[58]

BOTTLENECKS

When the first railways were cut it was obviously speculation as to how much trade they would receive, not just over a year but in a day. With only two tracks, main trunk routes soon reached a point where more capacity would be needed. This was easily accomplished where there were few physical impediments, however all main trunk routes had viaducts, bridges and tunnels that might need duplication. In the case of the London and Birmingham Railway, which was absorbed into the London and North Western Railway, a proposal was mooted as early as 1857 to lay an extra track from the north end of Watford Tunnel to Bletchley. *The Times* reported:

> in the case of the two short tunnels at Leighton and near Tring, some additional land would be required ... It was not thought necessary to build a third line through Watford Tunnel as ... no practical inconvenience would be experienced or delay caused by stopping the trains at the end of the north end instead of allowing them to travel slowly for a mile and a half.[59]

In fact, Watford Tunnel would not have been wide enough for an additional track, and a parallel bore was cut in the 1870s. On the busy London and Brighton Railway a start was made with a duplicate bore at Merstham Tunnel. However plans to continue the duplication with a second bore at Balcombe in 1903 were still-born, and the Balcombe Tunnel and Viaduct and Clayton Tunnel have been minor bottlenecks ever since.[60] On the former Great Northern Railway the tracks between King's Cross and Peterborough have been duplicated in many places and tunnels duplicated outside King's Cross and at Hadley Wood, although bottlenecks remain at Welwyn with the two short tunnels and viaduct.

ENVIRONMENTAL CONSIDERATIONS

Hills were, of course, the major obstacle to the swift cutting of a railway, but a no less important obstacle might be the sensitivity of a particular urban environment, whether from historical, archaeological or scenic circumstances. Brunel faced this problem at Bath with the tracks curving between an embankment through the Sydney Gardens with appropriately designed bridges and a cut-and-cover tunnel. Another historically sensitive town was Tunbridge Wells on the South Eastern Railway from Tonbridge to Hastings. The citizens, ever conscious of the beauty and peace of their former spa, were naturally a little concerned at the impact the railway would make on the landscape. Unlike Bath, there was not the room to take the railway on a viaduct round the extremity of the town since it lay on two sides of a narrow valley. *The Builder* noted:

> At considerable depth, it passes under the very centre of it. From the former station outside of the town, it branches some 250 yards through a deep cutting where it enters a tunnel 800 yards in length, which within 70 or 80 yards, bringing the visitor to the terminus ... The tunnel forms two curves and is said to be built with materials of great solidity ... The existence of the railway at Tunbridge Wells is scarcely perceptible.[61]

The line constructed in 1845 was therefore driven from one hill to another with the station at the lowest point of the valley between two tunnels. The station building was in the Italianate style with a rendered façade with corner rustication. The two tunnel portals were of brick with Italianate finishing to the buttresses.[62]

A new aspect to railway construction was the way in which the cutting of embankments and boring of tunnels revealed the geological structure of the area. At a meeting of the Institution of Civil Engineers in 1841 a Mr Sopwith brought members' attention to different geological strata presented by the railway cuttings and other works in progress; he gave as an example the North Midland Railway line, where the 'crops of the various seams of coal, with the interspersing strata, were displayed in the clearest manner, developing the geological structure of the country which the railway traverses'.[63] The cutting of Campden Tunnel on the Great Western also exposed a large number of fossils, while Red Hill in Leicestershire exposed a Roman camp. At Bletchingley Tunnel, Surrey, described as one of the most interesting sites for geologists, the resident engineer, F.W. Simms, was 'in possession of several interesting fossils'.[64]

Robert Stephenson's Chester and Holyhead Railway was a masterpiece of construction paying heed to the historical environment as well as fitting into the scenic coastline of North Wales and the backdrop of Snowdonia. At Conway it had to cut a sensitive path alongside the medieval town wall and castle as well as tunnelling through mountains and cliff-sides, exposure to the sea protected only by a stone wall. There will never be agreement as to whether the Conway Bridge should be classed as a tunnel or a bridge; it is certainly not a tunnel if the definition of a tunnel is a passage through earth or rock (renumber). Stephenson's construction was an iron tube hung between castellated towers.[65] It may best be described as a tunnel over the open water. Its design excited admiration from many quarters.

COLLAPSE AND ABANDONMENT

To the directors or proprietors of a railway company the ultimate fear was that of the collapse of a bridge, viaduct or tunnel with its possible consequences for travellers or maintenance workers. Most serious is obviously the collapse of a tunnel roof or lining. In the 1840s there are increasing references in the newspapers and journals such as *The Builder* to bad and hasty workmanship resulting in subsidence and collapse of railway structures; 1846 seemed to be a particularly unfortunate year for disasters. The normal or first assumption when such a accident occurred was one of bad workmanship or materials, as when the bridge over Oxford Road, Reading, collapsed. *The Builder* was quick to blame 'extreme haste in construction and the mixture of cement'.[66] Similar circumstances may have caused the collapse of the short tunnel on the Newcastle and North Shields line where the use of ordinary lime mortar instead of cement was blamed.[67] At Bramhope Tunnel in 1854 a collapse of rock actually hit a train and buried two locomotives. Although there were many injuries, there were no deaths. On another occasion at Bramhope twenty-four workers were killed. Given the complexities of constructing a tunnel, it is likely almost every tunnel claimed fatalities.[68]

On 3 March 1895 St Katherine's Tunnel, Guildford, collapsed. In the preface to the third edition of *Practical Tunnelling* Frederick Simmons claims the cause of this collapse was poor design and construction. He claimed it was due to water percolating from the drains of a house situated on the hill above causing structural timbers of the tunnel to rot, thereby weakening the brick arch.[69] The tunnel was built in 1849, at the end of a decade when perhaps due to the speed of railway construction shoddy workmanship became more commonplace. It is perhaps no coincidence that more faults in structures such as viaducts, bridges and tunnels were also reported in this decade.

If Kilsby tested the patience and ingenuity of Stephenson and Box that of Brunel, almost to the point of abandonment, was there ever an occasion where projects were abandoned? There were rare occasions such as that of Charlestown on the Leeds and Bradford Railway. Whishaw noted that work had stopped after considerable outlay, 'it being in a state totally unsafe for workmen to proceed, owing to a debris of the hill through which it was attempted to be driven, the side walls have collapsed and the masonry in parts literally crushed to pieces'.[70] As a result the route was realigned without tunnelling.

Perhaps foreseeing difficulties in construction, the proprietors of the Hereford and Worcester Railway proposed a route between the two towns running to the north of the Malvern Hills. This proposed route would have deprived the spa town of Great Malvern of a rail link. However, the Great Malvern town council insisted on a railway link. This meant driving the line through the hard rock of the hills in a single-bore tunnel near Colwall. The construction caused two firms to go bankrupt and the venture to be almost abandoned. The line was finally opened in 1861, but the tunnel 'built on a 1 in 28 gradient' was often flooded and filled with smoke. A loop-line avoiding the tunnel had been proposed as early as 1864.[71]

CELEBRATION

To the men who had undertaken such difficult labours there can have been few more satisfying sights than the pristine brickwork of a newly completed tunnel before the walls were quickly coated with layers of soot from the passing locomotives. The construction gangs might have celebrated with rounds of drinking in the local taverns, while the directors of the company and worthies of the county might have sat down to a banquet in the subterranean hall, having perhaps first processed from end to end behind a band. Just occasionally the celebrations would encompass everyone. On the opening of the Leeds and Bradford Railway in 1846, about 1,000 men employed by the contractors were 'liberally supplied with substantial dinners at inns in Leeds', while on the opening of the Glasgow, Paisley and Greenock in 1841, the directors provided about 90 gallons of whisky and then failed to see that it was shared out equitably among the 300–400 men. Inevitably some were greedy and a 'general battle followed'.[72] In spite of the numerous difficulties the success of the early railway tunnellers boosted confidence in tunnelling in such a remarkable way that there was a proposal to tunnel under the Mersey as early as 1839, and to tunnel under the Alps between Milan and Como in 1840.[73]

The South Eastern Company's decision in the early 1860s to shorten their route to the coast by cutting a direct line from Lewisham to Tonbridge involved cutting a number of tunnels through the Kentish hills at Chislehurst, Chelsfield, Polehill and Sevenoaks. The first, under the Sundridge estate, and the shortest, became the most problematic. It was worked 'at night and day six days a week', and when finished in January 1865 a 'celebratory dinner was held in the tunnel'.[74] The London and Chatham Railway extension from Rochester to Dover in 1866 involved a tunnel, over 1½ miles, through the chalk downs at Lyddon, which, although easier to cut than those through the chalk cliffs, was nonetheless a costly obstacle. When it was nearing completion a special party from London including the Lord Mayor of London and Mayor of Calais came down to Canterbury by train and proceeded to Lyddon in carriages, where they were drawn through the tunnel by horses.[75] This was obviously to show how important this link was seen in the competition for continental traffic with its rival, the London and South Eastern Railway.

BOX TUNNEL

Brunel's earliest biographers, Smiles, and son Isambard, painted a picture of a man loved and admired by all those who knew him, a view that has not been seriously challenged until recent studies, especially by Vaughan. Yet a study of his letters relating to the construction of the Great Western Railway and its tunnels reveal a very different picture. He was a man impatient for success, set impossible deadlines and blamed others when these were not met. He also drove a hard bargain over the cost of materials, and ballast for the track.[76] Perhaps, in mitigation, we must see that in the project to create the then-named Bristol and London Railway as early as 1834, as the second long-distance railway in Britain after the combined Grand Junction–London and Birmingham, the physical as well as the legal problems were not then fully understood. The Kilsby Tunnel was to hold up Stephenson's railway for over a year, and Box was also to delay the opening of the Great Western by over two years.

As early as 1835, Brunel was reporting with confidence the completion of the Bristol to Bath and London to Reading sections within twenty-four to twenty-six months from commencement. At this time he planned not only a long tunnel beneath Box Hill but also short tunnels between Bristol and Bath, and two further tunnels at Sonning and Purley.[77] In spite of apprehension by the directors, Brunel thought the whole line could be constructed for steam haulage.[78] The reality of the situation was that while the line between Paddington and Swindon presented few problems apart from the construction of Maidenhead Bridge, the stretch between Bristol and Bath involved tunnelling through rock. At the parliamentary enquiry Brunel was hesitant about the number of tunnels required between Bristol and Bath. He was asked to state which these were. They were Tunnel No. 1 of 407 yards, Tunnel No. 2 of 132 yards, and Tunnel No. 3, otherwise known as Fox's Wood, of 1,012 yards. He also said there was one at Saltford of unspecified length, however when questioned he said the total length of tunnelling was 2,079 yards, so Saltford would be 578 yards.[79] There was no mention of a long and a short tunnel at Twerton, making six. If we add Box and Middle Hill the total becomes eight.

With the rivalry between George Stephenson and Brunel, it has been suggested that since the former had driven Kilsby Tunnel over a mile through low Warwickshire hills, Brunel felt he had to drive a tunnel straight through the southern Cotswolds between Chippenham and Bath, a little under 2 miles in length, whereas he could have avoided a tunnel using the Avon valley, which would only have increased the length of the route by 3 miles. This was described in a popular Victorian magazine *'The Friendly Companion'* as 'a grand and gigantic mistake, which the engineer Mr Brunel fell into, to show his engineering skill'.[80] The magazine claimed he could have taken the line through Devizes and Trowbridge, so avoiding the necessity for a tunnel that held up the opening of the Great Western by more than a year.

He admitted the 30 miles at the Bristol end would necessitate a great deal of deep cutting and several tunnels, but this through chalk and freestone. He did not mention a long tunnel on a steep incline at Box, although in the published estimates of expenses he costed excavations and embankments including tunnels as being £835,000. He also costed £15,000 for lighting in the tunnels.[81] A picture created by a study of the documents is of a man of immense confidence in what, in 1835, was the longest railway tunnel proposed so far. In October 1835 he confidently predicted the line open from London to Maidenhead within twenty months, between Bristol and Bath by the end of 1837 or early in 1838, and the entire line by 1840.[82]

The Box Tunnel held up the opening of the Great Western in the same way that Kilsby held up the London and Birmingham, and details of its construction are worth further consideration. It is the most well-known of early railway tunnels and its progress was reported in the press. We also have a short account of its construction by a man who worked on the project: Thomas Gale, foreman for the 'great' contractor George Burge, whose recollections were published in 1884. Curiously, it hardly mentions Brunel but refers in almost reverend tones to Burge of Herne Bay, the new Chief Contractor, 'a very rich and able man of business'.[83] It is also useful as it mentions local personalities and events as seen from the humble workface rather than the boardroom. When the Great Western Railway Bill was launched it was denounced as the 'wildest scheme ever brought before Parliament'.[84] It was described in Parliament as having nine tunnels of unprecedented lengths. These would have included the tunnels on the proposed shared line with the London and Birmingham Railway from Euston to Kensal Green.

However, only Box can justifiably be described as unprecedented, as at that time it was the longest tunnel proposed in Britain. Box presented the greatest challenge, not only because of its length but also the rock strata to be bored and the gradient of the track. At nearly 2 miles long on a steep incline rising from the Avon valley, the challenge is set out in a watercolour section of the tunnel through the hillside showing the position of each shaft, with the gradient shown throughout as 1/100.[85]

The arch critic of early railways, Dr Dionysius Lardner, viewed Brunel's proposal for the tunnel at Box with its steep incline with trepidation, claiming that if the brakes failed on a train it would leave the tunnel at 120mph. Those proposing an alternative route described the proposed tunnel as 'monstrous and extraordinary' and predicted great difficulties in construction, if not financial ruin.[86]

As early as January 1834 the London Committee of the Great Western Railway proposed to 'secure the services of Mr Stephenson or some other engineer' to survey a possible route for the line and to start trial borings for Box Hill Tunnel.[87]

In view of the gradient it seems that the intention was to work the tunnel with stationary engines. A report in the *Morning Chronicle* described the working by rope 'five miles long' as the 'production of a dreadful and recurring sacrifice of human life'.[88] It is not clear why the *Morning Chronicle* refers to the sacrifice of human life, unless it may be assumed that the rope would break? The report, favouring the rival London and Southampton Railway promoting a branch line from Basingstoke to Bath, hoped the Great Western would lose the Bill. The argument was even pursued in a letter to *The Times*.[89] However, the last reference to rope haulage occurred in the *Bristol Mercury* of 3 September 1836, stating that 'two planes were to be worked by stationary engine, at Wootton Bassett and Box'. Perhaps it was George Stephenson who suggested the line could be worked throughout by a 'locomotive engine'. As a result, Daniel Gooch was appointed to be responsible for the development of locomotives powerful enough to tackle the Box incline. In a report to the directors on 13 June 1836 Brunel reported that 'between Bath and Chippenham active measures have been taken for proceeding with the principal work, viz, the Box Tunnel where temporary shafts have already been sunk, and arrangements for letting the contracts for its completion, some of which are advertised'.[90]

In March 1836 Brunel appointed William Glennie as assistant engineer with 'that part of work which I would wish to place under your immediate charge – the Box Tunnel'.[91] He was lured by a commencing salary of £150, raising to £250 and eventually £300, showing the esteem in which Brunel initially held Glennie. By June 1836 considerable progress on the construction of five temporary shafts had been made.[92] Brunel emphasised the importance of not only temporary shafts, but the importance of converting them into permanent shafts through which the materials for each section could be carried.[93] Material would be raised by horse-powered gin from depths of up to 300ft. Brunel was obviously anxious to get things right and of course had a vivid memory of what happened at the Thames Tunnel. In October 1836 contracts were offered to Messrs Overton and Paston for sinking seven shafts (one more than initially planned) at a proposed price of £20,000.[94] The contracts stated completion of the whole project was to be by February 1838. It seems extraordinary that the contract contained a target project completion date in 1838 given that working outwards from the shaft heads had only begun in 1836. A labourer on the project, Gale, stated work on the 'tunnel commenced in June 1838, and Mr Burge was bound to complete it in three years which he did'.[95] So, finally the project was completed three years late.

George Henry Gibbs, a director of the London Committee of the Great Western, had written in a gloomy mood to his brother Henry in May 1837:

> I can't help thinking that the Box Tunnel is operating a great deal against the Great Western. There is nothing like it, you know, upon any line, and connecting it with the name of Brunel, the difficulties of the Thames Tunnel are not unlikely to come into the people's mind.[96]

At first there were 'upwards of 100 workmen ... in the neighbourhood of Corsham, and near the village of Box, their wages are from 14s to 20s a week, an advance in the amount of wages within a very short period of at least one third'.[97] Later Gale says there were as many as 1,100 or 1,200 men continually working night and day while the tunnel was in progress, and not fewer than 4,000 'to hurry completion'.[98] Where did all these men live since they were from as far away as Cornwall? In the neighbouring villages of Box and Corsham and, being on day or night duty, as soon as one lot turned out, another turned in, so the beds were never empty.[99] He also mentions the frequent fights and drunkenness, and the employment of twenty-six inspectors who were sent to the different villages 'to keep the peace on Sundays, as well as they could, there being no county police in those days'.[100] It is worth remembering that the resident populations of Box and Corsham numbered several hundred, and Chippenham about 3,000, so the sudden influx of labour would have made a striking, if not unsettling, impact on the locality. As the project progressed Brunel frequently expressed his exasperation at slowness and frequent delays, especially to the contractors, Burge Lewis and Brewer. He was naturally watching carefully the progress on Kilsby Tunnel, which had also been delayed due to serious flooding. However, on its completion in September 1838 he wrote to specific assistant engineers recommended by Stephenson offering them employment at Box 'if you are disposed to offer your services'.[101] In this way he hoped to speed up the work with the help of proven and trusted employees.

At first the reports were very confident and reported in local and national papers; 'from the results of the openings of the trial shafts for ascertaining the nature of the soil, it appears certain that there can be no difficulty in completing the tunnel in three years'.[102] In spite of the confidence of reports at this time before serious excavations had been begun, according to Gale, the trial shafts took nearly two years to dig and line with bricks but he added the excavation was so difficult that the contractor, Horton, gave up.[103] The contract specifications also hint at possible difficulties ahead including water seepage. However, in order to cut through the rock of the seven permanent shafts, men were brought from the Thames Tunnel as the local labour force was more used to quarrying rather than tunnelling.[104] This was probably in view of the hard physical labour of excavating the long cutting leading to the tunnel. While the *Bristol Mercury* as late as February 1838 described the Box Tunnel as proving 'to be one of the finest specimens of scientific skill and boldness which this country can exhibit', it seems that confidence was quickly evaporating as the enormity of burrowing through this rock barrier became ever clearer.[105] If Brunel had the same confidence as Stephenson about his ability to complete it when first projected, he quickly became concerned about rising costs and the slow rate of progress.

Excavation from the shaft headings began in the spring of 1838 with the tunnel at its deepest, 293ft below ground, but with its passage through a number of strata including forest marble, fuller's earth, great and inferior oolite and lias clay, its construction led to many problems, and not least flooding, which held up the opening of this, the final section, between London and Bristol until 30 June 1841. Obviously there was a limit to the weight of loads hauled up so as not to damage the gins or cranes, and so stone pieces were not to exceed 5 tons weight.[106] On a very practical level the contract emphasised the need to keep a path clear of spoil on the north side of the shafts, not less than 10ft wide.[107] As much stone as possible was to be converted to ashlar, that is smooth rectangular blocks for dressing the portals. Fractured stone could be used for rubble infilling. Should the excavation of stone require additional expense, the contractor should be allowed fair compensation 'as determined by the engineers'.[108] Gale records how the sub-contractors Mr Stodhert, and Mr Lewes of Bath, were continually drowned out by water and got behind with their contract, and were obliged to give up. Sixty horsepower steam-driven pumps then had to be brought in. George Burge, with his hundreds of labourers and horses, worked night and day drawing the earth out of the tunnel.[109] Gale also mentions the practical side of acquiring local materials. He mentions a Mr Hunt who owned a brick field and kilns between Chippenham and the tunnel supplied a 'hundred horses and carts for bringing the bricks to the tunnel for three years'. Lime for mixing in the mortar came from Tanner's Lime Kiln, which produced five or six cart loads of lime daily and three or four loads of ashes a week. Sand was dug from a pit about 2 miles from the tunnel and mixed with the lime and ash to produce mortar.[110] The contract specified that the Roman cement (mortar) used was to be of the best quality from manufacturers approved by the engineers.[111]

The toll on human lives of the construction of Box Tunnel was also considerable. There were frequent newspaper reports of men falling from the top of shafts; if it was not men falling to their death, it could be a stone falling through the shaft killing and injuring men at the trackbed. Newspaper reports speculated that the increasing numbers of deaths showed workmen were becoming careless. The *Bristol Mercury* in November 1838 recorded nineteen deaths, although no specific time span was given.[112] There are likely to have been many more injuries that went unrecorded. Contemporary sources give conflicting numbers of fatalities and casualties. In 1839 a report described the 'destruction' of human life at Box Tunnel as 'awful; nearly fifty lives have been sacrificed … and one last week'.[113] Gale asserted that from the commencement to the finish 'just' one hundred men were killed in different parts of the works, and as many injured;[114] this might suggest this was below what he expected? David Brook stated that on the Great Western between Maidenhead and Bristol between May 1838 and May 1841, sixty-five men were killed and fifty-seven seriously injured, with nineteen killed and two injured in the Box Tunnel, which is at variance with a previous report of fifty lives lost there in 1839.[115] These figures of dead and injured need to be seen in the context of up to 4,000 men employed digging Box Tunnel.

After the completion of the tunnel there were fatalities among track gangers, for instance shortly after its opening in 1841, *The Times* reported a gang of thirty or forty men working shovelling ballast 'as an up and down train came upon them so suddenly that two of their number, unable to get out of the way, were knocked down by the trains … one of them died in an hour afterwards'.[116] The accident occurred in spite of the watchmen shouting to clear the way.

Was there a cause for the increasing cost to life and growing lack of care? For a start, work was almost brought to a halt by flooding by December 1838.[117] However, overriding this was the demand for contractors to meet the deadlines set out in contracts for working forward for each shaft. Financial penalties were imposed for failure to meet deadlines even though circumstances were beyond their control. Over a ton of gunpowder and a ton of candles were used each week. In total some 247,000 tons of oolite and earth were removed from the workings. Few apart from the actual workers could imagine the hell below. One who did was a journalist for the *Bath Chronicle* in 1839, who descended a shaft and graphically described his experience as like something out of a modern version of Dante. It is worth quoting at length:

> The descent by shaft No. 7, which is 136 feet deep, is effected on a platform, without any railings or any other security on the sides, attached to a broad, flat rope wound and unwound by steam engines, and is attended with no inconvenience (if the idea of a fall from giddiness, or from the breaking of the rope, be not allowed to intrude), except the hard bump with which your arrival at the bottom is announced to you. On stepping from the platform and escaping from the water which constantly drops from the aperture above, you find yourself in a temperature which, should the day be hot and dry, is agreeably cool, but in an atmosphere rendered oppressive and unpleasant by the want of a free circulation of air, and the smell and smoke of gunpowder. The dark, dim vault, filled with clouds of vapour, is saved from utter blackness by the feeble light of candles which are stuck upon the sides of the excavation, and placed on trucks or other things used in carrying on the works ... Taking a candle in your hand you pick your way through the pools of water, over the temporary rails, amongst blocks of stone and huge chains attached to the machinery which every now and then impede your way, happy and lucky if no impediment unobserved in the dull uncertain light, should arrest your progress by causing you to measure the length on the wet and rugged floor. Nor during all this time have your ears been idle, the sounds of the pick, the shovel and the hammer, have fallen upon them indistinctly; but as you advance the increase and the hum of distant voices is heard ... a busy scene opens before you, gangs of men are at work on all sides, and the tunnel, which to this point has been cut to its full dimensions, suddenly contracts; you leave the level of the floor, and scrambling up amongst the workmen, you wind your way slowly and with difficulty.
>
> Having been informed that a shot is about to be fired at the further extremity, you stop and listen to judge its effect. The match is applied, and the explosion follows, and a concussion such as probably you never felt before takes place, the solid rock appears to shake and the reverberation of the sound and shock is sensibly and fearfully experienced; another and another to follow, and with a slight stretch of the imagination you might fancy yourself in the midst of a thunder cloud with heaven's artillery booming around. You pursue your rugged path, and having arrived at that part where the junction was made between two cuttings, you have an opportunity of examining the roof, and of admiring the solid bed of rock of which it is formed, and of appreciating the skill which enabled the engineers to keep a true course under all the difficulties

of such a work. After traversing a considerable space within reach of the roof, you find your way to the bottom, among a gang of labourers who are working from the other end, and having arrived at the shaft at the Chippenham side of the tunnel, you step upon the platform, the word is given, and you are once more elevated to the surface of the earth, glad to breathe the pure air, and full of wonder at the skill, enterprise, and industry of your fellow men.[118]

As the months and years passed there was naturally growing impatience at the rate of progress, more so as the tunnel was actually made a little longer than originally intended. Brunel, in his report to shareholders in February 1841, promised the tunnel would be open throughout from the western face to shaft No. 8, which had always been considered as the eastern extremity, however 'the eastern end has been extended a few yards in order to diminish the quantity of excavation required in the open cutting'.[119] So the tunnel is 3,227 yards long, not 3,212 yards as originally intended. Mention of the start of construction is hard to find in the contracts since the tunnel would first be excavated from shafts. The start of construction of the actual faces would, it is assumed, be late in the whole operation. The tunnel was ready for the laying of track from 2 June 1841, and the order was given to stop visitors because they were impeding operations.[120] When it was finally opened on 30 June 1841 it had one track in use at first, but at least Bristol was now connected with London. Gale recalls the flags hanging across the tunnel mouth, banks and bridge, a band playing, and 'three hundred hogsheads of beer' being given away by the contractors. Several thousand people came to see the tunnel and the day ended with entertainments for the men at the Queen's Head, Box.[121]

The portals were included in contracts 2 and 6. Tantalisingly, however, the records are devoid of much information on the portals, which are hinted at rather than detailed. If we examine RAIL 252/1, which details cost for work on Box between April 1838 and May 1842, we find work on the east portal is only recorded from January 1840 with excavations at the east tunnel mouth. Quite obviously much work must have been undertaken over the previous years. Monthly accounts through to June 1841 record continuing excavations at the tunnel mouth shortly before the track was laid, and less than a month before opening. Only in October 1841 is there a record of the setting of ashlar (smooth stone) into the mortar, or the dressing of the tunnel face. This continues into May 1842 with costing of ashlar and rough work (stone) set into mortar. In the period 27 May to 18 August 1842 we have payment of 18s for 'lowering and re-using ribs on the tunnel face'. It also records backing in mortar for tunnel mouth, dry wall behind the face, and 'puddle over bell-mouth'. Expenditure for this period came to £175 18s 3d. This period of accounting ends on 18 August, when we can presume the portal to have been finished. If an attempt is made to simply add the expenditure devoted to the tunnel face, and excluding excavations, the amount is £1,324 14s 3d.[122]

Even reference to actual work on the west portal only starts in September 1840, and this is for timber for securing the tunnel face. The costing for work continues until 11 November 1841, and like the eastern portal, it includes rough stone set in mortar, as well as ashlar set into the mortar face. Payment for 86,000 bricks costing £189 9s 0d for the wing walls is included between May and November 1841. Taking the cost only of items directly related to the construction of the west face and excluding excavations, it amounts to £5,283 1s 4d (£309,217.89 in 2005 currency) (see Appendix 4).[123] This, as would be expected, is much more than for the eastern portal, and may be compared with the £7,000 for the Primrose Hill portal. It is unlikely that Brunel's portals would have exceeded this because he was using local stone for a start. Between Bath and Bristol it is impossible to separate each item of construction. However, in August 1841, nearly two months after the opening of the line throughout, Brunel estimated the cost of the Bristol Division from Swindon westwards to be about £465,000 with liabilities of £60,000. This would have included the Box Tunnel.[124]

The enormity of the Box Tunnel project was perhaps best stated in this report of the Board of Trade:

> The Tunnel is rather more than 1¾ miles in length, with large shafts numbered 1 and 8 afterwards enlarged into the openings or deep cuttings for the entrance of the tunnel at each end, so only six remained when the work was finished, which were about 25 feet in diameter and varied from 85 to 260 feet in height to the top of the tunnel. The whole of the tunnel from the western extremity to about 100 yards beyond No. 6 shaft is lined with brickwork. From there to the eastern mouth of the tunnel, a length of about 900 yards was formed by excavating the natural rock in the shape of a Gothic arch, no part of which is lined with masonry except at the eastern entrance and for a short distance in, where the sides are retained by walls and the roof by an arch built of the stone found near the spot. There were also five or six smaller shafts sunk during excavation but all are filled in on completion of the work.[125]

Since the Box Tunnel was not only on a major trunk route, but had also attracted much attention during its years of construction, and was for a time the longest railway tunnel in the world, any adverse news could damage the Great Western Railway and the reputation of Brunel. Shortly after the opening there were serious falls of rock from an unlined section. The possibility of collapse had been identified by the geologist, the Rev. William Buckland of Oxford, later Dean of Westminster, who asserted in 1842 that the oolite rock was of such a nature that large pieces were likely to be loosened or brought down by the 'concussion of the atmosphere' and vibration caused by trains. Within four years of opening his prediction became true with the collapse of rock near one of the shafts, which derailed a banking engine.[126] The cause was attributed to extremely cold air at the base of the shaft. After clearance of the debris and reopening the tunnel, Colonel Pasley wrote a long report to the Committee of Privy Council for Trade, proclaiming it safe.[127] He subsequently assured the House of Commons that he 'believed the roof was as safe as the roof of the house in which they were now assembled'.[128] It is hard to put a final cost on the Box Tunnel but Brunel was frequently to quote the figure of £100 per yard as he did to the GWR directors at Cardiff in 1844. Since the tunnel is 3,227 yards this would put the rough estimate at £322,700.[129]

As Brunel was celebrating the triumph of completing the Box Tunnel, a rumour was set in motion, perhaps by the anti-tunnel lobby, that the Great Western Railway Company had determined to take the top off the Box Tunnel. One journal described this as to 'un-box it, just as the Highgate arch people served their tunnel some years ago'.[130] The company was forced to publish a denial in spite of the impractical nature of the proposal, which would have required a cutting over 300ft deep.[131] Another rumour later in 1843 claimed that an atmospheric railway was to be laid through the Box Tunnel 'without delay'.[132]

Finally the question must be asked as to whether the tunnel could have been avoided if the line had been taken a mile or so to the north. Although not mentioned by E.T. MacDermot in his *History of the Great Western*, 1927, a correspondent in the *Railway Times* suggested Brunel had first contemplated a route to the north of the alignment of the Box Tunnel through a valley in the southern Cotswolds that would have necessitated cuttings but no tunnels.[133] This would have been following the line of the Box Brook, through the south side of Hartham Park and on to the north of Corsham Park towards Chippenham, needing a sharp curve in order to bring the line into Bath.[134] However, he was forestalled by the landowner Henry Joy, who owned Hartham Park. It is said that Joy refused to listen to any terms offered, including that of rebuilding the mansion 300 yards north of the proposed line. It was said the Great Western capitulated since they did not wish the defeat of the second Bill before Parliament.[135] A glance at a coloured contoured map such as Bartholomew's[136] shows the line taking a sharp, and what Brunel described as an objectionable, curve to the south of Corsham Park, the residence of Lord Methuen, whereas, had Joy been accommodating, the line could have run due west to the Box Brook to join the present alignment at Box, perhaps saving several miles in distance and certainly the tunnel (Appendix 3). On the other hand, Methuen, who had at first been violently opposed to the railway in any form, had been appeased by Brunel, who claimed it would not 'do the slightest injury to his property'.[137]

Others have suggested he could have taken a more southerly route utilising the Avon valley through Bradford, although Brunel insisted that this would have involved a mile-long tunnel beneath Claverton Down in order to reach Bath and that the country was 'very difficult'.[138] A rumour persisted until January 1836, when work started on the actual alignment of the tunnel, that the railway line was to be carried through Melksham and Trowbridge, joining the line from Salisbury following the course of the Avon to Bath, thereby avoiding a tunnel.[139] Such a route would have added a few miles to the distance between London and Bristol but would have saved money and would most likely have enabled the line to open throughout several years earlier.

The construction of Box Tunnel must be seen as throwing up almost all the problems in tunnel construction encountered anywhere in Britain during the days of manual construction except for a bleaker location such as the Pennines. It shows Brunel as a visionary with faith in a project that was costing increasing sums of money as flooding and collapse of rock were encountered. It also shows Brunel's weakness with his increasing impatience with the rate of progress in the face of difficulties he had not envisaged. He seemed at times to be blind to the difficulties of his labour force, and his treatment of his sub-contractors, especially Burge, was nothing short of disgraceful, more so as Burge had to sue for arrears of pay. Perhaps his impatience can be appreciated when the more heavily tunnelled section between Bristol and Bath was constructed without undue difficulty, and even the eastern section between London and Maidenhead involving the Warncliffe Viaduct and Maidenhead Bridge constructed with few problems and finished on time. While the construction of the Great Western Railway can be hailed as a masterpiece with some beautiful structures including viaducts, bridges, and of course tunnel portals, completed in a relatively short span of years, the Box Tunnel halted completion for at least two years beyond Brunel's projected date of completion. As we shall see in further chapters it became an object of either fascination or fear to passengers, and with its monumental western portal, it made a notable contribution to Victorian railway architecture.

Chapter 3
A RAILWAY, A LANDOWNER AND HIS ESTATE

This chapter examines the nature of opposition to early railways in instances where it was necessary to tunnel to satisfy either the needs of the landowner or of the railway company, whose chief aim was to drive a track in as direct a route as possible between two points. The negotiations between the Trent Valley Railway Company and the Earl of Lichfield at Shugborough are a classic example. The records of the parliamentary committees for the Bill in 1845 allow us a glimpse of the arguments and fears of landowners as well as the practical problems likely to be involved in construction, not least tunnels and gradients. As a result of the Trent Valley Railway Company's negotiations in the early 1840s to drive tracks through the grounds of a stately home, Shugborough Hall, at considerable

Ill. 4 View looking west from above portal of Box Tunnel, c.1840, J.C. Bourne, *Great Western Railway*, 1846.

financial gain to the occupant and no visual loss to the estate, it led to the creation of two of the most impressive railway tunnel portals in Britain.

Ian Whyte argues that early reaction to the railways and descriptions of them tended to polarise into strongly pro and anti groups.[1] Here the artist, the journalist and the book author could each have influence. David Cannadine has emphasised that opposition was mainly in the first two decades of railway development before 1850, citing a number of well-known instances of opposition that cost companies considerable expense.[2] It could be argued that in such cases the company would not be inclined to create pretentious architecture such as tunnel portals unless specifically directed by a landowner. He also emphasised that urban landowners, such as Lord Portman, could insist on tracks being concealed behind high walls or in tunnels, and 'all buildings to be seemly and ornamental', although in this instance this was for the Great Central in the 1890s and adjacent to Lord's Cricket Ground.[3] Leigh Denault and Jennifer Landis have suggested that opposition to railways was often a feud, even a bitter one, between landowner and potential railway company that rarely attracted wide public attention unless the proposed route was likely to endanger antiquities or historic buildings. They cited a number of examples of opposition from the University of Oxford and Eton College to the route of the Great Western Railway that did not involve a tunnel.[4]

In the early years of railway development, permission for tracks crossing over or running beneath a landowner's estate could be obtained, at its easiest, by financial compensation, but sometimes it required legal argument that might hold up the completion of a vital link in the net of iron rails, or even allow a rival to complete a parallel route some miles away. Some early illustrators dramatised the new railways and descriptions of them; *The Illustrated London News*, published from 1842, was foremost among the weekly journals to proclaim the progress of the system in vivid illustrations that could stir as well as allay the fears of a landowner, more so as the journal, not unlike the popular press of today, was quick to seize on the dramatic possibility of a crash or derailment involving death or injury. However, many early prints show the railway as a relatively unobtrusive feature of the landscape with banks or cuttings cleaned up and line-side trees, perhaps a little too mature for their years. While many by the 1840s could see the economic success of the system, both in exploiting and moving mineral resources, as well as moving the population in greater comfort and speed than hitherto, it did not stop William Wordsworth asking in a poem in 1844, 'is there no nook of England's ground secure from rash assault'?[5] All this may be expected from those who feared the destruction of their land and the visual spoliation of the countryside. Yet it may be argued with justification that quarrying, which had gone on since the Roman occupation, caused more dramatic and visual lasting damage. It is easy to portray all landowners as against the train in the 1830s and 1840s, not least because they might have interests in canals or even land transport, but many after the first decade quickly saw the railway as bringing benefits that might outweigh the inconvenience of sacrificing acres of land, such as access to mineral wealth, especially coal, in the neighbourhood, or, at a very personal level, quicker access to London. In discussing the role of the landowner in the routeing of early railways we may question whether such people were really more of a problem with regard to the provision of tunnels than the physical features of a landscape. It may be claimed that the impact of railways was visually less in the 1830s than the early motorways of the early 1960s. True, cuttings and embankments were like raw scars until the grass and trees grew, but subsequently they seemed to merge with the locality. Obviously there were cases where the landed aristocracy became a thorn in the side of railway developers in demanding that the railway be hidden from view by a short tunnel, as Brunel found with the Wiltshire family of Shockerwick.[6]

In spite of the views of some historians, we should not simply view the landowner as an obstacle that a railway company had to overcome; we should also see their contribution as positive, more so if it contributed to the railway companies doing their best to minimise the impact on the landscape. Since early railway pioneers like Stephenson, Brunel and Macatta, to name but three, saw themselves as setting out a modern version of a communications system to rival, and indeed exceed, that of the Romans, the buildings and structures had to be grand. In this they might be encouraged and supported by the landowner. What resulted was a new type of architecture utilising the current architectural fashions, classical or Gothic, or, especially for station buildings, using the vernacular style of the locality. By the time the railway age was under way the classical supporters had veered towards the Grecian with its stern simplicity, perfect for the entrance to Euston station. The Gothic, which some argue never really died, underwent a revival from the toy-like bauble of Horace Walpole at Strawberry Hill in the 1750s to the scholarly interpretation of Rickman and Pugin. This was the fundamental choice in taste confronting Stephenson, Brunel and Macatta; there was also a whiff of the Egyptian at Bangor, but this does not count as a 'railway style' due to its uniqueness.

In the early decades of railway development some landowners and other powerful influences were involved in the choice of style for the fabric of the system; a number of examples may be cited from the major companies. The Liverpool and Manchester Railway may be remembered for its pioneering civil engineering such as the cutting through Olive Mount and the conquest of Chat Moss but it did have several structures worthy of attention. While the tunnels at the Liverpool end attracted the local citizens as much for the experience of walking through a gas-lit passage as just looking at a tunnel, much more impressive were the Moorish Arch (now sadly destroyed), the skew-bridge at Rainhill, and the Sankey Viaduct.

PROPOSING A RAILWAY
Proposing a railway to a group of prospective directors in the candlelit back room of a tavern was one thing, seeing it through to completion was another. It was not just the physical side of the engineering that had to be contended with, but also the will or wishes of individual landowners who may or may not have wanted a railway to serve their own interests, or who did not wish to hear the noise of a train or see the smoke from the engine and insisted on the tracks going beneath their land or taking a large detour. Although there was some opposition to the construction of canals from the beginning of the canal-building era, such as the Duke of Bridgewater's Navigation having to pay Sir Richard Brooke compensation to cross his estate, and

the Grand Junction likewise to the Earl of Clarendon, it was with the construction of steam-hauled railways that landowner opposition really started, as in the period of horse-drawn haulage, a rail or wagon-way was of limited gauge and limited environmental impact in the wider sense.[7] The scale of a passenger railway, or one involving steam power, was very different, and therefore likely to make more visual and social impact. The most important imperative for a railway engineer, however, was to create as direct and flat a route as possible. Therefore crossing private property might need cuttings, embankments, tunnels, bridges or viaducts. With these circumstances, opposition was likely until the benefits were seen to outweigh the disadvantages. Tom Williamson and Liz Bellamy argued that landowners were rarely able to stop a railway being constructed but only in insisting it was hidden within a cutting or tunnel. Powerful landowners such as the Earl of Clarendon at Watford, Lord Braybrooke at Audley End and Lord Lichfield had to accept tunnels beneath their land, and there are many less celebrated cases.[8] The Duke of Devonshire at Chatsworth even invited Lord George Cavendish, promoter of the North Midland Railway, 'to come through any part of my park as long as you come through in a tunnel'.[9] At Stamford, Lord Exeter, fearing the disfigurement of his land and also the neighbouring market town of Stamford, succeeded in excluding the main London–York line, and when a branch was constructed from Peterborough to Leicester, forced it beneath the town in a short tunnel.[10]

Nonetheless, as Williamson and Bellamy further point out, the 'aesthetic dispositions of the landed classes could result in greater feats of railway engineering than those posed by geological or geographical factors'.[11] Ultimately if it were felt that it was in the national interest that a certain stretch of track should be built and that objections were unreasonable, landowners could be forestalled by compulsory purchase under an Act of Parliament. Most railway companies wanted as smooth a passage as possible, knowing that opposition could delay the required parliamentary enquiry and result in eventual defeat by certain landed interests. Therefore it was essential as far as possible to win over reasonable opposition. Peter Lecount, who was closely associated with the London and Birmingham Railway, in his *Practical Treatise on Railways*, 1835, was clear that in choosing the final alignment he 'should run through no more seats or ornamental pleasure grounds than possible and avoid towns and villages where land would be expensive', and should 'enter into all enquiries to enable him to choose the best line and construct it at the least cost'.[12] Smiles, in his life of George Stephenson, tells of a reverend gentleman who created such opposition that it was only when he was in the pulpit that the surveyors could work on his land, 'the surveyor concluded his task as he concluded his sermon'.[13] The incident may be apocryphal.

Before a railway could be constructed the directors and shareholders had to present a Bill to Parliament for scrutiny and approval under a process of Standing Orders governing the formal process of presentation and examination, before it could be enacted. It is therefore in the Parliamentary Archives that we should seek to learn the extent of opposition to a specific scheme, but all railway documents prior to 1835 were lost in the fire that destroyed the Palace of Westminster in 1834. From 1835 documents exist such as those detailing the Second Bill for the Great Western

Railway. The procedure of examination was sometimes tedious with various committee members asking the same questions of each witness, and in one specific example, the gradient of the tracks on the Box incline, and the effects of the Box Tunnel on passengers.[14] Many early proposals were composed of more enthusiasm than money and so foundered before presentation or at the committee stages.

By the early nineteenth century, a complex series of parliamentary standing orders and appeals had come into existence relating to the compulsory purchase of land for commercial purposes. In 1799 it was decided that standing orders relating to canals would be extended to cover any railway development that came before Parliament. This was first applied to the Surrey Iron Railway in 1803, and for the first two decades was largely confined to mineral railways in the north of England. In 1814 the interests of landowners were strengthened by the insistence that they should have a copy of the Bill and a map of how it affected their property in the handwriting of the proposers. Furthermore, maps also had to be deposited at parish level, thus ensuring that landowners would not be in ignorance of a proposal or that a Bill could be rushed through.

By 1836 the scene had changed from the planning of local mineral railways to national trunk routes conveying both goods and passengers. With the sudden expansion of proposals a 'Notice of Intent' to promote a line had to be published in both local and national newspapers in spring, and maps and sections of the proposed route of a railway had to be prepared and submitted by 1 March for the year preceding the relevant parliamentary session. The maps were to be of no less than 4in to 1 mile and the sections no less than 1 inch to 100ft, and they were to show all 'tunnelling or arching'.[15] In the vicinity of houses the scale was to be considerably larger and the powers of deviation lessened. Proposals were also to give estimates of expenses and information of financial backing for the venture. Bills would be promoted on the evidence of alignment provided on the maps, and there could be no subsequent deviation without parliamentary approval or a supplementary act. Further changes to the procedure occurred in 1842 with the date of submission brought back to 30 November and publication in newspapers to the autumn. In 1837 the House of Lords, realising the importance of committees, instituted new regulations for procedure; committees of both Houses were to consist of five members who would hear both sides and especially the opposition, and were to have powers to amend or reject proposals before the passing of an Act.

The railway companies were at their most vulnerable due to this and so employed skilled counsel to minimise the possibility of rejection. Finally, in the summer of 1844, a Railway Board was established 'whose duty was to examine every scheme to be laid before Parliament … and to report in favour, or against, each scheme to be laid before Parliament … for the guidance of the Select Committee'. It was to be concerned with the technical and commercial feasibility of each scheme, but not questions of land or private property, which was reserved for the Select Committee.[16]

Anthony Burton, in his *The Railway Builders*, emphasised the unscrupulous aspects involved in getting a railway Bill through Parliament; it could be expensive and time consuming, and 'a lot of people did very well out of it'.[17] Lawyers and

MPs thrived on bribes. By 1845 no fewer than 157 MPs sat on railway boards, and many of them received handsome sums to use their influence in Parliament.

DEFINITION OF A LANDOWNER'S DOMAIN

In order to understand the nature of negotiation between railway companies and the landed interest, we need to define what constituted a landowner's domain. A landowner might own many thousands of acres, so it might be debatable as to how far a railway, or indeed canal, might have a direct effect on his estate. After all, there is a difference between open farmland, a park and formal garden. No railway company would wish to go directly through a formal or family garden, nor indeed tunnel directly beneath it, as it would be in the vicinity of a large house. The park enclosed by boundary walls was a different matter, and a proposal to cut a railway through a park might need very careful negotiation: would it be sunk in a cutting or even carried through a tunnel? Beyond the park would be a public road with possibly extensive farmland, beyond which might be part of the owner's extended estate and so part of his property. For example, Brunel even considered cutting a tunnel for the Great Western Railway in the vicinity of Pangbourne to avoid Purley with its house and park. Several miles further on the tracks passed a few feet outside the gates of Sir James Sykes's Basildon Park, but across his property.[18] However, Basildon Park was well above the level of the railway, which would not be seen from the house. Against objections from a landowner between Bath and Bristol, Brunel argued that while the line passed through 'some meadows belonging to that gentleman' it would not be within sight of his house, indeed it was 'upwards of a quarter of a mile from the extreme boundary of the Park'.[19] Celia Brunel Noble, in her memories of her family, writes of her grandfather's concern to appease landowners in the vicinity of Brislington by 'tunnelling under Mr Owen's orchard', avoiding Mr Natham's ice house, and the orchards of Mr Northcote, who 'is to be bought by tunnelling under one corner and paying well for it'.[20]

A tunnel might seem an obvious way to keep the tracks out of sight on an estate and certainly could satisfy a landowner's wish to retain a favourite vista but there were disadvantages. It would be costly to a company and could only be constructed by first sinking shafts on the land. Until the excavations were connected from end to end, all the spoil had to come out through the shafts. Much of this would be dispersed in heaps or mounds in the vicinity, which might take some years to be hidden, for example by tree planting. Some shafts would be sealed while others would remain for air and form circular brick towers across the landscape, or at best be disguised by castellation like those at Kilsby in Warwickshire and Badminton in Gloucestershire, which look no more out of place than a folly, and at the very least excite curiosity.[21]

Rees Cyclopaedia, 1819, claimed canal builders were prepared to go round an obstacle such as a gentleman's park; however, a railway company could not necessarily afford to be so generous.[22] With the promotion of the London and Birmingham Railway in 1831, then the longest stretch of proposed track administered by one company, landowners' objections were anticipated from the start. To appease such trouble the company inserted an announcement in the

Birmingham Gazette: 'The utmost endeavours will be made to avoid all molestations to noblemen and gentlemen's seats near which the proposed line is intended to pass.' If alarm bells were sounding in the shires, the company added a sweetener, in which 'directions had been given to the surveyors to spare no expense for this purpose'. Further, the company was 'always ready and happy to confer with all parties who wish an alteration in the direction of the railway'.[23] In the case of this proposed line, accommodating the wishes of landowners involved several unnecessary tunnels at Primrose Hill, Kensal Green and Watford.

In the case of the Watford Tunnel, Freeling in his *Railway Companion*, 1838, could not understand why the railway should not run through Cassiobury Park, the estate of the Earl of Essex, as did the canal where the slow progress of the barges, and a 'set of men notorious for their half savage and predatory habits' caused a greater disturbance than the railway, which could be screened from the mansion.[24] Here personal interests had intervened, the 4th Earl was on the Board of the Grand Junction Canal when it was cut. An anonymous account by a civil engineer published in 1868 captured the atmosphere of the moment:

> Through this tranquil and old fashioned spot … rumour spread the intelligence, that a railway was to be constructed from London to Birmingham … Some readers of *The Times* may have known of a Bill for the purpose, having just been thrown out by the House of Lords, in consequence of the opposition of a noble Earl through whose park Robert Stephenson, following the line selected by Telford for the Grand Junction Canal, had proposed to lead the railway.
>
> A second Bill had been avoided; the line crossing the valley of the Colne by an embankment of what was, in those days, unprecedented magnitude, and thus boring beneath the woods at a distance from the mansion, by an equally unprecedented tunnel of nearly a mile.[25]

Landowners aside, railway constructors had to be aware of potential gradients and the physical limits of locomotives at the time, a point which Brunel had to argue at great length to the 1835 parliamentary commission when he proposed an incline through the Box Tunnel.[26] On a road of 1:100, an additional force of 1:3 was needed to pull a given load. On railways, a 1:100 slope required four times more force to pull the same load up. Brunel was conscious of this and between London and Swindon he kept his tracks to no more than 1:1,320, or 4ft to a mile, what became known as 'Brunel's billiard table'.[27] Sometimes therefore, a company had to balance the cost of a diversion that would involve greater distance and perhaps gradients, with the alternatives of a tunnel or compensation, which could be extortionate if the landowner was shrewd.

THE NATURE OF OPPOSITION?
The railway would 'spoil our shires and ruin our squires' was the familiar cry.[28] It was put even more forcefully in the House of Lords by Lord Broughton in a House of Lords debate in 1844:

> To be driven from one's home, to find it impossible to remain in a place where they and their ancestors have resided for perhaps 800 or 900 years, in consequence of a railway being formed there. To this they were exposed by the intrigues of attorneys, land measurers, land-surveyors and land jobbers, who under the pretext of consulting the public good, were pursuing their private interest – and if they could trench your gardens, your pleasure grounds, or your woods, without control, what was to prevent them from driving a railway through your hall or sitting room?[29]

Another concern of many landowners was the threat to the pleasures and pursuits of rural life and the damage to hunting. F.P. Delme Radcliffe, in his *Noble Science, A Few General Ideas on Foxhunting*, 1839, claimed that railways were an iniquitous attack on the rural way of life, 'to us sportsmen, the intersection of any community by canal, or railroad furnishes food enough in itself for lamentation, we bewail the beauty of a district spoiled, and as an obstacle to our amusement, we denounce the barrier hostile to our sport'.[30] This selfish attitude, oblivious to the broader public good, was a reason why some landowners were reluctant to sell.

Why was there to be more opposition to railways rather than canals or even roads? Perhaps the following, rather narrow view of Lord Fitzwilliam, holds a clue to contemporary feeling that railway companies were only interested in their own profit.

> Railways are speculations embarked on with a view to profit, without any collateral view to the interests of the district which the railways traverse; and here is to be observed a marked distinction between them and the canals and roads, which have always looked more to the benefit of the neighbourhood than to their own, except in as much as they might be incidentally benefitted. With the railways it has the reverse. The profit of the spectator is the motive; the advantage of the public is the incident.[31]

Thompson, in his study of the nineteenth-century landowners, states that Fitzwilliam disliked the Great Northern Railway because its proposed route was not the shortest route from London to York, missing important towns such as Stamford and Lincoln, yet intended to cut across his woodlands needed for hunting. He even sent his surveyor to map out a quarter-mile deviation near Peterborough.[32] The neighbouring 6th Duke of Rutland at first strongly resisted attempts to build a railway across his 33,000 acres of land in the 1860s; however, with the discovery of deposits of iron in 1870, he dramatically changed his views and courted the Great Northern Railway, and then the Midland Railway, without success. In 1871 he was approached by a private backer who offered to build the line from Newark to Leicester via Melton Mowbray and lease it to the Great Northern Railway. Before it came before Parliament the Duke had laid out the route himself and chosen the engineers![33]

Was this contemporary feeling fair? Obviously a railway had to be planned with a view to profit, if only to service the infrastructure and rolling stock. To say that the railway companies had no interests in the districts they traversed is certainly not true. Naturally proprietors had to balance the planning of the most direct route taking into account costs, while at the same time trying to mould the tracks to the locality. Certainly Brunel was aware of environmental factors. Also, a company needed to serve as many localities as possible if it was to maximise profits, again, a point Brunel made forcibly to the parliamentary committee, citing towns the track would serve or pass within 10 miles.[34]

The railways were a new phenomenon and the prospect of hundreds of construction workers or 'navvies' crossing or camping on land would obviously provoke opposition, certainly in the short term. At the height of the railway boom in the 1840s there were over 40,000 at work, so it is little wonder that landowners were in constant fear of destruction and pillage. As *Frazer's Magazine* wrote:

> Landowners were kept in a constant state of anxiety by rumours of the course each railway was likely to pursue. Young gentlemen with theodolites and chains marched across the fields; long white sticks with bits of paper attached were carried ruthlessly through the fields, gardens and sometimes even houses. [35]

Yet one can understand the fear of landowners when at night during the construction of Clay Cross Tunnel on the Midland Railway in Derbyshire 'huge fires that blazed on the summit of the ridge, lit up the rugged outline of the gangs of men, gave a strange and lurid colouring to the spectacle, and helped to make the spot the great wonder of that countryside'.[36] At Sevenoaks, the South Eastern Railway burrowed beneath a corner of the Knole estate without causing any problems to the Sackville family, but with rather more impact on the small market town through the influx of labourers.[37]

The view of the Duke of Cleveland of Raby Castle, County Durham, might be typical of the 1820s and '30s: 'O here now is a fine track of countryside, and no railway to interfere … there is none here, nor I hope will ever be, no one will ever think of making one here. I shall have nothing to interfere with my comfort.'[38] He even employed 'watchers' to stop surveyors for the Newcastle and Carlisle Railway crossing his land before the railway won the day. However, by the early 1840s, the fears and objections diminished as the anti-rail and anti-tunnel lobbies were gradually won over by the speedy and commercial advantages of the train.

The parliamentary Act for the Newcastle and Carlisle empowered the appointment of thirty directors, three of them nominated by the Earl of Carlisle, and it forbad the use of steam locomotives and the use of stationary engines within sight of several properties, the agreement of the owners having been vital to the obtaining of the Act.[39] The first stone was laid by Henry Howard of Corby Castle on 25 March 1830. As planned it was to have three tunnels, at Farnley of 170 yards, Whitchester, and Cowran Hill of 840 yards, as well as a number of viaducts and a bridge across the Tyne at Warden. By the time the line was completed in 1835, a supplementary Act had been granted allowing steam locomotives to be used anywhere without restriction. In the end only two tunnels, those at Farnley and

Whitchester, were constructed, that at Cowran Hill proving so difficult that work was temporarily abandoned and in the end it was turned into a deep cutting.[40]

In the 1830s Herapath's *Railway Magazine*, which supported the anti-tunnel lobby, expressed the fear of landowners. In Kent the routes from London to Dover could not avoid tunnelling due to the Weald and North Downs. Lyddon Hill between Canterbury and Dover was proclaimed as 'perfectly inaccessible to anything but the handihood of the south eastern mountaineers, besides, parks and pleasure grounds would be invaded, and among others, that of the Honourable Member for Dover'.[41] On the other hand, Joshua Richardson, a contributor to the *Railway Magazine* under 'Railroad Intelligence', wrote in 1836:

> An opinion has been entertained by some that the value of an estate is depreciated by a public railway passing through it, and that a reduction in the rental must take place in consequence. With the exception of cases where a railway approaches near a country mansion, or goes through a country park, the reverse of this is the general result, and in nine cases out of ten, is considerably enhanced in value. This cannot be better evinced than by the way some of the occupiers of lands and mines in the vicinity of the intended Leeds and Liverpool Railway have prepared to pay an increased rent in the event of the railway being established; and that very considerable increase has actually been offered by the tenants of a nobleman through whose property it is to pass for several miles.[42]

Hepple, in his thesis on landowners' attitudes to railway alignment, cites Lord Sefton, who had initially been one of the major opponents of the Liverpool and Manchester Railway but on seeing its success, supported the proposal for a railway from Liverpool to Leeds that would also cross his estates.[43]

From the angle of a railway company, the obstruction to the proposed path of a railway by a Bill could spell all but financial ruin, or at the very least several extra years of construction. Brunel was aware of this and in his survey for the route of the Great Western in 1835 emphasised that he had made 'every endeavour so as to impair ornamental property as little as possible', even though it 'occasioned a considerable increase in the estimate of cost'.[44] Faced by opposition from landowners, the result could be the same. Many early railways were not met with universal approval and in the case of the London and Birmingham Railway, Robert Stephenson had to face not only opposition from landowners, resulting in the collapse of the first parliamentary Bill, but also opposition from the proprietors of the new Kensal Green Cemetery. The reaction of landowners could influence whether a track was to cross a specific area or estate by embankment, cutting, tunnel or viaduct, and this would obviously govern the eventual cost that could 'make or break' a railway company.

PERSONAL GAIN OR NATIONAL INTEREST?

Some opposed the railways as they wished to keep the landscape as it was, either to preserve its beauty, or to preserve their land. This is not to say that there was no justified opposition, especially when the proposed course of tracks encroached on sites of antiquity or went near recognised historical buildings. In such cases the demand for a tunnel or cutting could be fully justified.[45] Once reconciled to the construction of a railway across or beneath their land, landowners might be able to dictate the style of any civil engineering works; was a structure to be classical or Gothic, what material was to be used and how far did it fit in to the 'colour' and atmosphere of the locality? The best example is the Fellows of Eton College requiring the east portal of Primrose Hill Tunnel to be in the Italian classical.

The cost of compensation instead of a diversion had to be measured against the physical restriction of creating a gradient of no more than 1:100.[46] Leigh Denault and Jennifer Landis suggest that many cases of opposition to the railways remained as a dispute between landowner and prospective railway proprietors and rarely attracted widespread public attention unless antiquities or national monuments were endangered.[47] The historical geographer David Turnock argued that popular historical accounts have harshly judged landowners' objections, and exaggerated the significance of the more notorious cases.[48] However, Robert Stephenson put forward the view that 25 per cent of railway construction costs were for the purchase of land and he was fiercely critical of landowner's 'extraordinary demands for compensation'.[49] According to Samuel Smiles in his *Life of George Stephenson*, by as early as 1833, the promoters of railways had acquired the art of conciliating the landlords.[50] J.C. Jeaffreson, the first biographer of Robert Stephenson, said he accepted financial conciliation as fair game.[51]

Robbins, in *The Railway Age*, claimed that few voices were raised purely on the grounds of natural beauty or amenities being destroyed; more likely they were to extract more money in compensation, very useful in a time of agricultural recession.[52] Even Benjamin Disraeli, in his novel *Sybil*, took a cynical attitude to railway compensation; when Lord de Mowbray mentions news that Lord Marney has consented to the passage of a railway through his estate, Lady Marney replies that her husband had not consented 'until the compensation was settled … George never opposes them after that'.[53]

Landowners were the literate and powerful class who, even if they personally did not care much about artistic taste, could nonetheless be influenced by the cultural critics of the day such as Ruskin and Pugin, the latter condemning the version of Gothic such as used at Temple Meads as 'engineers' architecture … at once costly and offensive and full of pretension'.[54] The Duke of Wellington famously railed against railways for the simple fact that they would allow the masses or wrong classes to move about too freely, and insisted that no railway station should be opened within 3 miles of his home, Stratfield Saye, without his consent, although later he relented when a neighbour prevailed on him to accept Mortimer, 3 miles away, 'as commodious as his grace may think fit to require'.[55] When Brunel was anxious that the Great Western Bill should pass through Parliament at the second attempt in 1834 he wrote to the Duke of Wellington enlisting his support. The Duke replied questioning whether the project should be carried forward without first 'ascertaining whether it is practicable for them to carry it into execution, consistent with the rights of property and the views of others'.[56] Ruskin condemned the railways on social as well as aesthetic grounds, producing a furious blast against the Midland Railway Company for running its line through the Derbyshire Peak District and ruining Monsal Dale; 'every fool in Buxton can be in Bakewell in half-an-hour, and every fool in Bakewell in Buxton'.[57] He also described the railway as the most 'loathsome form of devilry now extant … destructive of all natural beauty'.[58] The poet Wordsworth at first thought the benefits outweighed the marring of the lovely countryside until the Lake District was threatened by the Kendal and Windermere Railway.[59] They objected to the noise of the construction gangs or navvies, and uncouth behaviour in the rural countryside where there was perhaps nothing for them to do in their spare time except drink, or even pillage the nearby properties. Those who drew revenue from local turnpike trusts or a nearby canal saw the railway as introducing new competition. George Stephenson, when first surveying the route of the Liverpool and Manchester Railway in 1824, complained of the opposition from lords Derby and Sefton and one Bradshaw 'who fires his guns in the course of the night to prevent the surveyors coming in the dark'.[60]

ECCENTRIC AND UNUSUAL OBJECTIONS

It is easy to cite eccentric objectors such as the Duke of Cleveland, who was against the Stockton and Darlington Railway simply because it would pass close to one of his fox coverts, but this did not reflect the views of the landowning classes at large.[61] There were other cases of similar eccentricity: when the East Lancashire Railway came to extend its line from Chatburn to Hellifield in 1877, Lord Ribblesdale would not allow the railway to pass through the grounds of Gisburn Hall because it might frighten his horses. The result was a 156-yard-long tunnel built as a cut-and-cover structure. At least the Lord's resistance led to the creation of two elegant castellated portals in the local red sandstone.

Ill. 5 **Gisburn Hall** Tunnel, former East Lancashire Railway. *Private photo*

In 1847–48 the Blackburn, Darwin and Bolton Railway (shortly afterwards absorbed into the East Lancashire Railway) had to contend with the wishes of James Kay, who owned the estate of Turton near Blackburn. He insisted on a castellated portal to Sough Tunnel as well as an elegant castellated bridge flanked by rectangular machicolated turrets and arrow slits piercing the parapet, to carry a driveway. Kay was a director of the company and employed Terence Flanagan as the Resident Engineer, who had worked under Joseph Locke on the Trent Valley Railway with its grand tunnel portals and bridge at Shugborough Hall. Sough Tunnel North Portal does not quite have the grandeur of Shugborough North Portal, but the bridge certainly does.

Not all, however, were as mad or as bad! There were some very influential figures who supported the railways, although none more surprising than George Godwin, a seventeen-year-old junior architect and later editor of *The Builder*. His *An Appeal to the Public on the Subject of Railways*, 1837, was aimed at the professional and land-owning class. He appealed to readers to see the 'intrinsic goodness of railroads'.[62] He claimed that any disfigurement of the landscape would be more than compensated by the embellishment of railway buildings including bridges and viaducts.[63] Other influential voices, not least George Hudson, the so-called 'Railway King', saw money to be made from an expanding railway system. Cannadine cites Thomas Arnold's welcome to the railway at Rugby as making virtue out of necessity. He saw it bringing noise and smoke but enabling masses of ordinary people to travel distances hitherto undreamed of, and this as essential to feed the industrial revolution.[64] Another advantage in favour of Government support was that railways could transport troops from one side of the country to the other within hours.[65]

Perhaps the spirit or enthusiasm of the local MP, especially if he were also Prime Minister, could help sway opinion and therefore speed the progress of construction. At the commencement of the Trent Valley Railway to provide a direct link between London and the north, thereby avoiding Birmingham, Sir Robert Peel thanked landowners for their co-operation:

> I assure them that there are many persons in this neighbourhood who have no scruple to sacrifice private feeling and comfort by consenting to their land being appropriated. They have given their consent from a conviction that this undertaking was one conducive to the public benefit, and that considerations of private interest should not obstruct the greater one of public good.[66]

Sometimes there was disagreement within the landowning families. Thus, the Earl of Lichfield of Shugborough Hall objected to the passage of the railway through his estate, whereas his brother Colonel Anson, who was also an MP, was present at the start, as well as at the opening celebrations in 1847, to be discussed later in this chapter.

Likewise, in Derbyshire we witness two generations of a family taking opposing views towards railways. The 5th Duke of Rutland insisted that the Manchester and Midland Junction Railway burrow beneath the grounds of Haddon Hall, but here the result is certainly less grand than at Shugborough. In August 1847 the Duke had written to the Vicar of Bakewell that he 'always wished that no railway should pass through our beautiful country, yet when it was proved to me that the Town of Bakewell, the Public in general, and the project would be alike benefited by its completion, I gave way as was my duty to do'. The Duke's seat was at Bevoir Castle in Rutland, and Haddon was then uninhabited, yet his wishes were complied with, and a tunnel of 1,058 yards was constructed by the cut-and-cover process in 1860–61. At one point it was only 3ft below the ground, yet during its construction, five workers were killed by the ground collapsing above.[67] The project was supported by the engineer Joseph Locke, who was engaged by the Duke of Rutland in opposition to a proposed deviation by the 6th Duke of Devonshire 'to go by Chatsworth'.[68] Yet in 1888 when the Midland Railway proposed to sink shafts for Totley Tunnel on the Chatsworth estate, his cousin, the 7th Duke of Devonshire, objected, but eventually relented on the condition that work should cease during the grouse shooting season from August to October.

An unusual case of 'gamekeeper turned poacher' is Thomas Grissell, a businessman rather than aristocrat, who, having built up a fortune in public works, including the construction of the London and Birmingham and South Eastern railways, retired and bought the Norbury Park estate in the picturesque Mole valley in 1850. He there opposed the London and Brighton Railway's plans to drive a secondary line between Leatherhead and Dorking through his estate, along the route surveyed for a direct line to Brighton by Robert Stephenson in 1836. He insisted that the railway run in a cutting 'shielded by trees at least 15 feet high', and in a tunnel for 530 yards, with 'work to be completed within a maximum of two years, under a penalty of £50 a week for any work in excess'.[69]

One of the longest and most bitter land disputes was between Lord Braybrooke, incumbent of Audley End, and the Northern and Eastern Railway.[70] The two short tunnels beneath the Audley End estate in north Essex on the line to Cambridge are the result of a long dispute between the Great Northern and Eastern Railway and the landowner, Lord Braybrooke.[71] They were not physically necessary and a cutting would have sufficed through the low chalk ridge. He at first did not want the railway near his estate in any form; in the end the two short tunnels were a compromise, although he wanted a third. Perhaps the controversy might seem one-sided until the attitude of the railway company is examined. James Walker, the chief engineer, admitted he had difficulty in the alignment of the railway in the vicinity of the estate, and the promoter Nicholas Cundy claimed before the Select Committee of the House of Commons in 1836 that he had deviated to the west in an attempt to minimise the damage to the estate 'and had decided to use a series of tunnels … to remove or at least reduce, the opposition which was threatened by the noble lord'.[72] Cundy, on the other hand, was outspoken in his views on railway construction in a pamphlet addressed 'to those on the line and connected with the Great Northern and Eastern Railroad'. He believed that the public benefit of railways far outweighed private considerations and insisted on aligning the railway through the estate. Walker admitted, that 'nothing but something amounting to necessity would justify a line through Lord Braybrooke's

Park in a way Mr Cundy has carried it'.[73] It was only in 1844 after having been paid £120,000 for acres only worth £5,000 that Lord Braybrooke finally agreed to two tunnels with mouths 'to be made good and finished with a substantial and ornamental facing of brickwork or masonry, to the satisfaction of the Surveyor or Architect of the said Lord Braybrooke'. The arch of the south portal incorporates a frieze of stone adorned with Tudor Rose, and Beaufort portcullis motives on either side of a keystone displaying the Braybrooke family arms. Perhaps this could be described as architectural compensation![74] Since a cutting would have sufficed, a clause was introduced 'to prevent the soil immediately above or around from giving way or slipping down'.[75] It is not unlike the northern portal of Milford Tunnel built for the North Midland Railway.[76]

On the outskirts of Brighton, at Patcham, there was a similar instance of a tunnel being cut when it was physically unnecessary, but due to the objections of the landowner, Major Payne. He managed to get a clause inserted into the Act of Parliament requiring a tunnel instead of a cutting.[77] As Churton said, it is 'insignificant when compared with those we have enumerated as it is only four hundred and eighty yards in length'.[78] Because of the reason for its construction it was known as the 'Compulsory Tunnel'.

Another example of landowner resistance to the cutting of the Midland Railway was that by Lord Harborough at Stapleford Park between Melton Mowbray and Stamford. He prevented the surveyors from taking measurements in his park, involving a series of running battles with the result that several men were imprisoned and fined. The Midland, however, got an Act in 1845 for a tunnel

Ill. 6 **Audley End** Tunnel south portal. *English Heritage*

under his park. Yet because of inadequate surveying, the tunnel fell in, destroying sixty trees. As a result it was proposed to create a deep cutting, but Harborough prevented this, and even when the company purchased part of the Oakham Canal, of which Harborough was a major shareholder, as a trackbed for an authorised deviation, he was not placated and continued to obstruct work. He was eventually paid £22,000 compensation for damage to his estate. The building of the sharp deviation held up the opening of the line until May 1848, but without a tunnel saved £35,000.[79]

BRUNEL AND LANDOWNERS

There are frequent references in the archives to the handling of landowners by Brunel and the Great Western, much of it carried out in courteous terms. He was also aware of the attitude of potential passengers and felt a short tunnel would not be as objectionable to passengers as a long deep cutting. He claimed a tunnel could normally be passed in about a minute, whereas a long, deep cutting would cut out the light for longer.[80] Elsewhere, he claimed that tunnels were no worse than the rest of the line during the night, and that carriage lighting would be very costly.[81] What he did not reveal was that he did not intend any lighting for the carriages, so tunnels would be passed in darkness.

While Brunel was ever-confident at winning over opposition, there were some who had the potential to hold up the project. One member of parliament was Robert Palmer of Holme Park near Reading, who opposed the railway that Brunel proposed to carry beneath his estate in a tunnel upwards of a mile in length. At the 1835 parliamentary enquiry, Brunel asserted that the part of the track in open cutting would come no nearer to Palmer's house than ¾ mile.[82] He further claimed that there would be no obstruction to the view from the house except a field on the other side of the turnpike road.[83] He sent an agent with a sketch of the proposed route to Palmer, who lived for much of the time in North Wales. A public notice for the letting of a contract for the tunnel was announced in July 1836.[84] Palmer knew he could hold the company to ransom since the Thames flowed to the north of the estate and there were private residences to the south. He also tried to get the support of other Berkshire landowners in opposing the railway. The company were wrong in assuming he would readily accept a tunnel, however when serious geological problems occurred in 1838, Palmer finally consented to a deep cutting instead of a tunnel nearly 2 miles long and 60ft deep, and requiring the removal of 700,000 cubic yards of earth, more than removed from the Box Tunnel.[85] Had Brunel persisted with a tunnel the cost would probably have bankrupted the project.[86]

In the case of a proposed tunnel at Purley near Pangbourne, Brunel wanted it to avoid 'a park with a valuable House and Grounds'. He actually stated his reluctance to destroy the beauty of Purley Park, a distinguished house by James Wyatt. 'A tunnel could cost thirty thousand pounds to build.'[87] Although Brunel was undecided about the route for some months because the owners were abroad, in the end he decided to take the line in a cutting to the north and east of the house.[88] When the line was opened from Paddington to Maidenhead in June 1838, *The Times* noted that 'no tunnel occurs for nearly 100 miles from London'.[89]

At Saltford, 5 miles to the west of Bath, the line was to pass beneath the property of Major James, however when Brunel found the owner of the neighbouring property willing to sell, he bought it for 'a very moderate sum of £700 … and an acre of land'.[90] By this means Brunel hoped to diminish the length of the tunnel, or even substitute a cutting, except under the road, and obviously avoid the cost of tunnelling. Yet Major James proved a difficult individual, complaining that he was offended by the 'straight top' of the Bath stone parapet, which could be seen from his house, to which Brunel replied that the parapet wall formed an essential part of the ornamental front of the tunnel entrance and was in the style of other works in the neighbourhood.[91]

The building of Box Tunnel has been discussed elsewhere, however with the running of the tunnel in a straight line through Box Hill, Brunel encountered further opposition, this time from the Wiltshire family who farmed land to the west of the tunnel near the proposed alignment of the track.[92] William Wiltshire owned Shockerwick, a distinguished mid-Georgian mansion just across the Box Brook in Somerset.[93] This held up the construction of track in the vicinity on grounds of visual disturbance, although the Wiltshires did not actually own land crossed by the track. The Wiltshires' cause was taken up by a Mr Sturge, land surveyor, during the House of Lords Enquiry in 1835. He was asked where and how the proposed tracks affected the prospect from the house. Sturge replied that the tracks were to be 'at some distance in front of it … on the opposite side of the turnpike road … within view of the house … The valley on which the house stands is not a wide valley'.[94] He stated the track would then go into a deep cutting where it went 'over the brow of the hill', but this would be seen from the house. Sturge won the argument as the hill in question is Middle Hill and we may assume the short Middle Hill Tunnel was subsequently cut purely to satisfy the Wiltshire family of Shockerwick.

When it came to planning the route through Bath there was opposition at first from the land and property owners in the suburb of Bathwick, which had to be overcome even though the railway might come to the aid of what was then an ailing inland spa.[95] Such was the nature of the terrain with the River Avon and the Kennet and Avon Canal taking a curving route to the south and east of the urban development that Brunel took the tracks parallel with the canal, weaving a very delicate path through the fashionable Sydney Gardens, which was to have involved a cut-and-cover tunnel, and then across a spur of land at the south-east corner of the town. At the parliamentary enquiry in 1835 Brunel was quite outspoken about the route the railway would take through what he described as houses that were notorious in Bath for being a dreadful neighbourhood. Under questioning he described the inhabitants as being 'not merely guilty of being poor but something worse', and spoke of the railway 'operating' a great moral improvement to the city.[96] Brunel told the committee he intended to take the railway through the Sydney Gardens by a tunnel, as it passed beneath three roads.[97] When he was questioned on why the tunnel did not appear on the relevant section of the survey map, he claimed he had come to an agreement with the proprietors of the Sydney Gardens and local residents who were troubled by the potential inconvenience.[98] The committee was concerned that it was an area where property was very valuable, although Brunel thought not.[99] In a letter to Denis Osler, Secretary of the Bristol Section, in December 1837, Brunel was anxious to proceed as fast as possible but was concerned about boring holes through walls, which would damage the houses and buildings at the back of Raby Place, in order to set out the line.[100]

By January 1839 the Great Western Railway had managed to modify the proposed passage of the track with the proprietors. Instead Brunel proposed to carry the railway through the gardens by an open cutting instead of the covered way proposed hitherto. Since the ground on the east was at a higher level, also containing the course of the canal, it was proposed to secure it by a retaining wall, while the west was to be sloped towards the track by a terrace and low retaining wall. A bridge, 28ft wide, was to be constructed to carry the central walk from the Sydney Hotel to Sydney House over the tracks. Two smaller bridges of cast iron or wood were also to cross the tracks at points such 'as the proprietors may determine'.[101] The proprietors insisted that top soil not required for the slopes and any gravel obtained from the excavation were to be used for landscaping on any parts selected by them.[102] They also insisted on the bridges and retaining walls being constructed to fit in with the character of the surroundings. Negotiations dragged on for a year as this was finally confirmed by the Committee of Proprietors in January 1840, with the total width of the cutting being 69ft.[103] The verdict of *The Civil Engineer and Architect's Journal* was praise indeed, 'everywhere things seem to harmonise in splendour, even here we find the line of works adjacent adding to the general magnificence'.[104] It seems that for a short period it was proposed to erect a station in the gardens, although this caused concern to the residents of nearby New Sydney Place.[105] It is likely that this was in addition to the station only half a mile to the west on the peninsular that opened in late 1840, the building of which must have been under way at this time.

Even though the idea of a cut-and-cover tunnel had been abandoned, there was still the problem of taking the tracks beneath Church Street and the terrace in Raby Place. This was by the short Bathwick Tunnel, not initially referred to, as we have seen in the parliamentary enquiry. However, it appears as a drawing in an 1839 sketchbook.[106] It was under construction from at least August 1838, and by December a newspaper reported the commencement of the permanent way.[107] It was only a hundred or so yards and so would not have taken long to cut.

Between Bath and Bristol the line follows the valley of the Avon through extensive woodland and grand scenery that attracted visitors from London.[108] It was necessary to penetrate small hill spurs with short tunnels, including two at Twerton under land owned by Charles Wilkins, the owner of a local cloth mill and a major employer in the locality. The construction also necessitated an alteration to the alignment of the main street of the village and the destruction of a number of cottages and buildings connected with the mill.[109] Wilkins was most accommodating and happy with the compensation as well as the proposal to build him a new residence to replace his original house called 'Tiverton'. The new house was erected some yards away, only for it to be totally destroyed by fire shortly after he had moved in. The fire was discovered by a workman of the Great

Western Railway, who succeeded in alerting the family. Wilkins saved family papers but his furniture was totally destroyed. It was never discovered as to how the fire started.[110] The house was subsequently rebuilt by the Carr family, who purchased the mills.

OTHER PLANNING INTERESTS OR CONSTRAINTS

So far, most examples cited have been instances when the railway traversed the grounds of an estate containing a mansion or seat of nobility or powerful landowner. However, there were also other unusual circumstances in the early decades of railway building where the obstacle was not a gentleman's seat. In 1847–48 the Great Eastern Railway wished to cross Newmarket Heath, open heathland used since its institution by James I as a racing track for horses, and therefore considered sacred by the racing fraternity, who were of course powerful and influential landowners and Members of Parliament. The Duke of Portland, who owned the heath, insisted the line had to be dropped in a cutting and covered over. The resulting tunnel, 1,099 yards in length, has remained the longest in eastern England and remains single track.[111]

Two miles beyond Primrose Hill Tunnel the tracks of the London and Birmingham Railway pass beneath the outer perimeter of the then new Kensal Green Cemetery. Here the landowners were the proprietors of one of the new metropolitan cemeteries that were then being laid out around the metropolis. The complex negotiations between the cemetery committee and the Directors of the London and Birmingham Railway were discussed by Ruth Richardson and Stephen Curl in their magnificent study of the cemetery and its architecture.[112] As they put it beautifully, the idea of trains rushing through the site 'must have put the fear of God into the Provisional (cemetery) Committee, for to have express trains rushing through the Field of Repose would have destroyed just about everything the infant company was hoping for'.[113] The Cemetery Committee could not acquire or move their land southwards as it was already passed on the south by the Grand Junction Canal. In any case the cemetery had been consecrated in January 1833. The Provisional Committee instructed its solicitor to procure an insertion in the Birmingham Railroad Act that the Rail Road Company should 'make a Tunnel as per plan and section' and the Railway Company was to pay 'adequate compensation for the land forming the site of the tunnel, and for the dangers which the Cemetery Company would suffer'.[114] As the railway company at first refused to move from its initial route alignment, 'wishing to pass through the grounds with steam carriages', the Provisional Committee threatened to petition Parliament for an insertion in the London and Birmingham Railway Bill then going through the House of Commons, and if necessary to mount further opposition in the House of Lords.[115] As this was likely to delay final parliamentary approval, the Railway Company climbed down by simply moving the route to the northern boundary of the cemetery and placing it in a short tunnel. The Provisional Committee agreed to this simple compromise.[116]

The potential threat to historical or antiquarian sites was another reason for opposition to the railways. One of the most sensitive environments to be penetrated by the railway is the centre of Edinburgh, where the trackbed runs directly below the Castle rock across the former course of the North Loch drained in the late eighteenth century. Here, in spite of opposition from the Scottish Society of Antiquities and the proprietors of Princes Street, the solution came in the form of a short tunnel through The Mound, directly beneath the classical Scottish Institution. In London, in 1864 the District Railway wished to pass within 200ft of Westminster Abbey but was forced to make special arrangements for tunnelling that imposed additional financial burdens on the company.[117] A mile to the east the London, Chatham and Dover Railway was allowed to pass across Ludgate Hill by means of a bridge, thus intruding on one of the finest views towards St Paul's Cathedral. It was condemned in 1869 by the *Imperial Gazetteer of England and Wales* as having 'utterly despoiled one of the finest views in the metropolis, and is one of the most unsightly objects ever constructed in any situation'.[118] It was to be another 140 years before the tracks were taken underground in a tunnel.

The battle lost by the landowner against the construction of a railway might not in time be seen as a battle lost. It could eventually enhance not only the value of the land in being on a line of communication, but, with the resulting economic prosperity of an area, could enhance the popularity of the landowner. If landowners played their cards right they might hold out until the right financial terms were offered, or the railway company agreed to take the tracks through a tunnel in return for not opposing the parliamentary Bill. One of Stephenson's early biographers admitted that he saw landowners' actions in holding out for the highest price from a company as fair game since costly litigation, if eventually won, could hold up construction for months or years.[119] As early as 1851 W.E. Aytoun, in *Blackwood's Magazine*, defended the landowners' case, that since they wished to preserve their property from the 'spectacle of engines roaring at all hours of the day and night close to the bottom of the lawn' they should resist the railway companies' attempts to buy the land at agricultural value and hold out for the highest price on the basis that this was speculative development.[120] The most notorious case is of Lord Petrie receiving £120,000 from the Eastern Counties Railway for land valued at only £5,000.[121] Yet, as Barbara Kerr remarked, some of those who received these vast sums kept them in their pockets, or at least away from local lawyers, who did the spadework for little reward.[122] During the railway mania of 1845, Kerr says, ' the two Houses (of Parliament) were an Eldorado to certain favoured lawyers who were alternately paid for speech and silence with reckless profusion, and some London lawyers sat back with handsome salaries of £250 per annum'.[123]

THE IMPACT OF LANDOWNER OPPOSITION ON THE EARLY RAILWAYS

Whenever any new technological or even social advance is put into the public domain there is hesitation and opposition. This is natural as the human instinct is to see if a thing works first before accepting it. The railways were perceived as noisy and therefore likely to destroy the hitherto rural peace. It was therefore to be expected that early railway pioneers would have to fight their case against entrenched opposition; proprietors could only speculate on financial profits and the good to the local and national economy once the track had been built. It was the building of the Liverpool and Manchester Railway that put railway construction on a national stage and to which many landowners looked with some fear and trepidation. It was successful, and as we have seen many landowners quickly saw the financial benefits of a linked national railway system, especially in the 1830s and again after the economic recovery in 1842.[124] Obviously there were some who held out longer than others often for more personal or selfish reasons, even as late as the 1870s such as Tonge of Morants Court near Westerham, who did not want to see 'a train pass even at a distance of 1,000 yards … I want to protect my estate for my children after me.'[125] There were those also in the early days of railway promotion who had shares in canal companies and could see the railway's potential advantage for the transport of goods in both speed and weight.

Another factor that bred opposition was the fear on the part of the landed aristocracy that their social class was under attack, a fear fostered not just by the increasing number of projected railways coming before Parliament but the growing movement for increasing parliamentary reform. J. Francis, in *A History of the English Railway: its Social Relations and Revelations*, 1857, feared the House of Lords might have taken petty revenge on the commercial classes for the enforced acceptance of the Reform Bill by rejecting William Gladstone's Railway Bill aimed at improving the efficient running by companies of trains and provision of covered third-class accommodation passed in 1844.[126] Francis was outspoken in his criticism of some landowners, who were 'rapacious' in their extraction of the maximum compensation for land.[127] Those who promoted railways were perceived as representing a growing commercial and industrial society. A dramatic rise in population and new centres of population, especially in northern England, needed an expanded railway system. Hepple, in his thesis, points out that while the numbers of the so-called aristocracy remained fairly constant, their power within society as a whole was considerably eroded in spite of the increase of private parkland as late as the 1880s.[128] They watched Parliament increasingly siding with railway proprietors working in the national interest; indeed by 1834 Parliament had conceded the necessity of railways. Hepple cites O.F. Christie in his *Transition from Aristocracy 1832–1867* as claiming the enthusiasm for railways was supported by those who supported parliamentary reform, whereas those who opposed reform also opposed the expansion of railways.[129]

By the 1840s, many landowners could see the national benefits of a linked railway system and had identified how the railway might help them personally, especially if they had mineral assets on or near their land. Railway engineers for the most part were very civil and tried to be as accommodating as possible with landowners' wishes while accepting the constraints of financial backing from the proprietors. The process of obtaining a parliamentary Bill might be a course of compromise to accommodate the wishes of a landowner by a deviation rather than facing the possibility of opposition and consequent failure to obtain the Bill. After all, both the London and Birmingham and Great Western railways failed at their first attempt. The aim was obviously to drive as straight a track as possible and with the least gradient. If a tunnel could be avoided it would be, but might have to be introduced to placate the landowner, who may well have known that the company had no alternative route. We have seen how Brunel wished to preserve landscape by initially proposing to tunnel beneath estates at Sonning and Pangbourne, as well as keeping tunnelling to the minimum between Bath and Bristol. At Middle Hill he even introduced a tunnel rather than a cutting to satisfy the sight lines of a nearby estate. On the branch from Swindon to Gloucester he pacified Robert Gordon of Kemble House, who, in spite of assurances that he had taken care as the engineer to get the best alignment possible, insisted that the track be covered by a short tunnel to obscure it from the house.[130] Here was a chance for compensation, as seen at Audley End. However, as we have seen, before a railway could be built, the promoters had to argue their case before Parliament, when opposers were given a fair hearing and the alignment could be amended rather than a Bill rejected.[131] Consequently, the number of tunnels actually cut between 1830 and 1870 to appease a landowner who was not happy with compensation may not have numbered more than a dozen.

SHUGBOROUGH AND THE EARL OF LICHFIELD

Perhaps one of the most successful results of a landowner's intervention in the proposed course of a railway is the crossing of the Shugborough estate in Staffordshire. It may be described as a model of the integration of a railway with the landscape. Lord Lichfield may claim to have been among the earliest landowners confronted by a railway company wishing to cross his estate. It is essential to understand the historical background to his situation. The Shugborough estate, which was originally owned by the bishops of Lichfield, was acquired by the Anson family in the seventeenth century and a modest house was constructed in the 1630s. It was rebuilt in about 1693 and formed the nucleus of the present house, transformed by architect Thomas Wright in 1748 for Thomas Anson, brother of the famous Admiral George Anson. The village of Shugborough was demolished in stages from the 1730s and the grounds landscaped from the 1750s with a number of monuments and follies in the architectural taste of the period.[132]

The family was sufficiently powerful to have the ancient road from Lichfield to Stafford diverted so as not to divide the estate. It was Thomas Anson, 2nd Viscount Anson, who was created 1st Earl of Lichfield in 1831, who had to confront the railway age, and he was not keen on its potential implications for his lands, which extended to a number of estates. While he was a public servant, having first been MP for Great Yarmouth in 1819–20, he later held office as Master of Buckhounds in Lord Grey's Government, and Paymaster General under Lord Melbourne. Much of his life centred on gambling and lavish entertainment. In 1820 he purchased the estate of Ranton Abbey near Stafford where he built Abbey House, which was to prove his financial undoing.[133] It was here that he lived from 1839 rather than Shugborough until his departure for the Continent for some years with debts of some £600,000. In April 1841 it was even proposed that the Queen Dowager (Adelaide) who found Sudbury Hall, her then residence in Derbyshire, too small, might move to Shugborough as the house and its grounds appealed to her.[134] She subsequently

Ill. 7 **Shugborough Tunnel** north portal. *Private collection*

decided against this on the grounds that the house was too close to the Trent.[135] The Earl of Lichfield's first confrontation with a railway was as early as 1831 when the fledgling Birmingham and Liverpool Railway wished to cross the Anson estate of Hidcot Hall.[136] George Baker, on behalf of the company, was granted permission to 'make and maintain at their own cost and charges … a tunnel not to be less than 250 yards, and to guard and protect it'.[137] The company was also to pay the Earl of Lichfield 100 guineas for every acre of land taken for the railway.[138] This venture came to nothing and the company was superseded by the Grand Junction Railway, given parliamentary approval in 1833 and the line to Birmingham from Liverpool took another route when constructed between 1834 and 1838.

However, in 1844 the Grand Junction faced a more serious situation when it was proposed to follow the Trent Valley in the vicinity of Colwich and to cut through the spur of low hills on the Earl's Shugborough estate. The aim of the newly created Trent Valley Railway Company was to provide a direct mail route to Ireland, so avoiding transfer of mail and passengers in Birmingham.[139] In normal circumstances the Earl would have been as justified as any landowner in fearing the presence of the railway because his estate was celebrated for its monuments reflecting late eighteenth-century taste. However, he was not then living on the estate, its contents having been sold to pay debts at an enormous sale in London and at the house in June and August 1842.[140] After the sale the house became the residence of Colonel George Anson, the Earl's brother,[141] who was to look after the Earl's affairs. He took a more sympathetic view to the expanding railway system, although the Earl continued to oppose the railway from afar. Through documents surviving in the Staffordshire Record Office we can trace the somewhat tortuous negotiations between the Earl's representatives and the railway company. The company had its headquarters at 23 Bond Street, Manchester, and had appointed John Locke as chief engineer. Locke had to balance the interests of the railway company with the practicalities of construction, but he was not unsympathetic to the interests of landowners and would never consider a tunnel if it could be avoided. He was, according to his modern biographer, a man who could be trusted 'for good engineering with economy of speed of construction'.[142]

However as difficulties were anticipated, Locke in his report made it clear that it was scarcely possible to form a railway in that direction without interfering with some of them (private properties), the chief consideration then had been to lay out a line as to lessen the aggregate amount of interference, and to pass by a tunnel or covered way those portions of it that might otherwise fairly be considered objectionable.[143]

He proposed three routes, the first to the south passing through Haywood Park, the property of the Marquis of Anglesey. The second, in a wide northerly swing, would pass along the Sow valley and through Shugborough Park via a tunnel. Locke pointed out that as the line should run only ¾ mile from the house, it would be concealed in a tunnel. The third route was through Tixall, Lord Talbot's estate. However the curve or deviation not only cost more money but increased the time it would take a train to cover the distance, and thus lessen the advantage over the old route via Birmingham. Locke behaved as the perfect gentleman; wishing to satisfy his masters, the directors, yet at the same time he was very conscious of the feelings of landowners, even if the disruption to their land was to be temporary. He emphasised that he was most anxious about cost but also about providing the most direct route to London and stated:

> Considering what has already passed and what is now passing in reference to the desire of the government to shorten the connection between London and Dublin … I think it would be imprudent to lay out a scheme now contemplated without calculating on the Stafford and Rugby line … Believing that such a line will eventually be made, I would provide for it by adopting now the first proposal and make it as direct as possible.[144]

The company felt the great difficulty lay with Lord Lichfield[145] and may have sensed his precarious financial situation because it was not long before financial inducement came into play. In a letter from the company to the Earl's representative, Lord Hatherton, it was suggested that 'perhaps £10,000 including land might be given'. However, Lord Hatherton 'thought that double the sum Mr Swift offered would not be sufficient inducement to Lord L. to go through Shugborough'. The company expressed a slight feeling of exasperation 'wishing you could manage this matter for us … we could do without Shugborough if we could get permission to go through Tixall'. It suggested the company would have the backing of Lord Anglesey of Haywood Park, who did not wish the railway to cross his land but was naturally happy to see it 'get leave to go through Shugborough'.[146] Anglesey, in a letter to Hatherton on 29 March, clearly expressed his objection to the railway crossing his park at Hayward.[147]

Writing in April 1844 from Chesterfield House, London, to Harvey Wyatt of Acton Hall, Stafford, Land Agent for Shugborough, Lord Lichfield, perhaps sensing that the company might lose patience and find another route, stated that, though he was not prepared to accept any sum less than £20,000, the inducement to take that compensation would be chiefly 'upon the ground that the Company might take another line … and for which I would get no equivalent. I have no doubt that if it is of real consequence to the Company … that is if the line is carried, and less expensive than my offer, they will not allow compensation of £50,000 more.'[148] Could the Earl afford to lose the offer? It seems that he left the country shortly after for a prolonged stay in Italy. In November 1844 the Earl wrote from Naples to his brother Colonel George Anson hinting at personal depression, yet even in a detached way, still objecting to the line through Shugborough estate:

> You know from what I have before written that I have no wish ever to live there again, and therefore in decidedly objecting to the proposed line, I have been able to consider it without any special partiality to the place itself. I took it as a prime matter of damage and compensation and have no hesitation in saying that I think £20,000 no compensation whatever in proportion to the damage. I put it simply, would anybody who saw Shugborough now, and

again when the line is completed give so much for it as a country residence by £20,000 with line as without it. I do not think they would by £40,000.[149]

He raised no objection to the line running through Tixall Meadows, his neighbour's (Earl of Talbot) estate, which would be 'no nuisance' to him and his own estate! 'The more I consider it, the more objectionable it appears and the compensation offered … out of all … too little … I shall be very uncomfortable till I know that your consent is not given.' He was happy for the line as long as it was separated from the house by 'two rivers and a food plantation'.[150]

Colonel Anson could see the advantages of the railway. In writing to the company on 12 November 1844 he stated he did not believe the railway was as great a nuisance as the Earl imagined, however he shared his belief that the railway would lessen the value of the Shugborough estate and that it would not fetch £40,000. He was sure the Earl would take £40,000 compensation, although he feared the company would now go round Great Haywood. On the other hand, he was unhappy with the route as it stood as it crossed the park near the Lichfield Lodge on a 12ft-high embankment, which, nearer the river, would be twice as high. He concluded by stating that the only plan that would be free from objections would include a tunnel.[151] Two days later the secretary of the Trent Valley Company wrote to Anson expressing their wish to avoid further controversy and hoped that his Lordship would confirm in a letter that the terms of the arrangement respecting his property would be sufficient.

The company wrote to the Earl's representatives on 19 November what may be seen as a final letter to guard against further misunderstandings, disagreements and delays. In it the directors emphasised the line had been altered from its original course at the suggestion of Colonel Anson and Lord Hatherstone, as 'being acceptable to Lord Lichfield'. The company hoped the compensation to be paid to His Lordship would be to the satisfaction of his representative, Colonel Anson, and that the plans would now be acceptable without further delay. Also, and this was perhaps the most important point of all, since the line through Shugborough had involved arrangements with other influential landowners, the directors hoped that the Earl would not go back on his word and withdraw his sanction, which would materially damage the company.[152]

In December 1844 the Earl wrote another letter to Colonel Anson from Italy suggesting that, while he still felt the 'injury' to Shugborough was 'incalculable', time was running out, and that he would 'take £30,000 if the Directors like to give it, but … not take a farthing less', repeating in a final cry he would have 'preferred the railroad through Tixall or Haywood a hundred times'.[153] Anson wrote to Harvey Wyatt on 16 December 1844 to say that while Lord Lichfield was still as opposed as ever to the railway, he would give in if the compensation was £30,000. He concluded by saying the Earl had given his assent to the line proposed through Shugborough.[154] The company's minutes recorded a satisfactory arrangement having been made for the passage of the line through Shugborough Park,[155] and later in the month a deputation from the board of the Trent Valley Company agreed to meet 'parties appointed on behalf of the Earl and Countess of Lichfield'.

The year 1845 proved decisive in the tortuous negotiations between the Earl's representatives and those of the railway company. The Trent Valley Railway Bill was passed by Parliament on 29 April 1845 and two days later, on 1 May, an agreement was signed with the Earl's trustees.[156] It stated the railway was to pass through the estate on the line marked in red ink on the map, and that the parties should 'pay the said Earl and trustees in lawful money, the sum of thirty thousand pounds for the land required for the purpose of the said railway'.[157] Colonel Anson then requested a plan of the railway as it was to 'go through the whole of the park at Shugborough made out with the bridges, ornamental parts and showing how the lodges would be placed in respect of the line'.[158] The estate promised to give as much land as was necessary for the railway including the slopes of the embankment, which were to be maintained by the company. The Earl, wishing to get every pound of flesh, insisted on a 'further sum of sixty pounds for each and every acre of land … in order to lay spoil and top soil'. Should the land become unfit for husbandry as a result of railway work the company would pay a further £110 per acre. Also the land was to be returned to a fit state for husbandry within six months of the completion of work and covered with soil 'no less than nine inches in thickness'.[159] The sum of £30,000 was considerable, particularly as the fourteen-day sale of the contents of Shugborough Hall in 1842 had only fetched £18,344 13s 11d.

Later in the document the treatment of the landscape around the southern entrance to the tunnel is discussed. 'The entrance to the tunnel near the Stafford approach road shall be properly and sufficiently guarded for a length of forty yards by a screen or fence of close paling to hide the sight of the trains as they pass in and out of the southern entrance of the Tunnel to be neatly faced with stone.'[160] The company was to complete the work within a period of eighteen months. There is no mention of specific ornamentation, although possibly Locke as chief engineer, and certainly John Livock as company architect, would have been sensitive to the location and its monuments in the park. Indeed the tunnel passes almost directly beneath the Triumphal Arch, one of the follies of the park. Also the company was to provide a policeman 'on the line of the railway through Shugborough Park and grounds to prevent trespass and damage' on the Earl's property.[161] The agreement also provided a clause for the construction of a 'neat and handsome' stone railway bridge over the carriage drive from the Lichfield Road Lodges, of a suitable and convenient height with 'battlements or stone walls above the level of the line of the railway of a sufficient height to prevent the danger of horses being alarmed'.[162]

Colonel Anson, unlike his brother, the Earl, being more alert to the future advantage of the railway, also suggested a station 'somewhere near to the house for the occupiers of Shugborough'.[163] The station was never constructed, but at Colwich, the nearest public station to the hall, under an agreement between the Earl and Trustees of the London and North Western Railway, a passenger train could be stopped upon the giving of twenty-four hours' notice.[164] A letter of 5 July 1845 announced the staking out of the line and advised landowners [165] that the first sod was to be cut near Tamworth by Sir Robert Peel, an ardent supporter of the new line, on 13 November 1845.[166]

The Trent Valley Railway was completed in under two years, and there was a trial train ride on 28 April 1847, at which 'the beauty of the Trent and other bridges, the entrances to the tunnel, and the elegance of the stations excited much admiration'.[167] The cutting of the tunnel proved a swift operation after the tedious negotiations of the two years, and by 31 October 1846 the passage was opened from both ends. To celebrate the event the 500 men working on it were given a substantial dinner of roast beef at the Clifford's Arms, Haywood.[168] The opening was set for 24 June, with goods traffic scheduled to commence on 1 July.[169] The formal opening was celebrated with a grand reception at the Queen's Hotel, Birmingham, at which Sir Robert Peel likened the route of the Trent Valley Railway to the Roman Watling Street and its north-western route from London to Chester by Julius Agricola. In his speech Peel was profuse in thanking the landowners who 'had not scrupled to sacrifice private feeling and comfort, by consenting to their land being appropriated … they have given with a conviction that the undertaking was one conducive to the public good'.[170] We can be sure that if they all behaved like the Earl of Lichfield, they extracted a fair price from the company.

The start of full services was, however, held up due to the collapse of Chester Bridge on the Chester and Holyhead Railway, and the need to check bridges on the Trent Valley line. With the railway finally open to all traffic in December 1847, 12 miles were cut from the previous route to the north through Birmingham, and crucially it became the mail route to the north and Scotland. Since August 1846 the Trent Valley Railway had been subsumed within the expanding network of the London and North Western Railway. This may have held up the payment to Lord Lichfield, as according to the Trent Valley Railway minute book, it was only ordered in February 1847 that he receive his compensation.[171] Meanwhile, the Earl and Countess of Lichfield only decided to return to Shugborough Hall in June 1848, by which time the trains were safely running through their park and under the hill.[172]

The tunnel is only short at 777 yards with excavation from six shafts and headings at both ends. The shafts were filled in on completion of the excavations as any structure or spoil hill would have disturbed the delicate classically landscaped hillside overhead.[173] In spite of being on a curve, the excavation was relatively straightforward as the 'miners' hewed and blasted their way through gravel held in a matrix of red marl, which was so compact as to require gunpowder to excavate it and the bore stood alone before the lining by brickwork was started.[174] In terms of construction the tunnel is wholly unremarkable, however John Livock designed the two ornamental portals of stone, which can only be described as sensational. In spite of the written documents being remarkably free of reference to their architectural richness, drawings including beautiful watercolour drafts survive in the Staffordshire Record Office and are worthy of close examination (Chapter 6). So impressive were the portals that they became known as the 'Gates of Jerusalem'.[175]

Had the Earl held out and the company refused his demands, would a diversion have made as significant a difference as at first thought? The key were the London and Birmingham and Grand Junction companies as these were against the scheme to protect their own interests. From the *Map of Projected Lines of Railway through the Trent and Churnet Valleys*, published in 1845,[176] it can be seen that a diversion could have been made to link with the Churnet Railway at Tixall and then follow the River Anker to Atherstone, perhaps adding no more than 3 miles to the route. In any case, the interests of the rival companies were eradicated by the amalgamation of the London and Birmingham, Grand Junction and Trent Valley companies in 1846 to form the London and North Western Railway. As a result, Birmingham lost its status as Midland rail 'post capital' in favour of Tamworth.

Shugborough is a fine example of where an impoverished and anti-railway landowner reluctantly accepted considerable financial compensation while allowing the railway company to secure a more direct route between the north and London. The prevarications of the landowner on the other hand ensured the passage of the railway through the estate caused absolutely no detriment to the landscape. Indeed it could be argued that the nineteenth-century ornamental tunnel portals make as comparable a contribution to the landscape as those eighteenth-century follies to the park, including the Arch of Hadrian and Temple of the Winds (Ill. 7).[177]

The Shugborough case is not typical of all disputes between company and landowner but threw up some interesting 'twists'. The most direct route was obviously through the Earl's park but he preferred it to go either south or north of his estate. The latter would have involved greater distance, although by crossing Lord Anglesey's land to the south the distance would have been the same. Anglesey, on the other hand, preferred the tracks to cross the Earl's land. The Earl hated the ideal of a railway but was in debt and needed money. His brother, then resident in Shugborough Hall, was sympathetic to the railway company's case. With negotiations the Earl got considerable financial compensation in return for the Trent Valley Company being able to cross the park and tunnel beneath the hillside without detriment to the landscape, and thus cutting the distance between Stafford and Rugby. For the company it may have only saved 3 miles between Rugby and Stafford but it allowed through-trains to run between London and Holyhead, the Irish mail route, without change of trains at Curzon Street, Birmingham.

As Denault and Landis said, feuds rarely attracted public attention unless antiquities were involved, and a growing public had little sympathy for landowners who obstructed what may be called technical progress as well as parliamentary reform. Obviously there was a mixture of fear of moving trains as well as the need to preserve what was seen as ancient, God-given, or at least monarch-given, land. But increasingly landowners and Parliament saw the opportunity to exploit mineral resources beneath land, especially coal, which could be transported quickly by the new railway system. This could provide income lost from declining agricultural rents, or loss of turnpike or canal dues. Where there was likely to be the potential for dispute, there was a parliamentary process of enquiry to hear both sides of the argument before an act was passed. In any case, committees did not necessarily record everything in debate, and landowners' objections were only one of a number of matters to be weighed in the balance. Agreement therefore could be reached behind closed doors, which could avoid costly litigation and without leaving much secondary evidence.[178]

Since money was involved, it was in the interests of railway company directors to work as closely as possible with landowners, many of whom also sat in Parliament and had the power of veto. Railway companies did not want to lose as appeals were costly; likewise landowners, especially those sitting in Parliament, felt their power increasingly eroded as a result of parliamentary reform and the election of a new class from merchant and business backgrounds who saw the potential of a national railway system.

As the decades passed certain individuals who were involved in the construction of railways and who had made money out of this activity, and who had some respect for the powerful landowners whom they may have encountered at the parliamentary enquiry, saw themselves as future landowners; George Stephenson, George Hudson, Joseph Locke and Isambard Brunel each purchased landed estates. By their actions they so perfectly represent the changing social background of landowners as the railway age progressed. Whatever may have been the feelings of landowners, and even poets, Robert Stephenson was able to sum up the situation on behalf of his railway engineer colleagues with confidence in a speech delivered at Newcastle upon Tyne in 1850, stating that:

> hills have been cut down and valleys filled up, and when these simple expedients have not sufficed … tunnels of unexampled magnitude have pierced them through, bearing their triumphal attestation to the indomitable energy of the nation, and the unrivalled skill of our artisans.[179]

Chapter 4
THE FASCINATION OF EARLY RAILWAY TUNNELS

A tunnel dug by man through earth and rock is a very special place. Its shape is a reaction to the forces of nature and the texture of its construction bears the seal of man. This must be respected, not covered up to make the place look like any other building. One must be able to feel being underground, and make it a good experience.

Sir Norman Foster, Metro *Bilbao Touristic Guide Map*, 2011

Having discussed the objections of landowners to the construction of early railway tunnels, it is now time to examine the fascination or spell such structures held for some, if not all, early spectators and passengers. Another chapter will examine the fear felt by passengers, who had not only to overcome the apprehension of the

Ill. 8 Clayton Tunnel north portal. Charles Harper, *The Brighton Road*, 1922.

human body being propelled at a hitherto unexperienced speed, but also the terrors that might await them in the smoke-filled darkness. What then is the fascination of a railway tunnel? Charles Harper, in his *The Brighton Road*, 1922, captures it beautifully in his description of the northern portal of Clayton Tunnel: 'The Gothic battlemented entrance looms with a kind of scowling picturesqueness well suited to its dark history, continually vomiting steam and smoke like hell's mouth (Ill. 8).'[1]

However, since this fascination with dark tunnels pre-dates the railway era by a century or more, it is best to look first at the early fascination with darkness through several literary descriptions of caves and early canal tunnels and then to examine the impact the early arch and railway tunnel portal made on the spectator, not just traveller. Railway companies, very aware that they had to win over public confidence, were grateful for the early handbooks and guides to reassure the public of this new form of travel, so a few of the most outstanding will be examined for their reference to tunnels. Reassurance to the travelling public was given by the appearance of railway prints, some of which were published in specific books on railway companies such as those of J.C. Bourne. These on one hand could be seen as an extension of the popular prints of dockyards and seaports that extolled the power and success of our navy or the daily toil of our fishermen. As we examine the fascination for railway travel, and indeed the experience of penetrating the darkness of a railway tunnel, we should remember that those who left us accounts of such experiences were the literate travelling middle, and in some cases, upper class. They were the successors of the Grand Tourist of the previous two centuries who had visited Italy in search of sublime landscape redolent of classical history and mythology, and who, where the opportunity arose, gazed into dark caverns, and even antique Roman sewers.

While there has been relatively little published on the architectural character of the tunnel portal, the web has a number of sites contributed by persons and groups who make it their pastime to explore old and abandoned railway and canal tunnels.[2] They record their subterranean exploits in still photographs by the light of torches and by film, even recording the drip of water from above to a trackbed strewn with rubble or refuse. Perhaps such persons see a beauty in the discoursed brickwork, sometimes bulging under the pressure of the earth wall behind, or the sudden flashes of light from the air shafts where they remain. Or do they hear the ghostly sound of long-gone express trains, or the labouring of a heavy goods train advancing towards them, enveloped in smoke? Whatever it is, tunnel exploration is alive, and those who prefer a journey by boat into the recesses of a canal tunnel can hear the sound of trains rushing past unseen in the Sapperton and Standedge railway tunnels, which were driven above the line of earlier canal tunnels. Tim Warner has argued that the fears tunnels engendered in Victorian travellers can be linked, on a more poetic level, to an extension of the 'Sublime', a sensation of the 'tingling spine' or 'bristling hairs' caused by the sight of wild mountain scenery, dark and narrow valleys, and caverns that inspire emotions of awe, wonderment and fear.[3]

The sublime and its relation to early railway journeys was discussed by David Nye in his *American Technological Sublime*.[4] While there is only a passing reference to tunnels in Chapter 3 on the early railroads, he drew some interesting distinctions between American and English attitudes to the early railways. In America there was agitation for railways for twenty years before the first, the Baltimore and Ohio, was opened in 1830.[5] Their economic potential was seen not only for a locality, but ultimately also for uniting America from coast to coast. As in England there was opposition, principally from turnpike operators, inn keepers and canal boat owners, but in England there was more of an ambivalence to new technology; Nye cites the crowds at the opening of the Liverpool and Manchester Railway, where some came to jeer rather than cheer. Indeed many of the upper class in England viewed industrialisation including railways in terms of satanic mills and Frankensteinian monsters, whereas the Americans emphasised the moral influence of steam power, and often sought to harmonise nature and industrialisation.[6]

It was not only the natural landscape that could create a sense of the sublime with its mountains, gorges, waterfalls and caves, but also the steam locomotive, which had many times the power of a horse yet was under human control. Its power, and even its potential danger, became, as Nye said, an essential part of this new form of the sublime. Nye quotes a number of authors who elevated the sight of railroads and locomotives to the ultimate of the sublime. Walt Whitman, for instance, addressed a poem *To the Locomotive in Winter*, in which he invoked the sound of the mechanical parts as the locomotive 'shrieked' its way past rocks and hills, and a *Scientific American* reporter called the sight of a rushing train at night 'sublime and terrific'.[7] The railway builders tamed the panoramic vistas of mountains with technology and intertwined the natural sublime with technological conquests.[8] While English travel writers used poetic terms to describe the journey from London to Birmingham, or the piercing of the hills of Derbyshire, the American saw his railroad in the full sense of the sublime, a technological wonder inspiring beauty, grandeur and awe in a landscape of almost incomprehensible size. Yet it was J.M.W. Turner in his *Rain, Steam and Speed*, 1840, who first translated the power and romance of the steam-hauled train into something truly sublime, even if the viaduct at Maidenhead did not have the wildness of the American Midwest.

THE EARLY FASCINATION WITH CAVES AND GROTTOES

For many Grand Tourists wishing to acquire a souvenir of their journey such as a landscape by Claude or Poussin or a follower, an indispensable feature was a bridge spanning a lake or river. There might also be a triumphal arch and the ruins of an aqueduct in the distance. Horace Walpole described to his friend Richard Bentley the beauties and associations of Hagley Park, Worcestershire, by specifically linking them to paintings by Poussin. These features were translated into the English landscaped garden of the eighteenth century such as Stourhead and Painshill, and the results gave rise to a new word, 'picturesque', first used in 1748 by William Gilpin in front of ruined arches in the gardens at Stowe.[9] And for these creations of arcadia there was also the added *frisson* provided by a grotto: somewhere dark in which might lurk a nymph or something more fearsome. The darkness played on the visitor's imagination, for example Leonardo da Vinci said 'having remained at the entry for some time, two contrasting emotions arose in me, fear and desire – fear of the threatening dark grotto, and desire to see whether there are any marvellous things within it'.[10]

Dante, in his famous *Inferno*, created a vision of a multi-layered subterranean kingdom entered through descending levels of concentric tunnelling, at the bottom of which lived a community of demons. The idea of a tunnel to the centre of the earth was of course to be taken up by Jules Verne in his *Journey to the Centre of the Earth*. Perhaps the idea of a concentric tunnel may be more in keeping with some of the engineering masterpieces of the Swiss railway system, rather than our own country, but visions of Dante were to be invoked by early nineteenth-century travellers and writers on Britain's railway. Unlike a canal tunnel, the railway tunnel with smoke issuing from a portal could evoke the image of a monster lurking within, breathing fire. Perhaps Edward Bradbury, writing under the pseudonym of 'Strephon', invoked this vision as well as any subsequent travel writer did when describing a journey through Blea Moor Tunnel: 'We are plunged into a darkness so dense that it may not merely be felt, but literally cut through.' And on the approach of another train, 'two great glaring eyes – one lurid red, the other a sickly green – are fast advancing through the gloom, and something which I should take for a fiery dragon, did I not know it to be an "up" goods train, rushes past, and enhances the sensation of poetic horror quite Dantesque'.[11]

However, the quality or aesthetic pleasure of darkness was part of what Edmund Burke described as a feeling of the sublime.[12] A tunnel or grotto mouth would obviously create this, as well as perceptions of obscurity, immensity, and for those forced to venture inside, a sense of the horrific. Thoughts provoked on the labours of construction might provoke a further sense of awe. A subterranean cavern or secret tunnel was a key feature in the opening chapter of Horace Walpole's *Castle of Otranto*, first published in 1764:

> The lower part of the castle was hollowed into several intricate cloisters, and it was not easy for one, under so much anxiety, to find a door that opened into the cavern. An awful silence reigned throughout those subterranean regions, except now and then, some blasts of wind that shook the doors … and which grated on the rusty hinges, were re echoed through the labyrynth of darkness.[13]

Grottoes have been part of the landscaped garden since classical times to the nineteenth century, as discussed by Naomi Miller in her study *Heavenly Caves*, in which she cites that many remarkable examples remain from the Italian Renaissance including the grotto at Bomarzo known as the 'Gate of Hell', which takes the theme of a dark entry to a new height of visual, and dare one say physical, sensation, in the form of a large monster-face known as the 'petrified scream'.[14] It is meant to be enjoyed from a distance rather than entered or climbed into. In England grottoes played an important part in the eighteenth-century garden, although the first one is said to have been at Nonesuch Palace in about 1588. One of the earliest to survive is that created by Alexander Pope in the tunnel he constructed beneath a road to link his villa to his landscaped garden at Twickenham. In 1725 he wrote that he had put the last hand to his works 'happily finishing the subterraneous Way and Grotto'. In this grotto he 'then found a spring of the clearest water, which falls in Perpetual Rill, that echoes Thru' the cavern day and night'. A further development was his decorating it with coloured rocks and stones, 'and shells interspersed with Pieces of Looking-glass in angular forms … at which when a lamp is hung in the Middle, a thousand pointed Rays glitter and are reflected over the place'.[15] Attractive as it was to most contemporaries, Dr Johnson derided the idea of creating a feature exploiting darkness and gloom:

> A grotto is not often the wish or pleasure of an Englishman, who has more frequent need to solicit rather than exclude the sun, but Pope's excavation was requisite as an entrance to his garden, and as some men try to be proud of their defects, he extracted an ornament from an inconvenience, and vanity produced a grotto where necessity enforced a passage.

There was also a grotto at Virginia Water that appears in a number of watercolours of the estate by Paul Sandby.

Ornamental gates also had great powers, especially if set against a dark backdrop that could well create a tunnel effect, such as the entrance to the Garden of Venus at the Villa Torrigiani at Lucca, which is made the more powerful by the rusticated flanking masonry. This could even be applied to ornamental plates or books. The frontispiece for the publication of Thomas Gray's *Elegy Written in a Country Churchyard*, 1753, was engraved with a Gothic vaulted arch as the entry to a churchyard. Cemetery gates had a certain attraction, and perhaps also fear. Was this due to a fear of being sucked in, rather like gazing into the darkness of a seemingly impenetrable tunnel, like a near-death experience? To some people the process or experience of death is liked being sucked through an endless tunnel. Many gates took the Gothic style, perhaps because it was associated with death, although there are some impressive classical examples.

THE CASTLETON CAVERN

While grottoes and gates were, of course, man-made attempts to create a feeling of pleasure, awe or the sublime, nothing could rival nature herself. The eighteenth century, as we see from the writings of Burke, Pope and Johnson, was a time of writing about the physical sensation of nature, and especially experienced through travel. By the middle of the century travellers were discovering the wonders of the Derbyshire Peak District and one of its then greatest attractions, the Castleton Cavern. It was painted by the local-born artist Joseph Wright of Derby, who had visited Italy and painted several oil versions of *A Grotto in the Gulf of Salerno, Sunset*, 1778 and 1781.[16] The German pastor, Karl Moritz, who spent some months in England in 1782, describes in graphic detail his visit to Castleton Cavern in words that would have appealed to Brunel as he tunnelled through the rugged scenery of the Avon valley fifty years later:

I stood here a few moments, full of astonishment at the amazing height of the steep rock before me ... At its summit are the decayed wall and tower of a castle which formerly stood on the rock, and at its foot, the monstrous aperture or mouth to the entrance of the cavern, where it is pitch dark, when one looks down even at mid-day.[17]

Perhaps Brunel wanted to achieve the same feeling of awe with the western portal of Queen Anne Park Tunnel with its ruinous wall in a rocky cutting. The early traveller entering a railway tunnel with the smoke seeping into the carriage may have felt like Moritz as he reached a chamber with a steady drip of water from the roof into a stream below. Bradbury perhaps had similar feelings in mind as he exaggerated the experience of passing through the short Ampthill Tunnel, prompted by Dante's visions:

The darkness, that might be of the valley of the shadow of death – the clammy coldness ... the flakes of fire ... that flutter along, and reveal the wet walls flying past like a rushing river. The tunnel is a Styx, the train is Charon's boat. The engine driver, standing in a statuesque attitude at his post, is Dante's infernal ferryman.[18]

Others also wrote and illustrated their experiences of the cavern. In the 1790s George Woodward produced a drawing that was published as an engraving *View in Peak Hole*, in which a large party of men hold flaming torches to light up a huge chamber described as 'beyond the first river'.[19]

THE ATTRACTION OF EARLY MINING TUNNELS

The Industrial Age could not have flourished without the increasing excavation for coal, not as hitherto by open-cast mining but by the pit and adit or tunnel method. It was physically very hard and dangerous with frequent flooding or collapse of shafts, and as certain parts of the country were turned into a wasteland of spoil heaps and wagonways, many landowners exploited the mineral wealth for their own ends. Occasionally artists depicted this 'new hell' as some saw it, but it was not necessarily on the itinerary of visitors. Whereas a cave was assumed to be safe from collapse, a mine adit or tunnel was not, and few were visited, or considered attractions for visitors. One such, the Duke of Bridgewater's mine workings at Worsley, inspired this allusion to Dante:

We went in a pleasure boat down ye navigation, sailed rivers and highroads and at last arrived at ye Styx, where we embarked on board Charon's boat and sailed 1,000 yards underground by ye twinkling of a few candles.

We then arrived at a highway leading to ye infernal regions where we met one of ye furies of Darkness as black as ye Devil. By him we were conducted, having left our boat, 150 yards almost upon our hands and knees till we came to ye Coal.[20]

Another early experience for the keen subterranean explorer was Kitty's Drift from the East Kenton Colliery to the Tyne at Scotswood. Abraham Rees, in his *Cyclopaedia*, 1819, suggests the tunnel was more than just for mining purposes; he quotes a description first published in 1807 that reads like an account of what was to be experienced, as well as how to prepare for a visit:

> It would be advisable to take with you a change of dress, as, from the dirt you are likely to contract in a mine, you may feel uncomfortable without removing, at least, your upper clothes. Strong boots, to keep your feet dry, and an old hat, are also necessary. Being thus prepared, proceed to the staith, which is at the river side, about four miles above Newcastle (Scotswood), a pleasant excursion by water.
>
> Here you got into a wagon to be drawn through the tunnel by horse. As soon as you are placed with your candles lighted, you set off at full speed, with a boy in the first wagon, for your charioteer, into a tunnel, or subterranean passage, six feet high, about the same breadth, and three miles long … it is particularly necessary to guard against putting your hands suddenly out of the wagon, as the tunnel, in most places, is only wide enough to admit the wagon and horses.[21]

The speed was about 10mph and mostly through a rock-cut tunnel, with water draining in a channel at the side of the track. Because of the length of the tunnel there were passing places for loaded wagons coming down; the light of the candle of the boy on the approaching wagon appearing like a star in the gloom. Lest the thought of such a journey might create a sense of claustrophobia in the reader or potential traveller, they were assured that the air in the tunnel was 'cold but perfectly pure', and that it had been visited by many ladies who were 'drawn in small empty coal wagons, capable of containing two persons each, seven of which are drawn along a railway by one horse'.[22]

So from this we can see how the arrival of the 'human cavern' or man-constructed tunnel fitted perfectly the place taken by the concept of the 'Sublime Landscape', a point made by Warner.[23] Perhaps it could be argued that there was not much difference between the sensation of riding through the exposed rock sections of the Box Tunnel and wading through the Great Cavern at Castleton, except that the former was straight and there was the possibility of seeing light at both ends.

JOSEPH WILLIAMSON AND HIS PASSION FOR TUNNELS

If the man-made mine tunnel or adit such as Kitty's Drift could hold a fascination through the mood or sensations created by such a structure, then the eccentric creations of the Liverpool merchant Joseph Williamson went one stage further; tunnels for what might be termed the entertainment of 'mind and mood' rather than any practical purpose. Born in 1769, Williamson made his wealth in the tobacco trade and settled in the then wealthy Edge Hill district on the outskirts of the town. Here beneath his house in Mason Street he proceeded to excavate a series of brick-vaulted chambers and passages hewn into the bed of sandstone. The one directly beneath his house he called the 'Banqueting Chamber'. He bought more land on Mason Street and erected houses over a brick-arched terrace, from which he gradually tunnelled back into the hillside. There seems to be no known rational reason for this behaviour and extravagance, since the cost of labour and brick must have been considerable. It has been said that he sought solace from the death of his wife in tunnelling, that it may have provided shelter from predicted Armageddon, or that he wanted to provide work for the poor. The only visual parallel may have been the creations of subterranean chambers in the engravings of Piranesi. Williamson's tunnels were subsequently lost or forgotten for nearly a century as many were bricked up. In recent years some have been partially excavated.[24] Ironically the railway tunnel driven from Edge Hill to Lime Street in 1836 went directly beneath his house!

Even before a railway was opened a tunnel attracted the attention of the public, especially in or near towns. In 1840 crowds flocked to walk the 12 miles between Bristol and Bath, which included the thrill of a number of tunnels built to Brunel's gigantic dimensions, entered along dramatic rock cuttings. Such was the response as the opening date drew closer that the directors of the Great Western gave orders prohibiting the further admission of visitors to any part of the line between Bristol and Bath unless accompanied by a director or authorised officer of the company.[25] We can only imagine the thrill of gazing by candlelight at the virgin rock face or brickwork of a tunnel and the excitement of the dark. A similar order was issued for Box Tunnel because visitors were hindering track-laying, just a week before the train services between Bristol and London opened, and long before work finished on the portals.[26]

THE IMPACT OF A GIANT PORTAL

The portal of a railway tunnel, though larger than that of a canal tunnel was, of course, not the only type of arch to fascinate, or indeed suggest a sense of awe during the eighteenth and early nineteenth centuries. The eighteenth century had seen the building of extensive naval dockyard walls punctuated by large gatehouses; that at Chatham from about 1720, attributed to Vanbrugh, is notable, but nearer the railway age is the entrance to the Royal Victualling Yard at Plymouth by John Rennie 1823–33. Brunel was acquainted with Rennie and knew his aqueduct at Freshford, and may well have known his work at Plymouth. One can sense some of the gravity and weight of Rennie's work in Brunel's Box Tunnel western portal. Having received part of his education in Paris, an early influence on Brunel may have been the portals to the city wall including the Port S. Martin from the 1670s and the Arc du Caroussel, 1808, in front of the Louvre. From these and the Marble Arch, London, 1828, it is but a short step to the concept of an Italianate eastern portal for Primrose Hill Tunnel of 1837–38. Whilst triumphal arches had scale, the railway tunnel portal had another dimension, the darkness within!

Although many early travellers faced the prospect of a train journey with fear and trepidation, to the static observer, especially a child, there is, a thrill in looking towards a monumental tunnel portal, a point made in *Peter Parley's Annual* shortly after the completion of Primrose Hill Tunnel:

> Peeping out before you, you can see through Primrose Hill Tunnel, for it seems such a little way, that one can hardly fancy it should be so dark, but after entry, the light becomes dimmer, and although for a moment a gleam of light comes from the shaft, in another moment it is profound darkness again.[27]

We can picture this because we have the Bourne drawing with the other end distinctly seen. The early fascination with this portal was exploited in several popular prints of the crowds at Primrose Hill, and also in an early cartoon of crowds waiting at the western entrance to Box Tunnel to see the sun supposedly rise through the eastern portal. It is to Box that the accolade must be given for the most frequently mentioned tunnel in newspapers and journeys of the Victorian era; not just reports of accidents – mercifully there were few – but also as a theme running through stories set on railway trains. It was also the theme of questions in general knowledge journals of the day; it is remarkable how hard it was to ascertain its correct length. Why was it that Box captivated the imagination in the way it did? Perhaps partly it embodies the personality of Brunel. He was a confident leader and believed almost anything could be accomplished. He was not just a builder of railways but of bridges and steamships as well, and indeed accomplished the first transatlantic laying of a cable. He had his critics, and he got things wrong, such as persisting in the broad gauge when the rest of the country adopted the gauge chosen by George Stephenson. However, between Chippenham and Bristol he cut a sequence of tunnels with magnificent portals imaginatively engineered to fit into the local landscape.

THE LIVERPOOL TUNNELS
Perhaps it is appropriate that the leap from Williamson's fanciful tunnels built for the delight of mind and mood, to ones that served a very practical purpose, the transit of the first passenger railway, should have taken place in Liverpool. The long tunnel from Wapping to Edge Hill and the shorter one from Crown Street Station instantly became sensations for the Liverpool public and Williamson's tunnels became quickly dwarfed, if not forgotten. Both were considerable feats of physical labour let alone engineering. Henry Booth noted that the short tunnel was cut through various strata of red rock, blue shale and clay, but that the geologist would be disappointed because the walls were whitewashed to reflect the gas illumination.[28] Being through rock, there was not the problem of potential flooding.

As excitement in Liverpool mounted for the opening of the Liverpool and Manchester Railway, the tunnel at Wapping seems to have been an attraction for visitors at least a year before the official opening of the railway. Newspaper reports described large crowds visiting the tunnel at every opportunity. *The Times* of 3 August 1829 reported the opening of the 'grand railway tunnel under the town of Liverpool from the back of Edge Hill to Wapping' and the short tunnel from Crown Street. The short tunnel to Crown Street was also open; at the mouth was placed a temporary rail and door 'where the admission money, a shilling a head, was received'.[29] It would seem that visitors started at Crown Street on foot through the short tunnel and then 'at Edge Hill' joined wagons for the long descent through Wapping Tunnel. *The Times* reported:

> Although daylight penetrates this entrance tunnel which is 270 yards long from end to end, it is feeble in the middle, and there, for some extent, a row of candles was fixed on each side to relieve the obscurity and to enable the visitors to inspect the workmanship. At 2 o'clock, the worshipful mayor, in company with some friends, alighted from his carriage … and proceeded on foot through the small tunnel. Groups of elegantly dressed ladies and gentlemen had already arrived, and when his worship and his friends had reached the extensive area into which the two tunnels open, the scene was lively and interesting.[30]

Ill. 9 Entrance to the tunnels, Edge Hill. T.T. Bury. The portal in the middle is the Wapping Tunnel, on the right is the Crown Street Tunnel. The arch on the left was originally for symmetry and used for storage. It was later continued as a second tunnel to Crown Street goods depot. *Coloured Views on the Liverpool and Manchester Railway*, Ackermann, London, 1831. *Science Museum Group*

George Stephenson wrote proudly to the Ironworks owner Michael Longridge on 23 August 1829:

> Next we went to the tunnel, where a train of wagons was in readiness to receive the party. Many of the first families in the county were waiting here to witness the process which was accompanied by a band of music, occupying one of the Wagons.
> We descended in grand style through the tunnel which was brilliantly lighted up, the gas lights being placed at intervals of 25 yards.[31]

Another early visitor was the composer Felix Mendelssohn, who described in a letter to his father how he was driven through the tunnel in a wagon.[32] He started to walk into the long tunnel:

> But since I couldn't even see the end from inside I found it a bit intimidating. I spoke to the watchman and finally persuaded him ... to allow me the use of a wagon to go through Liverpool all the way to the harbour ... a workman climbed up on the back, and off we went at fifteen miles per hour, there was no horse and no engine ... the wagon ran on its own, gradually working itself up to the wildest speed. Two lamps were burning in front, the daylight disappeared, the wind blew out the lamps and then we were in pitch darkness and for the first time in my life I saw nothing ... all the while the wagon raced faster and faster. Halfway along the route we passed a coal fire ... there the workman stopped and lit up a lamp ... it was also bitterly cold in the passage; then the red warm daylight came streaming in from afar, and I was standing by the harbour as I stepped off.

While it appears that the wagon was not attached to a rope or had any system of braking, and Mendelssohn's experience was fraught with danger, the goods service would be operated by rope haulage.

James Scott Walker, in his 1830 description of the railway, wrote a vivid account of the long tunnel:

> The stranger who first explores this magnificent and apparently interminable arch, cannot fail to be impressed by feelings of awe and admiration ... the road being formed of sand is as smooth as a bed left by a summer sea with the rails rising an inch above the level. Painted on the whitewashed walls for promenaders, were the names of the streets below which they were walking, and gas jets every fifty yards lit up the scene.

Here Walker's imagination touched extraordinary heights of imagery:

> The effect was grand and beautiful ... no great stretch of the imagination was required by the enthusiast, to entertain the pleasing delusion that he traversed the splendid passages of a magnificent eastern palace, in which the

fair inhabitants of a hundred harems were permitted to ramble in unwonted freedom among the lords of creation.[33]

Since most of the construction was finished by early June, the directors made plans for a number of trial runs and excursions over part or whole of the route. This was primarily to give the engine drivers practise in working the engines, but also to advertise the joys and comforts of train travel to the public. On 18 June the directors were given a preview of the whole route. 'After passing through the small tunnel (from Crown Street) seven carriages laden with stone were attached to the engine. The weight of the coaches with passengers was about 5 tons.'[34] They arrived back from Manchester in 'one hour, 34 minutes. The average speed of the return was 20 miles per hour.'[35]

The then eighteen-year-old actress Fanny Kemble, who was fascinated by tunnels, gave a friend a detailed account of her trip on the Liverpool and Manchester Railway in 1830, including facts about the tunnels at Edge Hill.[36] 'I am most anxious to be there for the opening of the railroad which takes place on Wednesday.'[37] Her parents were well-known in acting and influential circles, which paid dividends in a spectacular way, not least in knowing the Earl of Wilton at Heaton Hall near Manchester. They were invited to take a trial trip as far as the 15-mile viaduct and Fanny was even allowed to sit beside Mr Stephenson.[38] The train was, of course, rope-hauled between Crown Street and Edge Hill and left Crown Street on a slight downward incline to the entrance to the tunnel 'which forms the entrance to the railroad'.[39] Fanny wrote at length about this tunnel and its neighbour:

> This tunnel is four hundred yards long (I believe), and will be lighted with gas. At the end we emerged from darkness and, the ground becoming level, we stopped. There is another tunnel parallel with this, only much wider and longer, for it extends from this place which we have now reached (Edge Hill), and where the steam carriages start, and which is quite out of Liverpool, the whole way under the town to the docks. This tunnel is for wagons and other heavy carriages; and as engines which are to draw the trains along the railroad do not enter these tunnels, there is a large building at the entrance which is inhabited by steam engines of a stationary turn of mind, and different constitution from the tunnelling ones which are to propel the trains through the tunnels to the terminus in the town without going out of their houses themselves. The length of the tunnel parallel to the one we passed through is (I believe) two thousand two hundred yards long.[40]

She then went on to explain the change from rope to steam haulage:

> We were then introduced to the little engine which was to drag us along the rails, (but as) the steam horse being ill adapted for going up and down hill, the road was kept at a certain level, and appeared sometimes to sink below the surface of the earth, and sometimes to rise above it.[41]

Another early diary record of a journey on the Liverpool and Manchester Railway by Lord Broughton in August 1834 described the effect as:

> I was more affected by this display of human power than by any other work of art, the Simplon Road or Menai Bridge not excepted. There was something awful, bordering on the terrific, in our moving through the last tunnel, but all portions of the work seemed performed with such accuracy as to diminish much the sense of danger.[42]

By the 'last tunnel' he meant the short rope-hauled one to Crown Street Station as the longer one to Wapping was only for goods traffic.

The opening of the line to Lime Street in 1836, necessitating a 2-mile-long tunnel from Edge Hill, was again rope-hauled, which provided drama at the commencement or end of the journey. Striking a positive note, *Frazer's Magazine*, April 1838, likened the journey between Liverpool and Manchester to a series of 'entertainments, surpassing any in the Arabian Nights because they are realities, not fictions'. It saw the journey as a series of acts or 'epochs', which are 'peculiarly exciting'. It saw the journey through the tunnel as:

> really electrifying … the deafening peal of thunder, the sudden immersion in gloom, and the clash of reverberating sounds in a confined space, combine to produce a momentary shudder, or idea of destruction, the thrill of annihilation, which is instantly dispelled on emerging into the cheerful light.[43]

Perhaps we may view this as highly exaggerated but this was still the first decade of passenger rail travel! The American novelist Nathaniel Hawthorne, who was Consul in Liverpool in 1843–58, kept a copious diary of his experiences here and frequently records his railway journeys, or it seems the track-side landscape, describing one such journey from Lime Street in 1856 as 'monotonous as usual'.[44] Yet this journey would have begun with rope haulage through a 2-mile long tunnel. Nowhere in his diaries does Hawthorne mention the experience of travelling through a tunnel.

THE EARLIEST PASSENGER EXPERIENCES OF TUNNELS ELSEWHERE

Between 1830 and 1832 Stephenson was contracted to supervise the short Leicester and Swannington Railway, which involved the boring of Glenfield Tunnel, 1,796 yards long. This opened in 1832 and was a single-track bore to bring coal from the neighbouring mines. When the tunnel was finished in March 1832 it appears to have been a considerable attraction to the local people, so temporary gates were erected 'so as to keep out intruders on Sundays until the permanent gates can be put up'.[45] Later a signalman's house was set up at one end, while the other was closed by gates. The announcement of the opening of the line was made in the *Leicester Journal* on 13 July 1832. 'The opening of the Railway will take place on Tuesday next, the 17th instant. The Locomotive engine with a train of carriages will start from the Augustine Friars at 10 o'clock and proceed to Badgworth.'

The opening was not without incident:

> The inaugural train, drawn by *Comet*, and consisting of an open wagon specially covered for the use of the Directors, the company's only open second-class carriages and ten new coal wagons with improvised seats, conveyed in all about 400 passengers. Slight delay was caused by the engine's chimney striking the roof of the tunnel at a point where the platelayers had temporarily raised the track to pack a depression in the ground. The train was halted specially at Glenfield Brook to enable the passengers, especially the ladies, to remove the effects of the enforced sojourn in the tunnel.[46]

The directors were relieved to know the fault did not lie with the construction of the tunnel and could easily be rectified by lowering the track. As an added precaution the chimney of the locomotive was lowered by 6in.[47] According to Wishaw, there were frequently up to seventy passengers a day travelling on the railway, but he is not clear as to whether they actually travelled through the tunnel.[48]

If the Glenfield Tunnel was the first tunnel to be used by steam locomotives hauling coal wagons from its opening in 1832, the Marsh Lane Tunnel, cut through Richmond Hill for the Leeds and Selby Railway, must be the earliest tunnel used by passenger traffic from its earliest days. *The Times* struck a positive note: 'there is an intercourse of passengers amounting to 400 per day … and generally speaking, they do not object to go through the tunnel with a locomotive engine. The fuel used is coke'.[49] Sir George Head wrote what must be the earliest experience of a traveller on a steam-hauled train in a tunnel. He described the tunnel at Leeds as 'admirably excavated; eight hundred yards long of ample dimension … well bricked and whitewashed'.[50] He did, however, admit that, in spite of three shafts that let out the smoke, a considerable 'part of the transit is performed in utter darkness'. With the expansion of tracks in 1894 the tunnel was opened out to be replaced by a deep cutting.

THE ROLE OF THE EARLY RAILWAY GUIDE

Hitherto reference has been to diaries and newspapers, however with the advent of railways came a new form of literature that added a visual dimension to the experience and joy of travelling: the travel guide. Some, including Simmons and Freeman, have argued that it had two purposes: to publicise the route of a particular company and to act as a vehicle for advertising, such as the popular guides of George Measom from the 1850s. The earliest guide was *Liverpool and Manchester Railway* by John Scott Walker, 1830. It was purely textual. However as the railway system developed so they took on the form of both a guide to the respective company and a description of the 'antiquities' to be seen at first from the carriage window, and then by alighting at an intermediate station and taking a horse-drawn carriage.[51] The London and Birmingham Railway saw four publications alone upon opening in 1838 and three more in 1839. While the carriage guide today is of little use because of modern speed, in the early days of railways they were really only useful for the window seat passenger; how far guides were actually taken on a journey is open to question. Also, these guides were written and purchased by the middle class, who would have travelled in a closed carriage and could therefore see a spell in the darkness of a tunnel as exciting, with only limited smoke penetrating the carriage; for the poor third class in open wagons it was a different experience, noisy at best and at worst choking, cold and possibly wet from water dripping from shafts.

The passenger who did purchase such a work was obviously keen on viewing the landscape, so the prospect of being plunged into darkness as a tunnel was traversed might not have great appeal. While Measom often illustrates tunnel portals, his references to tunnels are often purely factual, such as approaching Edinburgh 'we dash through a tunnel, 420 yards perforating the Calton Hill …'[52] Other early writers were more imaginative in their description, perhaps because in the first two decades of railway travel tunnels were still a novelty that could invoke fear as well as excitement with the glow from the dim oil lamps, where such were carried, playing on the tunnel walls. Few could compare with Edward Bradbury, or Strephon, on the Midland Railway, 1879. Others, especially those on the London and Birmingham Railway, tended to repeat extracts that have to be read in the context of what was then seen as an engineering achievement to rival the Pyramids, at least by the railway companies.

THE GLORIFICATION OF THE LONDON AND BIRMINGHAM RAILWAY

While the Great Western has over the decades become mythologised, and Brunel's achievements, both mechanical and structural, received great praise, it was the London and Birmingham and subsequently the London and North Western Railway that was the subject of a number of early railway guides or companions that included descriptions of features, not least the tunnels. This was after all the first long-distance railway from the capital and which, by linking with the Grand Junction in Birmingham, provided nearly 200 miles of track to Liverpool. The company was not short of publicity, firstly from the newspapers, and secondly the guide books, which were to whet the traveller's appetite and hopefully increase enthusiasm for some of its wonderful structures, not least the eight tunnels. Some guides copied passages from each other but the message was the same: sit back and enjoy the landscape and the 'wonders of the rail-road', although because of size, some were more suited to the library rather than the carriage. Even before the line had fully opened, Thomas T. Bury published a series of six high-quality prints of the southern section of the line, no doubt cashing in on the popularity of his earlier prints of the Liverpool and Manchester Railway.[53] J.C. Bourne's *The London and Birmingham Railway*, 1839, is the most celebrated book, with beautiful views of the track by Bourne and a commentary by Edward Britton, best known for his antiquarian essays on cathedrals.[54] It was meant more for the gentleman's library, both in size and content, whereas Freeling's *Guide to the London and Birmingham Railway*, 1838, was intended for the carriage passenger. Sensing that tunnels might threaten confinement to the uninitiated, he described them as 'spacious and lofty galleries'.[55] The following year saw the publication of two guides, Thomas Roscoe's *Guide to the London and Birmingham Railway* and Peter Lecount's *History of the Railway connecting*

London and Birmingham. Roscoe proclaimed it as 'unquestionably the greatest public work ever undertaken, either in ancient or modern times'.[56] He was particularly keen to emphasise the magnitude of the engineering and architectural aspects of the journey. On the other hand, Lecount was accused of lifting large sections from Roscoe's history.[57] Many more superlatives were written, some perhaps a little extreme or hard to verify. One was that it 'is observable that all the tunnels and bridges on the line invariably present their most handsome front to those leaving the metropolis'.[58] Several, including Francis Goghlan's *Great Iron Road* published in 1838, were more concerned with the scenery than railway features, emphasising gentlemen's estates rather than features of engineering, although 'there is scarcely a mile throughout the whole length in which cuttings or embankments are not necessary'.[59] Another writer, Samuel Sidney in *Rides on the Railways*, 1851, actually shows little enthusiasm for railways, but rather concentrates on the history and topography through which the journey passes.[60]

Some guide books could be quite lyrical, for example J.W.W. Wyld's *London and Birmingham Railway Companion*, 1838. Although full of exciting facts about the journey, its poetic language about the tunnels en route might have put off some of the more hesitant passengers. This also applied to James Drake's *Road Book of the London and Birmingham Railway*, 1838. *The Times* commented that the railway:

> is buried between lofty embankments, that nothing can be seen by the sides of a trench, and this is more particularly the case where the prospect of the seats and parks of the nobility and gentry would be most desirable. Another disagreement is passing through the tunnels, of which in the whole line there are seven.[61]

Right from the commencement of the journey from Euston there were things to see. While the impression for many miles northwards is now one of the uncontrolled sprawl of the London suburbs, those early travellers were greeted by the first tunnel beneath Primrose Hill with its monumental eastern portal. Being then on the outskirts of London, it naturally attracted attention, where crowds gathered to watch the trains plunge into the ornamental mouth, not least when a royal train carrying the Queen and Prince Albert was cheered 'into the recesses of the cavern'.[62] However, the tunnel was built as a passage for a train, not as a static architectural backdrop, and some descriptions might be calculated to instil a slight fear in the mind of the passenger, although to Freeling its portal 'allays the fears of the nervous passenger when entering these subterranean galleries'.[63] It received a eulogy by 'Mr Humphrey' in the *Architectural Magazine* in which he praised the good taste of Mr Stephenson, while dismissing the classical Euston terminus by Hardwick as having little 'that fits peculiarly for its locality and purpose'.[64]

Drake, in his *Road Book of the London and Birmingham Railway*, is perhaps near the truth in describing the experience, and certainly by those in open wagons:

> If the passenger should happen to look out of the carriage he will see, stretching across the line, the noble entrance of Primrose Hill Tunnel, ... If

however, the traveller should prefer keeping his seat and closing the window, he will find himself suddenly plunged, without a moment's warning, into worse than the Cimmerian darkness, and hurried along through clouds of smoke and vapour; amid flying sparks, jarring atoms, and every sign of elemental strife, whilst stunning sounds, and the rattling, clashing din from a hubbub that which Satan heard in his flight through the realms of Chaos and old Night could scarcely be more terrific.[65]

The timid travellers were invited to close their eyes for a minute until they were safely restored to the light of day, while the bolder passenger could contemplate the 50ft of earth above their heads. Drake may intentionally have underestimated the length at only 360 yards.

Beyond the tunnel it was still open country and Roscoe is quite poetic about the sensation of the journey:

After clearing the tunnel and excavations, the traveller, on reaching the levels, almost universally experiences a sensation of freedom and elasticity, like to that which the pilgrim feels when he has surmounted the heights

Ill. 10 Primrose Hill Tunnel east portals from adjacent garden. The original portal is on the right. It is virtually impossible to view these grand portals from another viewpoint in total contrast to the embankments crowded with sightseers when the railway was first opened. *Railway Heritage Trust*

that have long engaged his toiling steps. Such however is the rapidity of movement that little time is allowed for any feeling but that of a pleasant kind … Distance lends enchantment to the view.[66]

The writer Joseph Wyld was at his most dramatic as the train approached Watford Tunnel:

We arrive at the entrance of Watford Tunnel into which we are helplessly dragged by the belching monster that has hitherto spirited us safely along, but who now appears to be treacherously carrying us as victims to the subterranean retreat of some hideous gnome or ogre … It is cut through an earth composed of sand and gravel, which causes a great difference of temperature to be felt by the traveller on first entering; but the light given from the lamps carried on the train, and the reflection of the engine's furnace, dissipates in some degree the fear of lurking danger and the horrors of a living burial. Yet it is melancholy to reflect, that, in forming this stupendous work, and rendering it secure for passage to and fro, the lives of many human beings were sacrificed.[67]

The Morning Chronicle reported on the second day of opening in 1837 that Watford Tunnel was so straight that the exit could clearly be seen and that the 'passengers were shot through it, as out of a huge gun'. George Osborne, in his *Guide to the London and Birmingham Railway*, 1838, observed that:

in railway travelling, one of the most distinguishing traits is the magic celerity with which the different scenes are changed. At the moment we are gazing at the beauties of the delightful neighbourhood of Berkhamstead.

And then:

the scene is suddenly shut out of view by the train plunging into a cutting through chalk … deeper and deeper still, until the reverberation produced by the engine entering an arch is heard, and immediately we are in the darkness of North Church Tunnel.

On leaving the tunnel the passenger is told that:

on looking backwards, a large quantity of chalk, taken out of the tunnel in boring it, may be seen in a heap on the top of the hill, where it lies as spoil by the sides of the shaft through which it was drawn out.[68]

Between Tring and Rugby the tracks pass through four tunnels, Northchurch, Linslade, Stowe Hill and Kilsby, the latter a formidable undertaking for the period. Roscoe commented that Northchurch 'has two handsome fronts of stone, with sidewalls of brickwork, and is the same height and proportions as the Watford

Tunnel',[69] while Wyld considered it too short 'to conjour up any subterranean horrors'.[70]

Linslade Tunnel 'south of Bletchley' was noted by *The Times* as the only curved tunnel on the line.[71] The original intention was to take the route through Leighton Buzzard, however this met with opposition from landowners.[72] Indeed had the tunnel not been insisted on, a deep cutting could have been substituted.[73] Although short, only 285 yards, the tunnel had to bore through a belt of limestone under Jackdaw Hill, necessitating considerable blasting with gunpowder. The internal shoring up of the tunnel was depicted by Bourne. Its shortness inspired Wyld to his most poetic, 'we are borne with no more inconvenience than is occasioned by the temporary passing of some gloomy cloud, or the darkness which precedes the dawn upon the thousand hillocks of some glorious land'.[74] Samuel Sidney gives directions as to how to obtain the 'greatest sensation' when passing through Linslade Tunnel on the London and North Western Railway:

> We strongly recommend some artist fond of 'strong effects' in landscape to obtain a seat in a coupe forming the last carriage in an express train, if such are ever put on now, sitting with your back to the engine, with windows before and on each side, you are whirled out of sight into twilight and darkness, and again into twilight and light, in a manner most impressive yet which cannot be described. Perhaps the effect is even greater in a slow rather than an express train. But as this tunnel is curved the transition would be more complete.[75]

With the completion of Kilsby Tunnel, the principal delay of the middle part of the line, the route from London to Birmingham was opened in September 1838. However, before this there were a number of special trains; *The Midland Counties Herald* reported the journey from Birmingham on 20 September of directors and proprietors along the entire line. Kilsby Tunnel

> has excited the greatest interest and admiration. When the party arrived at the central shaft which has a diameter of sixty feet, they were saluted with hearty cheers from a number of workmen who had stationed themselves at its summit far above the subterranean travellers who responded to the welcome.[76]

When the passenger service started a few days later, its impact was quickly felt on what had hitherto seemed the stable coaching traffic between the provinces and London. In little over a month the number of coaches running between London and Birmingham was cut from twenty-two to four.[77]

By the 1840s rail travel had been accepted as a safe and quick form of transport by an increasing proportion of the public. As we have seen, there were a number of books on the London and Birmingham Railway likening it to the greatest of engineering feats in the whole course of history. On a simple but very useful level Henry Cole published the *Railway Chronicle Travelling Charts* from 1846 to cover the principal railway routes from London. These consisted of a simple line representing the tracks down the centre of the extended sheets with every bridge, viaduct, and tunnel marked. Alongside was a brief commentary of the major landmarks, both physical and man-made, seen from the carriage window, along with key historical facts. Tunnels sometimes received a special comment: Kilsby was described, perhaps with some slight exaggeration, as 'one of the most remarkable engineering works but difficult as it was, far greater difficulties have since been conquered by Mr R. Stephenson; the works at Holyhead and Conway put those at Kilsby in the background'.[78]

However, not every commentator on early rail travel was enamoured of tunnels or the sensation of riding through them. Even the wonder of the Kilsby Tunnel seemed to be short-lived, at least for one writer, Samuel Sidney, as 'after Weedon we pass through Kilsby Tunnel … which was once one of the wonders of the world; but has been, by the progress of railway works, reduced to the level of any other dark hole'.[79] He did, on the other hand, include a view from what was claimed to be the top of the tunnel looking towards Rugby with a group of sightseers, including women standing behind the parapet of a turret, which the portals of Kilsby never had! James Drake, perhaps having exhausted all his literary skills on the passage of Primrose Hill Tunnel, comments on the periodic gleams of light from the shafts, and how, in looking down one of these huge caverns from the top of the hill, it produced a 'sense of an awful sublime and terrific nature'.[80]

The final tunnel between Coventry and Birmingham is the Beechwood Tunnel, 292 yards in length, which Roscoe described as having a large ventilation shaft near the centre. Wyld was rather dismissive, stating 'this tunnel, extending about 300 yards, is insignificant compared with those which have occurred in our journey, and is not therefore calculated to excite the uneasiness which may have possessed us when entering the yawning gullets of Watford and Kilsby'.[81]

THE GREAT WESTERN RAILWAY

Great an achievement as it was, Kilsby never attained the familiarity of Box, which could be casually woven into a story in a newspaper or popular journal as if it were a memorable landmark on any railway journey, or at least known to the wide public, perhaps taking on an almost mythical character like the *Titanic*. That it was on the Great Western Railway helped, and the Great Western, never having been short of publicity from earliest days, was described as 'the most gigantic work, not only in Great Britain, not only in Europe, but in the entire world'.[82]

Brunel's architectural achievements on the Great Western between Paddington and Bristol have already been discussed, but as the route may be described as passing through beautiful, if not dramatic scenery, threaded by the Thames and Avon, it was worthy of literary description for the traveller. George Measom obliged with *The Illustrated Guide to the Great Western Railway*, 1852, which combined informative text with delightful engravings. The commentary is westwards from London to Bristol, however when it reaches the Box Tunnel 'timid lady-travellers' were told to 'screw up your nerves for a rush through the Box Tunnel. No, – not this first one: – it is only a short preliminary taste, before we enter the real stone-cut gallery beneath the Box-Hill'.[83] In reality though, coming from the east the longer Box Tunnel comes before the shorter Middle Hill Tunnel!

So much has been written about Brunel, who was the driving force for the project and its completion, that his name is synonymous with it, just as his father is forever associated with the Thames Tunnel. The idea that Brunel orientated his tunnel so the sun could shine through it on his birthday, 9 April, has been argued from almost the day it was opened. In 1842 *The Times*, quoting a Devizes newspaper, described how the sun was shining through it 'as though the whole tunnel had been lit', but added that 'the only other period when this occurs is on the 3 and 4 September'.[84] This fact was raised again in a letter to the *Daily Telegraph* on 12 April 1859:

> It is a curious fact that annually on the morning of April 9 the sun's rays penetrate through the great Box Tunnel of the Great Western Railway, and on no other day of the year, and it is still more remarkable that April 9 is the birthday of Brunel, who was responsible for the construction of the tunnel.[85]

This correspondence may have provoked the *Daily Telegraph* to commission a rather fanciful drawing of the western portal with a locomotive rushing out, much in the manner of the frontispiece for Bourne's *Great Western*, however with a motley crowd of ladies in crinolines and holding parasols, and gentlemen in stovepipe hats (Ill. 11).[86] Were they there to see the sun's rays through the tunnel, or just to experience the excitement of a train bursting out of the tunnel portal, an event depicted at the opening of Primrose Hill Tunnel in 1838 ?

In his biography of his father, published in 1870, Brunel's son Isambard does not mention this tradition. The topic has been the subject of several academic papers combining mathematics with a study of astronomical tables from the period of the tunnel's construction, and disproving the fact.[87] The other argument relating to Box, but ultimately one easier to prove, was its length. This was the subject of a number of questions in the most unexpected of journals. An answer section in *The Girl's Own Paper* in 1886 emphasised the fact that Box was not then the longest tunnel in Britain; Woodhead at 3 miles and 26 yards was longer.[88] Yet in the *Young Folk's Paper* in December 1889, in response to a question as to which was the longest tunnel in the country, the answer was given as Box at 3,227 yards. This was, of course, wrong; by then the Severn Tunnel was open, at over 4 miles.[89] In 1857 it featured as a short story by Charles Read called appropriately *The Box Tunnel* and set precisely on the 10.15 departure from Paddington on 7 May 1847, in which a young cavalry officer, following a bet with a fellow officer, kisses the lady opposite while passing through the Box Tunnel. Eventually they meet in Bath, where they subsequently fall in love and marry, and set off through the Box Tunnel on their honeymoon. A delightful story, but the one vital point is that the carriage was still at that time without any light, so they were in total darkness for several minutes: Measom's advice to timid ladies perhaps being fully justified![90]

Perhaps J.C. Bourne's collection of lithographs of the building of the *London and Birmingham Railway* published in 1838, and his *A History and Description of the*

THE FASCINATION OF EARLY RAILWAY TUNNELS • 99

Ill. 11 **Celebrating Brunel's** Birthday? Box Tunnel, *Daily Telegraph,* 12 April 1859.

Great Western Railway, 1846, were as much records of the triumph of the Victorian railway navvies as publicity to allay the fears of the public. Bourne used the picture of a locomotive emerging from the arch of Tunnel No. 1 just to the east of Bristol as the frontispiece for his *History of the Great Western*. An express train pulled by a great steam-powered locomotive roaring out of a stone dressed neo-classical tunnel entrance in a cloud of steam was sublimely terrible, full of energy, flaunting its power, and announced by noise; it conveyed a new sense of purpose and a conquering dynamism.[91] In the case of Tunnel No. 1, the bore was near the surface and was opened out into a red sandstone cutting in 1887.

From his earliest sketchbook drawings we can see Brunel's fascination with the idea of tunnel portals. In 1851 Edward Churton described the western portal of what he called the *Ivy-Mantled Tunnel* or No. 2 as 'long considered one of the principle attractions of the neighbourhood'.[92] At Twerton the two tunnels have portals like the entrance to a gigantic castle. The shorter is more like a very long gate to a gentleman's estate, however the 'long' one was described in the *Bath Chronicle* to excite its readers as 'darkly yearning as if wishing to swallow up whatever might have occasion to approach its wide and gloomy jaws'. It was contrasted with the 'low browed petty perforations' that were found on some canals, as a 'spacious excavation … forming a noble arch of nearly three hundred yards through'. The reader was reassured by the fact that although it was slightly curved and therefore dark in the middle, it was 'only a little dark'. Less reassuring for those in open carriages was that 'water drops slightly from the top in two or three places'.[93]

CROSSING THE SPINE OF ENGLAND
As the system expanded, so the natural barriers to be overcome became greater and none less so than the Pennine Hills, which for centuries had acted as a barrier between the east and west towns of northern England. It was seen as essential to link Manchester with Sheffield and Leeds, then major rising centres of industry and commerce, and the most direct way was by tunnelling. The first tunnel was Summit, opened in 1840, at just over a mile in length and driven beneath bleak moorland. It was described as approaching the Moorish arch in its forms. It was for a short time proclaimed as the longest tunnel in the world and as 'no abatement of speed is made in passing through … the train will therefore be not more than three minutes and a half or four in passing through the tunnel'.[94] The experience of passing through was contrasted with the smaller works at Edge Hill, Liverpool, but here passengers have but a 'faint conception of this splendid construction'. No praise was too great, surpassing Kilsby: it was so well ventilated that 'the general dryness of the interior will make the tunnel one of the pleasantest in every respect that can be traversed'.[95] This account is a good example of how early writers, if pro-railways, could be carried away to the point of exaggeration. On the other hand, its desolate situation provoked a sense of Gothic horror in poetic souls like Edwin Butterfield in his description of passing through it:

> The rapidity of the flight, the screech of the warning signal from the engine, the overhanging column of mingled smoke and steam, the rush of air,

together with the lurid glare and innumerable sparks thrown up by the flambeaux which the train carries, and others born by persons stationed in the tunnel conspire, with the feeling that we are passing through the body of a huge mountain, to excite and awe the mind.[96]

His mention of persons stationed in the tunnel at intervals holding lamps suggests a very lonely occupation in view of its location beneath the Pennines where there are fierce winters and where it is extremely damp and cold for much of the year, in total contrast to the previous description.

Even longer were the two single-track bores at Woodhead, over 3 miles long, described by the *Sheffield Iris* as a 'wondrous triumph of art over nature' and the 'greatest engineering work of the kind which has yet been completed'. On 20 December 1845, General Pasley, the Government inspector of railways, inspected the tunnel by torchlight, proclaiming it to be 'one of the finest pieces of engineering he had ever seen'. Two days later the inaugural train took ten and a quarter minutes in 'passing through this great subterranean bore. And on entering into the region of light at Woodhead, the passengers gave three hearty cheers'.[97] We may wonder whether the cheers were for the magnificence of the undertaking or simply reaching fresh air! It was not viewed with any admiration by footplate crews with its narrow single bores and choking smoke.[98]

DANTE'S INFERNO, OR A MODERN VISION OF HELL

The Midland Railway crossing the Derbyshire Peak district had the perfect ingredients for railway literary romance as the landscape changed from the relatively flat Midlands to the peaks of the northern hills and narrow valleys and gorges studded with fast-flowing rivers. The opening of Clay Cross Tunnel in 1840 had inspired a poetic description of a 'vault-like ancient runic cave' opening before the passage 'like a grave'.[99] For those of a literary bent and who wanted their train journey spiced with a little more than the observation that we 'are now passing the seat of Lord *so-and-so*, except that you cannot see it because of a tunnel or cutting', interesting or important as this might be, Edward Bradbury, writing as Strephon, was just the man. He wrote a series of *Midland Railway Sketches*, published in 1879, in which he relished the description of journeys through tunnels, invoking literary and artistic references.[100]

Is it fanciful to think that he might have borrowed literary images from Drake's description of the passage of Primrose Hill Tunnel? For some timid readers his words were enough to spread a sense of fear rather than comfort. Has anyone felt the short Ampthill Tunnel thus:

The darkness that might be the valley of the shadow of death – the clammy coldness, the furious whirlwind, the unearthly noises, the flakes of fire that flutter along, and reveal the wet walls flying past like a rushing river; these supply a sensation that elevates the railway ride into the regions of the romantic. The tunnel is a Styx. The train is Charon's boat. The engine driver standing in a statuesque attitude at his post is Dante's infernal ferryman.[101]

When we get to Milford Tunnel we see the 'folds of red smoke flying along the roof and the face of the driver, reflected in the glass in front of which he peers with strained eye, make a fine picture in which the artist souls of Rembrandt or Dore would revel'.[102] Further north the journey takes us through the Peak District, where there is a rapid sequence of tunnels and valleys crossed by viaducts. 'Don't protest my friend against the tunnel robbing us, like a Scotch mist, of a fresh gleam of Fairyland. It will give us a splendid compensation in a minute.'[103] He makes reference to the tunnel under the 'hallowed towers of Haddon Hall', where at the insistence of the Duke of Rutland 'the line passes under the wooded hillside upon which the feudal walls are reared'.[104]

If the timid passengers had survived up to now, they still had to face the 2-mile long Dove Holes Tunnel before arriving at Manchester:

> The bleak obscurity now envelopes us ... the darkness may be felt. Sulphur fumes are added to the damp earthy smell. Now and again an air shaft in the tunnel roof sends down a delusive glimmer of day. Right in front is the tunnel mouth; now it assumes the dimension of a three-penny bit; it gets larger, now it assumes the dimensions of a sixpence; it grows into a shilling, soon it appears like a florin, and presently, it resembles a five shilling piece. Another half minute in this vile vault and then we burst into the summer and sunshine again.[105]

On the other hand Bradshaw, in his *Handbook*, 1863, described the nearby High Tor tunnels as dry and comfortable, with the gloom being dissipated for a couple of seconds by daylight in the opening between the two bores.[106]

There were many more poetic descriptions of tunnel experiences, for instance Devey describes emerging from Joseph Locke's Bishopton Tunnel near Glasgow as magical as if 'suddenly emerging from the regions of Erebus into the loveliness of Arcadia'.[107] More recently, Webster describes Summit Tunnel, near Wolverhampton on the Grand Junction Railway, at only 186 yards as 'long enough to give the travellers an impression of darkness and a thrilling feeling that they were burrowing under the earth'.[108] However, it is approached from the east by a cutting 2 miles long that grows in depth to the entrance to the tunnel.

A TRIP BENEATH CLIFFS AND DOWNS

As we have seen in the case of the sequence of railway tunnels between Bath and Bristol and in the Derbyshire Peak District, they could inspire considerable flights of literary eloquence. In the case of George Measom in his *Illustrated Guide to the South Eastern Railway*, 1853, the route between Folkestone and Dover with its penetration of the Shakespeare Cliff inspired quotations from the bard himself. From *King Lear* he described the cliff,

> Whose high and bending head,
> Looks fearfully on the confined deep.

Measom was aware that the train journey could only give a brief glimpse of the landscape and sea while passing between the three tunnels. He wrote:

> to realise the bard's description, however, the tourist must ascend to its summit, 576 feet high, and then, if he has nerve to withstand the grandeur of the scene below he will see the truth of the following grand description:
>
> How fearful
> And dizzy 'tis to cast one's eyes so low …
> The fishermen that walk upon the beach
> Appear like mice; and yon tall bark,
> Diminish'd to her cock – her cock a buoy.[109]

However, when the South Eastern Railway started to tunnel through Shakespeare Cliff in 1838 there were, as the anti-tunnel *Railway Magazine* wrote, 'rigid classics who rail loudly against the Vandalism of the company'. Yet the magazine supported the company in this instance as tunnelling could not be avoided. While opponents cited *King Lear*, the magazine hinted that the secretary of the company might have not only the interest of completing the railway, but also an appreciation of the classics.[110] The following issue assured 'admirers of our great bard' that the cliff that bears his name still 'rears its 330 foot head undisfigured, and, as they would say, undesecrated'.[111] Whishaw, in his *Railways of Great Britain*, published when the line was still under construction in 1842, stressed the scientific significance:

> To the geologist the excavations in the Dover Cliffs afford ample scope for the exercise of his all searching investigations, to the civil engineer, the works carrying on are replete with interest throughout, presenting in the distance of about six miles, almost every variety of work which falls within the pale of construction (Ill. 36).[112]

Even before the line opened it received the acclamation of newspapers, travel journals and guide books alike. The bore of Shakespeare Cliff Tunnel was completed as early as November 1839 'with its lofty Gothic arches beginning to shadow forth its ultimate effect'.[113] The *Railway Times* suggested, perhaps implausibly in view of the working conditions, that any person visiting Dover should 'stroll through this tunnel', which would 'afford the highest satisfaction' and that he would be 'filled with awe and amazement at the various strata of chalk'.[114] Indeed, the Duke of Wellington accompanied by the Marchioness of Duoro and Lady Wilton paid an unexpected visit to Dover on 1 November 1843 and walked through the entire length of the Shakespeare Cliff Tunnel. The Duke expressed himself 'highly delighted at the construction of the tunnel … a marvellous piece of engineering and a lasting testimony to man's ingenuity in almost impossible conditions'.[115] In contrast the *Gentleman's Magazine* described the tunnels as 'dreary', although the nearby Abbot's Cliff Tunnel was considered to be the 'finest specimen of tunnel brickwork in the kingdom'; but then it had few competitors at this early date.[116] On its opening to Dover in February 1844 *The Builder* praised the South Eastern Railway and Mr Cubitt for creating a line of such 'extraordinary and novel character'.[117] The two tunnels 'have been cut through the chalk and formed in the soundest parts of it with a considerable height of thickness of chalk, not only above, but also between them and the sea'.[118] They were seen as the final means of linking London and Paris and reason for 'jubilation for the whole nation and ports'.[119] Churton, in his *Rail Road Book of England*, recommended that those interested in such works should first ride in an open third-class carriage between points Dover and Folkestone and then walk back on the summit of the cliffs along the pathway on the edge of the cliffs.[120] So while some looked with dismay on what was seen as the marring of this visual bastion of England by a 'useless invention', others saw this 'slight injury to the picturesque' as amply compensated for by bringing the Continent and Paris nearer to London.[121]

Reference has been made earlier to the concern over the number and length of tunnels on the London and Brighton Railway, even to the extent of a proposed route without tunnels; it was after all linking London with the then major seaside social centre in England. However, the depth and length of the cuttings increased the feeling of enclosure and claustrophobia; even popular railway guidebooks commented on the extensive earthworks sometimes exaggerating their depth, as at Mersham where 'a mighty excavation about two miles long and 120 feet in depth' approaches the tunnel.[122] Cole, in his *Travelling Chart* for the London-Tunbridge-Dover route, also commented on this cutting through the chalk, but exaggerated it, claiming that its deepest part was 180ft.[123] Further on travellers 'catch a glimpse of the towering heights ahead and plunge into a cutting and the deep recesses of Clayton Tunnel ... which penetrates the base of the mighty South Downs'.[124] Even well into the twentieth century the northern portal was receiving praise that took romantic travel writing to extremes; 'the Gothic battlemented entrance looms with a kind of scowling picturesqueness well suited to its dark history, continually vomiting steam and smoke like a hell's mouth'.[125]

As construction neared completion the newspapers frequently reported on the state of the tunnels. The short branch to Shoreham was opened first, which included a short tunnel. The report in the *Brighton Herald* of the opening in May 1840 included an engraving of the train leaving the 200-yard-long tunnel. It went on to say how the engine rushes, increasing 'with every momentum in speed to the tunnel'.[126] From this we may infer the fear or excitement with which passengers faced the prospect of the longer tunnels to London when the main line opened in September. Another correspondent for the *Brighton Herald* reported how he walked over the hill to see the train emerge from Patcham Tunnel. The first indication was a cloud of steam rising from the mouth of the tunnel and in the next moment could be seen 'a long dark object ... swiftly gliding along the line and rapidly increasing in size and distinction'.[127] Such a scene had the power to capture the attention of this early Victorian observer, just as one hundred years later Michael Mansfield QC felt there was nothing that could be compared to the sensation of standing on the bridge at Oakleigh Park, a few miles from King's Cross, and hearing the distant roar of the *Flying Scotsman* as it burst out of nearby Potters Bar Tunnel.[128]

Although the passage from light to darkness was often so sudden for the passenger that the portal of the tunnel was never seen, to the pedestrians on a road or walker across a fell, the line of shafts might indicate something more sinister, or even romantic beneath. Notable locations include the bare clifftop above the Shakespeare Cliff tunnel and the Blea Moor near Settle. Mention is made elsewhere of the architectural character of the shafts of Kilsby Tunnel visible from the A5 and M1 trunk roads. Early railway writers such as Coghlan commented on them; at Watford for instance the 'torrent of smoke and steam issuing from these shafts after the passage of a train had a singular effect; it is frequently ten minutes before the tunnel is completely clear'.[129] He also hints at the mischievous side of human nature where there is the temptation to throw objects down them, so consequently they had to be protected by high walls.[130] Perhaps very reassuring but hard to imagine is the claim that the tunnel policeman could by 'placing his eye close to the rail at one end detect even a pebble on the rail'.[131] Perhaps an instance of vivid imagination overtaking scientific fact?

FICTION

So far all the accounts have been factual or based on real tunnels. Dickens, not the most enthusiastic of tunnel travellers, wrote a short story, *The Signal-Man*, in which he set a tunnel at the end of a long cutting; we have no precise location for his inspiration but we might imagine the scene to be set somewhere like Merstham on the London and Brighton Railway with 'a gloomy entrance to a black tunnel, in whose massive architecture there was a barbarous, depressing and forbidding air … that it had an earthy, deadly smell'.[132] Simon Bradley suggests it was Higham near Dickens's home at Gads Hill, although here the cutting opens out to contain a station and derelict canal.[133] Scotland's R.L. Stephenson was inspired by the earliest railway tunnel in Scotland, the Scotland Street Tunnel cut beneath the Georgian New Town in the early 1840s. He made this interesting observation in his *Edinburgh Picturesque Notes*:

> The tunnel to the Scotland Street Station, the sight of trains striking out of its dark mass with the two guards upon the brakes, the thought of its length and the many ponderous edifices and open thoroughfares above, were certainly things of paramount impressiveness to a young mind. It was a subterranean passage, although a larger bore than we were accustomed to in Ainsworth's novels, and these two words, 'subterranean passage' were in themselves an irresistible attraction, and seemed to bring us nearer in spirit to the heroes we loved and the black rascals we secretly aspired to imitate.[134]

THE TUNNEL IN ART

Literary descriptions could, as I have demonstrated, range from the topographically accurate laced with historical fact to the grossly exaggerated that was meant to 'raise the hairs on one's back' or give that extra *frisson* of excitement, when for instance travelling through the tunnels of the Peak District on the Midland Railway.[135] The artistic depiction of the tunnel was intended to produce a feeling of confidence in the potential travelling public, especially if the artist was employed by a particular company to assuage public fears.[136] Before the age of mass-produced travel posters, which really only appear from the 1880s, the early railways needed good pictorial publicity, and this was supplied in a number of ways from paintings turned into popular prints, extolling the wonders of the new age of transport, to jigsaw puzzles, children's games and earthenware jugs. A humble bridge could be turned into the form of a triumphal arch. The standard of draughtsmanship varied from the highly professional of such artists as J.C. Bourne and A.F. Tait to crude depictions hurriedly created for popular magazines. Depictions ranged from locomotives and carriages, line-side locations and features such as tunnel portals to the sights seen from the carriage window. However, Simmons claimed that to render a train accurately was quite a new challenge, and was not accomplished successfully in the pictures of the Liverpool and Manchester Railway, but his statement that artists did not attempt to draw locomotives in detail or displayed little interest in them is not quite true.[137] Isaac Shaw produced engravings of specific locomotives of the Liverpool and Manchester Railway and animated pictures in pen and brown ink of the opening day in 1830. However, Simmons rightly classed the pictures of the London and Greenwich Railway as inferior to those of the London and Birmingham Railway.[138] He cites David Octavius Hill's depiction of the terminus of Glasgow of the Glasgow and Garnkirk Railway in 1832 as the first picture to set a new sense of accuracy in detail. The hustle and bustle of a railway station was perhaps the most ambitious form of depiction; at the other end of the scale were popular children's games illustrated by Freeman, such as *Cousin Chatterbox's Railway Alphabet* from about 1845 in which *T is for Tunnel* with a crudely drawn locomotive bursting from an elegant portal, perhaps inspired by Littleborough, opened in 1845.[139]

When it came to placing the railway in a landscape, artists sometimes used compositional devices to monumentalise the location or proclaim the triumph of the railway engineers against what was hitherto hostile territory. While Bourne was essentially proclaiming the triumph of the engineers in his *London and Birmingham Railway*, 1839, by 1846 his *Great Western Railway* placed greater emphasis on the landscape with architectural triumphs such as the viaducts and tunnels, complete and moulded into their natural setting. Artists such as Edwin Dolby in his lithograph of the South Eastern at Abbot's Cliff Tunnel and others depicted railways in similar situations threading their way along the coast as at Dawlish or in North Wales, often reducing tunnel portals to small holes in a greatly exaggerated cliff (Ill. 36). Where appropriate, cows and sheep graze peacefully and fishermen cast a rod into a country stream as if to confound the critics who condemned the railways as a disturbing invention of the devil casting a permanent blight on the landscape. Palmer and Neaverson, in *Industry in the Landscape, 1700–1900*, emphasise the integration of country people into railway scenes such as those by Tait of the Manchester and Leeds Railway, as if to confirm the blessings the railway may bring to the rural poor.[140]

Unlike the draughtsmen who created sections and profiles of tunnel portals in fine detail down to the last course of bricks or stone, the artist was allowed latitude and he could emphasise the tunnel as an architectural entity or submerge it in the broader landscape, approached along a deep cutting or burrowing into a range of hills, sometimes exaggerated to the proportions of a minor mountain range. The railway had to sit in the landscape rather than create a scar, the very situation railway opponents often cited.[141] As was to be proved more than with any other addition to the landscape, the scars of cuttings and embankments could heal quickly as trees grew to hide rocks and steep escarpments, and could add to that sense of mystery and excitement as the cutting grew higher and steeper, accompanied by the shrill of the whistle as the locomotive hauled its excited or apprehensive passengers into darkness, or at best, the flicker of carriage lamps against the tunnel walls.

When looking at these illustrations, whether published as plates in books such as those by Bourne or published in *The Illustrated London News*, they were for an essentially middle-class audience, not a mass market. Some cost as much as 10s, more than a week's wage for an agricultural labourer.[142] By the end of the nineteenth century Bury's *Coloured Views of the Liverpool and Manchester Railway*, published in 1831, was fetching over £10.[143] Bourne's *London and Birmingham Railway*, published as a hardcover book, was 94s 6d, so aimed at a gentleman's library.

The Illustrated London News is a remarkable visual record of the history of Britain and its Empire for over a century. Published weekly, its earliest editions

Ill. 12 Sevenoaks Tunnel on the London & South Eastern Railway, approached through a long cutting into the chalk Wealden hills. This watercolour possibly dates from the 1870s shortly after the line was opened. *Science Museum Group*

were illustrated by woodcuts and steel engravings, often surprisingly crude at first, although draughtsmanship and reproductive printing techniques improved dramatically from the 1850s. It frequently featured early railway events from the earliest editions in 1842, which caught the imagination of its upper middle-class readers. Tunnels and other railway structures were included, often with a text full of superlatives, especially with regard to viaducts, which after all made almost as much impact on the landscape as surviving Roman aqueducts. This was, of course, before we have Swiss masterpieces of viaduct construction, not simply across river valleys but deep chasms, hundreds of feet deep. Many illustrations were accompanied by eulogies placing railway construction on the same level as that of the Pyramids.

THE EARLIEST RAILWAY ILLUSTRATIONS

Although the earliest steam-hauled railway was the Stockton and Darlington opened in September 1825, and commemorated shortly after by a lithograph and letterhead featuring the Skerne Bridge, it did not have a tunnel.[144] Rudolf Ackermann of *the Strand* was quick off the mark in seeing the potential for this new market in visual material, in which not only might prints be used for corporate advertising, but could also boost the reputation of their specially commissioned artists. It was a new market that was a bridge between the topographical and the technological. Ackermann's earliest set of railway prints celebrated the opening of the Liverpool and Manchester Railway in 1830 and included the *Entrance to the Tunnel at Edge Hill*, and *Interior of the Tunnel at Wapping* (Ill. 13).[145] Most of his prints were essentially railway landscapes proclaiming the triumphal conquest of the railway through rocky cutting and across barren moorland.

A number of early books on railways were illustrated with engravings. The earliest, published in 1836, was a commentary on the dramatic northern landscape, *Views on the Newcastle and Carlisle Railway*, illustrated with lithographs after drawings by J.W. Carmichael.[146] The line must rank as one of the most picturesque in Britain, ranging from lush green fields and meadows to bleak moorland. It has two short tunnels, which is surprising for the terrain it crosses, and opened up to the Victorians an area that had rarely been visited except by shepherds. One engraving depicts the western entrance to the Haltwhistle Tunnel.[147] Perhaps the ingredients are perfect for a picture; the tunnel is a small feature in the total composition. Our attention is first drawn to the road on the left of the two tracks with drovers with horse and cart. The tracks have the obligatory labourers, both working and relaxing.

The earliest passenger railway hauled partially by steam was the Canterbury and Whitstable opened on 3 May 1830, which included the earliest public railway tunnel in Britain under Tyler Hill, just north of Canterbury (Ill. 14). The face of the tunnel is not recorded in a picture, however there were two prints made of the railway, one from above the tunnel of the first train descending into Canterbury by rope and another published in *Railway Magazine*, October 1835, using a bit of imagination, is set a few feet inside the tunnel, and is useful for showing the central rope for hauling the trains up the steep incline from the original terminus in North Lane. In reality, however, the Cathedral was well to the right of this angle!

Above: Ill. 13 **The Wapping** Tunnel, Liverpool, T.T. Bury. *Science Museum Group*

Right: Ill. 14 **Tyler Hill** Tunnel, Illustration by Henry Lewin, *Early British Railways*, 1925.

ILLUSTRATING THE LONDON AND BIRMINGHAM RAILWAY

As we have seen, the next major railway to be opened with tunnels of a striking appearance was the London and Birmingham Railway, in September 1838. The railway naturally attracted a number of writers to produce travelogues for passengers as well as artists to depict the enormity of construction and major points of interest. It is through J.C. Bourne's illustrations that we are most familiar with its construction (Ill. 15) (Boxmoor Tunnel). How he came to produce it left much to good fortune. Born in London in 1771, he was the pupil of the landscape engraver John Pye, and at the age of fourteen was attracted to the excavations for the new railway at Camden Town. His drawings were seen by the writer and antiquary John Britton, who saw a commercial possibility in a book that might also allay the fears of the anti-railway lobby. He sent Bourne to draw the excavations for Watford Tunnel with the understanding that he, Britton, would write the text. Britton had already had success with his *History of the Antiquities of Wiltshire* and his volumes of *Cathedral Antiquities*. Bourne produced thirty-four views translated into lithographs, of which no fewer than twenty-eight feature static engineering feats, and sixteen of these are of construction scenes. Several show the deep cuttings, perhaps, as Freeman notes, taking their cue from Shaw's pictures of Mount Olive cutting on the Liverpool and Manchester Railway.[148] He introduces a quality of the sublime with an emphasis on light and shadow, as well as the enormity of

Ill. 15 **Boxmoor Tunnel,** interior, wash drawing, J.C .Bourne. *Science Museum Group*

cuttings and brick retaining walls appearing to seem almost shear, while some occasional overhanging ledges suggest the impression of a cavern.[149] Even in his architecture there was to be nobility; the parapets of bridges and tunnel portals were coped in stone, and even the Locomotive Engine House at Camden has Doric strength with buttress-like pilasters beneath a continuous entablature. Most important of all, they look professional, with as much accuracy devoted to the locomotives as the lineside architecture.[150] Something of the flavour of Bourne's 'on-the-spot' depiction of construction can best be seen in his depiction of the work inside the short Boxmoor Tunnel.

Other artists depicting the construction include George Scharfe and R.B. Schnebbelie, who provide accurate and indeed dramatic views of the construction from above the embankment or retaining walls as well as at track level.[151] Interestingly, we have Dickens's descriptions of the excavations at Camden Town in *Dombey and Son*, which Simmons noted matched John Bourne's delicate and precise record.[152] As discussed elsewhere, there were a number of guide books or companions to the journey between Euston and Curzon Street, in many respects copying each other. The first was Osborne's *Guide to the London and Birmingham Railway*, published in Birmingham in 1838. The text included a number of steel engravings that, although very informative in terms of detail, lacked the accuracy of draughtsmanship shown by Bourne a year later. Some of the illustrations by the then-renowned Samuel Williams bear a striking similarity to depictions of the same theme by other artists, in the same way that early railway authors also copied from each other.[153]

With the completion of the railway the greatest attraction within a mile or so of the terminus was the tunnel beneath Primrose Hill, then the only one in London. Several contemporary prints show crowds of sightseers on the embankment beside the eastern portal. After all, as Bond said in his introduction to *Stokers and Pokers*:

> when the railways were first established, every living being gazed at a passing train with astonishment and fear: ploughmen held their breath; the loose horse galloped from it, and then, suddenly stopping, turned round, stared at it, and at last snorted aloud.[154]

An examination of several depictions of the eastern portal poses the question, was the tunnel open for traffic before the masonry of the portals was completed? The most accurate records are the drawings and lithographs by Bourne made between 1836 and 1838, the earliest therefore dating from before the railway actually opened. His earliest depiction, probably from late 1836, shows the arch in place and a section of the adjacent buttresses along with the stone courses for the wing walls (Ill. 16). This work is particularly valuable in showing the cranes and winches used for raising the stone. The track is already in place, including a temporary sliproad on either side for trucks to bring the stone.

The track is barely indicated, just the suggestion of the rails. The tunnel parapet and upper stage of the buttresses are missing, although the wing walls are finished.

Above: **Ill. 16 Primrose Hill** Tunnel, east portal, 1836?, wash drawing, J.C. Bourne. *Science Museum Group*

Below: **Ill. 17 Primrose Hill** Tunnel, east portal, April 1837?, wash drawing J.C. Bourne. *Science Museum Group*

Against the right buttress the crane and winch remains in place. He conveys the bevelled stone courses in the arch of the tunnel. The signalmen's huts are not yet in place. The National Railway Museum also has a fine study by George Scharfe, undated but probably late 1837, of the uncompleted eastern portal inscribed 'three quarters of a mile in length'.[155]

Another impressive study by Bourne, dated April 1837, is taken from between tracks showing the portal nearly complete but still masked by scaffolding (Ill. 17). Studies like this set the benchmark by which we judge other depictions of structures that are often secondary in railway art. The portal is almost complete along with wing walls, although the cranes are still in place. The slip tracks have been cleared and the retaining walls built on either side, while on the right embankment spectators watch the progress.

Yet another study perhaps days later (Ill. 18) from an identical position shows the tunnel with the scaffolding removed but retaining the same staffage.

An engraving by J. Cleghorn after a drawing by J.H. Nixon dated October 1837 shows a train leaving the tunnel with the parapet and side buttresses incomplete (Ill. 19). It should, however, be borne in mind that although the line opened throughout to Birmingham in September 1838, the first 24 miles from Euston Square to Boxmoor was opened in July 1837. If the date of this depiction is correct it would suggest Bourne's drawing is later as his masonry is in a more advanced state of completion. It is obvious from this picture that the embankments on either side of the track provided a popular viewpoint for this new attraction to the London population of either sex.

In a view from the opposite bank, Edwin Dolby again shows the setting as a spectacle attracting a large audience, some watching from behind the retaining wall, and in several cases climbing it to get a better view.

Ill. 18 Primrose Hill Tunnel, east portal watercolour, J.C. Bourne. *Elton Collection, Ironbridge Museum, AE 185.16*

114 • THE EARLY HISTORY OF RAILWAY TUNNELS

Above: **Ill. 19 Primrose Hill** Tunnel, coloured lithograph, J.H. Nixon & J. Cleghorn, October 1837. *Science Museum Group*

Below: **Ill. 20 Primrose Hill** Tunnel, Edwin T. Dolby. *Science Museum Group*

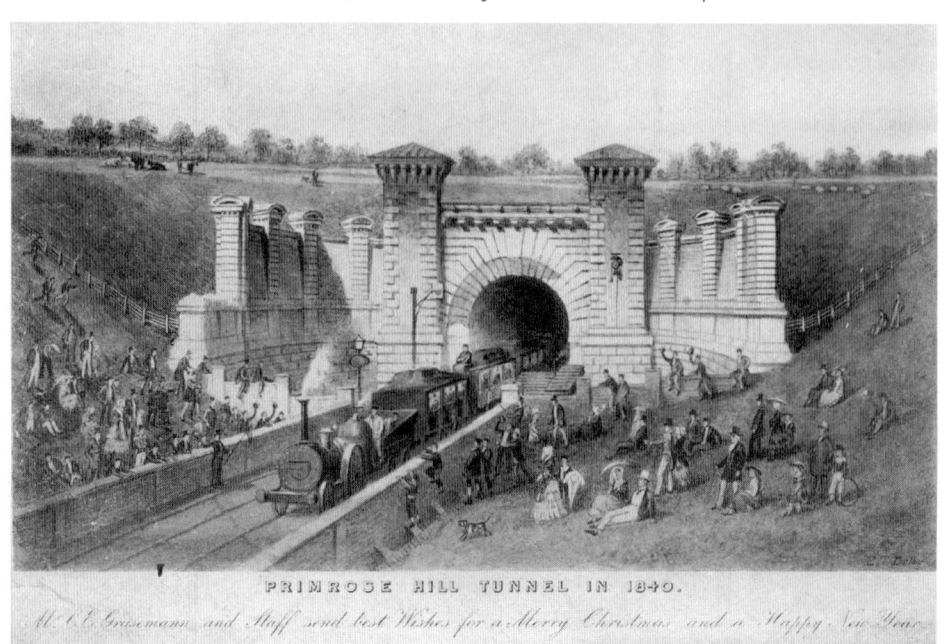

A number of crude versions of the same location show how popular this was for the early railway spectators. Some distorted the proportions of the portal or gave little hint of the landscape above or surrounding the tunnel entrance. Perhaps they were composed from the minimum of information gained on the spot, or the case of one artist copying evidence from another. None have the accuracy of Bourne's work here or at his other locations on the London and Birmingham Railway.

There is no doubt from these examples that the east portal of Primrose Hill was considered something special; the west portal is less impressive and there is no drawing of it by Bourne or indeed other contemporary artists on its opening. However, there is an ink and wash drawing of the west portal dated 12 July 1848 in the Elton Collection at Bridgenorth (Ill. 21). Again there are retaining walls and a tall signal in front of a policeman's hut. What is perhaps more interesting are the houses in Albion Road which were built since the tunnel's construction, showing how shallow the tunnel actually is beneath the surface.

Since the Kilsby Tunnel was the main reason for the delayed opening of the entire London and Birmingham Railway, it was right that Bourne should have depicted it during construction and near completion. His most dramatic views are from track level beneath one of the three large excavation shafts (Ills 22 & 23). He conveys a dramatic idea of the scale of the work with the light almost blinding, as we look beyond to the next section of tunnel. It brings to mind the

Ill. 21 **Primrose Hill,** west portal, 12 July 1848, anon. *Elton Collection, Ironbridge Museum*

Above left: **Ill. 22 Kilsby Tunnel:** working shaft, J.C. Bourne, *London & Birmingham Railway*, 1839.

Above right: **Ill. 23 Kilsby Tunnel:** giant air shaft, J.C. Bourne, *London & Birmingham Railway*, 1839.

drama of light and shadow in some of Piranesi's imaginary prison chambers and Joseph Gandon's depictions of Soane's sky-lit chambers in the Bank of England, to which no doubt Britton would have drawn his attention. The *Gentleman's Magazine* in its review of Bourne's book commended the two Kilsby pictures: 'In one a powerful light bursts through an excavation shaft as it enveloped a descending work load. At its foot two horses are silhouetted against the light whilst the trackside angle increases the vastness of the tunnel.'[156] Britton claimed the opaqueness of the atmosphere in the first picture (Ill. 22) arose from the 'want of ventilation' – but it is due to the dust caused by the works. In the second picture, showing the grand ventilating shaft, we peer beyond through the now clear atmosphere to the next section of tunnel and the distant white speck of the portal (Ill. 23).

It is surely no accident that a similar view of Kilsby Tunnel shaft was depicted as a steel engraving in Frederick William's *Our Iron Road*, published in 1852, and George Meason's *Guide to the North Western Railway*, 1859. Yet neither have the 'dynamic' quality of Bourne; indeed the locomotives, while introducing scale, gives the picture a somewhat naive quality.

THE FASCINATION OF EARLY RAILWAY TUNNELS • 117

Right: Ill. 24 **Waford Tunnel** coloured lithograph, T.T. Bury. *Science Museum Group*

Below: Ill. 25 **Watford Tunnel** south portal, 6 June 1837, watercolour, J.C. Bourne. *Elton Collection, Ironbridge Museum AE 185.17*

Ill. 26 Watford Tunnel south portal, J.C. Bourne, London & Birmingham Railway. 1839.

Ill. 27 Linslade Tunnel, north portal, *Drakes Road Book, 1839*, anon, woodcut.

No amount of romantic imagination can set Primrose Hill Tunnel in a dramatic environment, nor indeed Kilsby; however Watford southern portal was portrayed by T.T. Bury in 1837 from above the embankment, which was depicted as a man-made gorge looking freshly excavated (Ill. 24). Above the tunnel and to the right appear the white spoil heaps, which make for a more dramatic composition. However, for some unexplained reason the train appears to be leaving the tunnel backwards!

Bourne shows this portal under construction in a view dated 6 June 1837 in the Elton Collection, Ironbridge (Ill. 25).[157] The published lithograph differs from the preliminary drawing in that he introduced a number of wagons on the far track and considerably more labourers crossing the track and climbing the ladder beside the portal. He also increased the height of the winch in the lithograph (Ill. 26). In the drawing the masonry is suggested but in the lithograph he clearly defines the masonry as courses of stone radiating from the arch.

A naive woodcut of a train leaving the castellated north portal of Linslade Tunnel is of considerable historical value as perhaps the only visual record before the tunnel was expanded to three portals in a widened cutting (see Appendix 1).

THE ROMANTIC PORTAL: SHUGBOROUGH

Shugborough Tunnel on the Trent Valley Railway, on the other hand, presented both architectural distinction and a dramatic setting. The Trent Valley Railway as discussed in Chapter 3 was constructed to provide a direct line between Tamworth and Stafford, thus avoiding Birmingham, and has one tunnel that was created only because the route ran across Lord Litchfield's estate at Shugborough Hall. Since the landscaped park contained a number of monuments reflecting the taste of the eighteenth century, from a Roman triumphal arch to a Chinese dairy, the setting demanded something architecturally distinguished for the passage of the railway. The company rose to the occasion and produced two monumental portals. The north portal is especially outstanding and may be described as 'railway Romanesque'. At the time of its opening in 1846 it featured as a woodcut reproduced in the *Illustrated London News* (Ill. 28)[158] and in a watercolour heightened in white gauche by an unknown artist (Ill. 29).[159]

The watercolour is oblique, with the merest suggestion of the track with labourers and two top-hatted figures in front of what appears to be more a folly in a park than a railway tunnel. Considering the tunnel will have been completed recently, the natural surroundings seem remarkably undisturbed; perhaps the artist wished to create the air of antique calm. The woodcut depicts the portal face on, with the obligatory train leaving the tunnel watched by two figures from behind a fence on the low embankment. The accompanying description of the north portal in *The Illustrated London News* calls it:

a very striking architectural composition … a noble archway deeply moulded, flanked by two square towers, the whole surmounted by a battlemented parapet resting on arched corbel tables. The lofty trees clothed with the richest foliage rising from the elevated ground through which the tunnel is

120 • THE EARLY HISTORY OF RAILWAY TUNNELS

Left: Ill. 28 **Shrugborough Tunnel** north portal, woodcut, *The Illustrated London News*, 4 December 1847.

Below: Ill. 29 **Shrugborough Tunnel** north portal, watercolour artist unknown. *Science Museum Group*

pierced, give a depth of tone, and artistic effect to the whole scene, at once peculiarly imposing and beautiful, and form a remarkably fine feature in the scenery of the railway.[160]

The watercolour artist picks out the Romanesque detailing, the roll moulding with the arch resting on cushion capitals and flanking jamb shafts. The crenellated parapet above the portal rests on corbel blocks. He has also placed great emphasis on the buttresses pierced with narrow arrow slits. The woodcut on the other hand lacks the softness or mystery conveyed in the watercolour; the tree on the right, however, acts as a useful foil to scale and distance.

The south portal has received less artistic representation, perhaps because of the deep cutting causing shadow, and is difficult to photograph except during the summer when the sun is at the right angle.

BOURNE'S GREAT WESTERN RAILWAY

Bourne's *History and Description of the Great Western Railway*, 1846 was, of course, published five years after the line was fully opened, so the illustrations depict a completed railway with the emphasis on the railway setting within the landscape and the facilities provided, because as Freeman notes, the wonder had given way to the pleasures and convenience of railway travel. Unlike the *History of the London and Birmingham Railway*, this volume was not as successful; perhaps by now something of the wonder of railways had worn off, although the facsimile reprint of 1970 is as sought after as the original. The text this time was by Charles Cheffin. The frequently reproduced frontispiece is a lithograph of the locomotive *Acheron* bursting out of the Romanesque western portal of Tunnel No.1 near Bristol as if it were passing out of some ancient monument, to be hailed by the top-hatted men and their dog while other bystanders are less interested. They are all dwarfed by the enormity of the arch (Ill. 30). Klingender, in his *Art of the Industrial Revolution*, maintained that 'never before or since has anyone interpreted the simplicity and boldness, and drama of great engineering with such deliberate verve'.[161] Rather appropriately, the title of the book is carved into a huge block of stone over the arch, whose perspective increases the depth of the picture. (A similar theme was used about ninety years later in the frontispiece of *Railway Wonders of the World* edited by Clarence Winchester, in which a King-class locomotive is photographed posed at the entrance to Middle Hill Tunnel (Ill. 63)).[162] Bourne really emphasised the beauty of the landscape of the Avon valley between Bath and Bristol, as if to translate it into an Alpine journey with the tracks emerging from tunnels in gorges or beside a mountain stream.

It would be hard to improve on the grandeur of Box Tunnel's western portal as depicted in a lithograph from track level by Bourne, and published in his *History and Description of the Great Western Railway*, 1846 (Ill. 32), however there is an interesting sepia drawing in Bath's Royal Victoria Museum titled 'Making of the Box Tunnel' by William Walton (Ill. 31).[163] It is not dated and shows a giant hole like the entrance to a cavern cut into the hillside. This is before any masonry was added to the face, so there is nothing to specifically identify the location or

Ill. 30 Tunnel No. 1. Frontispice of J.C. Bourne's *Great Western Railway* showing the sadly destroyed Romanesque portal of Tunnel No. 1, 1846.

Ill. 31 Box Tunnel west portal under construction, pen & wash drawing, Bath, Royal Victoria Museum.

indeed the date. It is likely, however, to be of the western portal, judging by the light and breadth of cutting, which is deeper on the Chippenham side. On the hillside there is a factory and tall chimney but its function is unknown, possibly a brickworks?[164]

Bourne's lithograph depicting the western portal of Box from track level is without doubt the most frequently reproduced depiction of a railway tunnel portal, and perhaps any early railway illustration (Ill. 32). The low track viewpoint emphasises its grandeur while the rails form striking diagonals, drawing our eye beyond the emerging train to the darkness beyond. The scene is set in summer with strong afternoon sun casting shadows from the right of the picture, increasing the drama of the composition with the north abutment mostly in sunlight. A few feet in front of the tunnel on the left is a tall signal beside a small cabin. A coated figure stands beside the track with his right hand horizontal as the locomotive emerges from the tunnel mouth. A milepost beside the hut distinctly records ¾, presumably the distance from Bathford. Bourne has recorded the architectural features in great detail with the shadows emphasising the projected stages of the centrepiece, with the outer dressed at each corner with rusticated blocks. Above, the undulating hillside shows a group of farm labourers beside a track, possibly made by the construction workers, leading to a distant bank of trees.[165]

Ill. 32 Box Tunnel, west portal, lithograph, J.C. Bourne. *Great Western Railway,* 1846.

How accurate is this depiction? This question can be tested by reference to another picture, an engraving by J. Shury dated to about 1841, and published by William Everitt of Bath (Ill. 33). The position is the same as that of Bourne but how much earlier is it? It is without a train and so the eastern end of the tunnel can just be seen. While the track in the Bourne depiction is covered with earth between the rails, that by Shury shows longitudinal cross-sleepers with a V-shaped pit in the centre of each track, presumably for drainage. The signal and hut are in the same place with a top-hatted figure behind the hut. Behind him a figure appears to be bending down, as if to dig. The land above the tunnel appears as a pastoral hillside, seemingly undisturbed by any construction work beneath.

Did Shury create his picture before Bourne, or perhaps trade on the popularity of Bourne's work, which had in any case become popular through his depiction of scenes on the London and Birmingham Railway from 1837–38? A close examination of the detail of the tunnel façade will reveal certain differences, which suggest Shury was copying the basic impression of Bourne's depiction. The basic structure is obviously the same, even to the casting of shadow, although the flanking abutments in Shury's work have a sharper curve. The centrepiece is framed by rusticated stone work but of twenty-two courses, whereas Bourne's pictures depict twenty. The cornice in Shury's work is supported by eleven dentils, whereas Bourne's parapet has fourteen. In reality there are thirteen dentils. In the parapet, Shury depicts each division supported by four balusters, whereas Bourne shows six, which is accurate. The centrepiece of Shury's parapet is not central to the keystone of the arch beneath and is narrower than the outer divisions. I think we can assume Bourne was the model because even the Corinthian detail of the keystone is rendered accurately. On the other hand, is Bourne's rendering of the track accurate to the date of its depiction?

Since Box was hailed as the longest railway tunnel in the world when opened in 1841 – a distinction soon to be overtaken in the railway construction fervour – its gloom or rather its size and bore through solid rock was depicted by Bourne in the form of a gigantic cave with a chink of light at the far end (Ill. 34). In this picture it is tempting to see a parallel with the painter John Martin's illustrations to Milton's *Paradise Lost*, as if the train is entering Satan's palace down a long rock hewn tunnel like the entrance to a Welsh slate quarry. Martin was a friend of Brunel, and may have inspired Bourne and also Bury with his portrayal of the gas-lit railway tunnel at Wapping in 1830 (Ill. 13).

The east or less celebrated portal of Box was rarely seen except in early railway postcards and the occasional photograph, however an interesting early depiction

Ill. 33 Box Tunnel: west portal, steel engraving, J. Shury, c.1841.

Left: **Ill. 34 Interior of** the Box Tunnel, J.C. Bourne, *Great Western Railway*, 1846.

Below: **Ill. 35 Randall &** Saunders, Quarrymen, letterhead, c.1850.

CORSHAM DOWN QUARRY, EAST END OF BOX TUNNEL.

To Randell & Saunders,
Quarrymen & Stone Merchants.

of it is the use as a motif for a letterhead or invoice head by Randall & Saunders, Quarrymen & Stone Merchants, the proprietors of the Corsham Down Quarry (Ill. 35). The picture is of historical value because we see the tunnel with its original arch, before the later infill. On the right we see a rather ornamental portal to the quarry with a steam locomotive emerging with wagons.[166]

THE TUNNEL PORTRAIT

While Bourne's depictions of tunnels and viaducts showed accuracy in proportion and location, other artists exaggerated their illustrations by portraying a railway driven through a wild and romantic landscape. For dramatic locations artists turned to those stretches of line that ran along or above the seashore as these landscapes added that extra dimension of drama. Three such stretches are famous and include the track at Penmaen Mawr in North Wales, Shakespeare Cliff and the Warren between Folkestone and Dover, and the Great Western tracks at Dawlish Warren, which is in reach of the waves. Each have tunnels burrowing through the cliffs and depictions of the locality emphasise the natural surroundings rather than the tunnel mouths.

The construction of the line between Folkestone and Dover was not an easy undertaking, as referred to elsewhere in this book. Not least there was the constant danger of falling rocks from the chalk cliffs. The dramatic nature of this stretch of track was captured by artists at several points. E.T. Dolby, who had depicted the

Ill. 36 **The eastern** entrance to Shakespeare Cliff Tunnel near Dover, watercolour, E.T. Dolby. *London, Science Museum*

eastern portal of Primrose Hill Tunnel in 1838, produced another superb study of a train emerging from the eastern entrance of Shakespeare Cliff Tunnel (Ill. 36).[167] The composition has a high viewpoint as we look down from rocks on the right at the track with a gigantic cliff rising above the tunnel portal, exaggerated to dramatise an already dramatic location. What appear to be steps lead up the cliff face from the portal. The tunnel is further dramatised by it being in shadow, reinforced by the foreground folds of the cliff. The track appears to be well above the level of the sea, whereas in reality it is only a few feet. Distance is enhanced and scale reinforced by the minute yacht at sea and the couples on the clifftop and path.

The stretch of track between Dawlish station and Teignmouth on the South Devon Railway has been the subject of pictures and photographs from shortly after construction in the 1840s with its mixture of dramatic coastline and trains bursting out of the short tunnels. It remains a favourite spot for photography and inspired several railway posters during the 1930s, and even films. A version of this stretch conveying the air of a Victorian fashionable promenade was drawn by an unknown artist in about 1850, showing a steam train approaching Teignmouth.[168] The track is single and of course broad gauge, protected as now from the sea by a wall with a stone promenade above the sandy beach. Here, a group of fashionably dressed visitors stroll and watch the passing train. The scale of the cliff is exaggerated, giving the impression that the railway has just burrowed under a mountain.

The effect of these what may be termed 'seaside pictures' is to portray the tunnel mouth rather like a small cleft in a large cliff face. In the case of A.F. Tait's lithograph of Summit (Ill. 37) Tunnel it may be interpreted as the giant mouth to the passage to the 'other side' of the Pennines, which form the backbone of England.[169]

Constructed for the Leeds and Manchester Railway between 1837 and 1840, this was seen as the conquest of the backbone of England, which had hitherto held up communication between the east and west sides of fast-growing industrial England. We are almost at track level with the tunnel portal, the main feature of the composition beneath a towering pyramidal peak of rock. A sense of movement and life is created by a locomotive with a lamp hanging from the boiler, appearing from the gloom of the tunnel mouth, while two labourers climbing and descending the stairway to the right of the track also create a sense of scale. Freeman saw the navvy carrying a pickaxe as he ascends the steps as representing the triumphalism of engineering, a symbol of the 'eclipse of the creation story'![170] On the right side of the track is a watchman's hut while the left side of the picture is framed by a diagonal cliff face. The foreground displays a cluster of stone blocks on which lie what looks like a sketch book, pens and a furled umbrella.

Tait also illustrated Elland Tunnel, on the same line, although here the portal is more distant and seen beyond a bridge, which gives scale to the composition (Ill. 38). On the hill above the portal a ventilation shaft can be seen.

An intriguing painting in the Ironbridge Museum collection is signed 'Ambergate Tunnel', yet has the profile of the north portal of Milford Tunnel on the North Midland Railway. Perhaps dating from the 1840s, it shows a train crossing a three-arched bridge over what is probably the River Derwent. The north portal of

Ill. 37 Summit Tunnel coloured lithograph, A.F. Tait, 1845, *Views on the Manchester & Leeds Railway*, 1845.

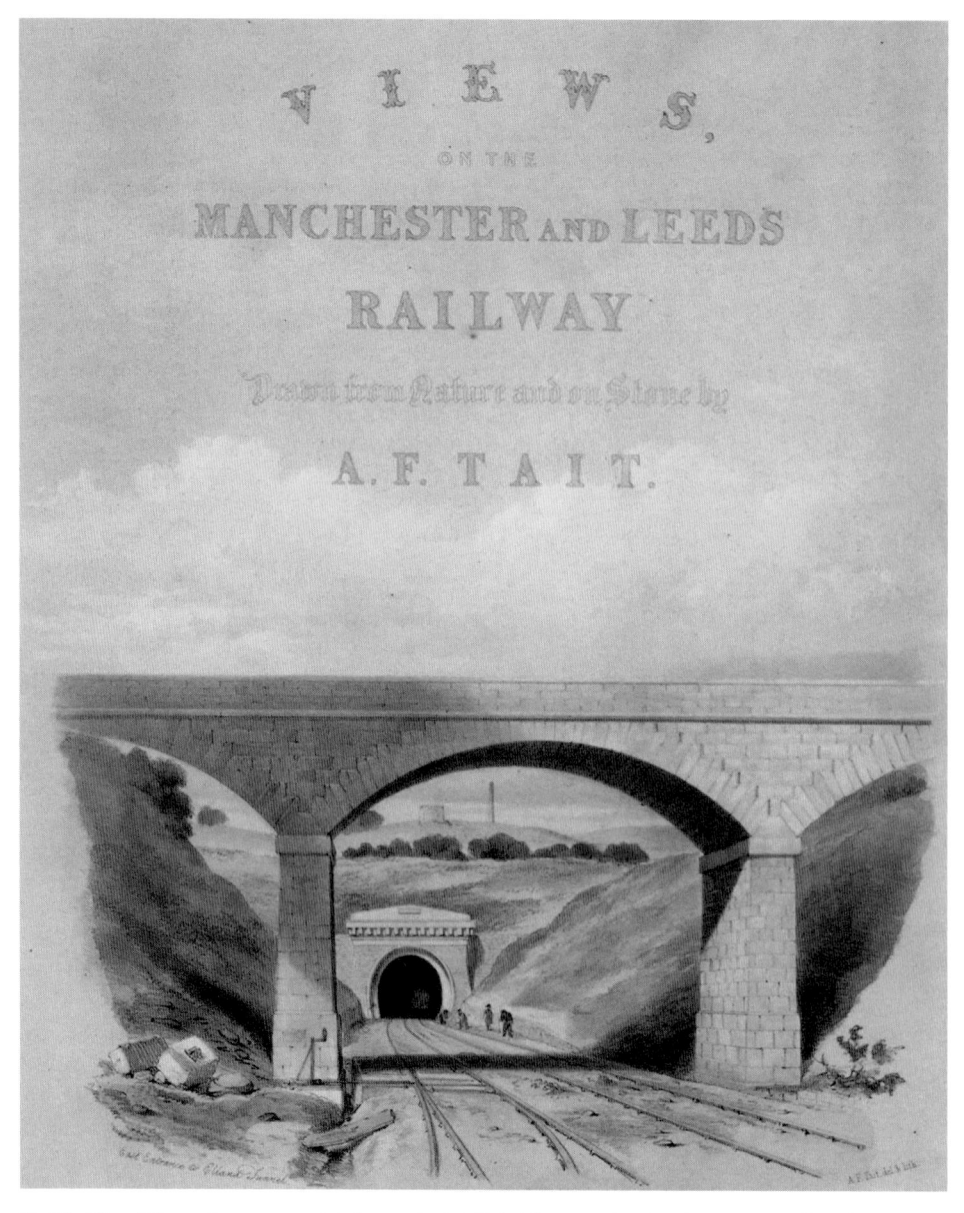

Ill. 38 Elland Tunnel, west portal, lithograph, A.F. Tait, *Views on the Manchester & Leeds Railway*, 1845.

Milford Tunnel is in a cutting, and the profile of the short Ambergate Tunnel has a distinctive stone face pierced by an elliptical arch. However, the Derwent crosses beneath the tracks a little to the north of Ambergate Tunnel (Ill. 39).

   As mentioned earlier, *The Illustrated London News* provides a record of the early development of railways with a series of woodcuts and steel engravings aimed at a middle-class readership and travelling public. Many illustrations involving

Ill. 39 **Milford Tunnel?** Artist unknown. Elton Collection, Ironbridge Museum, AE 185.39

railways emphasised an occasion such as an arrival of distinguished company or the opening of a station, but some featured outstanding structures such as stations and even tunnel portals. An early example of a crude woodcut shows a train emerging from the southern portal of Littlebury Tunnel beneath the Audley Estate in Essex (Ill 40).[171] This was included in a three-page section of the report on the opening of the Eastern Counties Railway. In this, the tunnel was described as having entrances which 'are good specimens of the bold and early style of arch, over which are … the armorial bearings of the noble house of Neville and Griffin, Lord Braybrooke'. This was followed by a long heraldic analysis because of his nearby residence, Audley End, and as a director of the company, 'he lent his weight and great interest to its perfecting'.[172] In this illustration two figures stand on the track in close proximity to the moving train. Early illustrations often give the impression of a fearless public or trackside workers wandering across tracks, far removed from the sense of fear on the part of the public suggested by some early commentators as they came face to face with the novel sense of speed and power.

On the London and Brighton Railway there was one tunnel whose northern portal stands out as one of the most impressive castellated portals. This is Clayton, piercing the South Downs and over a mile in length. Like Box Tunnel, which was visible from a nearby bridge, so also Clayton, which attracted artists in various mediums including watercolour, ink engraving and lithography. Two examples

Ill. 40 Littlebury Tunnel, Audley End, *Illustrated London News*, 2 August 1845.

include an engraving in George Measom's *Guide to the London and Brighton Railway*, published in 1853 (Ill. 41). It is of considerable artistic value in showing the tunnel with a crenellated parapet that was subsequently altered to hold a cottage for the signalman or tunnel keeper. The second from 1922 (Ill. 8) shows the portal as it has remained to this day. The portal will be discussed in greater detail later.

ENTRANCE TO CLAYTON TUNNEL.

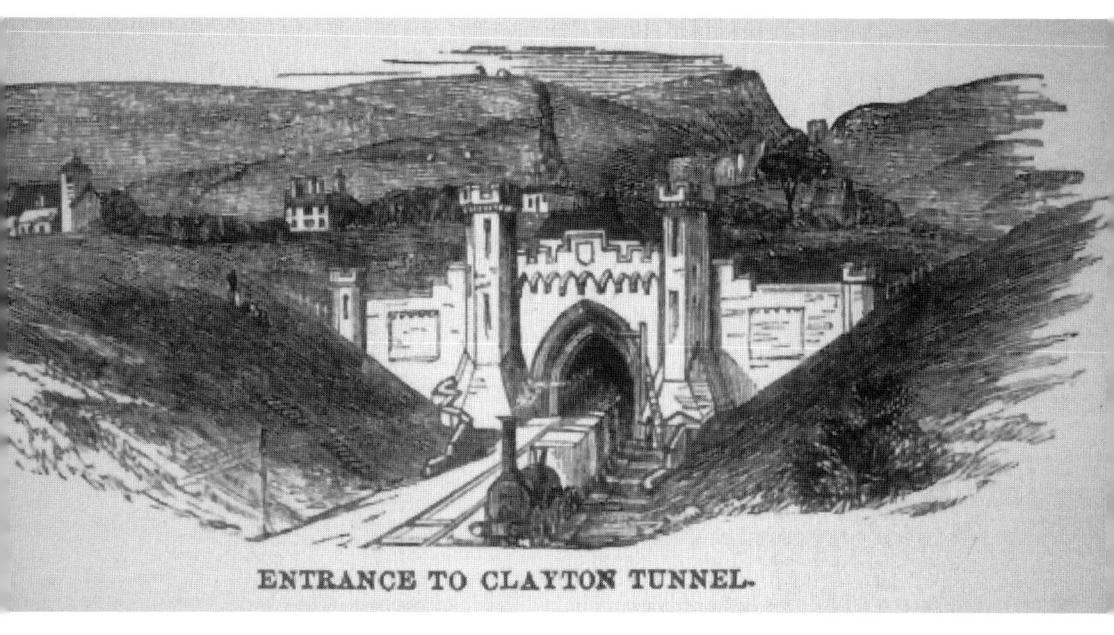

Ill. 41 Clayton Tunnel from George Measom, *Guide to the London and Brighton Railway*, 1853.

By the late nineteenth century the novelty of the rail journey had waned, perhaps overtaken by the novelty of sailing across the oceans on a coal-fired ship, which created its own sensations of exhilaration and fear as well as a new visual experience. The wonders and novelties of one generation become commonplace in the next, especially in the early nineteenth century, then in the grip of the Industrial Revolution and dramatic social change. The romantic descriptions of the flickering light of the carriage against a tunnel wall, or passengers shrieking in amazement against the sound of the whistle and screeching wheels as they were plunged into momentary darkness, receded in the face of public confidence in the railways. Publications such as *Bradshaw's Railway Guide* now devoted pages to purely factual information devoid of any sensation. Art changed as well; the initial popularity of prints specifically of railway features or trackside locations gave way to landscapes in which the railway became part of the grander setting. Even Bourne had changed emphasis between his views for the *London and Birmingham Railway*, where he emphasises the engineering, and his *Great Western*, where he emphasises the railway in the landscape. Increasingly the railway was depicted as at ease with the landscape, rather than destroying it, and where a tunnel appeared, it is at a point where the tracks burrow into a high hill or cliff face, perhaps in the far distance.[173]

This is not to say that the sensation of a railway journey had completely disappeared by the end of the nineteenth century. In 1904 the picture postcard firm Raphael Tuck issued a number of views of railway scenes including Shugborough Tunnel, and in 1906 a series of notable tunnel portals including Primrose Hill and Watford.[174] I only know of one railway travel poster, so much part of the station platform furniture of the past, that featured a train leaving a tunnel. In the 1950s

British Railways published a poster depicting a train on the former Malton and Driffield Railway leaving Burdale Tunnel, which was opened in 1853 on the now long-closed line between York and Hull. A letter in *The Times* in 1928 instanced specific situations and locations of track of tourist interest on the British railway system. Examples were cited of the proximity to water and rivers, walls of brick and rock, water troughs, bridges and viaducts, and not least tunnels:

> Tunnels are unforgettable landmarks on a night journey, and no one who notices these things could confuse the Clayton tunnel under the South Downs on the Brighton Railway, with that of Balcombe, with the ear-splitting crescendo of the last hundred yards at the southern end, due, it is said, to the peculiarity known as 'rolling rails' ... The old traveller on the South Eastern can tell off-hand whether the train is in the Sevenoaks or Chislehurst Tunnel.[175]

Chapter 5
THE FEAR OF A RAILWAY TUNNEL

Having shown what the fascination of tunnels and portals held for travellers and artists alike, I shall now turn to what was for many an intense dread of tunnels, and ask whether the experience of being in total darkness, or at best a dim light, provoked additional fears. Were these fears justified in the light of subsequent reports of accidents, and at worse, death. How many passengers actually died or were injured while travelling through a tunnel? Such perceived fear or hesitation has to be seen in the context of a rapidly expanding readership of newspapers and popular journals, whose journalists commanded considerable power to form popular opinion. Public opinion, of course, could spell the success or failure of a new venture, an aspect of early railway history discussed by Julie Wosk in her study of the influence of technology on the visual arts, *Breaking Frame*. Ironically, with the advent of railways, news travelled faster; newspapers and journals published in London reporting even minor railway accidents could be read throughout Britain within days.[1]

John Herapath's *Railway Magazine*, founded in 1836, was a formal record of railway development both at home and abroad. In its editions, at least for the first few years, he could not resist voicing his dislike of tunnels. Even in his first editorial, which concerned the Liverpool and Manchester Railway, he suggested that the experience of going through the short tunnel at Crown Street, Liverpool, in darkness, with the 'toot-toot of the horn', was as frightening as the experience that previous pre-railway generations had had of 'creeping through the narrow and dangerous lanes with horns and bells incessantly announcing each other's approach'.[2] We shall return to Herapath later.

THE FEAR OF SPEED
In the case of railway travel, the companies had to contend with not only a dislike of tunnels and the possibility of collapse but also a fear of speed. There was also the more likely possibility, present even today, that the train might be derailed, and that the then wooden carriages, which were viewed by some as 'unsteady, claustrophobic wooden boxes', might trap their occupants.[3] Ralph Harrington, in his 1994 *History Today* article, does not mention specifically fear of tunnels, but argues that the fear of travel by train was more general; some passengers feared the speed, although this lessened as the railways proved their ability to function safely.[4] He claimed that below the superficial acceptance deep disquiet still remained because many people were worried about the effect on the brain and

resulting nervous exhaustion due to constant vibration, and even the blur from the carriage window if passengers could not focus on specific objects because of the speed. Or, as R.L. Stephenson wrote in *From a Carriage Window*:

> Faster than fairies, faster than witches,
> Bridges and horses, hedges and ditches,
> Fly as thick as driving rain;
> And ever again, in the wink of an eye,
> Painted stations whistle by.

Wolfgang Schivelbusch's study of nineteenth-century rail travel, *The Railway Journey*, devotes Chapter 3 to the impact of speed, or what he called the 'annihilation of space'. He took his line from an article in the *Quarterly Review*, 1839, which spoke of the gradual annihilation, approaching almost to final extinction of that space, and of those distances that have hitherto been supposedly unalterably to separate the various nations of the globe. As distance was thus annihilated, the surface of our country 'would as it were, shrivel in size until it became not much bigger than one immense city'.[5] Schivelbusch cites Thomas Creevy describing a train journey and seeing the disadvantage of such progress as 'it is really flying, and it is impossible to divest yourself of the notion of instant death to all upon the least accident happening'.[6] He cites a text from 1845 that speaks of a certain constriction of the spirit that never quite leaves one. It was a fear of derailment, and not being able to guide the carriage, or indeed the whole train away from it. The passenger had therefore become a helpless victim.[7] Dickens described the passage through a long tunnel, especially for third-class passengers without the luxury of lamplight, as being like blindness.[8] Fear was compounded by the fact that in the early days of the railways passengers were even locked in carriages, a situation described in Parliament as 'pregnant with danger to vast numbers'.[9] J.G. Kohl, in his record of the King of Saxony's journey through England and Scotland in 1844, tells how they went through the Summit Tunnel near Manchester 'at full speed … We were exactly five minutes and fifteen seconds, and this may give some idea of the length of this subterranean work'.[10] It is, of course, likely that the King and his attendants would have had a lantern rather than enduring such a long period of darkness.

VIBRATION

The fear (mostly unjustified, as it turned out) was that the carriages might fall apart in a tunnel under the friction, or the engine might blow up. After all, a container filled with fire (a boiler) could be likened to a slowly burning fuse in a cannon. A fear, intensified in a tunnel, was the isolation of a carriage compartment, decades before the introduction of connecting corridors. In an emergency, there were no channels of communication with the outside world. Peter Lecount evoked the possibility of sudden illness and the only way the passenger might then gain attention would be if he were 'by accident in a carriage just under the guard', but even then 'he might exhort his voice in vain and … not possibly receive the least help if he were dying'.[11] Yet surprisingly, a little further on, he defends travelling through tunnels where 'there is positively no inconvenience whatever in them, except the change from day-light to lamp-light'.[12] In this instance he was referring to the report of several medical doctors regarding Primrose Hill Tunnel, and, with his reference to lamplight, was no doubt thinking of his 'first-class' reader passengers; he was, after all, Assistant Secretary of the London and Birmingham Railway and joint author with Thomas Roscoe of the *London and Birmingham Railway Guide*, 1839.[13] However, Roscoe pointed out that all rail travel, irrespective of whether the passenger was in a tunnel or not, meant that the passenger was shut out from all communication with the world.[14]

Gordon Biddle, on the other hand, laments the lot of the third-class passengers, who would be 'bouncing along on short iron rails and unyielding stone sleepers' with the only compensation of speed and relative cheapness, but enduring 'the sheer din of the blackness of a fume-filled tunnel deep below ground which could at best be alarming, to some terrifying'.[15] Catherine Hickie, in *The Permanente Journal*, in 2000, also quotes *The Lancet*'s fears for the discomfort of the poorer classes in third-class carriages.[16] The Great Western Railway conveyed its so-called third-class passengers as goods train passengers in open carriages, so the poor third class did not have lighting for many years. The seats for goods passengers were 18in high, and fitted in trucks with the sides and ends only 2ft above the floor; therefore standing up was very dangerous.[17] We can well imagine the terror of travelling through the Box Tunnel, with its eerie echoes against the walls of brick interspersed with naked rock.[18] It would have taken up to eight minutes to pass through it, based on Freeman's calculation of the speed of third-class trains on the GWR, as a result of an 1844 Act imposing a maximum speed of 12mph.[19]

Jill Matus, in a paper for *Victorian Studies*, argued that through rail travel the condition of trauma first became viewed as a medical condition worthy of notice, and therefore led to a study of the effects of modern technology on the human frame.[20] It was not until 1846, at the urging of Owen Chadwick, that legislation was passed by Parliament obliging railway companies to pay compensation to passengers or next-of-kin for those injured or killed in an accident.[21]

PUBLIC FEELINGS AND HEALTH

The Times reported the evidence of eminent scientists before a committee of the House of Lords in 1836. The proceedings were chaired by Sir Anthony Carlisle, Vice President of the College of Surgeons.[22] They expressed fears, some of an extremely lurid nature, as to the effects of tunnels on passengers, such as the difference of temperature in tunnels that would lead to colds, which in turn would lead to other disorders. One member would not permit his patients to go to Brighton by a railway that had a tunnel in it, since:

> it is impossible to change the atmosphere in a tunnel 600 yards long … the air is a commixture, with other gaseous substances; it is also damp air … sulphuretted, carburetted, and carbonic gases will be emitted from the burning of coke, and the steam would be condensing and would keep

the atmosphere damp, with effluvia of passengers, etc, so that a quantity of stagnant air would remain impregnated with poisonous gases. It might be scarlet fever or smallpox.[23]

Since it was impossible to get to Brighton by train without going through a tunnel, the doctor was obliging his patients to go by carriage.

Another doctor, Edward Griffiths, also would not allow invalids to travel by a railway in which there were tunnels, as from his own experience of the Whitstable and Canterbury Railway, he declared it 'would be extremely dangerous to a person in delicate health … The cold is very severe, and affected the skin and eyes.'[24] This was a short but narrow, single-track passage and the train was hauled by rope. Elsewhere, another contemporary claimed 'the deafening peal of thunder, the sudden immersion in gloom, and the clash of reverberated sounds in a confined space', would combine 'to produce a momentary shudder, or ideas of destruction, even a thrill of annihilation'.[25]

It is hard to gain an accurate picture of railway safety in the first fifty or so years of railway travel. In the 1830s it had been suggested that railway companies tried to hide numbers of injuries to allay the fears of potential passengers.[26] There was a suggestion in *The Times* as early as February 1839 that railway accidents were more frequent than actually reported in the press because 'railway companies prevent information respecting them being given to servants, and it is on record that an inspector on a certain line was actually discharged for giving information to a reporter with respect to an accident'.[27] Consequently the actual figures may have been higher.

Of the sixty-three incidents recorded by the Board of Trade between 1839 and 1870, only fourteen resulted in deaths. The largest number of fatalities occurred at Sutton Tunnel, 1851; Clayton Tunnel, 1861; and Blackheath Tunnel, 1864 (altogether thirty-seven fatalities). These are listed in Appendix 3.[28] Smiles, not an impartial authority, in his *Life of Stephenson* claimed that during the first eight years of the Liverpool and Manchester Railway no fewer than 5 million people travelled by its trains with only two fatalities (neither in a tunnel). He supported rail travel by rightly claiming that during the same period 'loss of life through stage-coach accidents was by far greater.'[29] We have, in any case, to distinguish death and injury as a result of a passenger's journey by train, or as a result of someone being on or near a railway track, such circumstances often occurring to railway employees, where a sudden slip or fall could mean a fatality. Harrington, in his 1994 article, quoted an article from the *Lancet* of 1862 stating that with 'accidents having become so frequent of late … railway travelling has become almost insupportable to persons of nervous temperament, whose thoughts are solely occupied during the journey by speculations on possible dangers'.[30] He cited the case of Dickens, who had a narrow escape without injury in the Staplehurst crash in 1865, but subsequently suffered an aftershock of fainting and sickness that affected his health for the remainder of his life. Harrington reinforced his article by reference to several ardent critics of the railways including Ruskin, who viewed rail travel, when it was not destroying the country, as transmuting 'a man from a traveller into a living parcel'.[31] Harrington concluded, however, with Kipling's positive view, who perhaps saw railways in the broader context of helping in the development of the British Empire and underpinning modern technological society. However, a study of the list of incidents in tunnels reported to, or recorded by, the Board of Trade reveals overwhelmingly that few resulted in death or injury. It is easy to quote the views of prominent Victorians who viewed the railways with disquiet for whatever reason, but the yearly increase in passengers would suggest that most of the public were won over by speed and efficiency; any discomfort was worth it for the reduced time it took to get to even the more remote outposts of Britain. In any case, by the 1880s there were even proposals to tunnel under the English Channel, which made all tunnels hitherto seem but minor inconveniences.

HOW MANY TUNNELS TO BRIGHTON?
Certainly the fear of tunnels was considerable in the first decade or so of rail travel. George Stephenson therefore initially proposed a route for the Manchester and Leeds Railway that avoided the use of tunnels (although the route eventually constructed involved several long ones).[32] There was intense competition to develop a London to Brighton line, with six rival routes being proposed between 1834 and 1838. One engineer, Cundy, sought to promote his line by stating it 'will require no tunnels, the loss of life from which has been so great as ought to make persons pause before they engage in lines where such are indispensable'.[33] The 'loss of life', of course, refers to the navvies, but Cundy may have phrased this deliberately ambiguously as scare tactics directed at the travelling public, in order to push through his plan. There had as yet been no passenger deaths in a tunnel, as there was only one tunnel in use for passenger trains at the time, on the Leeds and Selby railway, and no accident had occurred there. Robert Stephenson stated in evidence to the House of Lords in 1835 'until lately I was not aware of any tunnel in which a locomotive engine dragged a train with passengers'.[34]

On the other hand, Joseph Locke, then assistant engineer on the London and Birmingham Railway, wrote in support of Rennie's proposed direct line. He believed 'the gradients not exceeding 1 in 264 feet, nor the curves at a safe speed would prevent difficulties but most importantly, by the introduction of a tunnel at Merstham, and increasing the length of tunnels at Balcombe and Clayton, (Rennie) had reduced the source of objection'.[35] The directors of another proposed line, the South Eastern, Brighton, Lewis and Newhaven Railway, claimed they had been 'at some pains to fight "the Shadow" which ancient ladies are alarming themselves about, railway tunnels'.[36] In the final event, the London and Brighton Railway as surveyed by John Rennie was to have five tunnels, and that at Balcombe was shortened after revision by Rennie.[37]

Even before the London and Birmingham Railway was opened it had its critics, who questioned the chosen route by Stephenson with tunnels, over that without proposed by Rennie. The editor of the *Railway Magazine* wrote in December 1836: if 'Sir John Rennie had proposed a line from London to Birmingham without tunnels, why has a million of money been spent more than is needed, and on a line apparently every way inferior, why near a dozen curses to boot in the shape of tunnels'.[38] A report in the *Hampshire Advertiser* in May 1837 claimed the opening of the London and Southampton Railway would be the most favourable route from London, not only because of the scenery but because there would be no tunnels.[39] A letter to the *Railway Magazine* in April 1835 accepted there was no danger in a tunnel of up to two hundred yards, but the chill 'of a two mile subterranean passage' would deter any person of delicate health 'from ever venturing therein … the puffing of a high pressure engine … the clinking of chains … the dismal glare of lamps … convey a horror which weak nerves could never endure'.[40] This was when the completion of the London and Birmingham Railway was in doubt because of the flooding of Kilsby Tunnel.

When the Leeds and Derby Railway (later the North Midland) was proposed the proprietors claimed only one tunnel a mile and 200 yards long was required, as the railway could follow the line of the valleys.[41] In the event, the route as built involved at least five significant tunnels. In 1836, the Secretary of the proposed South Midland Counties Railway claimed that the most direct route between London, the Midlands and the north could be made without a tunnel, whereas the proposed London and Birmingham had no fewer than four, and was therefore highly objectionable to passengers.[42] Obviously it was in a company's interests to play down the significance of tunnels, although few could be avoided in hilly regions without adopting a costly and circuitous route. Also it is interesting that Herapath, the editor of the *Railway Magazine*, should have given a prominent platform to the anti-tunnel lobby – he just happened to be appointed assistant engineer of Cundy's proposed tunnel-less route to Brighton![43]

THE PROPAGANDA OF FEAR AND REASSURANCE

What provoked this fear other than the appearance of a dark arch? The debate for and against the perceived fear of tunnels was carried in a number of journals and newspapers including *The Times*, read by the very class whom it was essential to woo if companies were to succeed by attracting enough passengers. Even railway guides, such as Measom's *Great Western Railway*, which were produced to provide interest as the route unravelled before their window, could sometimes strike the wrong note for the nervous passenger, for example: 'The Sapperton Tunnel which cuts through the Cotswolds Hills before our arrival at Stroud is an object of terror,'[44] or: 'And now, timid lady travellers, screw up your nerves for a rush through the Box Tunnel,' a statement hardly likely to calm such persons and which was deleted from subsequent editions.[45] A letter in the *Railway Magazine* of April 1836 claimed a 2-mile subterranean passage would deter any person of delicate health from ever entering it. The second issue of the *Railway Magazine* in April 1836 carried an article by the editor, Herapath of course, entitled 'Tunnels ought to be especially avoided'. He warned against travelling through 'such holes of impurity'.[46] Higham Tunnel, on the Thames and Medway Canal, and the short tunnel on the Canterbury and Whitstable Railway were mentioned. Of the latter, he claimed that it was known in the neighbourhood as 'sink of colds, &c, that … very few will venture into it at all, and the railway consequently carries scarcely any passengers'. Of Higham the editor claimed that he walked through it with a companion on a fine bright day and that at first they 'found it light and not uncomfortable, but when (they) had reached about 500 yards, the darkness became so intense that (they) could neither see the path (they) trod, nor distinguish it from the water beside (them)'.[47]

If the sensation of passing through double-track tunnels was naturally likely to create a sense of claustrophobia to the unseasoned traveller, the action of passing through a single-track tunnel was even more likely to do so. As a result journals emphasised tunnels' widths almost in a spirit of rivalry; those on the London and Birmingham Railway were 24ft wide, while those on the Great Western would have a constant width of 30ft 'more with a view to diminish the objections to tunnels'.[48] A reference to the Box Tunnel in the *Penny Satirist* in September 1841, shortly after its opening, might be assumed to have put passengers' minds at rest: 'The three great desiderata of a tunnel, viz, absence from danger, darkness and damp, have been perfectly acquired; it is so dry within that one might walk through it in slippers.'[49] However, as we shall see shortly, all was not well at Box. In order to fully appreciate the implications of a passage through a tunnel we must realise that at a speed of, say, 30mph, it would take two minutes to traverse a tunnel 1 mile in length; those in the Pennines, at the end of a long climb such as Woodhead or Summit, therefore up to six minutes.

Railway companies bringing acts before Parliament were very conscious of public feeling in the early years of railway construction. When it was first proposed to build a railway from Leeds to Carlisle in the 1840s it was said the route would be 'thirty-seven miles long' and 'all in tunnel'![50] This gross exaggeration, perhaps to pacify influential landowners fearing the devastation of their moors, would have deterred most potential passengers. In fact the route, when finally constructed in the 1870s, was about 72 miles long, and included sixteen tunnels, mostly short apart from that at Blea Moor. On the Great Western a Bill was obtained 'authorising such a deviation of the line as enables the Company to avoid the intended tunnels at Sonning and Purley (Tilehurst), thereby leaving the railway without a single tunnel from London to Corsham, a distance of 96 miles … '[51] So, at Sonning where it was at first intended to tunnel, the line now went through a cutting 2 miles long and up to 70ft deep in places, longer and deeper than the proposed tunnel.[52]

VENTILATION, THE VIEWS OF LARDNER, HERAPATH AND STORER

Ventilation was of primary concern in the battle to woo early passengers to the prospects of a subterranean journey. The debate was started by Herapath in July 1835 with a paper in the *Mechanics' Magazine* on smoke in tunnels,[53] and a paper read at the Institution of Civil Engineers in 1836 as a result of tests on the air in Leeds Tunnel, which was deemed to be perfectly ventilated due to the three shafts.[54] This was sometimes emphasised in early railway guides to reassure the passengers. When passing through the relatively shallow Watford Tunnel, which had six shafts, Osborne says 'at the fourth … we can easily detect (the surroundings) from its magnitude, and the consequent broad and vivid glare of light which it throws into the tunnel'.[55] Yet it was claimed that it was frequently ten minutes before the tunnel was completely clear of smoke in spite of the six ventilation shafts.[56] In the case of Kilsby Tunnel, which was opened to passenger traffic in September 1838 and then the longest on the railway system, it was emphasised that 'for a few minutes after the engine and train had passed through, the vapour is carried up the shafts and the tunnel is rendered so clear that the other end may distinctly be seen'.[57] The King of Saxony must have admired this spectacle when he made a tour through England and Scotland in 1844 by road and rail, and took the latter northwards from Wolverton. 'His Majesty preferred remaining in an open carriage on the truck ... dragged along backwards by the snorting engine with such rapidity ... through long dark tunnels filled with smoke and steam.'[58]

The problem was not simply the length of a tunnel, most of which would be passed in less than a minute at a speed of some 30mph, but rather the adequate ventilation. Dr Paris, and Dr Walsh, Messrs Lawrence and Lucas, together with Mr Phillips, lecturer on chemistry, reported that:

> the air for many feet above their heads remained clear, and apparently unaffected by steam or effluvia of any kind, neither was there any damp or cold perceptible ... that the atmosphere of the tunnel was dry, of an agreeable temperature, and free from smell ... that the danger incurred in passing through a properly constructed tunnel, would be no greater than that incurred upon an open railway or on a turnpike road.[59]

In 1836 Dr Dionysius Lardner wrote an essay on *Examples of Steam Power* that was quoted at length in *The Times*.[60] In it he discussed the effects of passing through a tunnel hauled by a steam locomotive. He was writing at a time when few lines then open had tunnels penetrated by steam haulage. The readership of this journal would after all, form the bulk of the initial railway-travelling public, and their reaction to the experience could be crucial to the success or failure of a venture. He used two examples and admitted that they had so far little experience of tunnels that were open to regular passenger services.[61] The example he chose for passenger haulage was Leeds Tunnel just beyond the station:

> which is nearly level, the length of which is 700 yards, width 22 feet, height 17. It is ventilated by three shafts of about 10 feet diameter and 60 feet high. There is an intercourse of passengers amounting to 400 per day ... and generally speaking, they do not object to going through the tunnel with a locomotive engine, the fuel used is coke.[62]

The other example was the Glenfield Tunnel on the Leicester and Swannington Railroad opened in 1832:

> about a mile in length and nearly level. It is ventilated by eight shafts and I have frequently passed through it with a locomotive engine. Even when shut up in a closed carriage, the annoyance is very great, and such as would never be tolerated on a line or road having a large intercourse of passengers upon it.[63]

The comparison is perhaps a little unfair as Glenfield Tunnel was a single bore, which always caused problems of thick smoke lingering. In *The Times* article he said tunnels should be ventilated by shafts at intervals of no more than 200 yards, which is a situation likely to be impracticable from the construction point of view, if ideal for the traveller, when boring beneath a town or through belts of stone. An early passenger travelling through the single-bore Tyler Hill Tunnel on the Canterbury and Whitstable Railway who became fearful because of its dimensions rather than odours commented, 'when we had proceeded halfway through, a feeling of suffocation became perceptible, increasing so fearfully that had the tunnel been twice the length, I feel confident I should hardly have got through alive'.[64]

As we have seen, Herapath wrote a striking editorial 'Tunnels ought to be avoided' in *Railway Magazine*, April 1836, in which he not only expressed concern for ventilation and the effect on the passengers' health, especially of those of delicate constitution, but also the cost of construction including gas for lighting long tunnels.[65] In his view the way to avoid most tunnelling was the building of inclined planes, even if the initial and annual expense were much greater than with a tunnel.[66] However, his strongest criticism apart from ventilation was about noise. He described a journey through the Leeds Tunnel during which the train struck some scaffolding that had been used to whitewash the tunnel and came to a halt. The crash 'sounded like the report of artillery' and the passengers were so alarmed and frightened 'that they declared their apprehension of immediate death'.[67] He finished his editorial with a challenge to his readership to decide whether a tunnel of half a mile was a nuisance or whether they agreed with Mr Stephenson in seeing no objection to tunnels 20 miles long.

Herapath naturally encouraged letters supporting his views from readers of his journal; 'tunnels of two hundred yards admit of no valid objection … but the chill of a two mile subterranean passage will deter any person of delicate health'.[68] To his credit, however, he did publish three reports in support of tunnels, but prefaced them with the excuse that 'we insert the following reports for the amusement of readers. They contain the best specimens of twaddle we have seen yet on tunnels.'[69] This remark was picked up by *Fraser's Magazine*, April 1838, which suggested the views of the 'elite of London science' should be taken seriously.[70] The first report on Leeds Tunnel by doctors Davy and Rothman was positive in every aspect – quality of air, temperature, noise – however the darkness 'which though not dangerous, is to many persons unpleasant … It is understood to be in contemplation to attach lamps to the carriages.'[71] It was supported by Dr Williamson of Leeds Medical School.[72] The second report was on Primrose Hill Tunnel, which was not then open for through traffic but which was important because it was longer than the Leeds Tunnel and acted as a test for rail passengers on the London and Birmingham Railway. Several test runs were made through the tunnel for the committee led by Dr Paris, who found the atmosphere 'agreeable and free from smell' and the sensation 'experienced was precisely that of travelling in a coach by night between walls of a narrow street'.[73] This favourable report was also cited by Francis Whishaw in his *Analysis of Railways and Projected Railways*, 1837.

In a third report titled *On the Atmosphere in Tunnels*, Dr Reid, FRS, said he had no hesitation in expressing the conviction that the atmosphere in Primrose Hill was of no danger to passengers, being continually 'renewed by the currents' of air in the tunnel.[74]

A report in the *Bristol Mercury* in March 1838, when the tunnels on the Great Western were still under construction, drew attention to Dr Neil Arnott's publication on *Warming and Ventilation*, and claimed that opponents to the Great Western Bill in the House of Commons obstructed the 'new and almost miraculous means which the railway offers of forwarding human civilisation and happiness'.[75] He cited their six objections: temperature, impurity of air, moisture, rapid passage through the air, sudden darkness and noise. He claimed these simply caused alarm to the ignorant or inexperienced, in the same way as a 'child allowed to believe in ghosts may be tortured by fits'. Going through a tunnel was the same as 'passing through any narrow street at night'.[76] The Corporation of Bristol, having put so much faith in this venture, would naturally expect support from its local journal!

These positive reports were seized upon by several early railway authors; Francis Coghlan in his *Iron Road Book or the London and Birmingham Railway Companion*, 1838, in which he did his best to allay the fears of travellers on the London and Birmingham Railway when passing through the seven tunnels:

> The air that would be contaminated in a tunnel by a locomotive with its train passing through it, supposing there were no ventilating shafts whatever, is 1/450th part of the whole. The air of a crowded church or theatre is a thousand times more injurious, if indeed such a term can be applied to a railway tunnel.[77]

He was so confident that he proclaimed that 'in the tunnels now opened, not the slightest inconvenience is experienced in passing through, either from insufficient ventilation, or from any other cause. I can vouch for this for having been in a tunnel when a train was passing through.'[78] Bourne was also a confident supporter of rail travel, and in his *London and Birmingham Railway*, 1838, he referred to Primrose Hill Tunnel as exciting 'strong anxieties and terror in the timid mind' but allayed the readers' fears by assuring them that millions of people had passed through it.[79] Since the London and Birmingham Railway was the first long-distance line, and one with a number of tunnels of considerable length, it was either a test for passengers' fears for rail travel, or proof of how successful and comfortable it could be. So 1838 was a vital year, and the opening of the railway was accompanied by the publication of a number of supportive books and travel guides.

Not all journals were immediately won over by the positive medical reports. In 1843 *The Builder* reported that the public could not, or would not, understand that it was as safe to travel in a dark tunnel as in a carriage on a dark night.[80] As late as 1847 *The Builder* published a negative report on the Great Western Railway whose shareholders, arriving at Bath from Bristol after having 'like a mole explored (their) way through tunnels long and deep … will be so heartily sick, with foul air, smoke, and sulphur, that the very mention of a railway will be worse than ipecacuanha'.[81] Brunel, being obviously aware of the concern of influential persons and bodies and the consequences such reports could have on his potential passengers, composed an announcement published in the same issue:

> With the attraction also of the royal residence at Windsor, now made doubly attractive by the intention felt by our youthful Queen, there can be little doubt that of all the lines out of London the Great Western Railway will command the preference for pleasure excursions. When a ride of half an hour will land the holiday folk at Slough, and another ten minutes (at the outmost), carry them on to Maidenhead and its beautiful vicinity, we cannot suppose that any who ever leave London, will fail to make frequent excursions on this line, on which they will find no tunnels, and may be whirled along, probably if they wish it, at the rate of thirty-five miles per hour.[82]

By the 1860s tunnels of greater length than hitherto were planned in Europe and North America, and in 1862 American engineer Charles S. Storer visited England at the behest of the State of Massachusetts, then constructing the Hoosac Tunnel, nearly 5 miles long. Storer was keen to test the ventilation in tunnels such as Box and Sapperton, both with steep gradients. At Box he remarked that an up train was sufficient to fill the tunnel in spite of the shafts, to produce 'perfect darkness'. He concluded the quickest way to clear a tunnel was not the provision of ventilation shafts, but to run a fast down train with steam cut-off as 'a powerful agent for the dispersal of smoke'. At Sapperton he found it was common practice for the assisting or banking engine to run down the tunnel to clear the smoke. Tunnel maintenance workers supported his conclusion that ventilation shafts were of limited use, especially in fog, with the smoke trapped in the shafts, and eddies and currents interfering with the temperature in the tunnel. Shafts were also responsible for the accumulation of water and ice falling on to the tracks beneath.[83] Nonetheless it remained normal practice to include or retain shafts in all but the shortest tunnels.

There was also the problem of smoke inhalation if a tunnel was immediately beyond a terminal station platform, and where the engine might be fighting for speed and adhesion to the tracks such as at Lime Street, Liverpool. Here the 2,000-yard tunnel cut from Edge Hill to the new terminus, which opened in 1836, was built without ventilation shafts as the trains were rope-hauled up and down the steep incline. However, when in 1870 locomotives were sufficiently powerful to haul trains up the incline, the smoke rolled back into the station creating a very unpleasant atmosphere.[84]

THE FEAR OF COLLAPSE AND PROLONGED DARKNESS

A major fear, and a not unnatural one with a structure of such length, was that a tunnel might collapse and bury passengers alive. The geologist William Buckland had raised this very danger during a lecture at the Institution of Civil Engineers in 1842. In reply to a paper on Great Western Railway Tunnels by Charles Nixon asserting that tunnels could be safely framed without any masonry in unstratified rock, Buckland claimed that 'portions of the Box Tunnel ... having no roof of masonry would collapse as a result of the successive shaking of trains ... and some dreadful damage would arise'.[85] A writer to *The Times* urged railway proprietors to take notice of Buckland, 'a person so well qualified to give an opinion and render tunnels secure'.[86] In August 1842 no less a person than Major General Pashley, Inspector General of Railways, published an exhaustive report on Box Tunnel, in which he considered the portions of the tunnel unprotected by masonry or brickwork to be 'perfectly strong and safe'.[87] Buckland was right and Pashley was wrong in this instance, with rock falls on several occasions in Box in 1845. According to a letter from 'A Traveller', as the workmen cleared the rubble from the track, there were two further falls 'on some workmen, the weight of one of these blocks was about one ton, and the other about 12cwt. Fortunately the down mail train was delayed in the tunnel mouth'.[88] The debris was cleared and traffic was resumed after six hours. For a time, those passengers who feared travelling through the Box Tunnel had the alternative of taking a post chaise over Box Hill that was specially provided for them.[89]

At Bramhope, which was lined throughout, a section of roof collapsed in 1854 as a train was passing beneath. Fortunately it was on the locomotive; miraculously the driver and fireman escaped death.[90] On its reopening, *The Times* reported that it was now believed to be perfectly safe.[91] However, the Bramhope Tunnel, with its magnificent castellated northern portal, was seen as a fearsome and smoky experience (Ill. 73). In spite of this the Leeds and Thirsk Railway Company had boasted that the route cut the distance by 14 miles over other routes, and that it was 'intended to afford every facility to the public by the issue of day and season tickets at a moderate charge with the view to induce people to travel on the line'.[92] A local newspaper, *The Bradford Observer*, had questioned whether tunnels would fall down after constant vibration. It went on to describe the implications of 'burying alive some hundred passengers away from the light of heaven' and that it was not yet 'a horror generally imagined'. The article went on to lay the fault for such incidents hitherto at the door of the Government because 'for want of due examination, these "dark holes" are neglected'. It further claimed that this far from pleasant process was hampered by lack of sufficiently bright lighting.[93]

In the early 1840s the canal tunnel at Higham in Kent, then the longest in England, was converted for the Rochester and Gravesend Railway Company. As it was through chalk and unlined it was likely to cause concern in the future, even though shortly before its reopening in 1844 the safety of the tunnel was tested by firing a cannon several times without dislodging any rock.[94]

In a tunnel there was not only the fear of collapse and suffocation, but also the simple fear of being plunged into the dark, even if only for a few moments. *The Morning Chronicle* set the scene even when the London and Birmingham Railway was only partially open, 'the effect in the dark is not very agreeable', the passengers in the carriages feeling as if they were 'at the mercy of a huge monster of the engine ... dragging his victims into his cavern'.[95] It was perhaps natural that a machine with 'fire in its belly' should be likened to a monster, especially if it could explode and pour out fire, as some early locomotives did, and that a tunnel – big, long and dark as never seen before – should be his cavern. This fear felt by some passengers was not assuaged by the very publications that were intended to make this novel travel experience a joy. Osborne, in his *Guide to the London and Birmingham Railway*, described the entry into Primrose Hill Tunnel as causing:

> considerable surprise in most travellers; one moment we are in the midst of day – in the next the train is surrounded by a midnight darkness, which is scarcely penetrated by the rays of the dim lamps suspended at the top of the carriages, which though scarcely noticeable prior to entering the tunnel, are now found highly advantageous.[96]

Wyld, in his *Companion to the London and Birmingham Railway*, 1838, certainly stirs the romantic imagination of those entering the 'gloomy entrance of Watford Tunnel into which we are helplessly dragged by the belching monster that has hitherto spirited us safely along, but who now appears to be treacherously carrying us as victims to the subterranean retreat of some hideous gnome, or ogre'.[97] He is equally eloquent on Kilsby Tunnel:

> into which we need not like the Trojan hero on his visit to the Kingdom of Pluto, a skilful Sybil to conduct us, nor any golden branch to awe the gnomes, in our progress through the region of darkness; for our leader, who has hitherto conducted us, and iron hearted though he be, is yet faithful, and may safely be trusted in the gloom as in day-gleam.[98]

The experience of rushing through a tunnel at speed, and so experiencing total darkness followed by bright daylight was compared to being shot out of a huge gun.[99] The prolific railway guide book writer George Measom, who captured the travellers' attention with descriptions of beautiful countryside such as that on the London and Brighton Railway, sounded a warning to readers that on seeing the range of the South Downs growing gradually nearer readers were 'once again to leave the light of day and enter, as it were, into the bowels of the earth, passing through Clayton Tunnel, a work of extraordinary magnitude'.[100] Arthur Freeling advised passengers to 'shut their eyes as soon as they begin to see darkness and to open them very slowly as they come out'.[101] The more eloquent descriptions of experiencing tunnels from the carriage of a train have already been discussed in Chapter 4.

THE QUESTION OF LIGHTING

The question of lighting tunnels was faced from the start, although Herapath was sceptical as to how it could be accomplished.[102] If this could be done, he argued, then, in all but the longest tunnels, there might not be a need for internal carriage lighting. A month after the opening of the London and Birmingham Railway he described the tunnels as 'the worst blots on the line'. He claimed lights were to be carried in the carriages but this would make the 'intensity of the darkness more visible'. He concluded by what can only be described as a ridiculous plea, that the company should do away with these 'nuisances' and open them out as cuttings.[103]

One early expedient, although not effective for long in the age of steam, was to paint the interior of the walls white. Both the short tunnel from Crown Street and the goods tunnel from Wapping to Edge Hill were lit by gas from the start, although the editor of the *Railway Magazine* claimed that 'impenetrable darkness ensued, disturbed now and then by the gas, whose sickly glow seemed calculated only to render the horrors of the place more apparent'.[104] It was rumoured that Stephenson was to light all his tunnels, but Herapath doubted this even from 'the Pope of Engineering'.[105]

When the line was re-routed to the new terminus at Lime Street through a new tunnel this was not lit. It was 2,230 yards long, unventilated and on an incline of 1 in 93, so trains were lowered and raised by rope from Edge Hill. *The Times* reported the departure of the first train in which:

> by some strange oversight, no lamps were provided and the passage through the tunnel … a distance of a mile and a quarter, was done in total darkness, it was only a suspense of four minutes, and the passengers were enlivened … by the cheers of some of the workmen who had been suffered rather incautiously to hang on the steps of the carriages.[106]

Yet according to R.G. Thompson, when locomotives were uncoupled at Edge Hill, lighted oil lamps were hung on the outside of each carriage door for the descent through the tunnel to Lime Street.[107] Presumably this would only have been for first-class carriages. The ascent to Edge Hill would have taken about ten minutes.

Perhaps this account of passing through a tunnel by Squire George Osbaldeston really conveys the horror of prolonged darkness and the need for some form of lighting on the tunnel walls if not in the carriages:

> On our journey we had to pass through a tunnel … the carriages were not lighted, and there were a good many women in the one occupied. As we entered the tunnel … the women were most dreadfully alarmed and began screaming awfully. The guard had locked the door, and the gentlemen in the carriages had the greatest difficulty in preventing them from jumping out of the windows.
>
> They were pacified at last and their cries ceased. Just before we entered the station the driver blew his whistle … and it was so like the screams of the females that I thought they were frightened again, and said to my companion; what are those silly creatures screeching about now? I felt quite ashamed of my ignorance when he laughed and told me it was only the signal that we had reached our destination.[108]

The opening of the London and Brighton Railway was noted in *The Times*, both by a short report and by an announcement of the train times from London and Brighton. The time, which was rapidly to be improved on, was about two and a half hours, so one can appreciate the apprehension that early passengers had for long tunnels.[109] According to *The London and Brighton Railway Guide*, 1841,

Merstham Tunnel, at little over a mile, was measured at railway speed as being two minutes in length.[110] Lights were placed in the tunnels at Merstham, Balcombe and Clayton. Of Merstham the guide tried to be reassuring, if not so much to the passengers, at least to the driver of the locomotive. This might have been prompted by shareholders travelling in a special train to the temporary terminus at Haywards Heath and passing through two tunnels, each in about three minutes, and their fears for the passengers and especially those who would be travelling in open carriages.[111]

> It is, as the other tunnels on this line, whitewashed well throughout, and plentifully lighted with gas, which, though not of much value to the passenger (though in him it induces a feeling of confidence and cheerfulness), is to the engine driver, of utmost moment, enabling him to see the road throughout as well almost as in broad day, so well indeed, that any obstruction existing, which otherwise could not be observed, will by him be perceived and guarded against.[112]

It seems that a primitive form of gas lighting was used in the mile-long Calendar Tunnel on the Edinburgh and Glasgow Railway from 1842.[113] When completed in 1842, Bletchingley Tunnel was whitewashed throughout to allay the fears of travellers. In Leeds Tunnel, opened in 1832 and the first in the world through which passengers were drawn by a locomotive, copper plates were installed at the foot of the air shafts to reflect the light against whitewashed walls. It was even claimed that a newspaper could be read in the tunnel – surely an exaggeration.[114] In the tunnel between Sheffield and Leeds, the *Railway Magazine* reported, 'lamps will be affixed to the carriages while passing through the tunnel, as in the new passenger tunnel at Liverpool'.[115] However, at Kilsby Tunnel, *The Times* reported, 'there will be no lamps posted in it, as the carriages will have lights placed within them during the subterranean transit'.[116]

It is one thing to light a tunnel by a system of gas jets, as in Mersham in 1841, and it is another thing to provide lighting in individual carriages. There is no clear date for the general adoption of lighting in carriages, and which at first was considered only necessary for first-class passengers. However, one train or carriage that did have lighting was the royal carriage. In a description of the visit by Queen Victoria and Prince Albert to Burghley House in 1844 specific mention was made of a 'lamp with ground glass by means of which the carriage was illuminated in passing through tunnels'. The royal journey was from Euston to Weedon and the 'Primrose Hill Tunnel was passed through at great speed (about one minute)'; at Watford 'the long tunnel was passed through in a minute and forty seconds'.[117]

Box Tunnel, for a short time the longest tunnel in Britain, and certainly the most celebrated, was a subject of a number of pleas for lighting, and letters were written to *The Times* on the problem from 1841 until as late as the early 1870s. Brunel had been questioned on lighting in his proposed tunnels by the parliamentary committee in 1835. He seemed to think shafts were sufficient for the removal of smoke and for lighting, and that passengers would not feel danger from prolonged darkness, or 'two trains meeting' or colliding in the dark. He appeared to obstinately ignore the potential danger, even when several accidents on the Liverpool and Manchester Railway were cited.[118] Shortly after its opening in 1841 a train was derailed and the 'passengers continued to be boxed up for a few hours to their very great annoyance and terror'.[119] The *Penny Satirist* even noted that a correspondent to the *Railway Magazine* had called for the lighting of the Box Tunnel with gas.[120] In the report into a landslip on the Wootton Bassett Incline in September 1841, Sir Frederick Smith, the Board of Trade Inspector, noted that Box Tunnel lacked any form of lighting. He suggested that lighting would increase the comfort and safety of passengers.[121] A report in the *Bristol Mercury* in 1842 said the Box Tunnel was to be lit with Bude lamps, although there is no further report of this ever happening, even after later incidents.[122] With such a steep gradient through the tunnel there must have been frequent instances of the stalling of the locomotive. After one such incident a reader who had been delayed in the dark tunnel for two hours, called upon the company to adopt 'adequate means for pulling heavy trains up the tunnel'; presumably he meant double heading, or perhaps a 'shunter' at the rear.[123]

A 'Timid Female Traveller' wrote to *The Times* in 1842 to ask why, if lights were placed inside the carriages for the journey through the tunnel (Sapperton) between Swindon and Gloucester, why not in the down trains passing through Box Tunnel? She claimed the journey through 'this awful tunnel' was one of 'terror', and hoped her few lines might help to get the situation rectified.[124] A few weeks later 'A Frequent traveller on the Great Western' again called for lights because his train came to a halt for several minutes, and such an occurrence might deter many from travelling.[125] In 1852, the Great Western introduced eight-wheel carriages dubbed 'Long Charleys', which were fitted with primitive gas lamps giving limited light. However these were, certainly at first, restricted to the London and Birmingham service.

It may be that a letter to the Board of Directors by Lord Charles Thynne in June 1860 complaining of the 'want of lamp lighting in the carriage when passing through the Box Tunnel' prompted a review of the situation. An estimate of a Mr Gibson put the cost of lighting through the tunnels at £450 and the company, realising their prospects were improving and also fearing competition from rival companies, decided to introduce 'lighting with lamps' as soon as was practicable.[126] How long they envisaged this to be is unrecorded. A report in *John Bull* in 1868 said the Great Western had been placing lights in all carriages going through the Box Tunnel (which was exaggerated at 'more than three miles long'), however they had been ordered to light only first-class carriages.[127] In May 1870 the Rev. Francis Kilvert described how when passing through Box Tunnel:

> as there was no lamp, the people began to strike foul brimstone matches and hand them round to each other all down the carriage. All the time we were in the tunnel these lighted matches were travelling from hand to hand in the darkness. Each match lasts the length of a carriage and the red ember was thrown out of the opposite window, by which time another lighted match was seen moving down the carriage.[128]

A similar experience was reported by another passenger in a letter to *The Times* in 1872, when a delay of nearly fifty minutes 'in total darkness was … relieved by an occasional vesta or vesuvian. This was caused by some portion of the locomotive having broken off and the carriages having passed over it'.[129] According to *John Bull*, the writer was in a second-class carriage without oil lamps, which were by then almost universal in first class. Rudimentary electric lighting was only a few years away, being introduced into British railway carriages by the London, Brighton and South Coast Railway in 1881.

THE FEAR OF COLLISION

Certainly the greatest fear was that of collision, which could be caused by a train stalling, a derailment, or even hitting structure or debris in a tunnel. These and other incidents made the question of improving signalling a major topic and the reason for several prominent works including *Railway Dangers and how to Avoid Them*, 1853, by William Peters, and *Railway Collisions Prevented*, by Alfred Ogan, 1855. The first fatal tunnel accident, and the one to prompt Peters' treatise, was as a result of a triple crash caused initially by the overloading of an excursion train, causing it to fail in Sutton Tunnel on the Cheshire Junction Railway near Frodsham, on 30 April 1851 (see Appendix 3). The train of eighteen carriages was filled with about 900 passengers, too many for the power of the locomotive, causing it to stall. The guard signalled to the following train, hauling up to 450 passengers, to come up and push, but this proved impossible and it too stalled. With the tunnel filled with smoke and the tail lights of the second train being obscured, the third train, believing the tunnel to be clear, entered at about 20mph and ploughed into the back of the second one. Nine passengers were killed and over thirty injured. Subsequent newspaper reports spoke of 1,600 people crowding in the dark and smoke-filled tunnel; the coaches being unlit.[130] Normally the tunnel, which was dead straight, would have cleared of smoke within fifteen minutes, as trains on normal days passed through at two or three hours' intervals. The subsequent enquiry made a number of recommendations including installing an electric telegraph between stations at each end of the tunnel, and carriages to have lighting.[131]

In Clayton Tunnel, the longest on the London and Brighton Railway, two excursion trains collided in 1861, resulting in twenty-three deaths and 176 injuries. It provoked a number of critics of rail travel, especially as it happened on an August Sunday, to proclaim it as a 'judgement of God'.[132] The third fatal tunnel crash was in the mile-long Blackheath Tunnel in 1864, when a London-bound passenger train ran into a stalled ballast train, resulting in five deaths. According to *The Times*, the passenger train entered the tunnel at 40mph. The rescue team had to work in 'great heat and suffocating smoke' as the tunnel had no ventilation.[133] This crash prompted a correspondent to *The Times* to suggest a way of avoiding fatalities on the railway would be to have two luggage vans attached to the rear of trains filled with mattresses stuffed with cork.[134]

What could have been the worst disaster of all was in Welwyn North Tunnel in June 1864, involving three trains. It was at night so there was no way of knowing that this short tunnel was blocked when a down Midland Railway goods train ran into the back of a stalled Great Northern goods train, smashing the brake van and killing its two occupants, and forcing wreckage across the up track. Shortly after, an up meat train ploughed into the wreckage, completely blocking the tunnel. *The Times* carried several reports of the crash using dramatic language, more than sufficient to put fear into the timid, describing how the trains became 'ignited by fire in their furnaces' and the air shafts were turned into 'a species of burning crater'.[135] Yet on careful inspection it was found that the heat had done little damage to the brickwork and the services were quickly resumed. These incidents demonstrate the dangers to potential rail passengers in the most extreme circumstances, and fortunately led to a tightening of signalling trains on sections involving a tunnel. In these four accidents there were just thirty-nine deaths, many fewer than might have been expected in such a situation.[136]

The greatest fear then, as we have seen, was a breakdown or failure in a tunnel before a warning could be conveyed to the next train before it was too late. In such circumstances, there were some near-misses. On the opening of the North Midland Railway between Sheffield and Derby on 11 May 1840, the inaugural train broke down ¾ mile through Clay Cross Tunnel (1 mile and 20 yards). While a man was sent back on foot to recall the pilot loco from near the northern portal, some of the more excitable passengers climbed down from their carriages and began wandering about in the tunnel. George Stephenson began shouting to urge the 'jay walkers to resume their places in the train'.[137] Some, however, marooned in pitch darkness with no visible exit in either direction, ran back screaming through the tunnel, emerging in a state of great emotional distress.[138] The pilot locomotive arrived shortly after and the journey resumed to Derby. Fortunately there were no recorded deaths or injuries. This was, of course, before the operating of a full service but such a circumstance was obviously in the mind of a correspondent called 'A Traveller' writing to *The Times* shortly after the opening of Box Tunnel in 1841, who envisaged how a disaster might occur if an up train travelling in the London direction and 'propelled' by a banking engine was forced to stop suddenly in the tunnel:

> and a more horrible event can scarcely be imagined than the breaking of the leading engine running off the rails in the centre of the Box Tunnel, the rails being within a few inches of the brickwork on either side, (and) ... crushing all before it at a rate of 30 or 40 miles an hour.[139]

A similar event did occur in 1843 in Summit Tunnel between Manchester and Sheffield, which was reported in *The Illustrated London News*, when a train ran into the back of a luggage train 'smashing two or three carriages, but most providentially, not hurting an individual'.[140] In the early days personal carriages were conveyed by truck attached to the rear carriage, and in 1842 a gentleman who insisted on remaining in his carriage had a lucky escape while travelling through Balcombe Tunnel when:

> by some means the truck became disengaged and left the carriage ... The unfortunate occupant, perceiving the train leaving him, called after them but

in vain … He became dreadfully alarmed, being afraid to alight, and not knowing whether in a few minutes he would be dashed to pieces by the next train. He had not been long in this suspense when an engine entered the tunnel, his doom sealed, but the engine proved to be a pilot one sent to look after him, the truck and carriage having fortunately been missed on the train arriving at the next station.

The carriage and occupant were then conveyed to Brighton, where they arrived soon after the train, and the only inconvenience was the great fright the gentleman sustained.[141]

By coincidence, there had been two cases of trains breaking down in Blackheath Tunnel in 1850, which were the subject of two letters to *The Times*. In the first letter, the train stopped for ten minutes, moved forward 30 or 40 yards, then ran back some distance and stopped 'during which the greatest terror was manifested by the passengers'. When they eventually arrived at Blackheath, the guard informed them the cause was 'not sufficient power'.[142] The second letter reported another train on 'this miserably managed line stuck fast for nearly an hour in Blackheath Tunnel'. Nearly 700 passengers were for nearly an hour 'shut up … in a subterranean prison with scarcely air enough to enable them to breathe, or light enough (and that only in first class carriages …) to let them see … in peril of being hit by another train'.[143] On this evidence we may conclude that similar incidents happened elsewhere and with more serious consequences, and not necessarily because of a steep gradient into the tunnel but because the train was overloaded.

Another fear was that of the engine becoming detached from its carriages or trucks. An incident of this kind happened in Sapperton Tunnel, when forty-one trucks separated from the locomotive and ran down the steep gradient towards Brimscombe Station.[144] On another occasion, in Bramhope Tunnel the track was flooded causing a locomotive to come to a halt with 'the fire in the fire-box extinguished … but as the tunnel declines considerably to the north, the train by its own momentum slid out, and a fresh engine having been attached to it, it went by way of Knaresborough and York to Leeds'.[145]

It was, of course, not only passengers but also railway staff and servants who might be killed or injured in the course of duty. In Box Tunnel in October 1841 a 'ballast-man was crushed as he attempted to cross the tracks between a train and the banking engine'; presumably he could not see because of smoke.[146] *The Times* reported another unfortunate accident, though not deep inside a tunnel but at Lime Street Station, Liverpool, when a porter who was tying sheets to the top of a carriage jumped from the roof and was hit by a rope-hauled Manchester train emerging from the tunnel.[147] This was typical of the accidents reported in the more popular *Household Narratives* edited by Charles Dickens.

The Frodsham Tunnel disaster caused William Peters in *Railway Dangers and How to Avoid Them*, 1853, considerable alarm. It is the extension of an argument first raised in a letter to the *Daily News* on 10 October 1853, arguing that since 'self-preservation was the first law of nature [the writer] could not countenance a direction to sit still and be crushed', but 'that passengers should be urged, or even permitted in a body, to quit the train and run wild in a deep cutting or tunnel' – surely a recipe for disaster. Peters, in a reply to the *Daily News*, advocated that passengers should on the direction of the guard, 'get out, keep their left hand in contact with the tunnel wall, and go ahead of the engine, till they could place themselves beyond the possibility of mischief beyond the tunnel … I hope never to hear again the order "keep their places".'[148] This, of course, assumed the passengers could see in a dark, smoke-filled tunnel, a point taken up by another reader, in reply. Also there would be the fear, as in the Frodsham disaster, that another train might crash into their stationary one. The writer asked if Mr Peters had the courage to 'carry out such a project on an experimental occasion'. Even with a guard going down the track with a lamp to warn an approaching train he would not recommend even the most cautious to leave their carriages. Peters then proposed further ways of escape for passengers, including walking down the 6ft space between the tracks or between trains, if necessary lying down in the space as a train passed! As to the darkness, he claimed that lives, including those of platelayers and workmen, might be saved by lights in tunnels.[149] He recommended that hand lanterns or torches 'ought to be in abundance'.[150] He further mentioned certain (unspecified) tunnels as having 'holes' or recesses that could hold up to twenty people. He did at least advise that women and children should only leave a carriage under the guidance of a guard.

SIGNALLING
With tunnels of such length and in which a train would go out of sight in the darkness, a safe system of signalling was needed. At first it was by the very primitive method of placing watchmen or policemen with lanterns at intervals along the track. This was obviously subject to human frailty, as recorded instances show. For example, shortly after the Great Western opened the section between Bristol and Bath, a policeman in No. 3 Tunnel at Brislington was found to be asleep beside the track by the sub-inspector of police, who happened to observe him from a passing train.[151] At Liverpool, with the opening of the new tunnel from Edge Hill to Lime Street it was reported that:

> the communication signals can be made from one end to the other in twenty-five seconds by means of a very ingenious apparatus, by which a powerful current of air is driven through (a) tube with sufficient force to ring a bell or blow an organ pipe, which latter has been preferred.[152]

Also before entering the tunnel, both for the descent and ascent, the train crew had to observe a series of rules and regulations for the conduct of traffic on the London and North Western Railway, which had absorbed the Liverpool and Manchester:

> The tunnel-breaksman is to examine how many brakes there are on the train and must be perfectly satisfied that the requisite number are in good working order … the tunnel-breaksman must see that the Guard of the train is at his post before the train starts … no train may go down the tunnel without a

tunnel-breaksman ... trains are never to exceed ten miles an hour ... the brakes must be applied gradually ... when a train exceeds ten carriages, there must be an extra breaksman; if it exceeds fifteen coaches, two extra breaksmen ... .no train is to follow another down the tunnel without an interval of five minutes.[153]

Similar regulations were set out for goods traffic through the Wapping Tunnel:

Signal lamps and hand lamps must be kept properly trimmed and burning. A red signal lamp, lighted, must always be fixed at the rear of the last wagon going down the tunnel, and a green signal lamp lighted and fixed upon the most conspicuous part of the front wagon.[154]

Because of the steep gradient, in wet weather the rails could become slippery and sand, kept in readiness at Edge Hill, was to be sprinkled from the brake wagon on the descent.

The placing of lights in a tunnel or on the front or tail of a train will only avert a collision if the trains can be seen, and this was not necessarily likely in a smoke-filled enclosure that was the nature of a tunnel. A better, or safer, method of signalling was necessary. Experiments had been made with the electric telegraph system since the 1830s and was in use in Box Tunnel by the mid-1840s, however railway companies were slow to adopt this system.[155]

Alfred Ogan, in his *Rail Collisions Prevented*, 1855, was scathing in his criticism. He claimed that valuable suggestions for preventing railway accidents made by Government inspectors were lost in a mass of parliamentary reports, and so lost half their force. He cited figures for the year ending 31 December 1854 in which 233 persons were killed and 453 injured; of these, 283 were injured in collisions between trains. He strongly objected to the then current practice of allowing the passage of trains from or past a given point at five-minute intervals, as trains travelled at variable speeds, causing possible collision if the train in front slowed or stalled, as happened at Frodsham Tunnel in 1851 under this system. He mentioned another incident, in Stoke Tunnel on the Great Northern Railway, where two coal trains collided in December 1853, but without casualties. He urged the replacement or supplementing of semaphore signals with electric telegraph, as then being adopted on the South Eastern Railway.[156] This, however, was not carried out until after another collision in the tunnel on 7 March 1854, for which the Board of Trade report censured the Great Northern Railway for failing to adopt the new electric telegraph system for over two months.[157] Fortunately only one person was injured in these two accidents.

CRIME IN THE CARRIAGE
With the train plunging into darkness, or at the very least a state of gloom from oil lamps in the compartment, there was not just the possibility, even if remote, of injury by an accident, but also by some dastardly deeds committed by fellow passengers.[158] After all, the railway carriage brought together the so-called 'refined

people or class' with what *Frazer's Magazine* called, the 'swinish multitude' (i.e. third class).[159] Criminals were quick to see the advantages of the train in order to provide an alibi. The dangers possibly to be encountered while travelling through a tunnel were already hinted at in *The Railway Travellers' Handbook* for 1862: 'In going through a tunnel it is always as well to have the hands and arms disposed for defence so that in the event of an attack the assailant may be immediately beaten back or restrained.'[160] Schivelbusch, citing *The Globe*, 1863, mentions the fear that 'the loudest screams are swallowed up by the roar and rapidly revolving wheels, and murder, or violence or worse may go on to the accompaniment of a train flying along at sixty miles an hour'.[161] In 1855 there had taken place what could be described as Britain's first great train robbery, in which gold bullion was stolen from a train travelling at 55mph. This event had shocked the nation.[162] If this could happen in a moving train, what might happen in a tunnel? In the period before corridor carriages when passengers were confined to compartments, the possibility of criminal intent among fellow passengers was a serious reality. Ladies were unable to distinguish who they should avoid, and those who might be their protectors, while gentlemen constantly refused to travel singly with a stranger or a single woman. A hint of the diversity of society brought in close proximity on a railway journey was raised in a letter to *The Times* in 1853 as a result of prize fighters gathering on the Thames-side marshes to engage in combat. This attracted large crowds of spectators, 'the lowest of the low … these depraved people … the very scum and refuse of London', that 'no respectable lady dare travel on a Tuesday through the Blackheath Tunnel which is in perfect darkness except in the first class carriages'.[163] Two years earlier a man had been brought before the Central Criminal Court charged with having assaulted a woman 'in the third class' while passing through Blackheath Tunnel.[164] While in the same tunnel in 1864, a woman believed she had been assaulted by a man in the presence of other passengers. At the trial it was suggested that the steel frame of her crinoline, an 'article worn by a lady of fashion' but being an encumbrance in a confined space, and placed at an angle, 'might by the motion of the carriage have been pressed against her', and so caused her to believe she was being assaulted by a fellow passenger.[165] In 1862 a linen draper shot himself and subsequently died while passing through Blackheath Tunnel in an unlit third-class carriage, prompting a letter to *The Times* calling for lighting in all classes of carriage.[166]

The theme of the solitary lady being kissed by a suitor, or even worse an unknown man, as the train plunged into darkness was exploited in popular entertainment, becoming the subject of several silent films in the 1890s, perhaps inspired by an incident in 1865 in Merstham Tunnel in which a young man attempted to kiss a young lady while smoking a cigar.[167] There was even a case of murder on the same line in Balcombe Tunnel in 1881.[168] Perhaps a unique incident was the case of a prisoner under guard, taking advantage of the darkness to jump from a carriage while passing through Shugborough Tunnel on the Trent Valley line in 1866. His guard was amazed to find the door open upon leaving the tunnel. The prisoner survived, having injured himself against the wall of the tunnel, but was chased into a nearby village, where he was thought to be an escaped lunatic.[169] As expected, even the most serious situation could be reduced to humour, and jokes appeared in the popular magazines of the day. A cartoon in *Punch* in 1864 depicted a scene in a tunnel with the caption 'How to clear a carriage for a cigar murder in a tunnel?', meaning the perpetrator was looking to clear the carriage using cigar smoke of all but his intended victim.[170] There were reports of women putting pins in their mouths, point outwards, to repel unwanted approaches.[171] *Frazer's Magazine* told of a Scottish 'vicar of the Kirk' sitting opposite a rabid dissenter, with his brow steaming with anger and his fist shaking in the dissenter's face. Having been plunged into the tunnel 'dark as night' his anger was entirely dissipated by the time they came out; 'Don't speak against tunnels again,' the vicar said.[172]

FEAR AS ENTERTAINMENT

Before turning to the statistics of death and injury, it is worth mentioning how the fear of the subterranean railway traveller could be turned to drama on the stage for the entertainment of Victorian audiences. In the theatre the tension was heightened by changing lighting, obviously gas at that time, and simulated noise of trains accompanied by dramatic music. Nicholas Daly contributed a study of how railway travel played a part in the entertainment of the Victorian theatre, published in *Victorian Studies*, 1998–99.[173] Theatre audiences, now increasingly wanting dramas of contemporary urban life, 'demanded to see the very artefacts of modernity on the stage'. They wanted to be 'thrilled and chilled', and a play involving a train and a smoke-filled tunnel did just this. As the theatre journal *The Mask* remarked of the audience at the Princess's in 1868, they would 'applaud a real gaslight … longer than they would a sea-painting by Stansfield'.[174] He cited a number of successful plays on the London stage; one of the earliest being Dion Boucicault's *After Dark, or a Drama of London Life*, in August 1868[175] and involving the then new underground railway.[176] Daly makes the important point that in London many in the audience who came to see 'railway terror' would have come by the new underground railway.[177] This type of travel might be described then as almost a continuous smoky tunnel with occasional breaks of daylight. *The Times* was more eloquent:

> A subterranean railway under London was awfully suggestive of dark noisome tunnels buried many fathoms deep beneath the reach of light or life; passages inhabited by rats, soaked with sewer drippers, and poisoned by the escape of gas mains. It would seem an insult to common sense to suppose that people who could travel so cheaply on the outside of a Paddington bus, would prefer, as a merely quicker medium, to be driven amid palpable darkness through the foul subsoil of London.[178]

For *After Dark* a somewhat crudely drawn poster was produced to whet the audience's appetite for the fourth act, in which a train is seen rushing out of a tunnel towards a man tied across the track, with his saviour leaping to the rescue from the adjacent wall at the last moment. The poster was also used to sell a musical gallop composed to accompany the play.

However exciting as this must have been with the accompanying train noises and flats, the idea was 'lifted' from Augustin Daly's melodrama *Under the Gaslight*, which had been first performed in New York in August 1867. Daly actually won an injunction against its use in a performance in America but was powerless in England. Boucicault had seen the power of a train drama as part of a play but since his four-act play was an authorised adaption of Adolphe Dennery's *Les Oiseaux de Proie* first performed in 1854, he simply stole the idea to add sensation to his plot.[179] The *Times* review, as well as praising the dramatic tunnel rescue as the train swept across the stage, remarked on the reality of Victoria Station in an earlier act 'so closely copied as far as the eye is concerned'.[180] Martin Meisel, in an essay titled *Scattered Chiaroscuro*, sees these plays as exploiting a mid-century appetite for domestic perils set in an urban panorama. Audiences liked drama with a race against time, set against recreations of familiar London sights.[181] The theatre railway theme with its two-dimensional painted train plunged beneath the ground and enlivened with certain effects of lighting and sounds, perhaps crude by today's standards, had the power to thrill and chill. It provided a matrix for upstarts and scoundrels. Yet as Daly says, by the end of the nineteenth century it had lost its power to inspire anything but laughter.[182] In any case, by then a new form of entertainment, the cinema, had arrived and a real tunnel could form part of the entertainment.

An interesting point is made by the American scholar Julie Wosk regarding the different approaches between England and France to the depiction of the dangers in early railway travel in popular art. In England it was popular lithographs, and illustrations in the *Illustrated London News*, depicting explosions, collisions and derailments that caused the greatest fear among middle-class readers, the latter caused by speed, and often magnified in horror at the hand of the artist. Tunnels, however, do not appear in disaster illustrations but rather featured as objects of humour or discomfort as darkness envelops unwary passengers, and this for the most part in the pages of *Punch* outside my period of study. In France comical satires of the railways were popular, and especially the artist Daumier in *Le Charivari*, bringing the potential discomfort and horrors encountered travelling through a tunnel to the public in a way no English artist dared. Wosk cited Daumier's 1843 lithographs, 'Conducteur' and 'The Entrance to the large Tunnel', the latter with the caption: 'There hasn't been a trip without someone losing an arm, a leg, or a nose'.[183]

THE CHANCE OF DEATH IN A TUNNEL
I have hinted that the statistics could seem frightening if taken collectively; however, when analysed we see that the numbers of actual injuries and deaths was unexpectedly low from incidents in tunnels; the number of serious incidents such as the Clayton Tunnel accident were few indeed. But there were, of course, numerous incidents of injury and death elsewhere on the railway system. Statistics, if published in popular magazines, naturally fuelled a fear, especially those by Dickens, who started a special monthly section, 'Accidents and Disasters' in *Household Narrative of Current Affairs* from its first issue in 1850. In that year he

recorded thirty-three serious collisions, including one in a tunnel.[184] In 1851, he published an essay, 'Need Railway Travellers be Smashed', in which he argued vigorously and stridently for improved signalling and safety measures. This was fourteen years before he was caught in the Staplehurst crash.[185] A glance at any one month will show how he recorded everything from steam-boat explosions, balloon disasters and members of the public attacked by lions in a zoo; railway accidents were reported, but often involving public on the track, and not even a moving train, rather than the ultimate horror of a disaster in a tunnel. Norman Gash, in his *Robert Surtees and Early Victorian Society*, made the point that it does not appear that the public thought there was a disproportionate number of accidents on railways, though they were often more violent and more widely reported. Citing the year 1851, he claimed ten passengers were killed in instances outside their control; another twenty-two through their own negligence; also 120 employees of companies or contractors, and another sixty-four casual trespassers on the tracks, a total of 216, and this should be compared with an average of 250 persons killed on the streets of London every year alone during the 1860s.[186] In 1851 the actual chance of being killed on a railway was 1 in 420,437,[187] and by 1867 that was reduced to 1 in 6,998,885.[188] In the years 1830–70 there were sixty-three recorded deaths and 305 injuries (See Appendix 3). The figures for incidents in tunnels should also be seen against the totals of rail casualties from all kinds of accidents. Between 1830 and 1850 altogether ninety-five persons were killed and eighty-one injured, and between 1850 and 1870, 193 were killed, and about 411 injured. In the first six months of 1852 alone, 113 persons were killed and 264 injured, and in the first six months of 1853, 148 were killed and 191 injured.[189]

L.T.C. Rolt, in his classic study of railway accidents, *Red for Danger*, comments on the patronising attitude with which we view the acute trepidation that the Victorian traveller felt when travelling through a tunnel, and the often reiterated plea that tunnels should be lit. He rightly cited the possible consequences of such a disaster for passengers in the darkness of a smoke-filled tunnel, with tracks blocked, so impeding rescue attempts and ventilation shafts becoming furnace flues.[190] As I said at the beginning of this chapter, we must ask how far fear of tunnels was a serious deterrent to travel. We have statistics of all kinds of death and injury on railway property published annually by the railway department of the Board of Trade from 1839, but obviously these were not noted so much by the public at large compared to Dickens's reports for a popular readership in the monthly *Household Words* and its supplement *Household Narrative*.

For many the growing convenience of rail travel, as Godwin and others had urged, was obvious to see, and the prospect of injury or death on a railway had to be balanced against that from horse-drawn travel, or even on a steam boat when boilers blew up. As we have seen in a previous chapter, the more enlightened travellers even saw rail travel as an experience, creating a thrill or excitement, perhaps akin to the sensation of reading a powerful Gothic novel, which had to include a crypt or tunnel, and a supernatural experience. So some passengers might even have been found with guide book or travel compendium open on their lap, after all, did not Fanny Kemble describe her ride on the Liverpool and

Manchester Railway as 'uncannily smooth'?[191] And even Dickens in a moment of poetic lapse proclaimed the sensation of entering a railway tunnel as 'poetic and picturesque in the extreme'; he was travelling in a first-class carriage though.[192] The classic picture of middle-class railway passengers is of them clutching a newspaper, or more appropriately, a copy of Bradshaw's railway guide in their lap. The painter Augustus Leopold Egg produced what is sometimes seen as the most perfect advertisement for Victorian rail travel, *Travelling Companions*, 1862, in which two upper middle-class ladies sit opposite each other in a carriage, one little red guide book in hand, the other asleep, while through the window we see the sunlit French coast near Meudon.[193] These are calm and confident travellers without fear or worry, and, what is more, they must have travelled through a few tunnels to get there. By the 1860s the railway system had firmly established itself and had won over many who had been sceptical, or indeed fearful, in the first decade or so. So now, the ride over a viaduct, or more dramatically through a tunnel, could become an exciting part of the journey, and featured not only in books, but also as part of theatrical entertainment. In some instances the railway journey became a metaphor for life, as even our everyday journey was through 'tunnels dark and dreary'.[194]

ENLIGHTENMENT

As we have seen, the chances of suffering death or injury in a smoke-filled tunnel were actually remote in spite of the number of railway injuries recorded. Yet there was rightly public concern, and popular magazines published essays and periodic reports on railway accidents that did of course cause worry among the occasional, or sceptical traveller.[195]

In spite of the sense of foreboding over early rail travel, who were those who most ardently supported steam railways, or what we might call 'railway enlightenment', and therefore, because it could not be avoided, a journey through a tunnel? In 1837 there were two manifestos published in support of railways, Richard Mudge's *Observations on Railways with Reference to Utility, Profits and Obvious Necessity*, and perhaps the more prominent, George Godwin's *Appeal to the Public on the Subject of Railways* mentioned in Chapter 3.

Godwin saw railways as helping not only the hitherto coach-travelling public but also heavy industry, including the transport of stone to allow the creation of grand buildings instead of using brick. To landowners who opposed the railways he says they will 'insure the architectural embellishment of the countryside … with the decoration afforded by viaducts, bridges, depots … '[196] To play down the prejudice against a railway Godwin asks the reader to see it as 'a road provided with two bars of iron … ' and the step from Macadamised roads to railways is not as great as from the roads in which 'Prince George stuck fast in 1703, to the Macadamised roads of today'.[197]

He then introduces the amazing power of steam and counters against using absurd arguments as had been used one hundred years ago in opposition to earlier industrial progress. He cites the use of steam to power forges and power boats. He then takes a swipe at Dr Lardner, who in spite of his prejudices has had to admit to the number of passengers increasing fourfold due to the saving of time.[198] He criticises Parliament for rejecting Bills, by the 'frivolous attention to the letter, rather than the spirit, of standing orders'. He then rounds off his case by referring to the ignorance of past history, citing Galileo and Harvey, and counsels people to avoid making the mistakes of the past.[199]

As we have seen, a number of early travellers left positive accounts of their experiences including the actress Fanny Kemble, who was given a ride on a pre-opening train on the Liverpool and Manchester Railway in 1830, and described it in a letter to a friend:

> Nothing can be more comfortable than the vehicle in which I was put, in a sort of chariot … and there is nothing disagreeable about it but the occasional whiffs of stinking air which it is impossible to exclude altogether. The first sensation is a slight degree of nervousness and a feeling of being run away with.[200]

The battle was partly won, as Smiles claimed, as early as 1838, with the opening of the trunk rail link between London, Liverpool and Manchester of over 200 miles 'proving the fallaciousness of the rash prophesies promulgated by the opponents of railways'.[201] It was a great test of public confidence, a journey in a tunnel, in spite of the smoke. When subsequently there was a disaster those latent fears would be roused again, but only until they were compared with the daily accidents elsewhere reported in the press. By then, the public had embraced the message of George Godwin's *Appeal*.

Perhaps the final seal of approval was the journey from Slough to London undertaken by the young Queen Victoria on 11 June 1842.[202]

Railway literature, as we have seen, could stir the passenger to see a journey as a visual experience as the features of town and country swiftly passing the window, as if presenting a continuously moving picture. And as statistics and history have shown, the extreme horrors that were prophesied by Lardner and the anti-tunnel lobby, at its strongest in the 1830s, did not come to pass. We cannot know the occasions on which a guide book provoked the passenger to stand up and lean out of the window to see more, with unfortunate results, perhaps a fleck of coal dust in his eyes, or more serious, having his head shattered by coming into contact with the side of a tunnel or abutment of a bridge. In the first half of 1853 there were two instances of this alone.

By the end of the 1860s, the major system was complete and few citizens had not by then experienced a ride on a train. Although contemporary railway records and journals record numerous accidents involving death or injury to employees as well as the public, frequently on tracks rather than in trains, as the system expanded, so the odds of being killed on any single journey lessened. The few tunnel disasters claimed relatively few victims, and for the Victorian middle classes the railway was accepted as a natural and safe process, as it gradually became part of everyday life, and western Europe had assimilated it culturally and psychologically.[203]

Chapter 6

STYLE AND TASTE: UNNECESSARY SPLENDOUR; CLASSICAL OR CASTELLATED?

Previous chapters have discussed the construction of tunnels, the reaction of landowners, and the effect of tunnels on the early railway passenger. It remains to discuss the architectural character and variety of portal design, and reasons for introducing such extravagance when the tunnels' main purpose was to make the passage of the train as direct as possible. Schivelbusch among others sees the decoration of railway architecture, and especially stations, as typical of the nineteenth-century desire to disguise the industrial aspect of the railways; to make them appear friendly.[1] In considering these structures the question must be asked if they added appreciably to the cost of the whole project of tunnelling, and whether some may be considered a frivolous after-thought. Why build a tunnel portal to look like a castle or a triumphal arch? If railway companies were looking for an image of strength then the strongest type of structure is a castle, which is after all meant to be impregnable. The public needed to be reassured that a tunnel was sound and would not collapse. It further, suggested a hint of romance and mystery, although this, as shown elsewhere, was not how all early passengers saw such features of their journey. Of course, from the point of view of integrating the railway into the landscape, such a design as a castellated portal fitted perfectly into the age when gentry were building houses to look medieval without but with nineteenth-century conveniences within. For a definition of purpose we can do no better than refer to the engineer F.W. Simms' *Practical Tunnelling*, 1844, in which he claimed tunnel entrances:

> should be massive, to be suitable as approaches to the works, presenting the appearance of gloom, solidity and strength … It is plainness combined with boldness, and massiveness without heaviness, that in a tunnel entrance constitute elegance, and at the same time, is the most economical. The above conditions may be answered without cramping the taste of the engineer, so far as taste enters with the composition of such designs; for architectural display in such works would be much misplaced as the massive engineering works would be if applied to the elegant and tastefully designed structures of the Architect. Upon the London and Birmingham Railway and upon the Great Western Railway there are several very suitable structures of this kind.[2]

STYLE AND TASTE: UNNECESSARY SPLENDOUR; CLASSICAL OR CASTELLATED? • 163

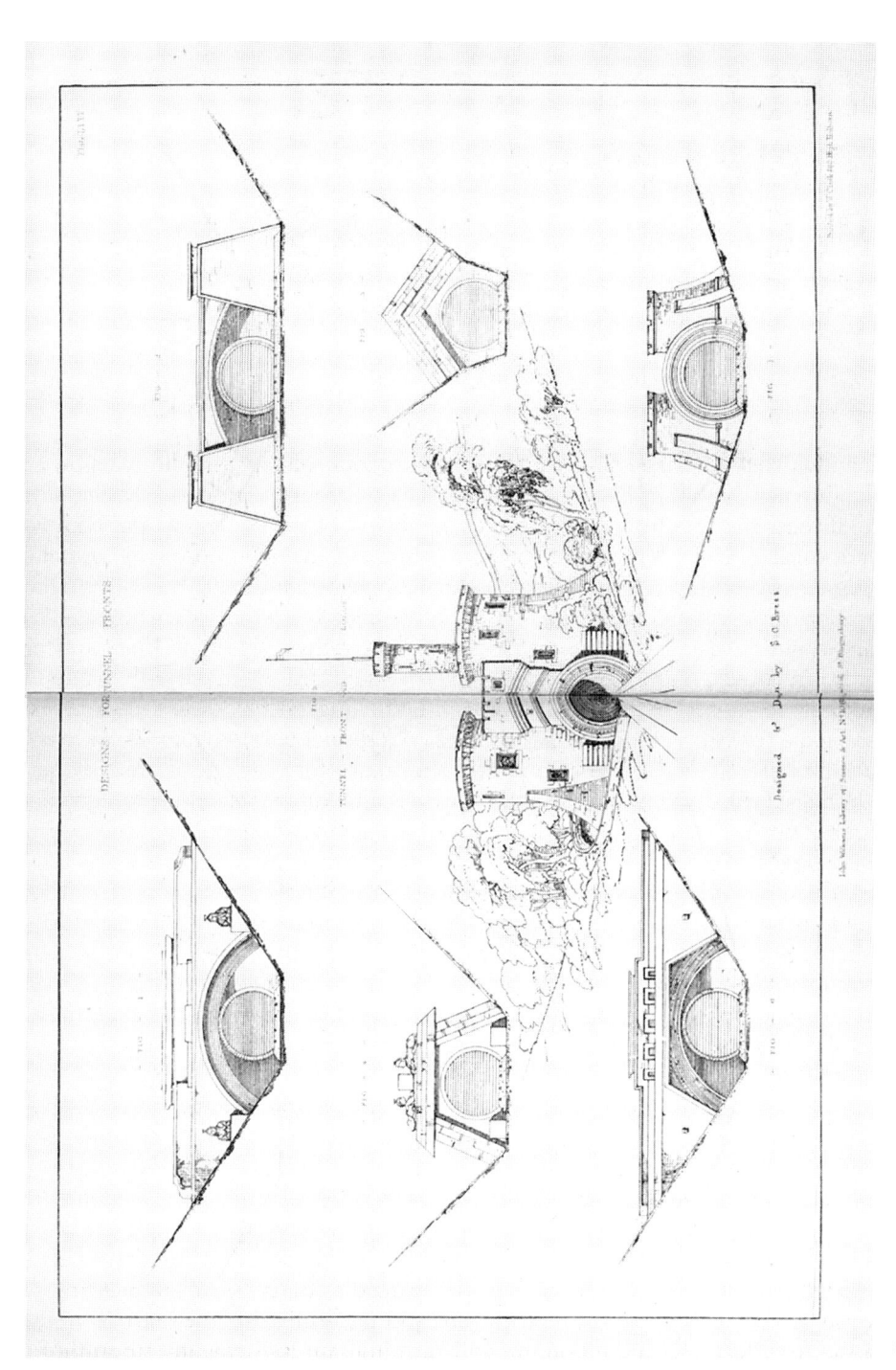

Ill. 42 **Designs for** Tunnel Fronts from S.C. Brees's *Railway Practice*, 1838.

Simms, as mentioned elsewhere, was responsible for the portals of Bletchingley and Saltwood tunnels on the South Eastern Railway, and his work ran into a number of editions until 1896. In spite of his writing of 'plainness' as a pre-requisite of a portal, he did contribute several designs for tunnel portals in the Gothic and Egyptian styles, which had they been constructed would have ranked among the most extraordinary of railway structures. He considered his Bletchingley portal to be a tasteful design.[3]

In the broader architectural sense there is a limited range of options open to the adornment of tunnel portals or even bridges and viaducts. For structural purposes, the bore or cover should be of circular or horseshoe form to deflect the weight of earth or rock on top; a horizontal cover would of necessity have to be of very limited span and this would be impracticable. So given that the portal is to be faced with a surround of brick or stone, necessary to hold back the slope of the earth or embankment behind, its adornment would fit into the vocabulary of architectural treatment used for the classical, Romanesque or Gothic styles as then currently interpreted for other forms of architecture such as gateways or triumphal arches (see Appendix 1). There were several examples where the then current fashion for the Oriental or Egyptian intruded but this is unusual in spite of Simms' inspirational suggestions. Even with these constraints, some railway companies went to astonishing lengths to give bridges, viaducts and especially tunnels considerable adornment, including surfaces of different materials or colours. As Gordon Biddle has written, a crenellated parapet or turret was certainly not necessary; it was a mixture of pride and company identity, although he states in *The Railway Heritage of Britain*, 'in order to convey confidence and reassurance they had to convey great strength. What better then, than to make them look like castles?'[4] Brunel certainly did this, although for him it was not simply to give the passenger reassurance, but also to blend with the surroundings; he saw his railway system as a work of art. The styles he used on the Great Western may be described as variations of Tudoresque Gothic overlaid with a slight flavour of Jacobean for his stations as at Temple Meads Terminus, and even Venetian for his atmospheric pumping stations at Dawlish. On the other hand, his tunnel portals varied from the pure classical of Box and Middle Hill to the castellated at Twerton and Fox Hill, and the Romanesque at Tunnel No. 1 at Brislington.[5] Away from Brunel's 'domain' there are several remarkable castellated examples that rank among the finest of functional, and at the same time romantic examples of early Victorian architecture. However, since Robert Stephenson is considered one of the fathers of railway engineering and was working in the capacity of chief engineer it is best to discuss his contribution to the development of the tunnel portal first.

STEPHENSON'S TUNNEL PORTALS

How far did Stephenson create a portal type? Unlike in Brunel's case, we do not have drawings or sketches in Robert Stephenson's hand showing preliminary ideas or thoughts on such structures, although since he took a personal interest in the design of bridges and stations, overseeing the drawings and discussing specifications with assistants, we may presume the same was with tunnels. In all, some 2,000 drawings were prepared for the London and Birmingham project, which include tunnel portals.[6] The highly finished pen and wash drawings in the National Archives were produced in the company's drawing office, the former Eyre Arms Tavern in St John's Wood, where twenty draughtsmen worked night and day to prepare the plans.[7] Unfortunately they do not have the names of the designer or those of the draughtsman, with several exceptions. We must presume that Stephenson would have kept a close eye on the appearance of the design of tunnel portals since they made an impact on the landscape as well as passengers as they approached what might be several minutes of darkness. In any case, from the inception of the project to link London with Birmingham the image was to be classical, starting with the Doric propylaea at Euston Square and finishing with the Grecian station building in Birmingham. Stephenson's hand was in any case forced at Primrose Hill and Watford tunnels with Italianate–classical designs, and the former's eastern portal by W.H. Budden. With this exception there is no evidence of specific direction as to the design of the portals. On the North Midland he may have delegated tunnel portal designs to Francis Thompson. However, the classical may stand as a badge or emblem of the company and of the directors' wish that the venture under Stephenson should be seen as the triumphal transport route from London to the heart of England, a new Watling Street.

The earliest specific record of Stephenson's attempt to give a tunnel portal a special architectural character was in 1829, when the Leicester and Swannington Railway was proposed, and a tunnel was found to be necessary at Glenfield. The directors, conscious of the nature and importance of this early railway undertaking, which was to be steam-hauled throughout, and of the attraction it would arouse, wanted the tunnel portals to be impressive but not too costly. The first designs 'were not thought sufficiently handsome', and more were called for.[8] On 29 October 1830 Stephenson put new designs to the directors with facings of Mountsorrel granite. However, with the rapidly escalating cost of the project, the portals and retaining walls were constructed of local brick crowned with stone coping, perhaps as well in view of the future of what was to become a minor branch line as the railway system developed.[9]

If we are to apply the term 'Stephensonian portal' to one, which can be described as loosely classical with a castellated flavour, it is the northern portal at Grosmont Tunnel, opened in 1834 for the horse-drawn Whitby and Pickering Railway (Ill. 43). When the line was converted to steam-hauled trains in 1848, a new and larger tunnel was cut alongside with a classical portal and the old tunnel relegated to a public passage linking the preserved station with the engine-shed.[10] Francis Wishaw described this portal with perhaps a slight degree of exaggeration, as forming a striking feature 'amid the romantic scenery of the Eske'.[11]

If the western portal of the Box Tunnel was to proclaim the grandeur of the Great Western Railway, those by Stephenson on the London and Birmingham Railway proclaim the confidence of the first trunk route to reach London. The east portal of Primrose Hill (Ills. 44–45) was a proud status symbol for the London and Birmingham Railway along with other major works including six other tunnels, major viaducts and several deep cuttings. Although the tunnel is 1,164 yards long it is only about

Ill. 43 Grosmont Tunnel original north portal. *Private photo*

45ft below the ground, and need not have been built at all, except at the insistence of the landowner, Eton College, since a contemporary gazetteer described it as only 'a small isolated hill'.[12] Until the early nineteenth century this was still a rural area where Londoners could come to breathe the pure air above the pall of London smoke. However, by the early 1830s the area was vulnerable to the fast-encroaching suburbs of north London, and in 1834 a passage in a local journal reported:

> The march of the railway has now begun its operations near the base of this hill, and in a few years the rattling machine with its bipeds and quadrupeds will usurp this land, and disposes the useful artisan of his moral walk; he will then look in vain for the green sward which cheered him after his daily or weekly toil.[13]

Although the Chalcot estate then consisted of only two houses according to a map of 1836,[14] the Fellows of the College, seeing the rise in property value in the locality, obtained an Act of Parliament to enable them to start a lease of land to the parishes of Hampstead and Marylebone.[15] However in 1841 the Crown was anxious to purchase Primrose Hill, and a public act was passed for an exchange with the college.[16] As a result the college gave up land on the hill in exchange for property in Eton.[17] However, by this time the tunnel was finished and the railway opened.

The Provost and Fellows not only insisted on a tunnel, built at considerable expense, but also that the mouth of the tunnel at the eastern end:

> shall be made good and finished with a substantial and ornamental facing of brickwork or masonry to the satisfaction of the provost and college, so as effectively to prevent the soil immediately above or round such mouth from giving way or slipping.[18]

The result is a magnificent portal designed by W.H. Budden in the Italianate style as specified by the college and considered sufficiently grand to be engraved for the frontispiece of F.W. Simms, *Public Works of Great Britain*, 1838, where 'the architectural character is original and participates in that of the massive Italian rusticated style'[19] (Ill. 45). It is tempting to ask how Budden got such a prestigious commission as he was only an assistant engineer and is not known for any other work. Was he inspired by contemporary watercolours of the arches proposed for the crypt of Soane's Museum? Praise of the tunnel portal by the nom de plume 'Mr Humphreys' in *The Architectural Magazine* suggests a supporter of Stephenson, seen as a mere 'engineer' against the establishment classical architect Philip Hardwick, who designed the nearby terminus at Euston. However:

> The entrance to the great tunnel under Primrose Hill is conceived in the right feeling, presenting exactly the effect required. On entering this subterranean road, bored through the very heart of the hill, whose super-incumbent weight seems ready to overwhelm and crush in any work Cyclopean, it was necessary to re-assure the timid passenger by such a parade of strength as is well expressed in the design of this entrance, every feature of which conveys the idea of force and strength. This and all the other architecture by an engineer.[20]

In fairness it must be accepted that a tunnel portal invites either a classical or Gothic entrance that by its nature is bound to be functional. How appropriate it is in a particular location is a matter of endless debate. Francis Whishaw, who wrote so eloquently on the tunnel portals of the Great Western Railway, claimed that some of those on the London and Birmingham Railway were of 'far too elaborate design'.[21] Yet, according to *The Times*, 'the masonry at the mouth of the tunnel by Primrose Hill, will cost £7,000. It is composed of the finest Portland stone, and when finished, will have a very handsome effect.'[22] Even an early Victorian children's book of knowledge, *Peter Parley's Annual*, included a few lines on the 'handsome brick and stone entrance', while noting that the western portal was very plain, but had a more 'picturesque look'.[23] On the other hand, Brian Morgan

Above: Ill. 44 Primrose Hill Tunnel, east portal, elevation, signed by John Shaw, 26 June 1836. *Network Rail Archive*

Below: Ill. 45 Primrose Hill Tunnel east portal forming the frontispiece of Simms' *Public Works*, London, 1838.

has described the portal as only being 'mildly decorative as the Stephensons had enough of the Puritan in their make up to avoid ornamentation unless there was good reason for it'.[24] Osborne noted that the tunnel is ventilated by a large shaft, which stood at least 12ft above the height of the hill like a tower;[25] this, of course, is now hidden by houses.

The effect of the eastern portal created by the lithograph in Simms' *Public Works* is one of grandeur. The stone-faced arch has a concave surround with gauged voussoirs radiating like the beams of the sun on either side of the keystone, and is surmounted by a projecting cornice on dentils. The portal is flanked by tower-like buttresses clasped in rusticated blocks and capped with small pyramids rising from a dentilled cornice, creating the air of the Italianate villas rising in the vicinity of Primrose Hill or to be found in Cheltenham; just what the college in fact wanted. The flanking wing walls curve to act as a visual curtain to the drama of entering the tunnel, obviously barely seen by the passenger in the moving train. These are divided into brick-filled panels by buttresses of stone capped by semicircular pediments. With increasing pressure on Euston as a London terminus there was, as early as 1852, the need to duplicate tracks and create a second bore.[26] This eventually happened in 1879 when the tracks were duplicated between London and Watford and the ornamental eastern portal was replicated. This second bore is to the south of the original and is slightly curved.[27] As already noted, the western portal is relatively plain in contrast and hard to see except from the bridge carrying the former Great Central Railway line from Marylebone.

As we have seen in an earlier chapter, the tunnel was a great attraction when first opened but now the line-side viewpoints have been eradicated by track widening and housing in adjacent streets.

Ill. 46 **Primrose Hill** Tunnel, west portal of original tunnel. *Author*

The next major tunnel is Watford (Ill. 47), which was cut through the Cassiobury estate at the insistence of the Earl of Essex. Like Primrose Hill, the line could have been taken in a deep cutting. There are no definite authors for this and the other tunnel portals; Budden might well have been involved, or they could have been the basic designs of Robert Stephenson. No drawings for the classical south portal have been traced.

The tunnel was constructed with great difficulty as it had to pierce strands of rock with loose gravel and running sand. The impressive southern portal contains a semicircular arch 25ft high and 24ft wide, set within a stone rusticated centrepiece beneath a triangular pediment, as described by Roscoe.[28] The flanking abutments are crowned by a cornice supported on dentils running across the tunnel face. However, to the architectural purist the portal looks slightly incorrect. The pediment that extends across the full width of the face should be supported by an entablature, which would be the case with a correct classical arch.

When finished this tunnel was to be the second longest on the London and Birmingham Railway at 5,374ft. Like Primrose Hill, the northern portal is less grand, which Roscoe described as similar to the latter.[29]

As mentioned in Chapter 2, even in Robert Stephenson's lifetime there was such an increase in traffic that the duplication of tracks and tunnels was considered in order to avoid bottlenecks. In 1873–75 parallel tunnels were cut at Primrose Hill and Watford. As at Primrose Hill, it would have been easy to have copied the original 1830s designs, however at Watford a much-simplified design was used with a date slab mounted on the crown of the arch.

Ill. 47 Watford Tunnel, south portal. *Private photograph*

At Stowe Hill and Kilsby we have what can be described as a machicolated parapet theme like the parapet of a castle wall. Stowe Hill is a rare example of a portal with the wing walls at right angles to the face, or parallel to the track.[30] The face of reddish brick inset with a semicircular arch of stone is surmounted by a boldly overhung parapet on machicolations, which is brought forward on both sides against the wing wall. The wall in turn is stepped down in stages, against which project stepped buttresses creating a slight effect of suction or of being drawn into the portal.

As already mentioned, the greatest undertaking on the whole of the London and Birmingham Railway proved to be the Kilsby Tunnel, which held up the complete opening of the line until September 1838. Here we have what might be described as the 'Stephenson type' of portal with the stone centrepiece pierced by a parabolic arch projecting well forward from the retaining walls but, like nearby Stowe Hill Tunnel, with a bold machicolated overhanging parapet virtually forming a viewing platform.[31] The splayed face of Kilsby is in stone with the stepped wing or abutment walls of brick dressed with stone coping. These walls are at about 30 degrees to the tracks.

These entrances have a quiet dignity, perhaps hiding the triumphal achievement that this construction was. However, Henry Humphreys felt the machicolated portals that were taken from an Italian model lacked the weight of Primrose Hill, and suggested Stephenson should have used a medieval model such as the machicolated gates of Carisbrook Castle or the city of Winchester, 'which by lowering the proportions would have made splendidly massive railway

Ill. 48 **Kilsby Tunnel** south portal. *Railway Heritage Trust*

entrances'. He felt the entrance to the Cloaca Maxima would have formed a capital model for a tunnel entrance.[32]

Even more than the portals to Kilsby Tunnel, the walls and treatment of the two large circular ventilation shafts are of interest. They are red brick towers finished with a machicolated parapet with crenelles that blend into the countryside like an eighteenth-century folly, perhaps reminiscent of Hawksmoor's mausoleum at Castle Howard, and even more the Mausoleum of Caecilia Metella on the Appian Way. They caught the imagination of Roscoe, who described them as 'perfect masterpieces of brickwork … leaving the tunnel entirely free from any offensive vapour immediately after the transit of each train'.[33]

Unseen by the rail traveller but perhaps a curious delight for the walker through Kilsby village is a model of the tunnel entrance at the entrance to Cedar Lodge, Main Road, made between 1833 and 1838 in brick with a rendered front to simulate the stone coursing and machicolated cornice. Like the real tunnel portals it is a listed structure.

At Linslade (see Appendix 1 for elevations) we see the original southern classical portal of 1837, flanked by further portals on either side due to the subsequent doubling of tracks in the 1850s. The north portal completed in 1838 by contrast is castellated and is the earliest main-line castellated tunnel portal by Stephenson, and so breaks with the preferred Stephenson fashion for a classical portal. This portal, of pinkish Bedfordshire brick, contains the horseshoe arch flanked by polygonal turrets. The crenellated brick parapet has a slightly raised merlon in the centre pierced by an arrow slit or loop.

Ill. 49 **Beechwood Tunnel**, east portal. *Science Museum Group*

STYLE AND TASTE: UNNECESSARY SPLENDOUR; CLASSICAL OR CASTELLATED? • 173

This 'Stephenson style' of classical portal is again seen with three similar versions at Beechwood near Coventry, Littleborough and Bramhope in Yorkshire. The short Beechwood Tunnel between Coventry and Birmingham, with a splayed projected face or centrepiece, is similar to Linslade and crowned by a parapet between two bowed cornices continued across the wing retaining walls. Here the arch is framed by a bowed inset, with the coursing radiating across the face.[34]

At Littleborough or Summit Tunnel on the Manchester and Leeds Railway the portal is set within a projected face of radiating stone courses. The horizontal parapet is set above a bevelled cornice. The frame of the arch is bevelled and is made the more dramatic along a deep cutting of almost vertical sides. We also see a lithograph of it in illustration 37.

At Elland Tunnel 'also on the Leeds and Manchester Railway' the arch takes up a greater proportion of the centrepiece or face than the other examples, and the heavy parapet is supported on boldly projecting brackets.

Stephenson must have influenced the design of the southern portal of Bramhope on the Leeds and Thirsk Railway opened in 1849, although, like the northern

Ill. 50 **Summit or** Littleborough Tunnel west portal. *Jeff Mills*

174 • THE EARLY HISTORY OF RAILWAY TUNNELS

Above: Ill. 51 **Bramhope Tunnel**, south portal. *Science Museum Group*

Below: Ill. 52 **Elland Tunnel**, west portal. *Private photo*

portal, it was probably designed by Thomas Grainger, the chief engineer of the company. The face is brought forward from the wing walls, and the rusticated voussoirs fan out from the arch to the corners of the face (Ill. 51).

From the examples so far of Stephenson's tunnel portals we see the classical as the image for his London and Birmingham Railway, apart from the northern portal of Linslade. Similarly, the southern portal of Clay Cross Tunnel on the North Midland Railway may be placed in a Stephenson stylistic classification with bowed banding to the arch. In sharp contrast, and rarely mentioned by railway historians and commentators, the northern portal finished in 1839, as at Linslade, breaks with any expected Stephenson norm and assumes the castellated form.[35] It may be by Francis Thompson who was appointed architect to the North Midland by the Stephensons.[36] This tunnel, at just over a mile long, was necessary to minimise damage to the town of Clay Cross, was twice as long as one initially proposed and cost an additional £34,000.[37] With its rough stone coursing blackened by nearly two centuries of smoke and Derbyshire rain, it looks mysterious and not a little forbidding, helped by its location in a deep cutting and therefore not easy to photograph or indeed see. From the drawings in the National Archive it is possible to see how the design was changed from drawing board to construction. The elevation[38] shows a smooth or ashlar stone castellated front with the arch set between circular drum towers crenellated at their summit. The conversion to deep channelled courses helps, I feel, to create a somewhat forbidding appearance. The turrets are converted from round to octagonal form, splayed at their base and pierced with mock slits or embrasures. The parapet is machicolated or projected over the arch on brackets. The parabolic arch is framed by a double band of bevelled moulding and flanked by boldly splayed castellated towers pierced by mock embrasures. In another drawing showing the elevation from above the tunnel portal we see the flanking wing walls were to have a slight curve of about 3 degrees terminating in turrets at either end.[39]

There had been concern expressed by shareholders that the cost of the North Midland Railway would exceed that of the original estimate like that of the London and Birmingham. The chairman rejected this, explaining that in the construction of the Clay Cross Tunnel they 'had provided against engineering difficulties'. Mr Swanwick, the assistant engineer, assured the shareholders that it would be completed by May 1839.[40] However its construction was described as a 'Herculean task' by the *Civil Engineer and Architect's Journal*.[41]

Another set of portals on the North Midland Railway that may also have been delegated to Thompson are those of Milford Tunnel beneath a hill called the Chevin, constructed in 1840. Two drawings in ink and pencil preserved at York show the north portal against bare rock overhang. They are Romanesque in style and consist of bands of semicircular rings beneath a boldly projecting hood cornice resting on low ashlar piers. The bore within is of horseshoe profile. One shows the intention to introduce a band of chevron ornamentation beneath the cornice but this is deleted from the version as built. A lithograph by S. Russell (Ill. 53) shows the northern portal under construction and in

176 • THE EARLY HISTORY OF RAILWAY TUNNELS

Ill. 53 Milford Tunnel, north portal under construction, lithograph, anon. *Science Museum Group*

the distance on the hillside the sighting tower, which still remains. The south portal differs in having its flanking wing walls. Biddle likens the portals to the Audley End south portal on the Eastern Counties Railway on which Thompson would later work.[42]

Is there therefore a clear Stephenson style-type, or only adaption of specific features? The conventional tunnel face to be adopted within a few years of the 1830s and perhaps fostered by the writings of W.F. Simms, consisted of a face or facade enclosing a semicircular arch and flanked by projected buttresses or rectangular piers. Beyond, on either side were wing retaining walls, either flat against the hillside or curving like embracing arms. Stephenson, on the other hand, projected his portal bay well beyond the wing walls without flanking buttresses, as we saw at Kilsby and Littleborough. This is splayed towards the base both sideways and outwards. Classical strength is further emphasised by the treatment of the arch, which may have a lip of bowed bands or rusticated voussoirs. The effect may be described as quiet elegance, far removed from Budden's eastern portal of Primrose Hill.

SHUGBOROUGH TUNNEL DRAWINGS, THE SOUTH PORTAL

There are no surviving preliminary drawings for Shugborough Tunnel as far as can be ascertained, and no preliminary doodles such as we may describe the notebook drawings by Brunel that show the fast-moving mind of the engineer-artist shifting

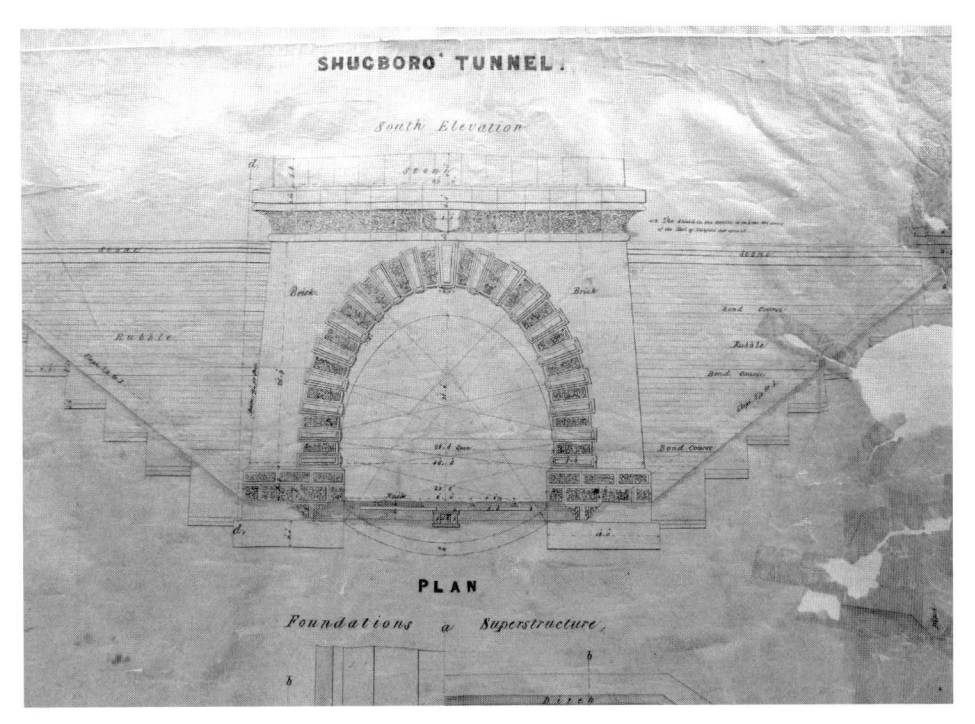

Ill. 54 Shugborough Tunnel south portal elevation, Staffordshire Record Office D615/M/10.

detail from one sketch to another. But instead we have the complete worked-up ink drawings, which are masterpieces of railway design art. In the case of Shugborough, it is unlikely that John Livock (if he was the designer) went through many preliminary changes of idea because, as he demonstrated with his station architecture for the Trent Valley Railway, he seems to have had an instinctive sense for locality and atmosphere. The railway cut through a low hill studded with monuments, some classical, which made an impact on the landscape, and here was an opportunity for the railway to contribute to the setting, to enhance rather than destroy, which had been the Earl of Lichfield's fear. To take the drawing for the south elevation first.[43]

It is in fine ink line with a colour wash applied to a side elevation. The style may be loosely described as classical, although it has also been described as Egyptian, with a boldly curved decorated overhang supporting the cornice, the centre of which is marked on the drawing with a blank shield to have the arms of the Earl of Lichfield carved upon it. As with Stephenson's tunnels on the London and Birmingham Railway, the brick centrepiece is brought forward of battered or sloping wing walls. Above the cornice is a parapet of stone rising by 6in towards the centre. The measurements of the arch give a ground-level span of 23ft 6in, and a height of 21ft 6in to the internal arch crown some 30ft inside the tunnel. The visual stability of the arch is reinforced by a surround of alternate bands of chamfered and vermiculated blocks standing on a stone base of vermiculated courses. The flanking wing walls are of broad courses of rubble stone interspersed with lines of bonded or finely cut stone beneath a stone cornice linked to corner posts of stone.

THE NORTH PORTAL

The ink drawing of the north portal clearly shows the portal's castellated Romanesque architecture (Ill. 55). The elevation is again in fine ink line and shows a stone screen set against the hillside rising in steps from the east (left) to west side on the right creating an effect like a gate in a town wall. The centrepiece has a deeply moulded arch supported on jamb shafts and cushion capitals. The face is dressed in finely coursed stone fanning out to the flanking side towers beneath a parapet supported by a corbel arcade. The flanking towers acting as buttresses splayed towards the base are pierced with arrow slits and roundels, and dressed at the corners with ashlar blocks. The left (east) wing wall is treated like a castle wall of rubble courses set between bonded courses and terminated on the left by a turret. The wall on the west (right) is stepped up the hillside in stages above the level of the portal face. Again it is dressed in bands of rubble and bonded courses. As with the completed portal, the turrets and central parapet have battlements.

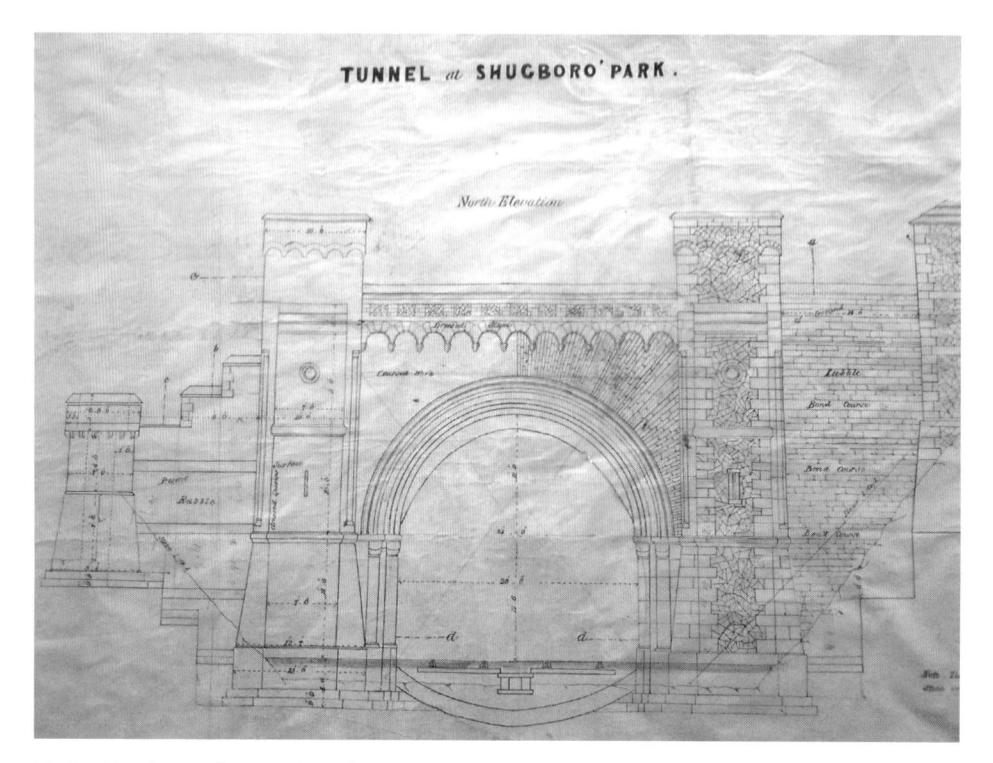

Ill. 55 **Shugborough Tunnel** north portal elevation, Staffordshire Record Office D615/M/10.

STYLE AND TASTE: UNNECESSARY SPLENDOUR; CLASSICAL OR CASTELLATED? • 179

Above: Ill. 56 **Shugborough Tunnel** south portal. *Private photo*

Below: Ill. 57 **Shugborough Tunnel** north portal London and North Western Railway postcard. *Private photo*

BRUNEL'S TUNNEL PORTALS

Apart from one article on Brunel's tunnel portals in *Railway Magazine* in 1909, there has been no specific study of the portals and their relation to surviving sketches in the Brunel Archive at Bristol.[44] These sketches, ranged over numerous notebooks and sketchbooks, reveal so much about the mind of this Victorian intellectual giant, and at the same time provide evidence of the process of design missing from Stephenson's work. The drawings range from screws, cranes and pieces of machinery to designs for flower beds in the garden of his house in Devon, to drawings of his steamships, his great bridge at Clifton, designs for railway carriages, station buildings, and, pertinent to my thesis, numerous images of tunnel mouths, some the briefest of pencil sketches while others in considerable detail in ink supported by notes. That Brunel was a brilliant draughtsman from an early age is revealed in Celia Noble Brunel's family study *The Brunels, Father and Son*, 1938, in which she mentions the series of beautiful sepia sketches in the then railway museum at Paddington for the bridge across the Clifton Gorge. She says he made the scene appear to be laid in an enchanted land and that the sketches 'almost incline one to think that the artist may have turned away from his true vocation to engineering'.[45] Obviously this judgement may be clouded by familial bias for admiration; however these sketches may date from Brunel's early twenties and show remarkable artistic skills by any standards. And, of course, they pre-date his appointment as chief engineer of the Bristol and London Railway in 1833.

What then do the sketches in the numerous sketch and notebooks surviving in the Bristol archive and watercolour drawings in the Network Rail Archive at York tell us? We may presume without question that Brunel was very familiar, indeed a subscriber, to S.G. Brees's *Railway Practice*. In Vol. 1, 1838, there are several pages of tunnel portals in various styles including Gothic and Egyptian, indeed more imaginative or bizarre than anything subsequently created. The sketches made between 1835 and 1839 show a remarkably mature vision of how the fabric of the railway should look. They show the evolution of his designs for specific tunnel portals, as well as several projected ones never carried out. One mystery that has perplexed students of Brunel, is who drew up the sketches into 'working drawings' in ink and washed in watercolour? There is hardly any reference in documents to external help, yet he must have relied on skilled draughtsmen for this task, as while his Clifton Bridge drawings show his ability to produce finished working elevations to the highest artistic standard, he would not have had the time, with his constant travelling up and down the track and daily correspondence with staff. William Westmacott is one name who appears in correspondence over the portal of No. 1 Tunnel (Brislington).[46] Westmacott was a partner in a Bristol firm of architects, but there is no record of him elsewhere in Bristol archives. Perhaps Brunel wanted his tunnel portals to be more personal and in any case there are more requirements and possible constraints in designing a station such as Temple Meads.[47] The mystery remains.

THE BOX TUNNEL DRAWINGS

Drawings survive in the Brunel papers at Bristol University for all the tunnels between Chippenham and Bristol except for Middle Hill Tunnel, a few hundred yards to the west of Box Tunnel, which is as impressive as Box but often overlooked in railway literature.[48] The reason will be addressed in due course. Watercolour drawings for the east and west portal of Box, Middle Hill and Twerton tunnels and several others between Middle Hill and Bristol are in the Network Rail Archive at York. Such is the elegance and detail of the design of some of these drawings, and especially the watercolours, that one might attribute them to a professionally trained architect rather than the railway company's chief engineer. As it is, a number of Brunel's drawings in his sketch books are on graph paper ranging from slight doodles to delicately worked out detailed drawings in ink and are too faint to reproduce. They show a mind committed to the challenge of designing the whole infrastructure supporting the railway and for this he must have looked at contemporary architecture and in particular gatehouses, lodges and arches.

In order to understand the tunnel portals on the Bristol or western end of the line we need to glimpse the challenge and constraints within which Brunel worked. In a letter of 13 May 1839 George Henry Gibbs, a director of the Great Western Railway, emphasised the importance of keeping down the cost of the Bristol depot (terminus), particularly of all the ornamental work.[49] This was an important point of difference between the London and Bristol committees. On the east division of the line (under London control) the construction did not face the daunting physical features, apart from Sonning cutting, faced by the Bristol committee west of Chippenham. At the west end construction varied, from the simple to the elaborate and expensive, using stone cut from tunnelling between Bristol and Bath as well as Box.[50]

THE EAST PORTAL

If the construction of Box Tunnel was to be seen as a triumph not only over nature but also his critics, Brunel had every reason to make the portals, and especially the western, the most monumental of classical entrances. While pencil drawings first appear in his 1835 and 1836 sketchbooks for the western portal, some years before the start of construction, a pencil drawing of the east portal appears in a sketchbook dated 6 January 1841,[51] which may suggest Brunel had given little thought to the actual appearance of the eastern portal until the excavation had been opened up into the deep cutting, although since there is another drawing for the west portal dated 9 March 1838, it is likely that both were in his mind at the same time. As the 1841 drawing is similar to the undated watercolour drawing of the east portal in the Network Rail Archive at York (Ill. 58), which would have been the working elevation for completion of work,[52] it is possible that the latter was finished about the same time, 1838.

The east portal, approached along a deep cutting, is less impressive now than in its original state depicted in Brunel's drawing, consisting of a tall arch of vermiculated stone voussoirs supported by a blank stone retaining wall, because in about 1900 a brick arch was inserted beneath the original portal and the intervening space filled with brick. The Bristol archives contain several more pencil drawings for this portal, including one with a rectangular plaque placed between the keystone at the centre of the arch and the parapet.[53] Another drawing shows the rusticated portal flanked by a rusticated buttress, however the parapet level is lowered with the omission of the plaque and with a total height of 48ft

182 • THE EARLY HISTORY OF RAILWAY TUNNELS

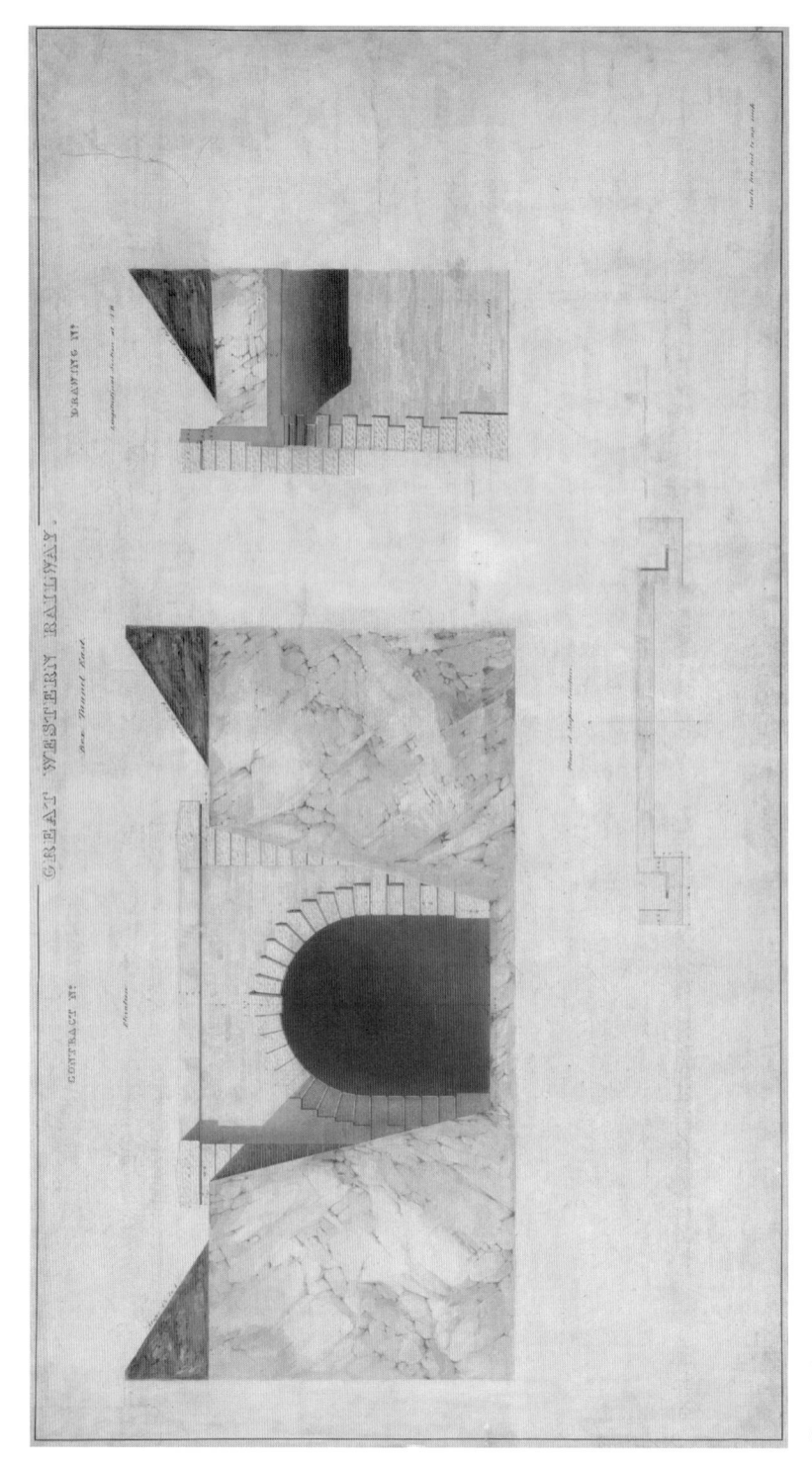

Ill. 58 **Elevation of** east portal, Box Tunnel, watercolour. *Network Rail Archive, York*

STYLE AND TASTE: UNNECESSARY SPLENDOUR; CLASSICAL OR CASTELLATED? • **183**

Ill. 59 This photograph of the eastern portal shows clearly the original dimensions of the arch, which has been decreased by the insetting of a smaller arch in brick. The entrance to the stone quarry is on the right. *Private collection* indicated to the top of the parapet.[54] This is similar to the dated pencil drawing[55] and therefore presumably from January 1841. All these features were carried out, but the east portal as built (Ill. 59) has lost some of its gravity, or, dare one say, monumentality by the insertion of the smaller brick arch and sloping retaining walls on either side of the approach. It is further damaged by the rectangular concrete entrance to the Box stone quarries on the right.

The watercolour at York in fine black ink line and delicate washes shows the arch of grey stone voussoirs set between stone abutments with an infill of yellow local Bath stone and shows the portal's original quiet monumentality.[56] The wing walls cutting the buttresses create the effect of a deep gorge, especially with the deep shadow cast from the left. As with the other drawings, measurements are added in black ink showing the arch from trackbed to crown is 36ft 6in high and 30ft wide. The sheet also includes a horizontal sectional elevation of the tunnel mouth with beautifully sensitive washes of grey to suggest the curve of the masonry within the portal. Later the stone wing walls were strengthened, especially on the left or south side, thus further diminishing the beauty of the structure.

THE WEST PORTAL

The west portal may be described as a showpiece for confidence in the newly burgeoning railway system because it could clearly be seen from the main London–Bath road. It is grand by any standard with a portal about twice as tall as a train. Although 39ft externally, the tunnel reverts to a smaller semicircular bore within. It was included in contract number 6 under George Burge. Like with the east portal, its construction is hard to date, but excavations at the western end must have commenced by 1838 with the need to divert the Corsham Road over a deep cutting. There are preliminary drawings that may date from 1835 as well as two in a sketchbook dated 9 March 1838, which, like the dating for those of the eastern portal, would suggest Brunel adapted the design to the space of the excavation or breaking through of the bore at each end. The finished watercolours of the portal and keystone and cornice details in the Network Rail Archive are undated.[57] At the west end the excavated area was wide and, with what would become a grandstand view from the Corsham Road, demanded, or certainly invited something grand.[58] There is a reference by Brunel in a letter from March 1839 to Assistant Engineer George Frère to 'having down a plan of Mr Northey's property' (Hazelbury Manor, Box) 'with some additions for the tunnel mouths',[59] which would suggest the plans for the portals were still not final. This could have referred to the portals of Middle Hill as well.

From the sketches it is clear that Brunel had the tunnel portals on his mind from early in the project; after all, these were the entrances to the most dramatic sections of the passengers' entire journey, and in the dark for most travellers until the 1870s. In the case of Box, it would be seen from the main London to Bath road and so would form an attractive feature of the landscape and act as the architectural entry to the Georgian city.

The earliest drawing c.1835 shows a semicircular arch resting on what appears to be a pilaster or column. The outer rim has a hood supported by dentils.[60] He suggests the parapet but without paired figures on each side as shown in the sketch on the

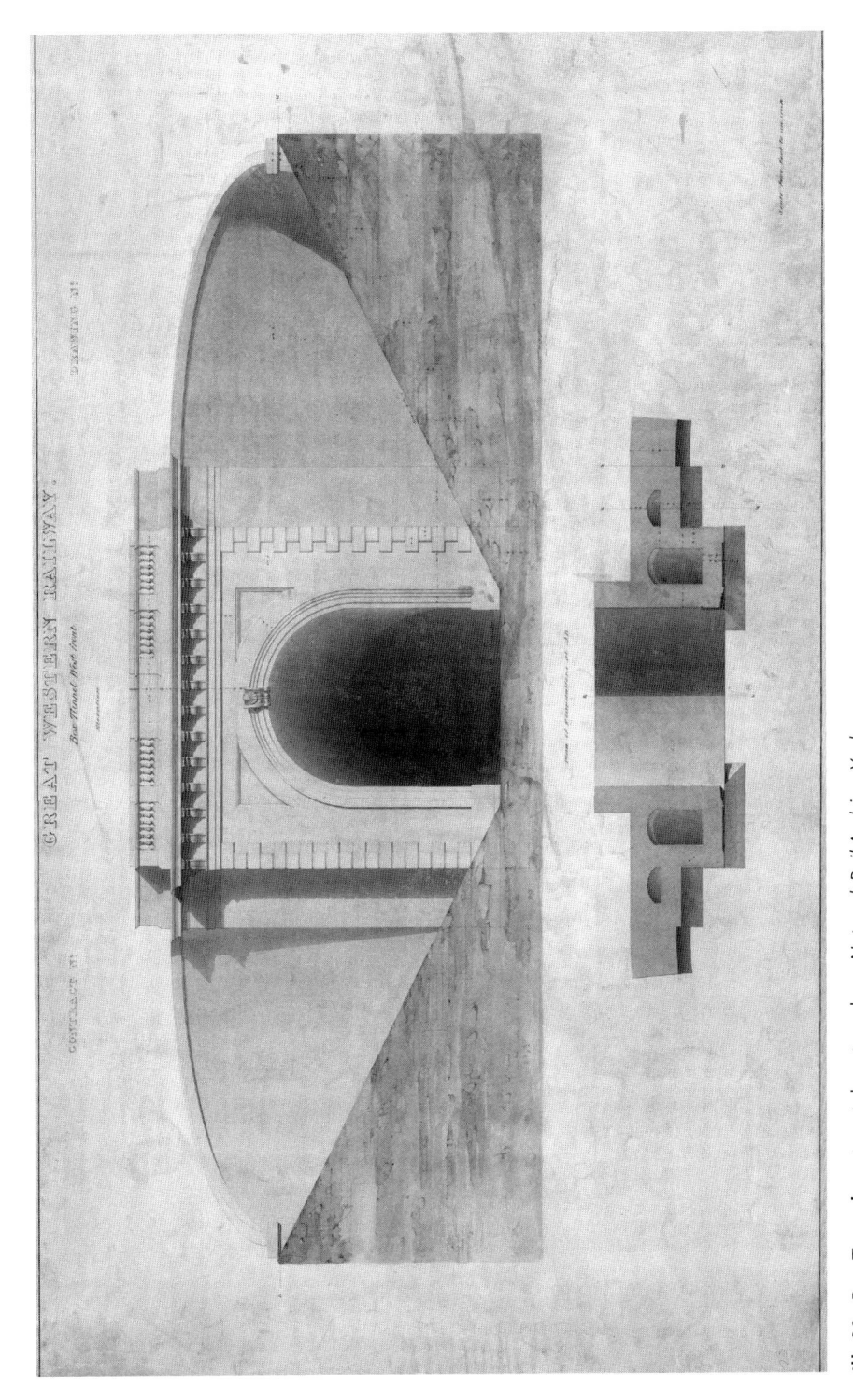

Ill. 60 **Box Tunnel** west portal, watercolour. *Network Rail Archive, York*

following page dated 9 March 1838.[61] At first glance this seems similar to the final version, however it is even grander with a sense of the Baroque. Here the arch is moulded without a break from base-stone to central embellished keystone, and in the spandrel areas between the arch and cornice is the suggestion of recumbent figures on either side of the keystone as if on a funeral monument; the one on the right with wings suggests an angel. Above the cornice is a balustraded parapet between corner pedestals supporting statues, whereas in the final version the face stands forward from the wing walls clasped in rusticated quoins. Here Brunel suggests, on the left side of the drawing, a vertical recessed strip, perhaps intended for classical fasces as at nearby Middle Hill Tunnel. The curving wing walls are terminated by a pier supporting an urn. However, beneath the corner pedestals the cornice is projected forward on brackets incorporating a swag or festoon. In the final pared-down version, as built and represented in a watercolour plan in the Network Rail Archive, the parapet figures are omitted, the cornice is unbroken on brackets and the walls are clasped with alternating quoins. The spandrel space has two triangular recesses without decoration, and the wing walls are without the pedestal termination.[62]

The watercolour in the Network Rail Archive shows the draughtsman, whoever he was, to be an exceptionally skilled artist, but tantalisingly we cannot attribute it to Brunel's hand. The central face is outlined in black ink and pale ochre wash to contrast with the deep golden ochre wash used to depict the curving wing walls. Shadow is introduced to create an effect of relief to features such as keystone, consoles or brackets beneath the cornice, and spandrel recesses. The artist depicts the centrepiece or tunnel face with the shadow falling from the right or south side, which adds drama to the projection. The individual stone quoins at the corners are emphasised by shadow against the white stone of the face. Unlike the east portal, however, the arch is framed in recessed bands like a Georgian window case. The dimensions given for the arch are 39ft to the crown of the arch from the trackbed and 24ft 4in wide.

There is a separate drawing showing details of keystone, brackets or what are called 'trusses' for the cornice and the balustrade (Ill. 61).[63] Here we can marvel at the care that has been bestowed on features that will barely be seen by the passing passenger, let alone the viewer from the Bath Road bridge without binoculars. Again the washes range across pale to deep brown with dramatic relief conveyed by shadow for the shell-like motif of the keystone and the flutes on the brackets or consoles beneath the cornice shown in blue-section. Brunel's Baroque Box flourish appears again in a drawing of a gate portal for features marked as 'Bristol Depot' in an 1838 sketchbook.[64] Was the classical intended for Temple Meads Terminus as well?

Praise for the completion of the tunnel came from many quarters, some of it in a slightly exaggerated tone of hyperbole common in Victorian England; *The Penny Satirist* called it a 'splendid monument of the industry and genius of this country' and 'the beauty of its two fronts built of picked Bath stone commands universal admiration'.[65] Perhaps its majesty and scale can only be fully appreciated if we compare it with the height of a three-storey façade in Bath such as the elevation of the Royal Crescent. Both are about 50ft from the ground to the parapet. The face of the portal was restored for the 150th anniversary of the foundation of the Great Western Railway Company in 1988.

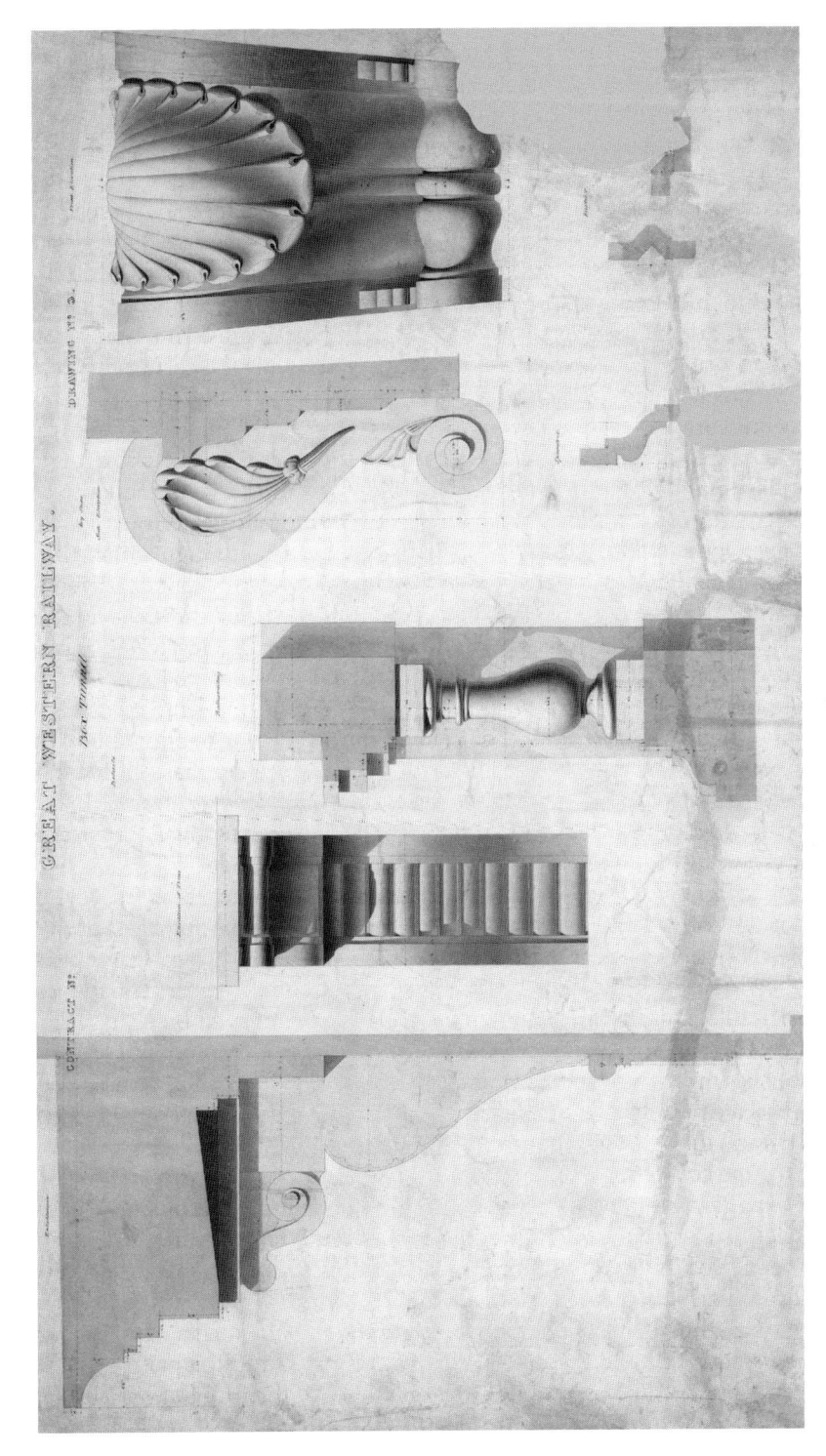

Ill. 61 **Box tunnel** west portal, details, watercolour. *Network Rail Archive, York*

That the tunnel was a costly project was not overlooked by *Punch*, who was even able to make a joke about the Great Western and 'how it is a wonderful triumph of cash and pick-axes over obstacles of fiscal as well as earthly nature. The tunnel at Box Hill proves that man can get through almost anything.'[66]

THE FORGOTTEN TUNNEL: MIDDLE HILL

A few hundred yards to the west of Box the tracks enter the lesser-known short Middle Hill Tunnel with stone-faced classical facades at both entrances. And here lies a mystery. There are no drawings for it in the National Archive at Kew, the Brunel Archive in Bristol, Swindon Museum or the Network Rail Archive in York, however there is a superb watercolour elevation in the Network Rail Archive (Ill. 62). There is no reference to the tunnel in written documents at Kew until 1839. It is also largely overlooked in studies of Great Western architecture, yet its portals bear comparison with its near neighbour. Buchannan dismissed it as simply a 'short tunnel under the shoulder of a hill as it approached the main tunnel'.[67] It is only 198 yards long and on a slight curve, and with a maximum cover of only about 30ft; obviously it has no shafts. It may be asked why it was constructed instead of an open cutting. The clue may lie in a report by Brunel to the directors on 17 October 1836, where he mentions a possible deviation in the Box valley depending on 'an arrangement being made with Mr Wiltshire of Shockerwick'.[68] The matter was still not resolved a year later, when Brunel reported 'that construction was seriously inconvenienced in consequence of the delay in Mr Wiltshire's business. Nothing prevents the contract from Bathwick to Box Tunnel being ready but this'.[69] This is the ongoing argument that had surfaced at the House of Lords enquiry in 1835, with the family owning not only land through which the track would pass but also the 'right to the view' as they saw it. Elizabeth Wiltshire farmed fields about a quarter of a mile to the west of the tunnel.[70] The fact that there are no drawings for the portals in the sketchbooks, yet there are two drawings marked 'Middle Hill Bridge' in an 1838 sketchbook, suggests there was never an intention to have a tunnel at this point.[71] As I have suggested in a previous chapter, the tunnel was made purely to satisfy the Wiltshires, who wished to retain the view of the existing hill rather than a violent visual gash in the hillside. Better a Georgian-style portal!

The first reference to the building of the tunnel occurred in March 1839, when there is a proposal to build the embankment east of Box Tunnel '40 feet wide',[72] however tenders to construct it were not submitted until September 1839, and in October the winning contract was awarded to George Findlater of Brislington, with J.G. Thomson as resident engineer.[73] The next reference is 3 January 1840, when a cheque for work on Middle Hill Tunnel was drawn in favour of Findlater, suggesting construction had just begun.[74] In February 1840 there is reference to the selling of stores belonging to the work at the Brislington tunnels because of their 'near completion' and transfer to Findlater at Middle Hill.[75] From September 1840 there were weekly reports of work on Middle Hill Tunnel noted in the sub-committee's record.[76] In February 1841 Brunel reported that the small tunnel called Middle Hill and the adjacent cutting were nearly finished.[77] However, work was noted in the weekly reports as continuing until September 1841. This also applied

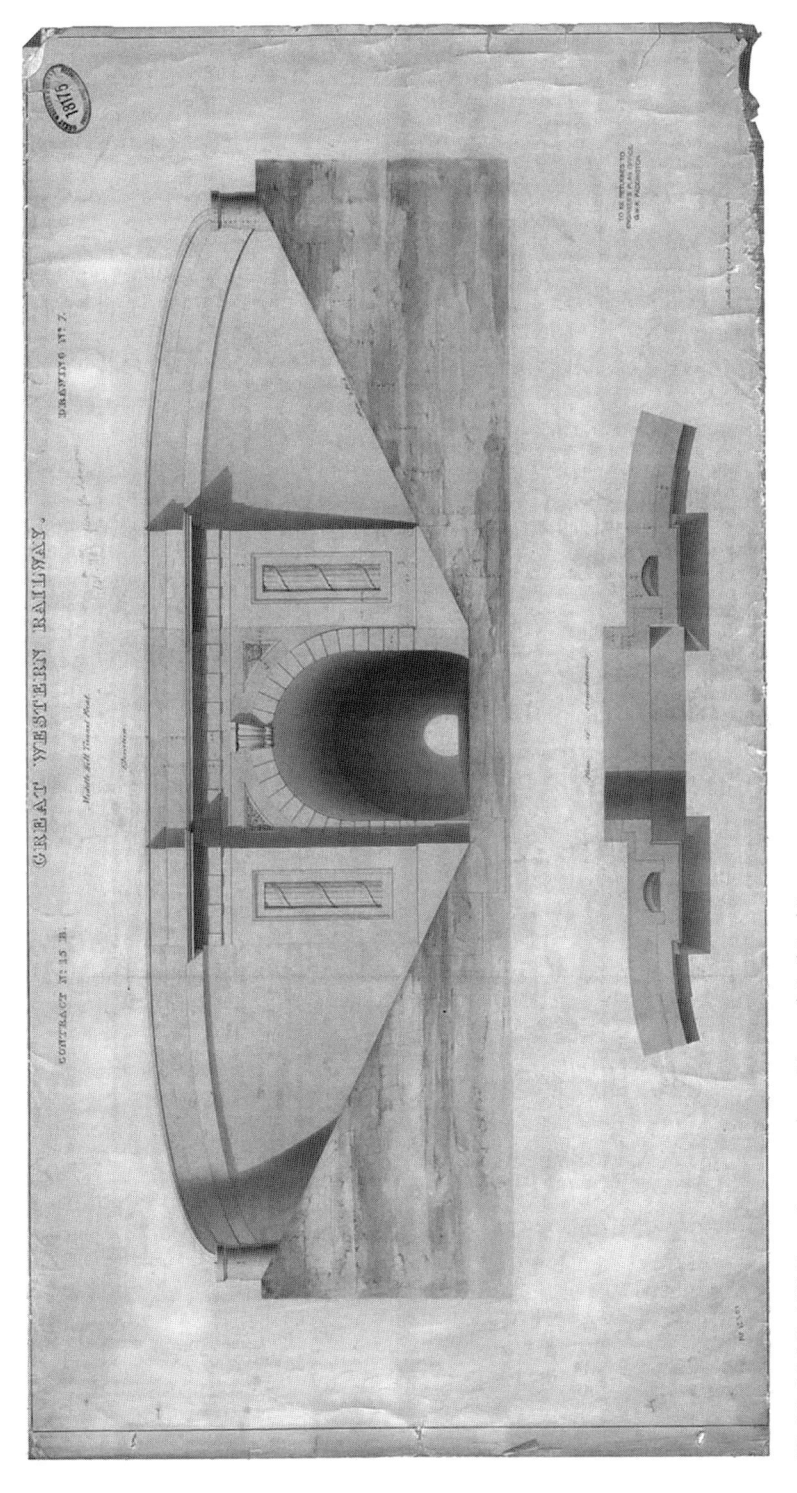

Ill. 62 **Middle Hill** Tunnel watercolour. *Network Rail Archive*

Ill. 63 Middle Hill Tunnel, west portal. GWR locomotive *King George V* posing for publicity photograph, *c.*1935. *Railway Heritage Trust*

to Box, and yet the line was opened throughout on 30 June, so this probably refers to further work on the portals.

The fact that there are no sketches for the portals of Middle Hill, their similarity to the western portal of Box (as shown by this one watercolour elevation of the portal), and the lateness of construction, suggest there was no time to design specific ones, and that Brunel therefore probably took the western portal of Box and duplicated it with minor variations such as the introduction of classical fasces on the buttress walls and a Doric entablature beneath the cornice. Also the surround to the arch is rusticated with scroll-patterned keystones at their crown. The spandrels between the rim of the arch and flanking pilasters have segmental recesses. The curved wing walls continue the line of the plain parapet.[78] The portals have roughly the same dimensions as Box but with minor variation in design in that the arches are flanked by buttresses displaying classical fasces. Why this tunnel is often overlooked is a mystery, perhaps because it did not involve the labour and hardship involved a few hundred yards up the track at Box.

Why these grand portals at Box and Middle Hill? Vaughan considers the three portals in Brunelian Roman Imperial style as suitable for such a Napoleonic figure as Brunel; they are like three triumphal arches to mark his victory over great odds.[79] A victory not only over nature but to assert himself over his rivals, the Rennies. John Rennie the Elder, as chief engineer of the Kennet and Avon Canal, had designed the magnificent Dundas Aqueduct, only a few miles away from Box, and this was not lost on Brunel. Rennie's son had built a grand portal to the Royal Victualling Yard at Stonehouse, Plymouth. Indeed, Brunel had written in his diary for 7 May 1828, 'the young Rennie ... will have built London Bridge ... while I shall have been engaged on a tunnel which has failed', a reference to his having helped his father on the Thames Tunnel, then temporarily abandoned because of flooding.[80] Brunel was conscious of the fact that a tunnel was really an unseen masterpiece, certainly as far as passengers were concerned, whereas a viaduct, aqueduct or bridge could take its aesthetic place in the landscape. So he wanted the western mouth of Box and the mouths of Middle Hill to be seen in the landscape and as an attraction on the main Bath–London road, even if not seen by passengers from within a railway carriage.

BETWEEN BATH AND BRISTOL: TWERTON AND BRISLINGTON TUNNELS

There is difficulty analysing the sketches for the section between Bath and Bristol as most sketches are not dated and do not refer to specific tunnels. One sheet, marked *tunnel mouths, Bristol end*, shows four pencil sketches introducing three pointed arches and one round or Romanesque, suggesting Brunel's mind was playing with ideas.[81] According to the *Bristol Mercury* in 1836, there were then four tunnels under construction, 'two of them might altogether have been dispensed with had not the wish to avoid injury to private residences interfered'.[82] This, on the other hand, may not be accurate since there were three tunnels close together and referred to as Brislington Tunnels or numbers 1, 2 and 3 in documents.

The first set of tunnels west of Bath are at Twerton, where the line passed through the estate of Charles Wilkins, a local mine owner who lived in

192 • THE EARLY HISTORY OF RAILWAY TUNNELS

Ill. 64 **Twerton Short** Tunnel, watercolour. *Network Rail Archive*

Wood House.[83] There is no mention of the intention of tunnels here in the 1835 parliamentary proceedings, yet there are drawings in the 1836 sketchbook. However, had it been built as first conceived, Twerton Long Tunnel, named Tiverton in the sketch, would probably have been celebrated as Brunel's most extraordinary tunnel portal. What was probably Brunel's initial idea, and may have been for the long tunnel, may best be described as a Gothic two-light window supporting a foiled roundel beneath a pointed hood. With a dividing pillar supporting the two arches it must be assumed that each was to take one track.[84] It is quite likely that he was undecided, certainly about the necessity for the short tunnel, which he describes in a sketchbook as 'Wilkins' covered way: bridge or tunnel?'[85] Brunel had actually expressed concern that he was interfering with the 'ornamental property', although Wilkins had given his consent.[86] However, what was eventually adopted for both tunnels were portals resembling castle gatehouses, and perhaps visually appropriate for the wooded nature of the immediate landscape.

The first tunnel approached on a curve is Twerton Short Tunnel, i.e. 'Wilkins' covered way'. *Railway Magazine* said it was to connect two parts of a plantation.[87] It appears that Wilkins was concerned about the preservation of the soil over the tunnel.[88] It rather looks like the opening in a castle wall, as it is so short. Watercolour drawings show a broad four-centred arch almost filling the whole face and flanked by angular castellated turrets.[89] As built it has a crenellated retaining wall with turrets on either side pierced with a quatrefoil arrow slit.

A short distance further on, the east portal of Twerton Long Tunnel is truly Gothic, with rusticated parapets and flanking semicircular battlemented turrets with tall projected base. In the 1836 sketchbook are several drawings that, although not specifically marked as Twerton, must be the germination of his design for this tunnel. In these Brunel introduces a Tudor four-centred arch beneath a machicolated parapet flanked by castellated buttress towers. The final result, although it omits the machicolated overhang, is among the finest castellated portals anywhere. The polygonal turrets are pierced by arrow slits and the height of the flanking abutments or wing walls is stepped down like a curving castle wall. Construction did not run smoothly in that the contract, drawn up in September 1837 between Brunel and the contractor David McIntosh, stated the arch to be 25ft high and 30ft wide. After work had been in progress for about three months, Brunel, for some reason, changed the specification to a height of 30ft but in 1838 he ordered the western entrance to be returned to the original 25ft. This, along with the alterations including the omission of crenellation to the parapet, must have led to additional expense for the contractor.[90] He also insisted that the contractor convert coursed rubble stone to smooth ashlar at his own expense, which McIntosh refused to pay.

This was not all, as in October 1838 Brunel learned with alarm that the east face of the tunnel was badly secured to the brown marl behind without any timbering. He cautioned David McIntosh against the delay a collapse would inflict for 'want of a little timber … you can expect no indulgence when it arises from your own neglect'.[91]

194 • THE EARLY HISTORY OF RAILWAY TUNNELS

Ill. 65 **Twerton Long** Tunnel, east portal. *Network Rail Archive*

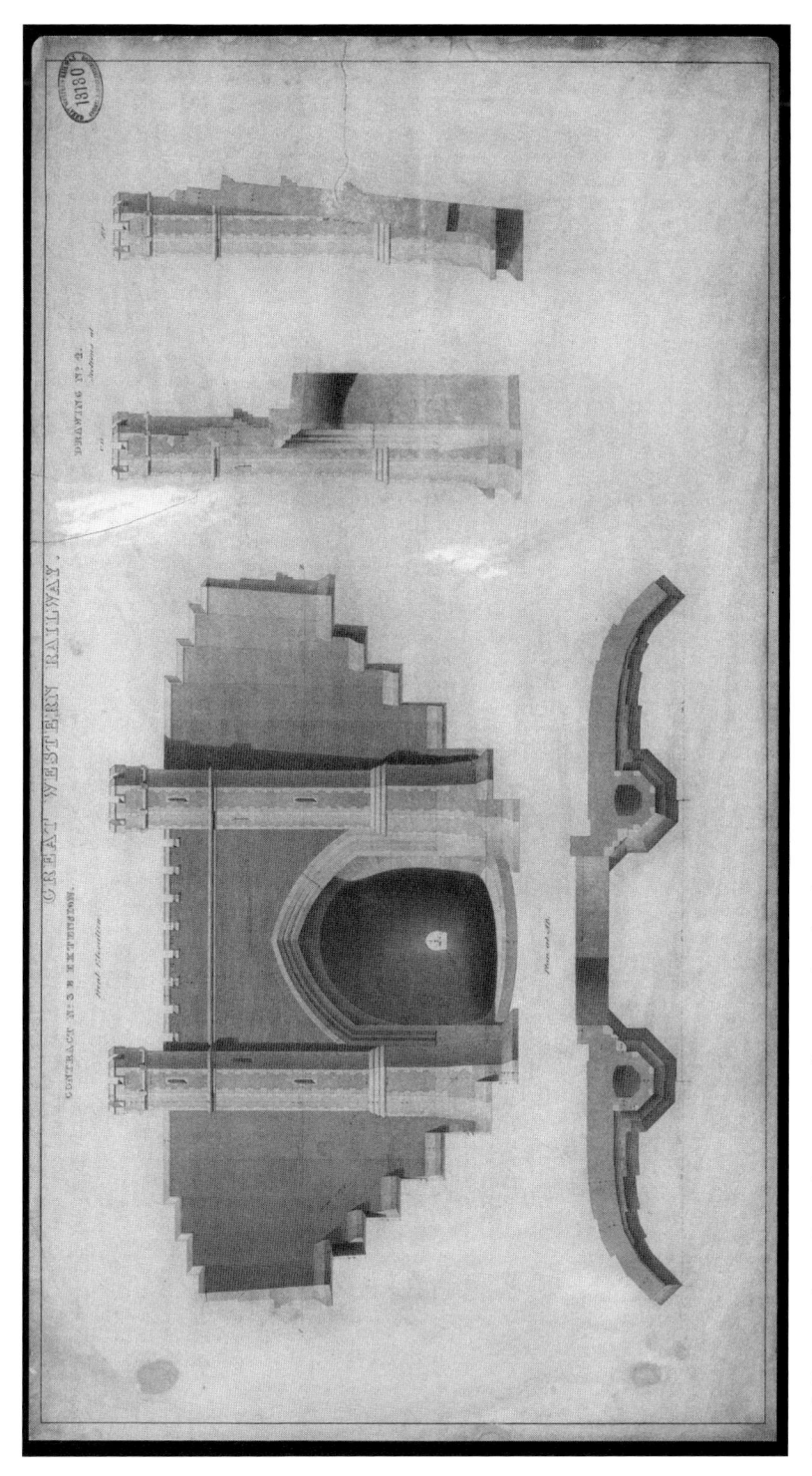

Ill. 66 **Twerton Long** Tunnel, west portal. *Network Rail Archive*

Ill. 67 Twerton Long Tunnel, east portal. *Private collection*

Beyond Keynsham both the Avon and railway run in close proximity through a deep valley, perhaps the most picturesque section of the whole route between London and Bristol. Originally the line ran through several tunnels that have been opened out, including the celebrated Tunnel No. 1 which adorned the frontispiece of Bourne's *History of the Great Western* (Ill. 30).[92] Those surviving from the Bristol direction are St Anne's Park Tunnel, also known as Bristol No. 2, Fox's Wood, also known as Bristol Tunnel No. 3, with a classical arch, and known originally as Long Tunnel, and Saltford Tunnel.

Reverting to the sequence westwards from Bath, we first come to Saltford Tunnel; at only 176 yards it is hardly noticed from a train unless it is passed at slow speed, however it would have been longer but for a landslip. It passed beneath land owned by Major James, who was upset because Brunel had failed to make prior arrangements for the work, as well as the road to Saltford village. As a result of a legal dispute, James was paid £605 for various rights.[93] Brunel made a number of ink sketches for the portal in an 1836 sketchbook.[94] It seems that, as with Twerton Long Tunnel, Brunel was unsure of the final dimensions, and in September 1837 raised the height of both portals from 25 to 30ft; this after construction had been under way for three months, then in 1838 ordered that the western portal be reduced to its original 25ft.[95]

The design is basically a four-centred arch set into a broad retaining wall of thin courses of rough stone. The arch is set in a rectangular frame with triangular recesses in the spandrels like a fifteenth-century moulding. Above the east portal is a horizontal parapet, while that at the west end has a slight inclination over the actual tunnel face. Another drawing that may be related but is unidentified, shows a similar-shaped arch with a broad rectangular panel or tablet between the crown and parapet.[96] It is not clear from correspondence as to which parapet Major James objected when seen from his house but he wanted the substitution of an iron railing, to which Brunel replied that such a feature would be very inconsistent over a Gothic arch.[97] The *Railway Magazine* described the east face of Bath stone as of 'good proportions, and which is seen from a great distance when looking westwards'.[98]

It is now that the route is at its most scenically dramatic with the Avon running through the narrow valley and virtually touching the railway embankment. Trains are normally running too fast for the passenger to appreciate the architectural merit of the tunnel portals. The next tunnel is Fox's Wood or Bristol Tunnel 3, for which a number of drawings survive but no watercolour elevations. It is the longest tunnel after Box at 1,017 yards and on a curve. The eastern portal is cut into naked rock without any retaining wall, made all the more dramatic by the narrow rock cutting approach. Brunel made a scribble in one of his sketchbooks of a Romanesque arch to a tunnel set in rock.[99] (He comes close to an arch set into a rock face in the southern portal of Wickwar Tunnel, 1844, on the then Bristol and Gloucester Railway.)

The western portal of Fox's Wood is by contrast set against a spur of hillside dropping to the river on the north. Here we perhaps have the perfect setting for Brunel to make his tunnel look like a piece of timeless architectural ornament appearing like a feature in a country estate (Ill. 69). It is hard to trace the origin of this idea as there are so many sketches of castellated features including turrets but no final watercolour elevation surviving. In his set of three drawings in his 1835 sketchbook in which he includes the Romanesque arch set in a rock face. He also includes another of a turreted entrance with the suggestion of a rock overhang breaking into the right turret.[100]

In some of his sketches for this portal Brunel takes the romantic ruin to extremes with a pencil sketch of a face with a Romanesque arch beneath a machicolated parapet broken on the left side as if the whole structure was crumbling away.[101] The merlons in the partly ruined battlement are pierced by arrow embrasures, adding to the charm. The retaining wall rising from a spur is suggested by deep shading on the left side. In sketches the following year titled Tunnel No. 3 West Front, he introduces the complete castellated theme with the portal face flanked by circular turrets.[102] One even has the hint of a bartizan, a projected corner turret seen on Scottish baronial architecture.

Ill. 68 Saltford Tunnel. *Network Rail Archive*

STYLE AND TASTE: UNNECESSARY SPLENDOUR; CLASSICAL OR CASTELLATED? • 199

The arch also goes through variations from the semicircular to the four-centred pointed. In another 1839 sketchbook he includes a drawing of the west portal of Tunnel No. 3 in which he has the semicircular arch as built, but with the projected parapet without machicolation beneath or crenellation above.[103] On the right is the suggestion of a buttress partially hidden by rock, but the left side has a circular spurred turret, again without crenellation, but decorated with narrow embrasures. To the left is a retaining wall dropping away in stepped stages. This treatment of the retaining wall, on the Avon or north side, appears in a drawing for an unidentified tunnel portal in the same sketchbook.[104] Here the turrets but not the parapet are crenellated. Yet another variant shows crenellated turrets of equal height with the left wing wall partially covered by rock or vegetation.[105] In Bourne's drawing for his *Great Western Railway*, 1846, this tunnel portal is a combination of treatment from various drawings with a semicircular arch flanked with a semicircular spurred turret on the left, and flat turret on the right side almost obscured by rock. This is similar to the photograph, ill. 69.

The final remaining tunnel before Bristol is St Anne's, or Bristol Tunnel No. 2, with two castellated portals with machicolated and crenellated parapets. There are no sketches specific to the design for this tunnel's portals, although two drawings in an 1838 sketchbook are marked Tunnel Front No. 2b.[106] One drawing, however

Ill. 69 Fox's Wood Tunnel or Tunnel No. 3 west portal. *Private photo*

has a four-centred arch, and the other a semicircular one as built. One also has a machicolated overhanging parapet without battlementing but flanked by a splayed flat-faced turret. The eastern portal, very hard to see except from a train window, is basically a broad rectangular retaining wall without a crenellated parapet but with a flat crenellated turret on the right or Avon side. The grander western façade is crenellated with machicolated overhang pinned into a slightly projecting buttress on the right. The crenellated parapet runs across the façade without interruption. The circumstances of its construction were set out by Isambard Brunel in his biography of his father published in 1870: 'During its construction a part of the ground behind slipped away, and it became unnecessary to complete the top of one of the side walls. It was therefore left unfinished, and was planted with ivy so as to present the appearance of a ruined gateway (Ill. 70).'[107]

It was described by Whishaw as representing the entrance to an old ivy-mantled castle, and is:

> the first, and we may say perfectly successful attempt in railway-work so to blend nature and art as to produce the most pleasing effect on the mind of the spectator … Within an easy walk of Bristol, the ivy mantled tunnel

Ill. 70 **Tunnel No. 2** or St Anne's Park Tunnel, J.C. Bourne, *Great Western Railway*, 1846.

will, no doubt, be long considered one of the principal attractions of the neighbourhood.[108]

Churton also echoed this view.[109] Unfortunately it was not allowed to remain in this state and the intended buttress was restored to the left side. A careful study of the left side will reveal the difference between the courses of rough stone and the machine-like finish of the buttress and part of the parapet.

Tunnel No. 1 at Brislington on the eastern outskirts of Bristol was perhaps the most monumental portal of all after that of Box Tunnel. It was chosen as previously mentioned for the frontispiece to Bourne's *History of the Great Western Railway* but at 330 yards was deemed sufficiently short and shallow to be opened out to form a long cutting in 1887. Here the flavour was Norman Romanesque and received praise from the normally anti-tunnel *Railway Magazine*, 'its simplicity and boldness was considered highly creditable to the taste of the engineer with its noble circular arch enriched by cable-twist moulding'.[110] The writer further considered the enlarged dimensions would help to dispel the public's prejudice and fear of tunnels. Wishaw, in his *Railways of Great Britain*, praised its 'bold and pleasing outline'.[111] The evolution of this tunnel portal can be followed in several sketchbooks, although the specific location is not always given. One sketch in ink (Ill. 71) shows the west portal for Tunnel No. 1 with a Romanesque arch supported on cushion capitals and jamb columns.[112] The face is dressed with what is suggested as rubble stone on the left and ashlar on the right. The parapet is surmounted at

Ill. 71 Tunnel No. 1 Bristol (13 December 1835), sketchbook, folio 37 DM 162/8/1/4. *Brunel Archive, University of Bristol*

each corner by what appears to be indication of turrets above a semicircular arch with a roll-moulded surround. Scale is created by a small figure within the arch.

In another drawing in pencil there is a projected parapet over a moulded overhang.[113] There is, however, slight confusion about a reference to Tunnel No. 1 in Brunel's letters. In correspondence to his draughtsman, William Westmacott, he refers to a drawing with two towers: 'The No. 1 will make a very pretty elevation. I should like to see the tunnel left heavy at the top so as not to form so striking a point of the outline, more as I have sketched the right hand over with slight alterations.'[114] This, of course, does not accord with either the style or what was built, and may therefore refer to Tunnel No. 2, which as we have seen was castellated. As built, the upper area of the tunnel face was treated in rubble stone without any dressing, perhaps part of the romantic nature of the structure. Perhaps Brunel became interested in the Romanesque when working under his father on the twin-bore Thames Tunnel, where its features were used for the transverse connecting arches (Ill. 72).

It is impossible to cite a specific example as the inspiration for this portal, however, the gatehouse at Penrhyn Castle in Caernarfonshire, by Thomas Hopper, was then under construction with a chevron arch on jamb shafts. (Norman arches

Ill. 72 Tunnel No. 1, opened out in 1896. *Science Museum Group*

of stone were to be used about twenty years later as entrances to several of the so-called Palmerston forts at Portsmouth and Plymouth.) As for the other castellated tunnel portals between Bath and Bristol, perhaps it is no coincidence that several portals resemble features on Blaise Castle near Bristol, and that its owner, John Harford, who was a Bristol merchant, funded the Great Western from its inception in 1833.[115] It is worth recording that railway companies elsewhere built overtly Norman Romanesque tunnel portals at Wansford near Peterborough, 1845, and Beacon Hill, Halifax, 1849.[116]

What can be learned from an overview of Brunel's tunnelling is that all subsequent examples built after the completion of the line between London and Bristol may be described as plain or modest, even on the picturesque stretch between Dawlish and Kingswear, where taking the railway along the beach demanded extensive underpinning; in places foundations were 17ft deep and 'faced in Babbicombe [Babbacombe] lime-stone rock of the finest workmanship ...'[117] Cost therefore must have entered into these subsequent ventures. To get to Plymouth, achieved in 1849, Brunel had to take the line over the foothills of Dartmoor, involving the South Devon Banks and a tunnel at Dainton with an arch of Box proportions. However, the face of the portals are of local stone and unadorned. A similar simple portal by Brunel is to the 742-yard tunnel at Newport completed in November 1842. Yet when completed it was pronounced to be 'equal to anything of its kind in the kingdom'.[118]

THE CLASSIC CASTELLATED PORTALS: BRAMHOPE AND RED HILL

The castellated theme perhaps reaches its peak, if such a term can be used, at Bramhope in north Yorkshire, on the former Leeds and Thirsk Railway, at Red Hill Tunnel near Nottingham, on the former Midland Railway, and at Clayton on the London and Brighton Railway. Two were necessary due to depth of hillside and one could have been avoided but for an eccentric landowner. Unfortunately no elevational drawings have been traced.

The northern portal to Bramhope Tunnel is often illustrated as the classic castellated portal on the British railway system and is on a different scale to the portals at Shugborough (Ills 54–55). The construction of the tunnel, over 2 miles long, could not be avoided if the Leeds and Thirsk Railway was to reach Harrogate from the south; the range of hills to be pierced were over 200ft high. The company obtained its parliamentary Act in 1845, and the tunnel took three years to construct. While the southern classical portal (Ill. 51) was described as 'handsome but somewhat impaired by the strong retaining walls which it was necessary to construct', that on the north is, like Red Hill, more like the entrance to the outer defences of a castle, except you cannot see the other end.[119] It is said that the castellated appearance owes its existence to local landowner William Rhodes, who also insisted on castellated ventilation shafts and wanted it to look like a large garden folly. It must be inspired by the earlier north portal of Clayton, as well as Brunel's Twerton Tunnel. Completed in 1849, the result can only be described as a masterpiece of the Gothic imagination. The 25ft-high arch is set into a stone face, and the voussoirs are set within a roll-moulded hood acting as a relief frame. The keystone is carved to form the head of a bearded man sometimes described as a Nordic warrior but also suggested to portray the local landowner Rhodes. Above is a cornice with parapet adorned in the centre with a panel displaying the arms of the Leeds and Thirsk Railway. On either side of the face are two crenellated towers that act as strengthening buttresses. That on the left or east side is the taller of the two and is pierced with embrasures and paired semicircular headed windows as this tower served as a residence for railway workmen. The tower on the right side is lower and is square with a buttress projection for the first 30ft, above which the upper stage is circular. The parapet is machicolated but not castellated, while the asymmetrical scale of turrets is a Brunel feature. However, the parapet has lost its upper courses, including the upright merlons. Without the darkness within the arch, it could pass as a grand entrance to a castle, or perhaps a structure to satisfy the romantic needs of a country gentleman. Like most tunnels at this time, their construction invariably led to injury and deaths with sudden collapse or flooding of workings. There is a memorial in nearby Otley churchyard to workmen killed in the construction of Bramhope.

Red Hill on the former Nottingham and Derby Railway is very short and was built at the insistence of an awkward landowner, J. Emmerton Westcomb

Ill. 73 Bramhope Tunnel, north portal. *Private photo*

of Trupston Hall. At first he would not entertain the presence of the railway in any form, considering 'the taking of even this small amount of land as symbolic of the breaking down of a barrier which secured his estate from unwelcomed intruders' – an instance of the power of a local landowner who was prepared to resist the advance of the railway because he feared it would 'spoil our shires and ruin our squires'.[120] Eventually in June 1838 he suddenly lifted his objection and allowed a tunnel but requested a private station near the Hall. This the company refused as there was to be a station nearby on the north side of the Trent. In the ensuing correspondence he proposed his own short railway link constructed at his own expense so that his carriage could be attached to the London-bound train. The matter was dropped when he conveniently died abroad!

The resulting northern portal is magnificent even though the tunnel is only piercing a low wooded hill for a mere 170 yards. The stone face with projected parapet is flanked by two circular turrets with the wing walls stepped to create the impression of hugging the hillside behind. The wider turret on a massive base was said to contain rooms for a policeman and another guardian for this section of the railway (Ill. 74).[121] With the volume of traffic the tracks had to be doubled, necessitating a second bore. This had identical sets of portals to the original.[122]

Ill. 74 **Red Hill** Tunnell, north portal, Midland Railway. *Science Museum Group*

When the line between Long Eaton and Loughborough was opened on 4 May 1840, a celebratory train set out from Nottingham for Leicester with a stop at the bridge over the Trent to allow the passengers to admire Vignole's handsome iron bridge and the castellated north portal of Red Hill Tunnel.[123]

THE MYSTERY OF CLAYTON TUNNEL
Some claim the north portal of Clayton on the London and Brighton Railway to be the most monumental castellated structure of all, or as Jobbins' *Guide* said 'as pretty a piece of Gothic architecture as can be desired'.[124] This was said to be due to the insistence of William Campion of nearby Danway Park, Hurstpierpoint, who also owned the manor of Clayton.[125] This was not a case where the company could have taken a circuitous route except by adding many miles to the journey. The South Downs were a formidable natural barrier and a tunnel was the most direct route. There is uncertainty as to who made the design. David Mocatta was architect to the company and designed some of the stations, but no portal elevation survives among the Mocatta drawings in the RIBA collection. According to David Cole in a paper in the *Journal of Transport History*, 1958, 'there is nothing to connect Mocatta with the elaborate castellated entrance'. He thought Mocatta, who had been classically trained under Soane, might have been unhappy with Gothic.[126] However, according to the diary of John Rastrick, the chief engineer, on 1 October 1840 he 'attended a meeting of the Directors (London & Brighton Railway) and laid a plan for the entrance of the Clayton Tunnel … which they approved'.[127] This suggests the north portal was only designed as the tunnel neared completion. Another entry in March 1842 refers to him visiting the works at Haywards Heath Station and Clayton Tunnel, suggesting that trains were running before stations and this tunnel were completed.[128] On the other hand, in 1839 Rastrick had put the whole of the contract in the hands of William Hoof, an engineer hitherto specialising in canal tunnelling.[129] It is tempting to suggest Hoof might have been responsible, just as the illusive Budden was responsible for Primrose Hill. It could, of course, have been a joint design between Hoof and Rastrick.

An undated, beautifully detailed watercolour of an unnamed portal in the Elton Collection at Bridgnorth shows Clayton Tunnel in its original state (Ill. 75). It is identical in almost every respect to the tunnel today except for the central bay between the octagonal towers, which is topped by an overhanging parapet with four slits between machicolation.[130] In 1848 £70 was granted for building a cottage over the tunnel portal between the turrets for the watchman or tunnel keeper and his family, and in 1849 conversion of the towers for use of the signalman.[131] George Measom, in his *Guide to the Brighton and South Coast Railway*, 1853, illustrates its original form without the house in situ (Ill. 41).[132] It is likely that the crenellated parapet was modified to allow the occupants more light as well as a view along the track. A stone corbel embedded in the north-east turret remains as evidence of the machicolation. The cottage may have replaced two small stone cabins on either side of the portal indicated in the watercolour, although an ink drawing by Rastrick for the octagonal chamber within the turret contains a fireplace and may have been the tunnel-keeper's original accommodation.[133] The 'arrow slit' windows in the turrets would indicate several chambers above each other. The cottage has been described as 'a rocking home to lull the keeper's children to sleep',[134] since it was said that at one time a family of eleven lived in it.[135]

The façade is of yellow brick, which from a distance looks like stone (Ill. 76). The company was able to obtain land nearby for making brick for the tunnel lining and portals. The portal is in the form of a double Gothic arch of Caen stone, the outer one of which is moulded. The flanking castellated turrets are splayed at their bases and capped with mock machicolation.[136] The grandeur of the original design as shown in the watercolour is reinforced by the trackside walls holding back the embankment, which may never have been built. In June 1841, *The Times* reported about 200 sightseers being conveyed to 'Clayton Tunnel … which will be finished in about a fortnight'.[137] When first opened the tunnel was lit by gas supplied from a retort at Merstham that also lit Merstham and Balcombe tunnels. Rastrick designed an elegant brick and stone classical building for this purpose.[138] It is not known how long this system survived as the passing trains blew the jets out. Several appliances survive in recesses within the tunnel walls.[139]

Ill. 75 **Clayton Tunnel,** north portal original elevation. *Elton Collection, Ironbridge Museum, AE.185.57*

Ill. 76 **Clayton Tunnel** north portal, as it is today with cottage built c.1850. *Author*

A little-known castellated portal is the west portal of Kirton on the former Manchester, Sheffield and Lincolnshire Railway. Opened in 1849, it is contemporary with the building of Bramhope north portal, and was probably designed by Sir John Hawkshaw, chief engineer of the line.[140] It is in red brick with sandstone ashlar dressings and has a wide facing wall with the horseshoe arch flanked by circular turrets, pierced by what may be described as 'fake' arrow loops with overemphasised machicolated parapets above. The outer walls on either side terminate in square turrets. While the eastern portal is plain and in a long cutting, and so virtually unseen, that of the west can be seen from Kirton in Lindsey Station.

There were other early ideas for ornamental portals that were inspired by the then antiquarianism and urge to both clothe the railways in respectability and perhaps satisfy a local landowner, which we have seen in Chapter 3. One of the most extraordinary must be the proposals by John Hawkshaw for Hipperholme Tunnel, Halifax, on the then West Riding Union Railway in 1840, which later became part of the Lancashire and Yorkshire. One proposal was for a pointed

Ill. 77 Clayton Tunnel north portal showing inner arch and watchman's cottage. *Author*

Gothic arch enclosing a portcullis resting on pilasters (Ill. 78). The inner bore of the tunnel was a conventional semicircular arch. A second design, perhaps for the other portal, was a Norman–Romanesque arch dressed with chevron decoration resting on a pillar and cushion capital on each side (Ill. 79). Perhaps Hawkshaw was inspired by the possible range of portal designs published by Brees in his *Railway Practice*, 1838.

By the 1860s this kind of monumental portal architecture was all but over with few exceptions. When the London, Brighton and South Coast and London, Chatham and Dover Railway companies wished to cross the Alleyn estate in south London in the 1860s they had to pay over £10,000 to the governors, and their architect, Charles Barry Junior, had to be consulted about structures, especially bridges. In the case of the often overlooked southern portal of Knights Hill Tunnel near Tulse Hill, the resulting design is impressive, in classic red brick and ashlar dressing and displaying the crest of Dulwich College.[141] However, not every landowner wished to bleed a company of its funds, sometimes there was the insistence of no more

ELEVATION

Ill. 78 Hipperholm Tunnel. *Network Rail Archive*

ELEVATION

Ill. 79 **Hipperholm Tunnel.** *Network Rail Archive*

than a stone tablet or metal plate with initials. Since the railways were here to stay, it was better to use them than oppose them, at a cost, and possibly lose. While there were still many thousands of miles to be laid, few had tunnel portals of any notable distinction. As we have seen, in the case of Stephenson and Brunel there was the need to drive the tracks in the most direct route possible, while taking account of landowners' opposition and wishes as well as the terrain. If we take the three most significant early railway systems to be the London and Birmingham, Great Western and London and Brighton, we can make a fair comparison of their handling of tunnel architecture. There were, of course, several other notable examples such as Bramhope on the Leeds and Thirsk, and Red Hill on the Midland Railway. In Scotland the crenellated portals of Killiecrankie Tunnel on the Perth and Inverness Railway by the engineer Joseph Mitchell, built in 1863, are perhaps one of the last ornamental railway tunnel portals in Britain (Ill. 80).[142]

Ill. 80 **Killiecrankie Tunnel** south portal. *Railway Heritage Trust*

THE COST, A NECESSARY ARCHITECTURAL EXTRAVAGANCE?

Were the examples described in detail – in other words the 'classic examples' – a costly extravagance, or did they add little to the overall cost of a project? After all, with tunnelling, the cost is estimated on time to be taken to completion, length of bore and basic materials needed including brick or stone. Lists of items for construction in company accounts do not include labour costs, which would be in addition (see Appendix 4). Permanent staff such as resident engineers would have a fixed salary, but not casual or seasonal labour, which might be increased depending on nature or speed of work. Cost was in any case governed by factors that were not necessarily apparent at the commencement of work such as the presence of water. Drysdale Dempsey, in his *Practical Railway Engineer,* 1855, gave several examples of cost: Kilsby estimate £40 per linear yard, actual £130; Box £100 per linear yard, Bletchingley £72 per linear yard; Saltwood, £118 per linear yard. Saltwood was the shortest at less than a third of the length of Kilsby, yet because of the waterlogged lower greensand, cost almost as much.[143]

If Brunel can be said to have put a sense of the 'great' into his tunnels, it was for other companies to follow or surpass if money allowed. It is perhaps worth examining the cost of just one example of monumental portals of which the cost can only be approximate; those of Bramhope, opened in 1849. Here at the north end, as we have seen, the castellated style reached its most impressive. We may gain a fair idea of basic cost for the two portals in the accounts up to October 1849.[144] The castellated northern portal cost £1,345 9s 6d – cheap compared with Box west portal at £5,283.[145] The flanking wing towers seem to have been more than just ornamental, and the circular larger one was intended to serve as a tunnel keeper's office with stone-flagged floors and lathe and plaster ceilings between floors. There were also additional costs involved in the portals, or 'entrances' as they are termed in the contract. At the north end these include for building a wall at 'Mr Rhodes' orchard' as well as for fence walling 'over the Bramhope Tunnel, £212 9s. 0d'.[146] The south portal in the classical style came to about £509, which may seem cheap compared with the east portal of Box at over £1,324. It was constructed of stone extracted from the working and so was on site, but here were additional costs, for example filling in and levelling the earth over the south entrance, '43,344 cubic yards, £1,213 7s 1d'.[147] So the overall cost was £3,280 5s 7d for work on the two portals.[148]

So was this all unnecessary extravagance? Given that the railway was a new form of transport involving, at its crudest, the haulage of humans by a machine belching smoke and fire from its boiler and perhaps exploding if treated wrongly, it could easily arouse fear in the anxious travellers. To allow themselves to be hauled into what seemed a huge and dark cavern needed trust. A well-constructed and ornamented portal could at least allay the fear of further horror through possible structural collapse of the tunnel beyond. The early portals therefore can be seen as statements by the companies of confidence in this new form of transport, perhaps, in certain instances, designed in accordance with the wishes of a nearby landowner. When new, and perhaps for a very short period before opening, with gleaming stone faces of local hue, they would have been attractive to the observer, even if he

Ill. 81 **Crystal Palace** Tunnel, sometimes known as Paxton's tunnel. *Author*

had no desire to venture inside. By the 1870s the railways were established, and tunnels of ever-increasing length were cut and accepted by most of the travelling public. While there had been crashes and fatalities in them, none had collapsed. Companies, increasingly in competition with each other, now turned to a more simple, if dignified portal, whose function was simply the elementary one to pin the hillside back, rather than to inspire confidence in fledgling passengers.

Sadly Londoners cannot saunter out on a summer's evening with their children and dogs to admire the classical portal of Primrose Hill Tunnel because it is now hidden by private gardens, but they can admire the Italianate portal of the appropriately named Paxton Tunnel on the former short branch of the Crystal Palace and South London Railway Company, now a car park. Treated with brick bands of different colours, it would look even more attractive if a more suitable cast iron grille could be designed for the arch.

Chapter 7
POSTSCRIPT

The age of heroic railway construction is over in which long tunnels and cuttings are dug by hand. The words of Victorian writers likening the achievements of the engineers and labourers to the ancient Romans or even the Egyptians seem by the standards of modern times to be very valid. We have moved from the age of the spade and shovel and horse-drawn wagons of spoil to a time of machines. This involved the production of millions of bricks for the tunnel lining let alone the bridges and viaducts that were the features of every main line. Tunnelling techniques were improved with the invention of a protective rectangular shield or casing of iron by Marc Brunel for the construction of the Thames Tunnel between 1825 and 1843. In spite of this the workings were flooded, holding up construction of what became the world's first subterranean tunnel for several years, and almost forced the project to be abandoned. Completed as a foot tunnel, it was converted to take the East London Railway between 1865 and 1869. It was originally brick lined but has been faced in concrete during restoration between 1998 and 2007.

The digging of the deep-level London underground system from the last decade of the nineteenth century marked the beginning of a new age in tunnelling. Improved tunnelling shields and especially the circular tunnelling shield invented by James Henry Greathead speeded up the whole process of tunnelling and was first used on the Tower Subway under the Thames in 1870, and a few years later on the first deep-level underground line in the world, the City and South London Railway. Tunnels were lined with steel casing bolted together to form a continuous underground pipe. No longer were millions of bricks needed and the labour force was lower. The last major railway to be built involving major brick-lined tunnelling was the Great Central from Nottingham to Marylebone Station in London, opened in 1899.

Now we have moved to another stage with huge boring machines that can cut the soil or rock face with an immediate follow-up system of precast concrete sheets being slotted into place to form the casing or walls of the tunnel. The spoil is sent back from the face of the excavation on huge conveyor belts to trucks waiting on the already constructed hard tunnel floor. So the speed of cutting has moved dramatically from 8ft per week on Brunel's Thames Tunnel to hundreds of yards. Another method was to encase the rock or earth face in a wire mesh frame and spray it with liquid concrete, a technique developed in America in the early 1900s and known as shotcrete.

The first major reinforced concrete-lined tunnel was the Maas tunnel in Rotterdam built between 1937 and 1942. It was built in steel sections in a dry dock and sunk into a trench cut into the river bed. These sections in effect formed a subterranean tube that was then covered with concrete. This was about one hundred years after the world's first successful tunnel beneath a river, Marc Brunel's Thames Tunnel beneath the Thames between Rotherhithe and Wapping opened in 1844.

This had been exploited on the continent of Europe with the cutting of high-speed lines in Germany and France involving extensive tunnelling and some of considerable length. This also applied to road tunnels and even large sewers such as the new Thames Super Sewer over 20 miles long under London and due to come into service in 2025. To a certain extent the achievement of cutting a tunnel under the English Channel between 1988 and 1993 to serve Britain's first high-speed service known as Eurostar was to eclipse everything that had gone before, although this achievement was marked by greater publicity and acclaim on the Continent. Now we see the cutting of long tunnels under north London and the Chiltern Hills to accommodate HS2.

Unfortunately the great age of railway building came several decades before the advent of photography, or at least when the camera could have been used to record the magnitude of such projects, involving armies of men, thousands strong; at Box, up to 4,000 men descending on the countryside. That the engineering of the London and Birmingham Railway was likened to the building of the Pyramids might seem to us exaggeration, as few of us when travelling through those many yards of darkness remember that this void in the earth or rock surface was cut by labourers with pick and shovel aided by periodic charges of gunpowder. Photographs do survive on the Settle and Carlisle section of the Midland of this large undertaking in the wildest and most inhospitable region in England. Here the workers were accommodated in shanty towns such as the one created at Ribble Head for the building of the large viaduct and nearby tunnel.

Where possible the surveyors chose the easiest route through a hillside because of the initial digging of shafts and rarely went above 300ft in depth, but under the Pennines the depth was up to 600ft, a frightening experience for those labourers being lowered into the candlelit gloom. Writers have compared the excavation for the railways in the 1830s and '40s to the motorway revolution in Britain in the 1960s and '70s, but that was done by machinery and is well documented by photography.

The advantage of modern concrete-lined tunnels is immediately apparent in that the maintenance needs are lower. Brick-lined tunnels are susceptible to damp and water seepage, and in the worst case flooding. A notorious example is Chipping Sodbury Tunnel, Gloucestershire, on the former Great Western Railway beneath the grounds of Badminton House, constructed between 1897 and 1902, which hit an underground aquifer and has proved a problem ever since. As we have seen, landowners could be very powerful in the early history of railway construction and the cost had to be weighed up of a costly detour or burrowing underground. At Shugborough there was an eventual compromise, to pay the Earl of Lichfield compensation to be allowed to burrow beneath his park, renowned for its ornamental classical features, including the 'Arch of Hadrian'. The portals were designed to add an additional feature to the surrounding landscape. At Littlebury

Tunnel on the Eastern Counties Railway the line was forced to tunnel by Lord Braybrooke of nearby Audley End, who even insisted the south portal bore his coat of arms and Tudor rose mouldings around one of the ornamental bands of the arch. It is grade II listed.

An ever-present danger is the movement of brickwork due to cracking, which if not immediately checked could lead to collapse. The fall of rock in the unlined sections of the Box Tunnel did in fact cause the tunnel to be closed for a time during the First World War. All the tunnels featured in my book 'if still in use' demand constant inspection. Even those on lines now closed have to be maintained and periodically inspected. Ironically, the oldest tunnel through which fare-paying passengers were conveyed, that of Tyler Hill on the former Canterbury and Whitstable Railway, partially collapsed in 1974, causing a building above in the University of Kent to also fall down. There have been proposals to restore it as part of a long-distance pathway and cycle track. This has happened with the former Combe Down Tunnel near Bath on the former Somerset and Dorset Railway. Other former tunnels in the Derbyshire Peak District have also been converted to cycle and footpaths and, of course lit, throughout. Walking through tunnels was often a pleasure to those who welcomed the railways in the 1820s and '30s. Fanny Kemble's visit to the Thames Tunnel in 1827 was not one to a demonic world like the description of Box, but one with 'lanterns flashing' along the 'beautiful road to Hades'.[1] Those first walkers through the gas-lit tunnels at Liverpool in 1830 must have been in awe with the effect of flickering lights on the clean brick walls. Brunel's tunnels between Bath and Bristol were open for pedestrians before the railway service started in 1838.

A tunnel on a vintage railway provides an added attraction and excitement to the journey, especially for children; notable examples but of no great length are to be found on the Bluebell Railway in Sussex, and the Severn Valley Railway near Kidderminster. They do, however, add to the yearly cost of the upkeep of the railway's fabric and are subject to the same stringent periodic structural examination as those on the main system.

As I have emphasised, many tunnels are not easy to see as they are along deep cuttings, but notable exceptions are Box west portal and Middle Hill in Wiltshire, both grade II* listed, and Clayton north portal in Sussex, grade II listed. The primary purpose of a portal was to provide entry to the tunnel as well as stabilising the structure of the hillside behind. Some, such as the castellated north portal of Bramhope Tunnel, are in need of costly restoration even though Bramhope is a grade II listed structure. The two portals at Tyler Hill, Canterbury, are grade II* listed but in need of dramatic conservation. Here it is not their aesthetic quality but their historical significance that justified this listing. Sometimes the ventilation shafts are as notable as the portals, especially if they are castellated, although many are simple circular towers of brick with wire netting across the aperture at the top. Sometimes they may be the only indication of a tunnel beneath and were created as ornamental features in the landscape to satisfy local landowners. The shafts at Kilsby in Northamptonshire seen from the nearby motorway and featured in the book are the largest of any tunnel and have a crenellated parapet. The two shafts are grade II* listed. Another feature similar to a shaft were sighting towers at the highest points of the ground above a tunnel so the line of construction beneath could be kept true. Two survive at Bramhope, grade II listed, and another at Mersham in Surrey.

This study has attempted to set the railway tunnel in the wider context of the traveller's experience as well as those under whose land they penetrated. To enter a tunnel was to experience a new type of space hewn out by the labours of man on a scale never undertaken before, and in conditions rivalling Dante's *Inferno*, which invoked fear for some, yet brought others the thrill of a new dimension of the technological sublime. And some portals were, as we have seen, on a scale or size much larger than the portal of a lodge or even a triumphal arch. The darkness within could excite or instil fear, yet the style and ornamentation at its grandest such as at Primrose Hill made them structures of considerable beauty.

GLOSSARY OF RAILWAY COMPANIES AND ABBREVIATIONS

Abbreviation	Full name
B&ER	Bristol & Exeter Railway
CALR	Caledonian Railway
C&H	Chester & Holyhead Railway
CR	Cheshire Railway
ECR	Eastern Counties Railway
ELR	East Lancashire Railway
GNR	Great Northern Railway
GWR	Great Western Railway
L&YR	Lancashire & Yorkshire Railway
L&BR	London & Birmingham Railway
L&BtonR	London & Brighton Railway
LBSCR	London, Brighton & South Coast Railway
LCDR	London, Chatham & Dover Railway
LNWR	London & North Western Railway
LSER	London & South Eastern Railway
LSWR	London & South Western Railway
L&TR	Leeds & Thirsk Railway
M&BR	Manchester & Birmingham Railway
M&LR	Manchester & Leeds Railway
MS&LR	Manchester, Sheffield & Lincolnshire Railway
MR	Midland Railway
NBR	North British Railway
NMR	North Midland Railway
P&IR	Perth & Inverness Railway
SEBL&NR	South Eastern, Brighton, Lewis & Newhaven Railway
TVR	Trent Valley Railway

Appendix 1
ARCHITECTURAL TERMINOLOGY

TUNNEL PORTALS

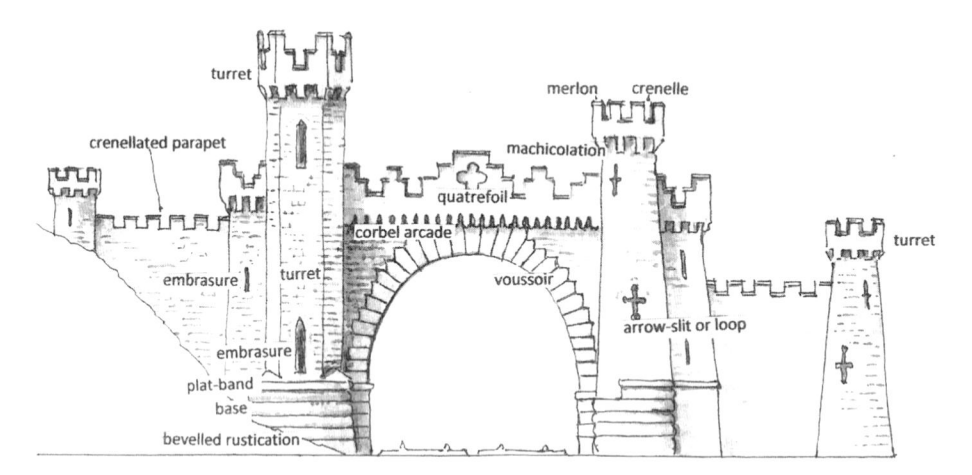

Red Hill Tunnel north portal 1840
castellated

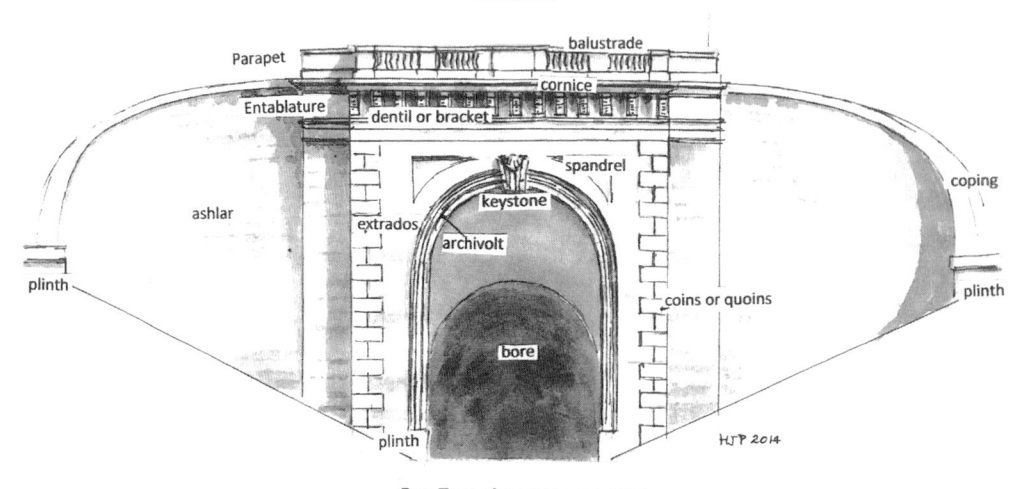

Labels: turret, crenellated parapet, merlon, crenelle, machicolation, quatrefoil, corbel arcade, voussoir, embrasure, turret, arrow-slit or loop, embrasure, plat-band, base, bevelled rustication

Box Tunnel west portal 1841

Labels: Parapet, balustrade, Entablature, cornice, dentil or bracket, spandrel, keystone, ashlar, extrados, archivolt, coping, plinth, coins or quoins, bore, plinth

ARCHITECTURAL TERMINOLOGY • 221

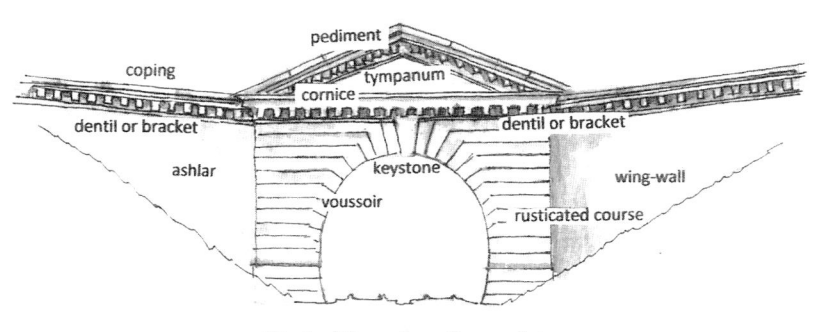

Watford Tunnel south portal 1837
classical

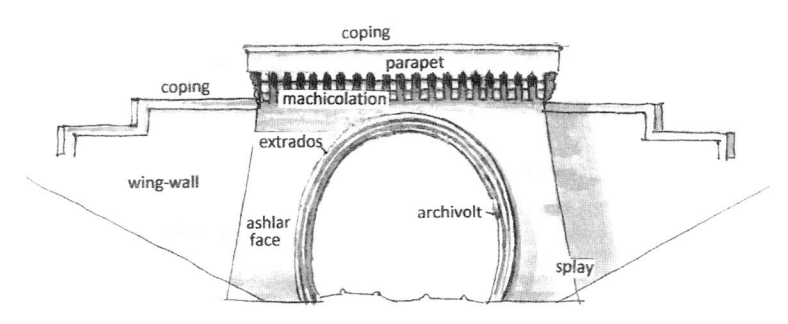

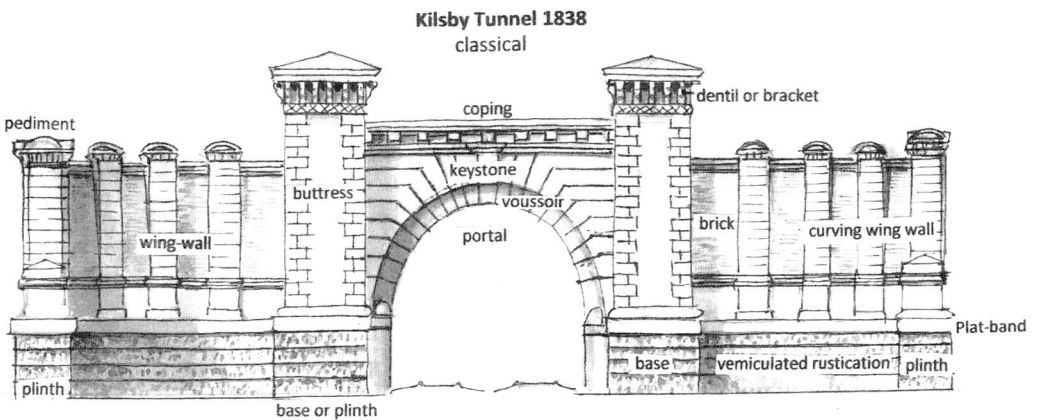

Labels: pediment, coping, tympanum, cornice, dentil or bracket, ashlar, keystone, voussoir, wing-wall, rusticated course

Kilsby Tunnel 1838
classical

Labels: coping, parapet, machicolation, coping, wing-wall, extrados, ashlar face, archivolt, splay

Primrose Hill east portal 1838
classical

Labels: pediment, wing-wall, buttress, coping, keystone, voussoir, portal, dentil or bracket, brick, curving wing wall, Plat-band, base, vermiculated rustication, plinth, base or plinth

HJP 2014

222 • THE EARLY HISTORY OF RAILWAY TUNNELS

Linslade Tunnel, London & Birmingham, & London & North Western Railway

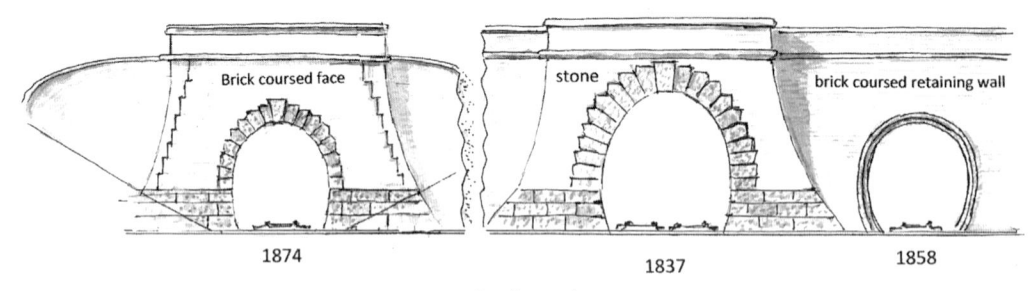

Brick coursed face — 1874
stone — 1837
brick coursed retaining wall — 1858

South portals

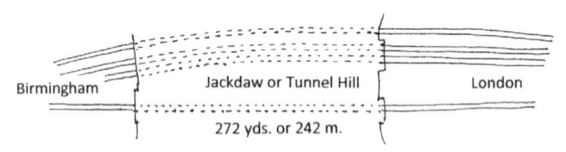

Birmingham — Jackdaw or Tunnel Hill — London
272 yds. or 242 m.

Route of tunnel beneath wood.

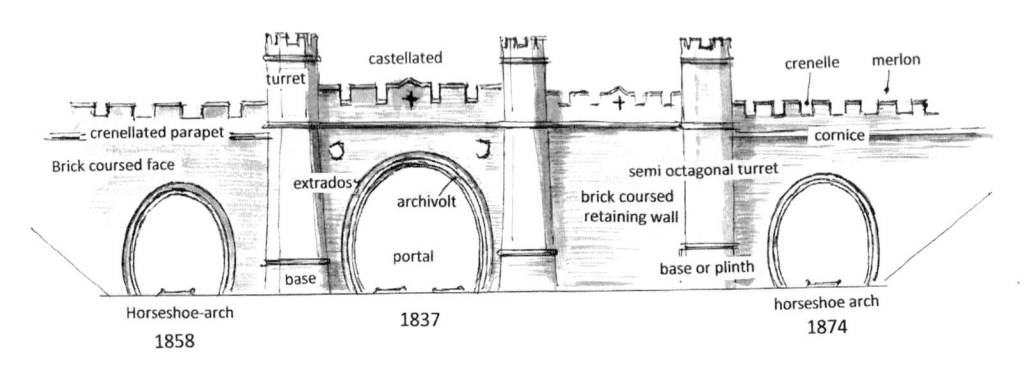

castellated turret — crenelle — merlon
crenellated parapet — cornice
Brick coursed face
extrados
archivolt
semi octagonal turret
brick coursed retaining wall
portal
base
base or plinth

Horseshoe-arch 1858 — 1837 — horseshoe arch 1874

North portals

TUNNEL PORTALS ARCHITECTURAL TERMINOLOGY

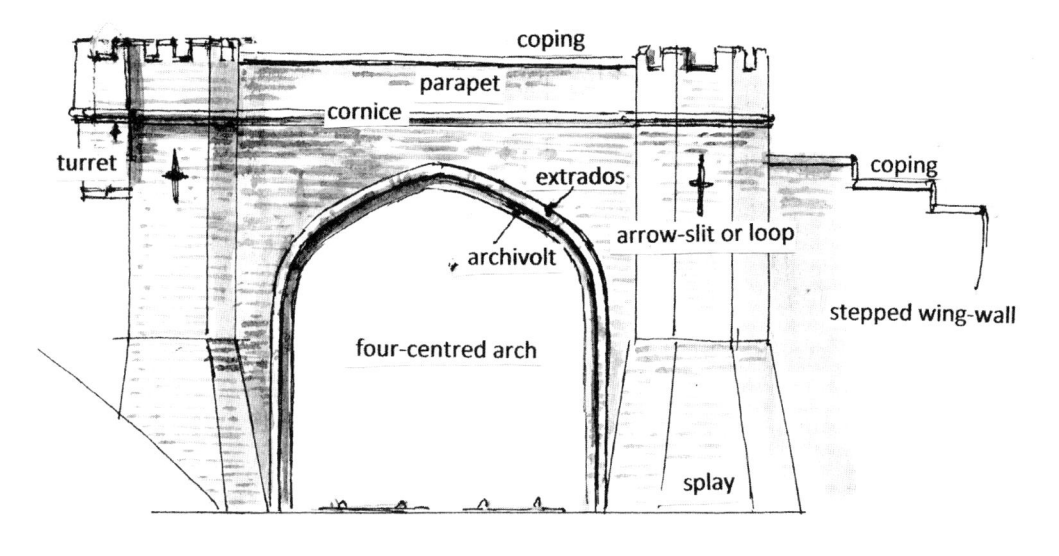

Labels on diagram: turret, cornice, parapet, coping, extrados, archivolt, arrow-slit or loop, coping, stepped wing-wall, four-centred arch, splay

Twerton short tunnel 1838

Appendix 2
TUNNEL PORTALS WITH DISTINCTIVE ARCHITECTURAL CHARACTER

Tunnel Name	Railway Company	Position	Style	Date of Tunnel Opening
Primrose Hill	L&BR	East portal	Italianate classical	1838
Watford	L&BR	Portal	Classical	1838
Linslade	L&BR	North & south portals	Classical & Gothic	1838
Kilsby	L&BR	North & south portals	Classical	1838
Milford	MR	North & south portals	Classical	1840
Toad Moor	NMR	North & south portals	Classical elliptical	1840
Clay Cross	NMR	North portal	Castellated	1840
Red Hill, Trent	MR	North & south portals	Castellated	1840
Elland	M&LR	West portal	Classical	1840
Summit/Littleborough	M&LR	West portal	Classical	1840
Twerton	GWR	East & west portals	Castellated Gothic	1840
Tunnel No. 1	GWR	West portal	Romanesque	1840
Middle Hill	GWR	East & west portals	Classical	1841
Box	GWR	West portal	Classical	1841

TUNNEL PORTALS WITH DISTINCTIVE ARCHITECTURAL CHARACTER

Tunnel Name	Railway Company	Position	Style	Date of Tunnel Opening
Clayton	LBSCR	North portal	Castellated Gothic	1841
Shakespeare Cliff	LCDR	East & west portals	Gothic lancet arches	1844
Bangor	LNWR	East portal	Egyptian	1844
Prestbury	M&BR	South portal	Classical	1845
Tunbridge Wells	LSER	South portal	Italianate	1845
Wansford	L&BR	East portal	Romanesque	1845
Nuttall	ELR	South portal	Castellated	1846
Shugborough	LNWR	North & south portals	Romanesque & classical	1847
Sough	ELR	North portal	Castellated	1848
Beacon Hill	GNR	West portal	Romanesque	1849
Branhope	L&TR	North portal	Castellated	1849
Kirton	MS&LR	West portal	Castellated Gothic	1849
Gisburn	L&YR	East & west portals	Castellated	1850
Killiecrankie	P&IR	North & south portals	Castellated	1863

Appendix 3
ACCIDENTS IN TUNNELS 1830–70 REPORTED TO THE BOARD OF TRADE OR IN THE PRESS

N.B. The notification of an incident or accident did not necessarily result in a formally published report. For some incidents, no documents survive; the number of fatalities and injured may therefore be higher.

Ref. Railway Archives, www.railwayarchive.co.uk

Date	Location	Railway Co.	Cause	Date	Fatalities	Injured
1839	Chalk Farm Tunnel ?	L&BR	Collision	11 Jan	0	5
1839	Beechwood Tunnel	L&BR	Derailment	1 Aug	0	4
1840	Claycross Tunnel	NMR	Stalling	?	0	0
1841	Box Tunnel	GWR	Stalling	?	0	0
1842	Waller's Ash Tunnel	LSWR	Minor collapse	2 Apr	4	?
"	"	"	Derailment	4 Apr	0	0
1843	Summit Tunnel	M&SR	Derailment	?	0	0
"	Clayton Tunnel	L&BtonR	No information	?	0	0
1844	Claycross Tunnel	[N]MR	Collision	29 Mar	0	0
1845	Clayton Tunnel	L&BtonR	Collision	8 Sep	0	0
1847	Kilsby Tunnel	LNWR	Derailment	30 Mar	0	0
1849	Walton Tunnel	L&YR	Collision	26 Nov	0	0

ACCIDENTS IN TUNNELS 1830–70 REPORTED TO THE BOARD OF TRADE

Date	Location	Railway Co.	Cause	Date	Fatalities	Injured
1850	Blackheath Tunnel	SER	Stalling	Jan	0	0
"	"	"	"	15 July	0	0
"	Primrose Hill Tunnel	LNWR	Derailment	7 Dec	0	4
1851	Sutton Tunnel, Frodsham	CR	Collision	30 Apr	9	30+
"	Brislington Tunnel	GWR	Mechanical failure	10 Aug	0	7
"	Cranberry Moss Tunnel (now known as Sough Tunnel)	ELR	Collision	21 Oct	0	1
1852	Perth Tunnel	P&IR	Collision	26 Aug	0	1
1853	Guildford Tunnel	LSWR	Collision	19 Jun	0?	0?
"	Bletchingley Tunnel	SER	Derailment	18 Jul	0?	0?
"	Stoke Tunnel	GNR	Collision	14 Dec	0?	0?
1854	Welwyn North Tunnel	GNR	Collision	19 Jan	2	0
"	Stockport Tunnel	LNWR	Collision	27 Feb	0	0
"	Stoke Tunnel	GNR	Collision	7 Mar	0	0
"	Clarborough Tunnel	M&SR	Collision	11 Apr	2	0
"	Bramhope Tunnel	L&TR	Partial collapse	19 Sep	0	0?
"	Stowe Hill Tunnel	LNWR	Collision	30 Sep	0	0
"	Calton Hill	NBR	Collision	7 Dec	1	0
1855	Strood Tunnel	SER	?	4 Jan	0	4
"	King's Cross Tunnel	GNR	Wheel failure	18 Jan	0	0
"	Summit Tunnel	L&YR	Collision	19 Aug	0?	0?

Date	Location	Railway Co.	Cause	Date	Fatalities	Injured
"	Whiteball Tunnel	GWR	Collision	2 Oct	0?	0?
"	Sapperton Tunnel	GWR	Train-split	29 Oct	0	0?
1857	Shugborough Tunnel	LNW Rly	Collision	1 Jan	0?	0?
"	Cambridge Batch Tunnel	B&ER	Collision	12 Oct	0	1
1859	Bowling Tunnel	L&YR	Collision	12 May	0	8
"	Bishopston Tunnel	Cal R	Collision	16 Jul	1	9
"	Bangor Tunnel	C&HR	Collision	15 Oct	0	0
1861	Primrose Hill Tunnel	LNWR	Derailment	4 Jan	1	?
"	Stroud Tunnel	SER	Derailment/ collision with structure	13 Jul	1	0
"	Clayton Tunnel	L&BtonR	Collision	25 Aug	23	176
1862	Chatham Hill Tunnel	LCDR	Collision	9 Jun	0	0?
1864	Blackheath Tunnel	SER	Collision	16 Dec	5	0?
1865	Ripchester Tunnel	L&YR	Collision	5 Oct	0	0
"	Clarborough Tunnel	M&SR	Collision	14 Nov	0	4
"	Blackboy Tunnel	LSWR	Partial collapse of tunnel	25 Nov	0	1
1866	Watford Tunnel	LNWR	?	21 May	0	0
"	Welwyn Tunnel	GNR	Derailment	9 Jun	2	2

Date	Location	Railway Co.	Cause	Date	Fatalities	Injured
1867	Watford Tunnel	LNWR	Derailment	6 Mar	0	7
"	Bowling Tunnel	L&WR	Collision	Mar	2	22
"	North Shields Tunnel	GNR	Derailment	6 Mar	0	7
"	Peak Forest Tunnel	MR	Collision	? Sep	5	5
"	Dove Hole Tunnel	MR	Collision	9 Sep	5	5
1868	Penge Tunnel	LCDR	Derailment	6 Jan	0	0
"	Diggle Tunnel	LNWR	Signalling error/ collision	19 Oct	0	0?
1869	Copenhagen Tunnel	GNR	Train misrouted	18 Jan	0	0
"	Lockwood Tunnel	L&YR	Collision	17 Mar	0	3
"	Colwyn Tunnel	LNWR	Collision	16 Jul	0?	0?
"	Glasgow Tunnel	NBR	Collision	23 Nov	0?	0?
1870	Watford Tunnel	LNWR	Collision	26 Nov	0?	0?
"	Guiseley Tunnel	MR	Collision	31 Dec	0?	0?
Total					63	305

Appendix 4
COST OF CONSTRUCTION

Box Tunnel				
RAIL 252/1 Box Tunnel contract No. 6, between 3 April 1840 & 11 Nov. 1841				
Location	£	Shillings	Pence	£2005 Value
East portal	1,324	14	3	77,535.42
West portal	5,283	1	4	2,984,569.19

Bramhope Tunnel				
RAIL 357/30 Leeds & Thirsk Railway: Bramhope contract, No. 18 from commencement to 12 Oct. 1849				
Location	£	Shillings	Pence	£2005 Value
South portal	509	0	0	27,791.77
North portal	1,345	9	6	78,751.38
Earth moving at south portal	1,213	7	1	70,017.62
Fencing and walling at north end	212	9	0	12,434.70

Primrose Hill Tunnel				
The Times 14 July 1837; *John Bull*, 17 July 1837				
Location	£	Shillings	Pence	£2005 Value
East portal	7,000	0	0	£3,954,518. 40p

BIBLIOGRAPHY

UNPUBLISHED PRIMARY SOURCES
Brunel Archive, University of Bristol.
Elton Collection, Ironbridge Museum, Coalbrookdale.
National Archives: RAIL.
Network Rail Archive, York.
Staffordshire & Stoke-on-Trent Record Office, Stafford.
Anson family archive.
Parliamentary Archives, House of Lords.
University of London, Goldsmiths Library (Special collections), Senate House.
Rastrick papers.
Wiltshire County Archives, Chippenham.

PUBLISHED PRIMARY SOURCES: BOOKS
Arnott, Dr Neil. *Warming and Ventilation.* London: J. & A. Churchill, 1838.
Bayne, A.D. *A Royal History of Eastern England.* Great Yarmouth: James Macdonald, 1873.
Bradbury, Edward. *Midland Railway Sketches.* Derby and London: Bemrose, 1879; reprinted by Midland Railway Society, Sheffield, 1999.
Blackmore, John. *Views on the Newcastle and Carlisle Railway, from Original Drawings by John Blackmore.* Newcastle upon Tyne: Currie & Bowman, & C. Tite, London: 1836; reprinted by Frank Graham, Newcastle upon Tyne, 1969.
Bradshaw, John. *Bradshaw's Handbook.* London: 1863: reprinted, Oxford: Old House, Botley, 2012.
Bourne, James Cook. *The London and Birmingham Railway.* London: James Cook Bourne, 1839.
Bourne, James Cook. *The Great Western Railway,* London: Tite & Bogue, 1846.
Brees, Samuel Charles. *Railway Practice,* 4 vols. London: J. Williams, 1837–47.
Booth, Henry. *An Account of the Liverpool and Manchester Railway.* Liverpool: Wales & Barnes, Liverpool, 1830, reprinted 1969.
Brunel, I.. *Life of Isambard Kingdom Brunel.* London: Longman Green, 1870.
Burke, Edmund. *A Philosophical Enquiry into the Origins of Our Ideas of the Sublime and the Beautiful,* 1757, edited by James Boulton, Oxford: Blackwells, 1998.
Bury, Thomas Talbot. *Views on the Liverpool and Manchester Railway.* London: Ackermann, 1831.
Churton, Edward. *The Rail Road Book of England.* London: Edward Churton Publisher, 1851; reprinted, London: Sidgwick & Jackson, 1973.
Cole, Henry. *Railway Chronicle Travelling Chart, No. 1, London-Wolverton-Birmingham.* London: Railway Chronicle, Wellington Street, Strand, 1846.

Coghlan, Francis. *Coghlan's Iron Road Book: London, Birmingham and Liverpool Railway Companion.* London: A.H. Baily & Co., 1838.
Croker, John Wilson. *The Croker Papers.* London: John Murray, 1884.
Cundy, N.W. *Observations on Railways, addressed to the Nobility, Gentry, Clergy, Agriculturalists, and particularly to those situated on the line and connected with the Great Northern & Eastern Railway.* Great Yarmouth: J. Palmer, 1834.
Dorchester, Lady. *Recollections of a Long Life, Letters and Diaries of 1st Lord Broughton, 1786–1869.* John Murray: London, 1910.
Devey, Joseph. *Life of Joseph Locke, Civil Engineer.* London: Richard Bentley, 1862.
Delme-Radcliffe, F.P. *The Noble Science, A few general Ideas on Foxhunting,* London: G. Routledge & Sons, 1839.
Drake, James. *Drake's Road Book of the Grand Junction and London and Birmingham Railway.* London: Hayward & Moore, 1839.
Drysdale, Dempsey G. *The Practical Railway Engineer.* London: John Weale, 1855.
Francis, John. *A History of the English Railway 1820–45.* London: Longman Brown, Green & Longman, 1857.
Freeling, Arthur. *Freeling's Railway Companion for the London, Birmingham and Liverpool and Manchester Railway.* London: Whittaker & Company, 1838.
Gale, Thomas. *A Brief Account of Making and Working of the Great Box Tunnel.* Cheltenham: private publisher, 1884.
Godwin, George. *An Appeal to the Public on the Subject of Railways.* London: J. Weale, 1837.
Gooch, Daniel. *Memoirs and Diary.* Edited by Roger Burdett Wilson, Newton Abbot: David & Charles, 1972.
Goodrich, S.G. *Peter Parley's Annual.* Boston US: S.G. Goodrich, 1840.
Gray, Thomas. *Observations on a General Railway, showing a Great Superiority over our Present Means of Conveyance.* London: Baldwin, Craddock and Joy, 1825.
Greville, George. *Memoirs of Four Reigns,* 2nd ed. London: Longman Green, 1875.
A Handbook for Travellers along the London and Birmingham Railway. London, R Groombridge, 1839.
Head, F.B. *Stokers and Pokers on the London & North Western Railway.* London: John Murray, 1849; reprinted Newton Abbot: David & Charles, 1968.
Head, Sir George. *A Home Tour through the Manufacturing Districts of England.* London: John Murray, London, 1835.
Jeaffreson, J.C. *Life of Robert Stephenson.* London: Longman, 1864.
Jobbins, J.B. *Jobbins' Guide to the London and Brighton Railway.* London: Jobbins, 1841.
Kemble, Frances Ann. *Memoirs of a Childhood.* Vols. 1 & 2. London: R. Bentley & Son, 1878.
Kohl, J.G. *The King of Saxony's Journey through England and Scotland in the Year 1844.* London: Chapman and Hall, 1846.
Lecount, Peter. *History of the Railway connecting London and Birmingham.* London: Simpkin Marshall, 1839.
Lecount, Peter. *A Practical Treatise on Railways.* Edinburgh: A. & C. Black, 1839.
Measom, George. *The Illustrated Guide to the Great Western Railway,* London: Richard Griffin, 1852; facsimile, Oxford: Oxford Illustrated Press, 1983.

Measom, George. *The Illustrated Guide to the Great Northern, Manchester, Sheffield, and Lincolnshire and Midland Railway*. London: Griffin, Bohn & Co., 1861.
Measom, George. *The Illustrated Guide to the London and South Eastern Railway*. London: W.H. Smith & Son, 1853; facsimile 1987.
Measom, George. *The Illustrated Guide to the Brighton and South Coast Railway*. London: H.G. Collins, 1853.
Moritz, Charles Philip. *Travels in England, 1782*. London: Humphrey Milford, Oxford University Press, 1924.
Mudge, Richard Z. *Observations on Railways with Reference to Utility, Profits and Obvious Necessity*. London: James Gardner, 1837.
Nottingham and Derby Railway Companion. London: Hamilton Adams & Co., 1839.
Ogan, Alfred. *Rail Collisions Prevented*. London: G.T. Pope, 1855.
Osbaldeston, George. *Autobiography, 1786–1866*. London: John Lane, The Bodley Head, 1926.
Osborne, E.C. *Guide to the London and Birmingham Railway*. Birmingham: E.C. & W. Osborne, 1838.
Parry, E. *Parry's Railway Companion from Chester to Holyhead*. Chester: Thomas Catherall, 1852.
Personal Records of English Engineers, and of the Introduction of the Railway System in Great Britain. By a Civil Engineer. London: Hodder & Stoughton, 1868.
Peters, William. *Railway Dangers and How to Avoid Them*. London: Effingham Wilson, 1853.
Pugin, A.W. *An Apology for the Revival of Christian Architecture in England*. London: John Weale, 1843.
Queen Victoria's Letters 1837–61, edited by A.C. Benson and V. Esher. London: John Murray, 1908.
Railway Traveller's Handbook. London: Lockwood & Co., 1862; republished Oxford: Old House, Botley, 2011.
Roney, Cusack P. *Rambles on Railways with Maps, Diagrams and Appendices*. London: Effingham Wilson, 1862.
Roscoe, Thomas. *Guide to the London and Birmingham Railway*. London: Charles Tilt, 1839.
Roscoe, Thomas. *Home and Country Scenes on each Side of the Line of the London and Birmingham Railway*. London: Charles Tilt, 1840.
Sidney, Samuel. *Rides on Railways*. London: William Orr & Son, 1851; reprinted with introduction by Barrie Trinder, Chichester: Phillimore & Co., 1973.
Simms, F.W. *Public Works in Great Britain*. London: John Weale Architectural Library, 1838.
Simms, F.W. *Practical Tunnelling*. London: Crosby Lockwood, 1844; 3rd ed. 1896.
Smiles, Samuel. *The Story of the Life of George Stephenson*. London: John Murray, 1857.
Stephenson, R.L. *Edinburgh Picturesque Notes*. London: Seeley & Co., 1878.
Stevens, Henry. *Sunday Traffic on the London and Brighton Railway; an Appeal to the Directors against their Efforts to Obtain Sunday Traffic*. London: Seeley & Co., 1863.
Tate, A.F. *Views on the Manchester and Leeds Railway*. Liverpool: A.F. Tait, 1845.
The Railway Traveller's Handbook, 1862. reprinted, Oxford: Old House, Botley, 2012.

Walpole, Horace. *The Castle of Otranto*. London: William Bath, 1811.
Whishaw, Francis. *Analysis of Railways and Projected Railways of England and Wales*. London: John Weale, 1837.
Wishaw, Francis. *The Railways of Great Britain and Ireland*. London: John Weale, 1842, reprinted Newton Abbot: David & Charles, 1970.
Williams, Frederick S. *Our Iron Road*, London: Ingram Cook & Co., 1855; republished London: Cass Library of Railway Classics, 1968.
Williams, Frederick S. *The Midland Railway, its Rise and Progress. A Narrative of Modern Enterprise*. London: Strahan & Co., 1876; reprinted Cambridge: Library Collection, 1968.
Williams, Peter. *Railway Dangers*. London: Effingham Wilson, 1853.
Woodward, George and Isaac Cruickshank. *Eccentric Excursions or Literary and Practical Sketches in England, Wales* ... London: Allen & West, 1797.
Wyld, J.W.W. *The London and Birmingham Railway Guide and Companion*. London: J. Wyld, 1838.

SECONDARY SOURCES: BOOKS

Allen, Cecil J. *The Great Eastern Railway*. Shepperton: Ian Allan, 1967.
Anderson, Roy. *A Pictorial Record of LMS Architecture*. Oxford: OPC, 1981.
Andrews, Malcolm, *The Search for the Picturesque*. Aldershot: Scholar Press, 1982.
Atkinson, Alan A. *London's Termini*, Newton Abbot: David & Charles. 1969.
Aston, Michael and James Bond. *The Landscape of Towns*. Stroud: Alan Sutton, 2000.
Awdry, Christopher. *Brunel's Broad Gauge Railway*. Oxford: Oxford Publishing Company, 1992.
Bailey, Michael. *Robert Stephenson – the Eminent Engineer. London:* ICE, 2003.
Barman, Christian. *Early British Railways*. London: Penguin Books, 1950.
Barman, Christian. *Introduction to Railway Architecture*. London: Art & Technics, 1950.
Barnes, E.G. *The Rise of the Midland Railway 1844–1874*. London: George Allen & Unwin, 1966.
Baugham, Peter. *The Chester & Holyhead Railway*. Newton Abbot: David & Charles, 1972.
Beckles-Wilson, Anthony. *Alexander Pope's Grotto at Twickenham*. Twickenham Museum, 1998.
Bennett, Alfred Rosling. *The First Railway in London*. London: Locomotive Publishing Company, 1912; reprinted Newton Abbot: David & Charles, 1971.
Biddle, Gordon. *Railways, their Builders and the Environment, Essays in Honour of Jack Simmons*. London: Ashgate, 2003.
Biddle, Gordon and O.S. Nock. *The Railway Heritage of Britain, 150 Years of Railway Architecture and Engineering*. London: Michael Joseph, 1983.
Biddle, Gordon. *The Railway Surveyors, the Story of Railway Property Management, 1800–1990*. London: Ian Allan & British Railways Property Board, 1990.
Biddle, Gordon. *Britain's Historical Railway Buildings*. Oxford: Oxford University Press, 2003.
Biddle, Gordon. *Railways in the Landscape*. Barnsley: Pen and Sword, 2016.

Binding, John. *Brunel's Bristol Temple Meads.* Oxford: OPC, 2001.
Binney, Marcus and David Perry. *Railway Architecture.* London: Bloomsbury Books, 1979.
Blower, Alan. *British Railway Tunnels.* Shepperton: Ian Allan, 1964.
Bonython, Elizabeth and Anthony Burton. *The Great Exhibition, the Life and Work of Henry Cole.* London: Victoria & Albert Museum, 2003.
Bowden, Mark. *Unravelling the Landscape.* Stroud: Tempus, 1999.
Bonavia, Michael. *Historic Railway Sites in Britain.* London: Robert Hale, 1987.
Bradley, Simon. *The Railways, Nation, Network and People.* London: Profile Books, 2015.
Bratton, Jacky. *Melodrama, Stage Picture, Screen. London:* BFI, 1994.
Brindle, Steven. *Paddington Station.* London: English Heritage, 2004; 2nd ed. 2013.
Brindle, Steven. *Brunel, the Man who Built the World.* London: Phoenix, 2006.
Brock, A.T. and A.E. Peace. *Bath Stone, a Quarry History.* Bath: Kingsmead Press and University of Cardiff Extramural Department, 1979.
Brooke, David. *The Railway Navvy.* Newton Abbot: David & Charles, 1983.
Brooke, David. *The Diary of William Mackenzie, the first International Railway Contractor.* Edited for ICE, London: Thomas Telford, 2000.
Brunel-Noble, Celia. *The Brunels, Father and Son.* London: Cobden-Sanderson, 1938.
Bryden, Tim. *Brunel the Great Engineer.* Shepperton: Ian Allan, 1999.
Buchanan, Angus. *The Life and Times of Isambard Kingdom Brunel.* London: Hambledon & Lowden, 2002.
Buchannan, R.A. *Industrial Archaeology in Britain.* London, Allan Lane, 1980.
Burman, Peter and Michael Stratton. *Conserving the Railway Heritage.* London: E. & F.N. Spon, 1997.
Burton, Anthony. *The Railway Builders.* London: John Murray, 1992.
Cannadine, David. 'After the Horse: Nobility and Mobility in Modern Britain, in Land and Society in Britain.' In *Land and Society in Britain 1700–1914*, ed. by F.L. Thompson, N.B. Harte and Roland E. Quinault, 213-4. Manchester: Manchester University Press, 1996.
Carlson, Robert E. *The Liverpool and Manchester Railway Project 1821–1831.* Newton Abbot: David & Charles, 1969.
Checkland, S.G. *The Rise of the Industrial Society in Britain.* London: Longman, 1964.
Clark, Kenneth. *Civilisation.* London: BBC, 1969.
Clayton, Antony. *Subterranean City: Beneath the Streets of London.* London: Historical Publications, 2010.
Clinker, C.R. *Railway History Sources: a Hand-list of the Principal Sources of Original Material with Notes and Guidance on its Use.* Bristol: Avon-Anglia, 1976.
Clifton-Taylor, Alec. *Buildings of Delight, 100 Masterpieces.* London: Victor Gollanz, 1986.
Connelly, Angela and Michael Hebbert. *Liverpool's Lost Railway Heritage.* Manchester: MARC, University of Manchester, 2011.
Chimes, Michael. *The Civil Engineering of Canals and Railways before 1850.* London: Ashgate, 1998.

Cossons, Neil (ed). *Perspectives on Industrial Archaeology.* London: Science Museum, 2000.
Christopher, John. *Track Topics, a Book of Engineering for Boys of All Ages.* London: GWR, Paddington, 1935.
Crook, J.M. *The Dilemma of Style.* Chicago: University of Chicago Press, 1987.
Crook, J.M. 'Ruskin and the Railway'. In *The Impact of the Railway on Society in Britain: Essays in Honour of Jack Simmons,* edited by A.K.B. Evans and J.V. Gough, 129-34. London: Routledge, 2003.
Curl, James Stephen. *Kensal Green Cemetery, Origins and Development of the General Cemetery of All Soul's Kensal Green, 1824–2001.* Chichester: Philimore, 2001.
Curl, James Stephen. *Victorian Architecture: Diversity and Invention.* Reading: Spire Books, 2007.
Dickens, Charles. 'The Signal-Man'. *In Mugby Junction, an Uncommon Addition to All the Year Round.* London: Chapman & Hall, 1866.
Disraeli, Benjamin. *Sybil.* Oxford: Oxford World Classics, 2008.
Dodds, John W. *The Age of Paradox, a Biography of England 1841–51.* London: Gollanz, 1953.
Dogshon, Robert A. and Robin A. Butlin. *An Historical Geography of England,* 2nd ed. Cambridge, MA: Academic Press, 1990.
Dunstone, Denis. *For the Love of Trains: The Story of British Train and Railway Preservation.* Shepperton: Ian Allan, 2007.
Dyos, H.J. and Michael Wolf, ed. *The Victorian City.* Vol. 1, London: Routledge, 1973.
Elvers, Rudolf. *Felix Mendelssohn, a Life in Letters.* New York: Fromm International Publishing Corporation, 1986.
Evans, A.K.B. and J.V. Gough eds. *The Impact of the Railway on Society in Britain, Essays in Honour of Jack Simmons.* London: Routledge, 2003.
Everitt, A. 'The Railway and Rural Tradition 1840–1940.' in *The Impact of the Railway on Society in Britain,* edited by A.K.B. Evans and J.V. Gough, chap. 14. London: Routledge, 2003.
Fellows, Reginald B. *History of the Canterbury and Whitstable Railway.* Canterbury: Jennings, 1930.
Freeman, Michael J. *Railways and the Victorian Imagination.* London: Yale, 1999.
Freeman, Michael J., and Derek H. Aldcroft (eds). *Transport in Victorian Britain.* Manchester: Manchester University Press, 1988.
Ford, Boris, (ed). *Victorian Britain,* Cambridge Cultural History Vol. 7. Cambridge: Cambridge University Press, 1992.
Gash, Norman. *Robert Surtees and Early Victorian Society.* Oxford: Oxford University Press, 1993.
Garrett, Bradley L. *Subterranean London: Cracking the Capital.* London, Prestel Publishing, 2015.
Girouard, Mark. *Cities and People.* London: Yale, 1985.
Gloag, John. *Victorian Architecture.* London: Adam & Charles Black, 1962.
Gordon, W.G. *Our Home Railways.* London: Frederick Warne, 1910.
Gray, Adrian. *The London, Chatham and Dover Railway.* Rainham: Meresborough Books, 1984.

Gray, Adrian. *The South Eastern Railway*. Midhurst: Middleton Press, 1990.
Grieveson, Lee and Peter Kramer. *The Silent Cinema Reader*. London: Routledge, 2004.
Grote Lewin, Henry. *The British Railway System, Outlines of its Early Development to the Year 1844*. London: Locomotive Publishing Company, 1925.
Grote Lewin, Henry. *The Railway Mania and its Aftermath 1845–52*. London: Railway Gazette, 1936; reprinted Newton Abbot: David & Charles, 1968.
Hamilton Ellis, Claude. *British Railway History, 1830–76*. London: Allen & Unwin, 1954.
Harper, Charles G. *The Brighton Road*. London: C. Palmer, 1922.
Harrington, Ralph. 'The Railway Journey and the Neuroses of Modernity.' In *Pathologies of Travel*, edited by Richard Wigley and George Revill. Amsterdam: Ridolphi, 1999, 236-37.
Hart, Brian. *The Canterbury and Whitstable Railway*. Didcot: Wild Swan Publications, 1992.
Hawthorne, Nathaniel. *Passages from the English Notebooks*, Vol. 1. Boston US: Houghton,
Mifflin & Co., 1870.
Heffer, Simon. *High Minds: The Victorians and the Birth of Modern Britain*. London: Random House, 2013.
Hill, Rosemary. *God's Architect*. London: Allan Lane, 2007.
Hitchins, Mike. *The Trent Valley Railway*. Stroud: Sutton Press, 2003.
Holland, Henry. *Traveller's Architecture*. London: Harrap, 1971.
Horton, Glyn. *Horton's Guide to Britain's Railways in Feature Films*. Kettering: Silver Link Publishing, 2009.
Hoskins, W.G. *The Making of the English Landscape*. Leicester: Leicester University Press, 1960.
Hyde, Ralph. *The A to Z of Victorian London*. London: London Topographical Society, 1987.
Hylton, Stuart. *The Grand Experiment: The Birth of the Railway Age 1820–45*. Shepperton: Ian Allan, 2007.
Hunt, John Dixon. *Studies in the History of Landscape Architecture*, 2nd ed. Cambridge, MA: MIT Press, 1997.
Ison, Walter. *The Georgian Buildings of Bath*. London: Faber & Faber, 1948.
James, Leslie. *A Chronology of the Construction of Britain's Railways 1778–1855*. Shepperton: Ian Allan, 1983.
Jones, Barbara. *Follies and Grottoes*. London: Batsford, 1953.
Jones, E. *Industrial Architecture in Britain*. London: Batsford, 1985.
Joy, David. *Regional History of the Railways of Great Britain, South West Yorkshire*, Newton Abbot: David & Charles, 1975.
Katy Jones. 'The View from the Viaduct: The Impact of Railways upon Images of English Provincial Towns, 1830–1857'. In *Perspectives in British Cultural History*, edited by Rosalind Crone. Newcastle: Scholar Press, 2007.
Kerr, Barbara. *County Professionals in the Victorian Countryside Vol. 1*. London: Routledge, 1981.

Kellett, John R. *The Impact of Railways on Victorian Cities,* Toronto: University of Toronto Press, 1969.
Kennedy, Ian and Julian Treherz. *Art in the Age of Steam.* London: Yale, and Liverpool: Walker Art Gallery, 2008.
Klingender, Francis. *Art and the Industrial Revolution,* 1947. Rev edition by. A. Elton, London: Routledge & Kegan Paul, 1971.
Lee, Charles E. *Passengers of Distinction.* London: Railway Gazette, 1946.
Leleux, Robin. *Regional History of the Railways of Great Britain,* Vol. 9, East Midlands. Newton Abbot: David & Charles, 1976.
Leleux, Robin. *Restoration Rewarded; A Celebration of Railway Architecture.* Brighton: Unique Books, 2019.
Lewin, Henry G. *Early British Railways.* London: Locomotive Publishing Company, 1925.
M.J.T. Lewis. *Early Wooden Railways,* London: Routledge & Kegan Paul, 1970.
Lindsay, Stafford M. *Perspectives on Industrial Archaeology.* London: Science Museum, 2000.
Macdermot, E.T. *A History of the Great Western Railway.* London: GWR, 1927.
Macready, Sarah and F.H. Thompson. *Influences in Victorian Art and Architecture.* London: Society of Antiquaries, 1985.
MacTurk, George. *A History of Hull Railways,* 1879, reprinted Naresborough: Nidd Valley Narrow Gauge Railway Ltd, 1970.
McFetrich, David. *An Encyclopaedia of Britain's Bridges.* Kettering: Priory Ash, 2010.
Maggs, Colin. *The GWR Bristol to Bath.* Stroud: Sutton Publishers, 2001.
Mansfield, Michael. *Memoirs of a Lawyer.* London: Bloomsbury Publishing, 2009.
Marshal, John. *A Biographical Dictionary of Railway Engineers.* Newton Abbot: David & Charles, 1978.
Martin, G.H. 'Sir George Measom, 1818–1901, and his Railway Guides.' In *The Impact of the Railway on Society in Britain,* edited by A.K.B. Evans and J.V. Gough, chap. 17. London: Routledge, 2003.
Marx, Leo. *The Machine in the Garden, Technology and the Pastoral Idea in America.* New York, Oxford University Press, 1964.
Matterson, Rosa. *Terror in the Tunnels, Britain's Dangerous Railway History.* Stroud, The History Press, 2017.
Mattingley, Neil and Gareth Slater. *Bradford's Railways.* Bradford: Bradford-on-Avon Preservation Trust, 2007.
Mengel, Ewald. *The Railway through Dickens's World, Texts from Household Words and All the Year Round.* Frankfurt-am-Main: Peter Lang, 1989.
Merriman, Peter. *Driving Space, a Cultural Historical Geography.* Oxford: Wiley-Blackwell, 2007.
Miller, Naomi. *Heavenly Caves, Reflections on the Garden Grotto.* London: George Allen & Unwin, 1982.
Moffat, Hugh. *East Anglia's First Railways.* Suffolk: Terrence Dalton, 1987.
Morgan, Brian. *Railway Relics.* Shepperton: Ian Allan, 1969.
Morgan, Brian. *Civil Engineering, Railways.* London: Longman, 1971.
Morriss, Richard. *The Archaeology of Railways.* Stroud: Tempus, 1999.

Moritz, Charles Philip. *Travels in England, 1782*, London: Cassell, 1895.
Mowl, Timothy and Brian Earnshaw. *A Trumpeter at the Distant Gate*. London: Waterstone, 1985.
Munby, Lionel M. *The Hertfordshire Landscape*. London: Hodder, 1977.
Nairn, Ian. *Buildings of England, Sussex*. London: Pelican, 1965.
Norden, Greg. *Landscapes under the Luggage Rack*. Northampton: GNRP, 1997.
Nye, David E. *American Technological Sublime*. Cambridge, MA: MIT, 1994.
Ottley, George. *Bibliography of British Railway History*, London: HMSO, 1966.
Ottley, George. *A Guide to Sixty-One Collections, Libraries and Archives in Great Britain*. London: Library Association, 1973.
Palliser, D.M. *The Staffordshire Landscape*. London: Hodder, 1976.
Palmer, Marilyn and Peter Neaverson. *Industry in the Landscape 1700–1900*. London: Routledge, 2002.
Palmer, Stanley H. *Police and Protest in England and Ireland, 1780–1850*. Cambridge: Cambridge University Press, 1988.
Perkins, Harold. *The Age of the Railway*. Newton Abbot: David & Charles, 1970.
Perkins, J.W., A.T. Brooks and A.E. Pearce. *Bath Stone, a Quarry History*. 3rd ed. Bath: Kingsmead Press & University of Cardiff Department of Extramural Studies, 1990.
Pike, Richard. *Railway Adventures and Anecdotes*. London: Hamilton Adams, 1884.
Richardson, A.E. *Early Victorian England 1830–65*. Oxford: Oxford University Press, 1934.
Read, Charles. *The Box Tunnel*. Boston, MA: Tiden & Field, 1857.
Rees, Gareth. *Early Railway Prints; A Social History of the Railways from 1825 to 1850*. London: Phaidon, 1980.
Rennison, R.W. *Civil Engineering Heritage, Northern England*. 2nd ed. London: ICE, Thomas Telford, London, 1996.
Robertson, Kelvin. *GWR, the Badminton Line, a Portrait of a Railway*. Stroud: Sutton, 1988.
Robertson, Martin. *Exploring England's Heritage, Dorset to Gloucestershire*. London: HMSO, 1992.
Robbins, Michael. *The Railway Age*. London: Routledge & Kegan Paul, 1962.
Rolt, L.T.C. *Red for Danger*. 2nd ed. Newton Abbot: David & Charles, 1966.
Rolt, L.T.C. *Isambard Kingdom Brunel*. Harmondsworth: Penguin, 1989.
Ross, David. *George and Robert Stephenson: A Passion for Success*. London: The History Press, 2010.
Sanstrom, Gosta. E. *The History of Tunnelling*. Texas US: Holt, Rinehart & Winston, 1963.
Schivelbusch, Wolfgang. *The Railway Journey, the Industrialisation of Time and Space in the nineteenth century*. US: University of California Press, 1977; Oxford: Blackwells, 1980.
Sherringham, C.E.R. *Economics of Rail Transport*. London: Edward Arnold, 1928.
Silvester, Reginald. *Official Railway Postcards of the British Isles*. London: BPH Publications, 1978.
Simmons, Jack and Gordon Biddle. *Oxford Companion to British Railway History*. Oxford: Oxford University Press, Oxford, 2000.

Simmons, Jack. *The Birth of the Great Western, Extracts from the Diary and Correspondence of George Henry Gibbs.* Bath: Adam & Dart, 1971.

Simmons, Jack. *The Image of the Train.* Bradford: National Museum of Photography, Film & Television, 1993.

Simmons, Jack. *The Railways of Britain, an Historical Introduction.* London: Routledge & Kegan Paul, 1961.

Simmons, Jack. *The Railway in England and Wales, 1830–1914.* London: Faber & Faber, 1986.

Simmons, Jack. *The Railway in Town and Country, 1830–1914.* Newton Abbot: David & Charles, 1986.

Simmons, Jack. *The Victorian Railway.* London, Thames & Hudson, 1992; rev. ed. 2009.

Skeat, W.O. *George Stephenson the Engineer and his Letters.* London: Mechanical Engineering Publications Inst. IME, 1973.

Smith, Stuart. *A View from the Iron Bridge.* Bridgenorth: Ironbridge Gorge Museum Trust, 1979.

Smithson, Alison and Peter. *The Euston Arch and the Growth of the London, Midland and Scottish Railway.* London: Thames & Hudson, 1968.

Steegman, John. *Victorian Taste, a Study of Art and Architecture from 1830–1870.* London: Nelson, 1970.

Straub, Hans. *A History of Civil Engineering.* London: Leonard Hill, 1952.

Stretton, Clement E. *A History of the Trent Valley Railway.* Tamworth, 1897; Burton on Trent: Chronicle & Gazette, 1901.

Swift, Andrew. *The Ringing Grooves.* Bath: Akemann Press, 2006.

Thompson, F.L.M. *English Landed Society in the Nineteenth Century.* London, Routledge, 1963.

Thornton, Robert, & Malcolm Wood. *The Architectural Legacy of British Railway Building 1825 to the Present Day.* Ramsbury: The Crowood Press, 2020.

Trinder, Barrie. *The Making of the Industrial Landscape.* London: Dent, 1982.

Trinder, Barrie. *Blackwell's Encyclopaedia of Industrial Archaeology.* Oxford: Blackwell's, 1992.

Turner, John Howard. *The London, Brighton and South Coast Railway.* Usk: Oakwood Press, 3 vols. 1977–79.

Turnock, David. *An Historical Geography of Railways in Great Britain.* Farnham: Ashgate, 1998.

Vale, Edmund. *LMS Route Book, No. 2.* London: LMS publishing, 1947.

Vaughan, Adrian. *A Pictorial Record of Great Western Architecture.* Oxford: Oxford Publishing Company, 1977.

Vaughan, Adrian. 'Brunel as a Creator of Environment.' In *Conserving the Railway Heritage,* edited by Peter Burman and Michael Stratton. London: E & FN Spon, 1997, 75-88.

Vaughan, Adrian. *Brunel: An Engineering Biography.* Shepperton: Ian Allan, 2006.

Vaughan, Adrian. *Brunel: The Intemperate Engineer,* Shepperton: Ian Allan, 2010.

Vaughan, Adrian. *I. K. Brunel: Engineering Knight Errant.* London: John Murray, 1992.

Vaughan, Adrian. *Railwaymen, Politics and Money.* London: John Murray, 1997.

Walton, Edward. *Old and New London,* Vol. 5, London: Cassell , Petter & Galpin, 1878.
Ward, J.R. *The Finance of Canal Building in Eighteenth Century England.* Oxford: Oxford University Press, 1974.
Webster, N.W. *Joseph Locke, Railway Revolutionary.* London: Allen & Unwin, 1970.
Webster, N.W. *Britain's First Trunk Line, the Grand Junction Railway,* Bath: Adam & Dart, 1972.
Wigley, Richard and George Revill. *The Railway Journey and the Neuroses of Modernity, Pathologies of Travel.* Amsterdam: Ridolphi, 1999.
Williams, Cliff. *Driving the Clay Cross Tunnel, Navvies on the Derby-Leeds Railway.* Cromford: Scarthin Books, 1984.
Williams, Rosalind. *Notes on the Underground.* Cambridge MA: MIT, 1990.
Williamson, Tom and Liz Bellamy. *Property and Landscape.* London: George Philips, 1987.
Whyte, Ian. D. *Landscape and History since 1500.* London: Reaction Books, 2002.
Winchester, Clarence. ed. *Railway Wonders of the World.* London: Amalgamated Press, 1935–36.
Woodall, S.J.R. *The English Landscape: Past, Present and Future.* Oxford: Oxford University Press, 1985.
Wosk, Julie. *Breaking Frame: Technology and the Visual Arts in the Nineteenth Century.* New Brunswick, US: Rutgers University Press, 1992.
Wyte, Ian D. *Landscape and History since 1500.* London, Reaktion Books, 2002.

GAZETTEERS
Biographical Dictionary of Civil Engineers of Great Britain and Ireland, Vol. 1, A.W. Skempton, London: ICE Thomas Telford, 2008.
Civil Engineering Heritage, regional volumes, London: Institution of Civil Engineers.
Imperial Gazetteer of England and Wales, London: A. Fullarton & Co., 1868.
National Gazetteer of Great Britain and Ireland, London: A. Fullarton & Co., 1838.
New Encyclopaedia of Brighton, edited by Rose Colis. Brighton: Brighton & Hove Libraries, 2010.
Parliamentary Gazetteer of England and Wales, Vol. 3. Edinburgh: A. Fullarton & Co., 1851.
Penny's Cyclopaedia of Useful Knowledge, edited by C. Knight, 1843.
Survey of London, Vol. 26, Lambeth, southern area, London County Council, 1956.
Victoria County History, Cambridgeshire, Vol. 10, 1989.
Victoria County History, Northamptonshire, Vol. 6. 2007.

PRIMARY SOURCES: CONTEMPORARY JOURNALS
Anon. 'Railroads, their past history, present condition and future prospects', *Frazer's Magazine for Town and Country.* (April 1838): 421-32.
Dickens, Charles. 'Need Railway Travellers be Smashed?' *Household Words,* Vol. 4 No. 88 (29 Nov. 1851): 217-270.
Herapath, John. 'Of the Smoke, Noise, etc in Tunnels.' *Mechanics Magazine, Museum Register, Journal & Gazette,* Vol. 23 (11 July 1835).

Humphreys, Noel. 'From a Provincial Tour, the London and Birmingham Railway.' *Architecture Magazine & Journal in Architecture Building Furnishing*, Vol. 5 (1838): 677-82.

Institution of Civil Engineers, *Journal of Proceedings*, April 1838, re: *Richmond Hill Tunnel, Leeds*.

Nixon. C. 'Description of the Tunnels situated between Bristol and Bath on the Great Western Railway, with Methods adopted for Executing the Works' *Proceedings of the Institution of Civil Engineers* (3 May 1842): 138-41.

'Railroads, their Past History, Present Conditions and Future Prospects.' *Fraser's Magazine for Town and Country* Vol. XVII (April 1831): 421-432.

Walker, J. and G. Smith 'On Ventilation and Lighting Tunnels, particularly by Reference to the One on the Leeds and Selby Railway.' *Institution of Civil Engineers Transaction* No. 1 (1836).

SECONDARY SOURCES: JOURNALS

Barnes, Martin. 'Maths throws light on Brunel Legend.' *New Engineer* (4 April 1985).

Barnes, Robin. 'A Royal Progress.' *Back Track,* Vol. 16. (June–July 2002): 343-50, 406-13.

Brook, David. *'The Equity Suit of Mcintosh versus the Great Western Railway,' Journal of Transport History*, 3rd ser. (1996): 141- 42.

Cameron, Ian. 'The Battle of Mickleham Tunnel.' *Cotswold & Vale Magazine* (April 2007).

Carr, David, P. 'Side Lights on the High Peak Railway.' *Newcomen Society Transactions,* Vol. 14 (1933).

Chrimes, Michael. 'The Civil Engineering of Canals and Railways before 1850,' *Institution of Civil Engineers, Studies in the History of Civil Engineering,* Vol. 7 (1997).

Chrimes, Michael. 'Robert Stephenson and Planning and Construction of the London and Birmingham Railway.' *Construction History*: Proceedings of the 1st International Congress, Madrid (Jan. 2003): 593-609.

Chrimes, Michael. 'Kilsby Tunnel – New Light on an Early Railway Masterpiece' *Early Railway Papers for the Seventh Early Railways Conference,* Early Railways Conference Committee (2022): 175-99.

Clinker, C.R. 'The Leicester and Swannington Railway.' *Leicestershire Archaeological Society Transactions*, vol. XXX (1954).

Cole, David. 'Mocatta's Stations for the Brighton Railway.' *The Journal of Transport History*, Vol. 3 (May 1958): 149-57.

Daly, Nicholas. 'Blood on the Tracks, Sensation and Drama, the Railway and the Dark Face of Modernity.' *Victorian Studies,* Vol. 42, No.1 (1998-99).

Dawes, Malcolm. 'Clayton Tunnel Cottage.' *Sussex Industrial Archaeology Newsletter* (June 2010).

Dendy-Marshall, C.F. 'The Liverpool and Manchester Railway,' *Newcomen Society Transactions*, Vol. 2 (1921).

Dendy-Marshall, C.F. *'Railway Engineering and its Impact on Civilisation.'* *Newcomen Society Transactions*, Vol. 36 (1963).

Denault, Leigh and Jennifer Landis. ' Motion and Means: Mapping Opposition to Railways in Victorian Britain.' *Holyoke College Graduate History Seminar Papers*, vol. 256 (Dec.1998). www.mtholyoke.ed./courses/rschwart/ind_rev/rs/denault.htm. (accessed 25 Aug. 2015).
Edmonds, Tim. 'Early Narrow-gauge Railway Tunnels in North Wales.' *Back Track* Vol. 9, No. 10 (Oct 1995).
Freeman, Michael. 'The Railway as Cultural Metaphor, What Kind of Railway History?' *Journal of Transport History*, 3rd ser. Vol. 20 (Sept. 1990): 160-66.
Gaye, Diana. 'My Ideal Home.' *Ideal Home* (June 1976): 52-3.
Gilkes, David. 'Joseph Locke and the Stephensons.' *Back Track*, Vol. 19, No. 6 (June 2005).
Gouvish, Terry. 'What Kind of Railway History did We Get?' *Journal of Transport History*, 3rd ser. Vol. 14, No. 2 (Sept. 1993): 242-51.
Gray, Adrian. 'The Clayton Tunnel Disaster.' *Back Track*, Vol. 23, No. 10 (Oct. 2009).
Green-Hughes, Evan. 'Tunnels.' *Hornby Magazine* (July 2010).
Harrington, Ralph. 'The Neuroses of Railways.' *History Today* (July 1994).
Hickie, Catherine. 'The Fatal Form of Contentment.' *The Permanente Journal*, Spring, Vol. 13, No. 2 (Spring 2000).
Hughes, John. 'Fourteen Tunnels to Lime Street.' *Back Track*, vol. 4, No. 4 (July/Aug. 1990).
Institute of Historic Buildings Conservation, May 2009, 'The Labyrinth at Edge Hill.'
Knight, Jack. 'Explaining Tunnel Construction by Joint mapping.' Proceedings of ICE Transport, Vol. 160, Iss. 2 (London: 2007): 47-51.
Lee, Charles E. 'Early North-East Coast Railways,' pt. 2 *Colliery Engineering* (London: July 1939).
Lee, Charles E. *'Railway Engineering and its Impact on Civilisation.' Transactions of the Newcomen Society*, Vol. 36 (1963): 113.
Linsley, Stafford M. 'Industrial Archaeology in the North East 1852–2000.' In Cossons, Neil. *Perspectives on Industrial Archaeology,* Science Museum (2000).
Mathams, Robin and Dave Barrett. 'The Trent Valley Railway.' *Back Track*, Vol. 28, No. 1 (Jan. 2014).
Matus, Jill. L. 'Trauma, Memory, and Railway Disaster, the Dickensian Connection.' *Victorian Studies*, Vol. 43, No.3 (Spring 2001).
May, Peter. 'Tunnels in Sussex.' *Back Track*, Vol. 2, No.1 (Spring 1988).
Mills, Keith. 'A Ducal Whimsy.' *Midland Record*, No. 3 (1995).
Millward, Pat. 'The Building of Balcombe Tunnel, 1838–41.' *Sussex Industrial Journal*, No. 30 (2000).
Moorhead, Claire. 'The Labyrinth at Edge Hill', *Historic Buildings Conservation Journal* (May 2009).
Leeds, Tessa. 'The Construction of Sevenoaks Tunnel.' *Archaeologia Cantiana*, Vol. 120 (2000): 187-200.
Philmester, James and Jerome Tait,. 'Corsham's Hidden Landscape.' *Landscape*, Vol. 15, No. 1 (June 2014).
Rennison, R.W. 'The Newcastle and Carlisle Railway and its Engineers, 1829–1862.' *Transactions of the Newcomen Society*, Vol. 72 (2000).

Richards, P.S. 'The Railway Influence on Leighton Buzzard.' *Bedfordshire Magazine*, Vol. 15 (1975).
Sharman, Frank, H. 'The Influence of Landowners on Route selection.' *Studies in the History of Civil Engineering*, Vol. 7 (1997).
St Claire, Roger. 'Earlier Tunnelling on the Kent Coast.' *Back Track*, Vol. 8, No. 2 (March/April 1994).
Timperley, Robert. 'Light at the End of the Tunnel.' *Back Track*, Vol. 29, No. 3 (March 2015).
Twining, E.E. 'The Original Tunnels of the Great Western Railway.' *Railway Magazine*, Vol. 25 (Oct. 1909).
Ward, J.T. 'West Riding Landowners and the Railways.' *Journal of Transport History*, Vol. 4 (Nov. 1960): 242-51.
Warner, Tim. 'Country House Railway Stations.' *Back Track*, Vol. 11. No. 6 (June 1997).
Warner, Tim. 'Leicestershire Landowners and the Railway: Resistance and Co-operation.' *Leicester Archaeological & Historical Society Transactions*, Vol. LXI (1987).
Warner, Tim. 'Monstrous Cavities, Victorian Fear of the Railway Tunnel.' *Back Track*, Vol. 3 No.5 (Nov/Dec. 1989).
Wells, Jeffrey. 'In Search of Light.' *Back Track*, Vol. 25, No. 1 (Jan. 2011).

CONTEMPORARY NEWSPAPERS AND PAMPHLETS REFERRED TO IN TEXT

Bath Chronicle, 1838 (various dates).
Blackwoods Magazine, Vol. 70, Dec. 1851.
Bradford Observer, 5 Oct. 1854.
Brighton Herald, 16 May 1840; 25 Sept. 1841.
Bristol Mercury, 1833–38 (various dates).
Civil Engineer and Architect's Journal, 1837–38, 1840–41.
Daily Telegraph, 12 April 1859.
Derby Mercury, 9 December 1840.
The Friendly Companion, December 1879.
Gentleman's Magazine, 1830, 1840, 1844.
Girls' Own Paper, 24 July 1866.
Hampshire Advertiser and Salisbury Gazette, 19 May 1837
Herapath's Railway Magazine and Annals of Science, various from 1836.
Household Narrative of Current Events
Illustrated London News, 4 Dec. 1847, Shugborough Tunnel; 26 July 1851, Battle of Mickleton Tunnel.
John Bull, 31 March 1839.
Kentish Gazette, 7 November 1843.
Lady Newspaper, August 1847.
Morning Post, 1835–1870 (various dates).
Penny Satirist, 4 Sept 1841, 11 Sept 1841.
Punch, 31 Aug. 1844.

Quarterly Review, Vol. 63, 1839.
Rail Engineer Magazine, 2008.
The Standard, Nov. 1844.
The Times, 1835–1870 (various dates).
Young Folks' Paper, 7 Dec. 1889

UNPUBLISHED THESES/DISSERTATIONS
Hepple, J.R. 'The influence of Landowners' attitudes on Railway Alignment in Nineteenth Century England.' unp. Ph.D. University of Hull, 1974.
Leeds, Trecia. 'The Sevenoaks Railway Tunnel: its Construction and Immediate Consequences.' University of Kent Diploma in Local History, 1991.
Roberts, Peter. 'British Canal Tunnels, a Geographical Survey.' Ph.D. University of Salford, 1977.

WEBSITES
http://bristol-rail.co.uk
www.IKBrunel.org.uk.index.php
http://.en.wikipedia.org/wiki/List_of_tunnels_in_the_United_Kingdom
www.forgottenrelics.co.uk/tunnels/index.html
www.buildingshistory.org/buildings/railway.shtml
http://sites.google.com/site/waggonways/history-northumberland
www.railwayheritagetrust.co.uk
www.oldrailwaystuff.com/northchurch-tunnel-1836-37
www.railarchive.co.uk
www.yeoldesussexpages.com/history
hwww.tunnelsuk.com

ENDNOTES

CHAPTER 1
1. John Steegman, *Victorian Taste: a Study of the Arts and Architecture from 1830-1870* (London: Nelson, 1970): 125.
2. Gordon Biddle, 'Historic Railway Structures in Britain: a Continuing Appraisal' *Conserving the Railway Heritage*, ed. Peter Burman and Michael Stratton (London: F. & F.N. Spon, 1997): 62.
3. Gordon Biddle, 'Railways, their Buildings, and the Environment,' *The Impact of the Railway and Society in Britain: Essays in Honour of Jack Simmons*, (Aldershot: Ashgate, 2003): 122.
4. Edgar Jones, *Industrial Britain* (London, Batsford, 1985): 74.
5. F.L.M. Thompson, 'Towns, Industry & the Victorian Landscape,' in *The English Landscape, Past, Present and Future*, ed. S.R.J. Woodell, (Oxford: Oxford University Press, 1985): 169.
6. E.W. Twining, 'The Original Tunnels of the Great Western Railway,' *Railway Magazine*, Vol. 25 (October 1909): 297-301.
7. Christian Barman, *Early British Railways* (London: Art & Technics, 1950): 18-24.
8. Ian Nairn, *Buildings of England, Sussex* (Harmondsworth: Penguin, 1965): 472.
9. *Economist*, 24 May 1969: For an excellent survey on the rise of the industrial preservation movement and interest at Government level, see Simon Thurley, *The Men from the Ministry* (London: Yale, 2013): 216-32.
10. R.A. Buchanan, *Industrial Archaeology in Britain*, 2nd ed (London: Allen Lane, 1980); J. Simmons, *The Railway in England and Wales 1830–1914*, vol. 1 *The System and its Working*, revised ed. (London: Faber & Faber, 2009); Henry Holland, *Traveller's Architecture* (London: Harrap, 1971): 36.
11. Marcus Binney and David Pearce, eds. *Railway Architecture* (London: Bloomsbury Books, 1979).
12. B. Trinder, *The Making of the Industrial Landscape* (London: J.M. Dent, 1982); G. Biddle and O.S. Nock, *The Railway Heritage of Britain: 150 Years of Railway Architecture and Engineering* (London: Michael Joseph, 1983).
13. Marilyn Palmer and Peter Neaverson, *Industry in the Landscape, 1700–1900* (London: Routledge, 1994): 166.
14. P. Burman and M. Stratton, eds. *Conserving the Railway Heritage* (London: E.& F.N. Spon, 1997.
15. Stafford M. Linsley, 'Industrial Archaeology in the North East of England, 1852–2000' in *Perspectives on Industrial Archaeology*, ed. Neil Cossons (London: Science Museum, 2000): 119.
16. G. Biddle, *Britain's Historic Railway Buildings: An Oxford Gazetteer of Structures and Sites* (Oxford: Oxford University Press, 2000).

17. *Industrial Archaeology Review* Vol. 4, No. 2 (Spring 1980).
18. Pat Milward, 'The Building of the Balcombe Tunnel, 1838–41,' *Sussex Industrial History* No. 30 (Brighton: Sussex Industrial & Archaeological Society, 2000): 2-25.
19. Frederick Walter Simms, *Practical Tunnelling* (London: Crosby Lockwood, 1844): IX.
20. Gosta Sandstrom, *A History of Tunnelling: Underground Workings through the Ages* (London: Barrie & Rockcliff, 1963).
21. Alan Blower, *British Railway Tunnels* (London: Ian Allan, 1963).
22. Roy Anderson and Gregory Fox, *A Pictorial Record of LMS Architecture* (Oxford: Oxford Publishing Company,1981).
23. Adrian Vaughan, *A Pictorial Record of Great Western Architecture* (Oxford: Oxford Publishing Company, 1977).
24. Richard Morriss, *The Archaeology of Railways* (Stroud: Tempus Publishing, 1999): 99-108.
25. Various authors, *A Regional History of the Railways of Great Britain*, 15 vols. (Newton Abbot: David & Charles, numerous editions, 1960 onwards).
26. Mike Chrimes, ed. *The Civil Engineering of Canals and Railways before 1850* (London: Ashgate, 1998).
27. Trecia Leeds, 'The Sevenoaks Tunnel: its Construction and Immediate Consequences' (Canterbury: University of Kent Diploma in Local History, 1991).
28. J.R. Hepple, 'Influence of Landowners' Attitudes on Railway Alignment in Nineteenth Century England', unpublished PhD thesis (University of Hull, 1974); Tim Warner, 'Leicestershire Landowners and the Railways, Resistance and Co-Operation', *Leicestershire Archaeological and Historical Society*, Vol. 61 (1987): 51-60. See also Jack Simmons, *The Railway in Town and Country, 1830–1914* (Newton Abbot: David & Charles, 1986): 307-08.
29. Rosalind Williams, *Notes on the Underground* (Cambridge MA: MIT Press, 1990).
30. Ibid.: 26.
31. Ibid.: 9.
32. Ibid.: 60.
33. Ibid.: 72-3; Kenneth Clark, *Civilisation* (London: BBC, 1969): 330.
34. Ibid.: 59.
35. David Nye, *American Technological Sublime* (Cambridge MA: MIT, 1994): 72.
36. Leo Marx, *The Machine in the Garden* (New York: Oxford University Press, 1964): 204.
37. Ibid.: 214
38. G. Mom, C. Divall and P. Lyth, 'Towards a Paradigm Shift? A Decade of Transport and Mobility History,' in G. Mom, G. Pirie and L. Tissot, eds, *Mobility in History: The State of Art in the History of Transport, Traffic and Mobility* (Neuchatel: Editions Alphil, 2009): 13-40, esp. 28-33.
39. Terry Gouvish, 'What Kind of Railway History did we get? Forty Years of Research,' *Journal of Transport History*, 3rd ser. Vol. 14, No. 2 (Sept. 1993): 125.
40. Jack Knight, 'Explaining Tunnel Construction by Joint Mapping,' *Proceedings of ICE Transport*, Vol. 160, Iss. 2 (London: 2007): 47-57.

41. Marilyn Palmer and Peter Neaverson in *Industry Landscape 1700-1900* (London: Routledge, 1994); see also Michael Robbins, *The Railway Age* (London: Routledge, 1962): 57-67; Ian D. Whyte, Landscape and History since 1500 (London: Reaction Books, 2002): 79.
42. J.R. Ward, 'West Riding Landowners and the Railways,' *Journal of Transport History*, Vol. 4 (1960): 242-51.
43. A partial exception is Michael Aston and James Bond, *The Landscape of Towns* (Stroud: Alan Sutton, 2000):176.
44. J. Morduant Crook, *The Dilemma of Style* (Chicago IL: University of Chicago Press, 1987): 98-132.
45. Simon Heffer, *High Minds, The Victorians and the Birth of Modern Britain* (London: Random House, 2014): 719.
46. Timothy Mowl and Brian Earnshaw, *Trumpet at the Distant Gate* (London: Waterstone, 1985): 36.
47. David Cole, 'Mocatta's Stations for the Brighton Railway,' *Journal of Transport History* Vol. 3, No. 3 (May 1958): 154.
48. Kenneth Clark, *Civilisation* (London: BBC/John Murray, 1969): 331.
49. M. Freeman, 'The Railway as Cultural Metaphor,' *Journal of Transport History*, 3rd ser, Vol. 20. (Sept. 1999): 162.
50. L.T.C. Rolt, *Brunel* (Harmondsworth, Penguin, 1989); Adrian Vaughan, *Brunel* (Shepperton: Ian Allan, 2006); Adrian Vaughan, *The Intemperate Engineer Isambard Kingdom Brunel* (Shepperton: Ian Allan, 2010); Steven Brindle, *Brunel, the Man who Built the World* (London: Weidenfeld & Nicolson, 2005); Angus Buchanan, *The Life and Times of Isambard Kingdom Brunel* (London: Hambledon & Lowden, 2002).
51. E.T. MacDermot, *History of the Great Western Railway* (London: GWR, 1927).
52. Mom, Divall and Lyth 'Paradigm Shift? 28-33.
53. Wolfgang Schivelbusch, *The Railway Journey: The Industrialization of Time and Space in the 19th Century* (Oxford: Basil Blackwell, 1980, orig. German ed, Frankfurt, 1977). For a telling but sympathetic critique, see Susan Major, 'The Million Go Forth, Early Railway Excursion Crowds, 1840–1860,' unpublished PhD thesis (University of York, 2012).
54. Julie Wosk, *Breaking Frame, Technology and the Visual Arts in the Nineteenth Century* (New Brunswick, US: Rutgers University Press, 1992).
55. Leo Marx, *The Machine in the Garden, Technology and the Pastoral Idea in America* (New York: Oxford University Press, 1964).
56. Paul Fyfe, 'Illustrating the Accident: Railways and the Catastrophic Picturesque in the Illustrated London News,' *Victorian Periodicals Review* Vol. 46, No. 1 (Baltimore: John Hopkins University Press, Spring 2013): 61-91.
57. Ralph Harrington, 'The Railway Journey and the Neuroses of Modernity,' *Pathology of Travel*, eds. Richard Wigley and George Revill (Amsterdam: Ridolphi, 2000): 236-37; see also R. Harrington, 'The Neurosis of the Railways,' *History Today* (July 1994): 15-21.
58. David Turnock, *An Historical Geography of Railways in Great Britain* (Farnham: Ashgate, 1998): 9.

59. Simon Bradley, *The Railways, Nation, Network and People* (London: Profile Books, 2015).
60. Susan Major, 'The Million go Forth' unpublished PhD thesis, (University of York, 2012).
61. Barman, *Early British Railways*: 21.
62. Steegman, *Victorian Taste*: 128. See also J.M. Crook, 'Ruskin and the Railway,' in *The Impact of the Railway on Society in Britain: Essays in Honour of Jack Simmons*, ed. A.K.B. Evans and J.V. Gough (London: Routledge, 2003): 129-34.
63. Crook, *Dilema of Style*: 288.
64. The National Archives, Kew (hereafter NA). RAIL 384/336.
65. The *Railway Magazine*, which has been published monthly since 1897, should not be confused with its earlier namesake.
66. For early railway journalism, see Elizabeth Bonython and Anthony Burton, *The Great Exhibition: the Life and Work of Henry Cole* (London: Victoria & Albert Museum, 2003): 66-77.
67. J.M. Carmichael, *Views on the Newcastle and Carlisle Railway* (Newcastle: 1839; republished Newcastle: Frank Graham, 1969).
68. This type of railway guide for the carriage window or armchair traveller was revived in 1948 by Stuart Pike with his *Mile by Mile* series for the LMS, LNER, and SR companies copying the same format as Cole's *Traveller's Charts* published by *Railway Chronicle*. Yet he omitted some significant tunnels from his maps.
69. *Civil Engineering Heritage,* six volumes covering Great Britain and Ireland (London: Thomas Telford, for ICE, 1981–2007).
70. Forgotten Relics: www.forgottenrelics.co.uk/tunnels/index.html.

CHAPTER 2

1. David Joy, *Regional History of the Railways of Great Britain,* Vol. VIII South West Yorkshire (Newton Abbot: David & Charles, 1975): 61.
2. *Times,* 26 Dec. 1861: 4.
3. Francis Bond Head, *Stokers and Pokers; On the London and North Western Railway* (London: John Murray, 1849): 27.
4. L.N. Munby, *The Hertfordshire Landscape* (London: Hodder, 1977): 218.
5. Edward Churton, *The Rail Road Book of England* (London: Edward Churton, Publisher, 1851): 18-19.
6. *A Handbook for Travellers along the London and Birmingham Railway* (London: Groombridge, 1839): 54.
7. See Barrie Trinder, *Blackwell's Encyclopaedia of Industrial Archaeology* (London: Dent, 1992).
8. See Charles E. Lee, 'Early North-East Coast Railways,' pt. 2 *Colliery Engineering* (London, July 1939).
9. Henry G. Lewin, *Early British Railways* (London: Locomotive Publishing Co., 1925): 3.
10. See Tim Edmonds, 'Early Narrow Gauge Railway Tunnels in North Wales,' *Back Track,* Vol. 9, No. 10 (Oct. 1995).

11. Lewin, *Early British Railways*: 1-2.
12. Surprisingly John Francis in his *History of the English Railway 1820–45*, 1851, does not include the Penydarren Tramway in his list of railways from 1801–25 on p.57, yet on p.50 he states, 'The first locomotive was in use in 1804, on a Welsh railway, drawing as many carriages as would contain ten tons of bar iron, at a rate of five miles an hour.'
13. Hindlow Tunnel was rebuilt to take two tracks after the line had been leased from the London and North Western Railway in 1860.
14. See David P. Carr, 'Side Lights on the High Peak Railway,' *Transactions of the Newcomen Society*, Vol. 14 (London: 1933): 179-81.
15. See Brian Hart, *The Canterbury and Whitstable Railway* (Didcot: Wild Swan Publications, 1992): 10-11, for references to building Tyler Hill Tunnel. It is said that Stephenson's incentive for visiting the line was to visit London to see his fiancée. Initially George Stephenson was appointed as engineer in 1825, however his son Robert took over in 1827. The locomotive Invicta was constructed by the Robert Stephenson Engineering Company of Newcastle as locomotive number 20 for the Canterbury and Whitstable Railway.
16. *Kent Herald*, 17 May 1827: 3.
17. The tunnel survives, although after the subsidence of the foundations of a University of Kent building directly over its path in 1974, it has been partially filled in and the portals bricked up.
18. By the end of 1830 trains had carried over 70,000 passengers between Liverpool & Manchester. The new station was built with a gift of £2,000 from Liverpool Common Council. The tunnel for rope haulage over a mile long was partially opened out in the 1870s.
19. Opened out into a deep cutting by 1881, apart from short tunnel length to west of Edge Hill Station that may lay claim to be the oldest tunnel used by the present-day railway system. For photos of this operation see www.nrm.uk/ourcollection/photogallery?group=Crewe
20. *Times* 20 Aug. 1844: 6 & 8 Dec. 1846: 7.
21. *Times*, 18 Aug. 1849: 7.
22. See Hamilton Ellis, *British Railway History* (London: Allen & Unwin, 1954): 31. For a recent appraisal of the present state of the Liverpool tunnels and a possible future bid for World Heritage status, see Angela Connelly and Michael Hebbert, 'Liverpool's Lost Railway Heritage', MARC discussion paper, University of Manchester, 2011. See also *Subterranea Britannica* website www.subrit.org.uk for photographs of current state of Liverpool's abandoned railway tunnels.
23. C.R. Clinker, 'Leicester and Swannington Railway', *Transactions of the Leicestershire Archaeological Society*, Vol. XXX (Leicester, 1954): 64-66.
24. For early history of the Leeds and Selby Railway and digging of Richmond Hill Tunnel, see Chapter 2 of G. MacTurk, *A History of Hull Railways* (1879), reprinted by Nidd Valley Narrow Gauge Railway Ltd, Naresborough, (1970).
25. For Strood tunnel conversion for use as a railway tunnel see Peter Roberts, 'British Canal Tunnels, a Geographical Survey,' Vol. 2 Ph.D, University of Salford, 1977, (copy at ICE): 546-47.

26. *Times*, 18 March 1847: 7.
27. Lewin, *Early British Railways*, 48. The line was to be worked by fixed engines from Princes Street to Trinity Pier, 2½ miles in length, with a branch of 1½ miles to Leith Docks.
28. This tunnel had a short life with the line from Princes Street to Canonmills, closing in 1868, and subsequently being used for growing mushrooms. The southern end of the tunnel was blocked by the building of Waverley Station in the 1860s. A small air shaft remains in the wall opposite platform 19.
29. Institution of Civil Engineers, *Proceedings*, 20 Jan. 1846: 36. This was mentioned by John Rennie in his presidential address.
30. Simms, *Practical Tunnelling*, 3rd ed. (1896). See Frederick Smeeton Williams, *Our Iron Road* (London: Ingram Cooke, 1855) Chapter 3, for early account of problems and methods of railway tunnelling.
31. *Encyclopaedia Britannica*, 7th ed. 1830–42. See also Fredrick S. Williams, *Our Iron Road* (London: Ingram Cook & Co., 1855): 147.
32. See G. Biddle, *The Railway Surveyors* (London: Ian Allan, 1990): 58-82, for what was involved in surveying the route of an early railway.
33. RAIL 386/57, report into excess costs of construction, 17 March 1842.
34. *Railway Magazine*, No. 2 (April 1836): 58.
35. *Railway Magazine*, No. XIII (March 1837): 191.
36. Head, *Stokers and Pokers*: 19-26.
37. John Francis, *A History of the English Railway* (London: Longman Brown, 1857): 189-90.
38. Samuel Smiles, *The Life of George Stephenson* (London: John Murray, 1857): 318.
39. *Times* 13 Oct. 1859: 7.
40. *Railway Times*, reported in *The Civil Engineers and Architect's Journal*, Oct 1837–Dec. 1838: 86.
41. Thomas Roscoe, *London and Birmingham Railway* (London: George Tilt, 1839): 105.
42. *Times*, 12 March 1841: 6.
43. *The Civil Engineer and Architect's Journal*, Oct 1837–Dec 1838: 51.
44. See *Railway Times*, 19 Oct. 1839: 832.
45. See *Railway Times*, 16 March 1839: 228.
46. *The Civil Engineer and Architect's Journal*, Oct 1837–Dec 1838: 46. See RAIL 386/46 & RAIL 386/51, London and Brighton Railway Company, J.U. Rastrick half yearly reports to directors.
47. Francis Whishaw, *The Railways of Great Britain and Ireland* (London: John Weale, 1842): 273.
48. University of London, Senate House Library, Rastrick Papers, MS 242, 111 (2).
49. *Times*, 21 Sept. 1841: 1.
50. Whishaw, *Railways*: 411.
51. *The Builder*, Vol. 1, 16 Dec. 1843: 546.
52. Jack Simmons, *The Victorian Railway* (London: Thames & Hudson, 1992): 22.
53. Churton, *Rail Road Book*, Vol. 1: 177.
54. *The Builder*, Vol. 1, 1 April 1843: 100.
55. *Times*, 27 Jan. 1843: 5.

56. *Times*, 27 Jan. 1843: 5.
57. See *The Builder,* Vol. 1, 16 Dec. 1843: 177.
58. When the South Eastern Railway duplicated the 1866 Chislehurst Tunnel in 1901–02, the crown of the old bore cracked and a section of the new bore collapsed due to the loose nature of the clay between the bores. The tracks were reopened in Nov. 1902. There were fortunately no fatalities.
59. *Times*, 21 Feb. 1857: 12. Report of half yearly meeting of shareholders at Euston Station.
60. John Howard Turner, *London, Brighton and South Coast Railway* (Usk: Oakwood Press, 1979): 151.
61. *The Builder* (5 Dec. 1846): 585.
62. The tunnel face at the north end of the station platform has been cut on its right (east) side by the creation of a large office block sometime in the 1930s.
63. Proceedings of Institution of Civil Engineering (12 Feb. 1841).
64. *The Civil Engineer and Architect's Journal*, Dec. 1840: 430.
65. See *The Builder,* Vol. 4, 1846: 357.
66. *The Builder,* 3 Oct. 1846: 476.
67. *The Builder,* 10 Oct. 1846: 484.
68. *Times*, 21 Sept. 1854: 6.
69. Simms, *Practical Tunnelling:* IX.
70. See Whishaw, *Railways of Great Britain*, 1842: 319.
71. *Times*, 20 Dec. 1864: 5. Colwell Tunnel was in danger of collapse by the 1920s and a parallel tunnel was finally cut and the original abandoned and bricked up.
72. David Brooke, *The Railway Navvy* (Newton Abbot: David & Charles 1983): 163.
73. *Times*, 9 Sept. 1839: 7 & 11 Jan. 1840: 7.
74. *Bromley Record,* 1 Sept. 1863; Adrian Gray, *The South Eastern Railway* (Midhurst: Middleton Press, 1990): 161.
75. *Times*, 8 Aug. 1866: 5; Adrian Gray, *The London, Chatham and Dover Railway* (Rainham: Meresborough Books, 1984): 27.
76. RAIL 1149/5: letter, 18 Jan. 1840.
77. RAIL 250/82 reports 14 Sept: 4-6 and 8 Oct. 1835: 13.
78. RAIL 250/82 report 8 Oct 1835: 13.
79. RAIL 1149/49: 50 & 67.
80. *The Friendly Companion* (1 Dec.1879): 276.
81. *Bristol Mercury,* 3 Aug. 1833; report of public meeting of Bristol and London Railway Company.
82. RAIL 250/2; Great Western Minute Book, 29 Oct. 1835.
83. Thomas Gale, *A Brief Account of the Making and Working of the Great Box Tunnel* (Cheltenham: 1884): 17.
84. *Morning Chronicle,* 5 May 1835: 3
85. NA, NRCA1 10029, dated 7 July 1838.
86. I. Brunel, *Life of Isambard Kingdom Brunel* (London: Longman Green, 1870): 72.
87. Brunel Archive, Bristol, DM 1758/11/10: 17 Jan. 1834.
88. *Morning Chronicle,* 5 May 1835: 3.
89. See *Times*, 2 April 1835: 4.

90. Brunel Archives, DM 162/10/2/folio 46-50.
91. Brunel Archive DM 162/10/1/folio 126-128, 3 March 1836.
92. Brunel Archive DM 162/10/2/folio 46-50, 13 June 1836: 50.
93. Brunel Archive, DM 162/10/2/folio 46-50, 13 June 1836: 50.
94. Brunel Archive, DM 162/10/1 folio 235 (10 Oct. 1836).
95. Gale, *Box Tunnel:* 9.
96. Jack Simmons, *The Birth of the Great Western, Diary and Correspondence of George Henry Gibbs*, MS.11021. Vol. 16 (Bath: Adam & Dart, 1971): 88.
97. *Railway Magazine,* No. V, July 1836: 190.
98. Gale, *Box Tunnel*: 8.
99. Ibid.: 13.
100. Ibid.: 12.
101. RAIL 1149/4 Letterbook, 15 Sept. 1838: 194-95.
102. *Railway Magazine,* No. VIII, Oct. 1836: 326.
103. Gale, *Box Tunnel:* 17.
104. *Bristol Mercury,* 15 April 1837: 3.
105. *Bristol Mercury,* 24 Feb. 1838: 2.
106. RAIL 1057/3731.
107. RAIL 1057 /3731.
108. RAIL 1057/3731.
109. Gale, *Box Tunnel:* 17.
110. Gale, *Box Tunnel:* 10.
111. RAIL 1057/3731.
112. *Bristol Mercury,* 10 Nov. 1838: 2.
113. *Champion and Weekly Herald,* 24 Nov. 1839: 7.
114. Christopher Awdry, *Brunel's Broad Gauge Railway* (Oxford: Oxford Publishing Company, 1992): 34.
115. David Brooke, *Journal of the Railway and Canal Historical Society*, No. 142, July 1989.
116. *Times,* 20 Sept. 1841: 6.
117. *Bristol Mercury,* 29 Dec. 1838.
118. *Bath Chronicle*, 18 July 1839.
119. RAIL 250/114 Weekly meeting of sub-committee on Progress of Work, 2 June 1841.
120. RAIL 1014/30 (22 June 1841).
121. Gale, *Box Tunnel:* 13.
122. RAIL 251/1, Box Tunnel contract No.2, between 12 June 1841 to 18 Aug. 1842.
123. RAIL 252/1, Box Tunnel contract No. 6, between 3 April 1840 to 11 Nov. 1841. See National Archives currency conversion tables.
124. RAIL 1149/5, 20 Aug. 1841: 268.
125. NA, MT. 6/1/226. Board of Trade Report, (12 Aug. 1842); included in Charles Knight, *Penny Cyclopaedia for Diffusion of Useful Knowledge,* 1843: 370; E.T. MacDermot, *History of the Great Western Railway,* Vol. 1, 1833–63 (London: GWR, 1927): 67.
126. *Times,* 29 March 1845: 5.

127. NA MT 6/1/226.
128. *Times,* 12 April 1845: 2. Colonel Charles Pasley, 1780–1861, was Inspector General of Railways.
129. *The Builder,* 23 Nov. 1844: 587.
130. *Jackson's Oxford Journal,* 28 Jan. 1843: 1.
131. *Bristol Mercury,* 28 Jan. 1843: 7.
132. *The Cornwall Royal Gazette,* 3 Nov. 1843.
133. See Kevin Robertson, *GWR, the Badminton Line, a Portrait of a Railway* (Stroud: Sutton, 1988): 4.
134. Wiltshire Record Office. WRO 197/Box/621 0321 920, 06/01/83.
135. WRO 192w/Box/621 0321 920, 06/01/83.
136. Bartholomew's revised 'half inch' contoured map, sheet 28, *North Somerset,* 1936.
137. RAIL 250/82, Brunel's Reports 1835–42 (17 Oct. 1836).
138. RAIL 1149/49, Parliamentary Committee of House of Commons on GWR, (25 March 1835): 81; & (26 March 1835): 110.
139. Herepath, *The Railway Magazine* (Jan. 1836): 314.

CHAPTER 3

1. Whyte, *Landscape and History*: 124.
2. David Cannadine, 'After the Horse: Nobility and Mobility in Modern Britain,' in *Land and Society in Britain 1700–1914*, essays in honour of F.L.M. Thompson, ed. F.L. Thompson, N.B. Harte, Roland E. Quinault (Manchester: Manchester University Press, 1996): 213-14.
3. Ibid.: 213.
4. Leigh Denault and Jennifer Landis, 'Motion and Means: Mapping Opposition to Railways in Victorian Britain,' History, Vol. 256, Holyoke College, Mass. (Dec. 1999) http:www.mholyoke.edu/courses/rschwart/ind_rev/rs/denault.htm (accessed Oct. 2016).
5. Whyte, *Landscape and History:* 124.
6. The Wiltshire family owned land on the Wiltshire-Somerset border near Box.
7. See J.R. Ward, *The Finance of Canal Building in Eighteenth Century England* (Oxford: Oxford University Press, 1974): 143-60.
8. Tom Williamson and Liz Bellamy, *Property and Landscape* (London: George Philips, 1987): 206.
9. HLRO Minutes of Evidence, HL 1847, Vol. 8 North Midland Railway: 159.
10. Michael Aston and James Bond, *The Landscape of Towns* (Stroud: Alan Sutton, 2000): 176.
11. HLRO Minutes of Evidence: 206.
12. Peter Lecount, *A Practical Treatise on Railways* (Edinburgh: A. & C. Black, 1839): 17.
13. Smiles, *George Stephenson*: 241.
14. See HL/PO/PB/5/1/1 (3 Aug. 1835): 902-30.
15. HL/PO/PB/5/2/2, 1836, Report from the Select Committee on Railway Bills: IX.
16. See J.R. Hepple, *The Influence of Landowners' Attitudes to Railway Alignment,* unpub. Ph.D, (Univ. Hull, 1974) chapter 5; also O.C. Williams, *The Historical*

Development of Private Bills and Standing Orders of the House of Commons Vol. 1(HMSO 1949): 65.
17. Burton, *Railway Builders*: 55.
18. RAIL 1149/49 House of Commons Select Committee on GWR (26 March 1835).
19. RAIL 280/34 Proof of Brunel surveying proposed lines between London and Reading and Bath and Bristol, Jan.–Dec. 1835. The property belonged to Mr Gore-Langton.
20. Celia Brunel-Noble, *The Brunels, Father and Son* (London: Cobden-Sanderson, 1938): 137.
21. Blower, *Tunnels*: 16-18.
22. See J. Farey Jnr, article on Canals in *Rees Cyclopaedia*, 1819.
23. *Birmingham Gazette*, 24 Jan. 1831.
24. *Freeling's Railway Companion to the London and Birmingham, Liverpool and Manchester Railway* (1838): 2-3.
25. Blower, *Tunnels:* 11.
26. See RAIL 1149/49, Parliamentary Committee of House of Commons on Great Western Railway (March 1835): 34-36, 75-80, 88-92.
27. Stuart Hylton, *The Great Experiment: The Birth of the Railway Age 1820–45* (Shepperton: Ian Allan, 2007): 127.
28. Leleux, *Regional History: The East Midlands:* 47.
29. Hansard 3rd series, House of Lords (20 May 1844) cols. 1297-99; quoted by Hepple, thesis: 172.
30. F.P. Delme Radcliffe, *Noble Science, A Few General Ideas on Foxhunting* (London: Routledge & Sons, 1839): 129.
31. Alnwick Ms. 3, Duke of Northumberland; Letter book (Nov. 1836–Aug 1844); Fitzwilliam Ms, Draft report by Lord Fitzwilliam as Chairman of Railway Land Compensation Bill (June 1845). Quoted by F.L.M. Thompson, *English Landed Gentry in the Nineteenth Century* (London: Routledge: 1963): 261.
32. Ibid: 259.
33. See Hepple, thesis: 315.
34. RAIL 1149/49: 3.
35. See Charles E. Lee, 'Railway Engineering and its Impact on Civilisation,' *Journal of the Newcomen Soc*, Vol. 36 (1963): 113.
36. Frederick S. Williams, *The Midland Railway, its Rise and Progress. A Narrative of Modern Enterprise* (London: Strahan & Co., 1876): 40.
37. See Trecia Hunt, 'The Sevenoaks Railway tunnel; its construction and immediate consequences', Univ.Kent. Dip. Loc. Hist. (1991).
38. (NA) PRO 30/22/2a, quoted by Anthony Burton, *The Railway Builders* (London: John Murray, 1992): 29.
39. See J.R. Ward, 'West Riding Landowners and the Railways,' *Journal of Transport History* Vol. 4 (1960): 242. See also 'Landlords, Family and Railways', www.richardjohnbr.blogspot.co.uk; (accessed Oct. 2016).
40. See R.W. Rennison, 'The Newcastle and Carlisle Railway and its Engineers 1829–1862,' *Transactions of Newcomen Society*, Vol. 72, No. 2 (2000-01): 203-13.

41. *Herepath's Railway Magazine* No. 1 (April 1836): 139. The then MP was John Monet Fector. The line from Chatham to Dover through Lyddon Hill Tunnel was opened in 1865.
42. See *Railway Magazine* No. 1 (April 1836): 101; also Joshua Richardson, *Observations on the Proposed Railroad from Newcastle upon Tyne to North Shields* (London: Longman Green & Co., 1834).
43. See Hepple, thesis: 99.
44. RAIL 280/34: Brunel's survey proposals for 1835.
45. G. Biddle et. al., *Railways, their Builders, and the Environment* (Farnham, Ashgate, 2003): 120.
46. Mike Chimes, 'The Civil Engineering of Canals and Railways before 1850,' *Studies in the History of Civil Engineering'* Vol. 7 (1997).
47. Denault and Landis, 'Motion and Means', History. www.mholyoke.edu/courses/rschwart/ind_rev/rs/denault.htm.
48. Turnock, *An Historical Geography of Railways*: 8.
49. Inst. of Civil Engineers, *Proceedings* (8 Jan. 1856): 19.
50. Samuel Smiles, *The Life of George Stephenson* (London: John Murray, 1857): 325.
51. J.C. Jeaffreson, *Life of Robert Stephenson* (London: Longmans, 1864): 269-70.
52. Michael Robbins, *The Railway Age* (London: Routledge & Kegan Paul, 1962): 58.
53. Benjamin Disraeli, *Sybil*, 1845 (Oxford: Oxford World Classics): 117-19.
54. A.W.N. Pugin, *An Apology for the Revival of Christian Architecture in England* (London: John Weale, 1843): 11.
55. Jack Simmons, *The Railway in Town and Country 1830–1914* (London: Faber & Faber, 1986): 308.
56. RAIL 1014/8/1 (25 Sept. 1834). Quoted in Celia Brunel-Noble, *The Brunels Father and Son* (London: Cobden-Sanderson, 1938): 118.
57. See Biddle, 'The Impact of Society in Britain', chap.8 in *Railways and their Built Environment* (Farnham: Ashgate, 2003): 121.
58. *Times*, 3 March 1887:9; J.M. Crook 'Ruskin and the Railways' in *The Impact of Railways on Society in Britain,* ed. A.K.B. Evans and G.V. Gough (Farnham: Ashgate, 2003): 129-34.
59. Biddle, *Impact of Society:* 122.
60. W.O. Skeat, *George Stephenson and his Letters* (London: Institution of Mechanical Engineers, 1973): 77.
61. Turnock, Historical Geography: 7.
62. George Godwin, *An Appeal to the Public on the Subject of Railways* (London: J. Weale, 1837): 9. See also Denault, & Landis, Holyoke College, Mass, Dec. 1990; www.mtholyoke.edu/courses
63. Godwin, *Appeal:* 41.
64. Cannadine, *After the Horse:* 212.
65. See Stanley H. Palmer, *Police and Protest in England and Ireland*, 1780–1850 (Cambridge: Cambridge University Press, 1988): 409.
66. *Times*, 14 Nov. 1845: 4 ; quoted in Rex Christiansen, *A Regional History of the Railways of Great Britain,* Vol. 7 The West Midlands (Newton Abbot: David & Charles, 1973): 136.

67. See Keith Mills, 'A Ducal Whimsy,' *Midland Record*, No. 3 (1995): 25-29.
68. *The Diary of William Mackenzie, the First International Railway Contractor*, ed. David Brooke (London: ICE, Thomas Telford, 2000): 26 Aug. 1847.
69. Simmons, *The Railway in Town and Country*: 307.
70. By the time the line was constructed, the Northern and Eastern Railway had been absorbed by the Eastern Counties Railway.
71. This was Richard Griffin, 3rd Baron Braybrooke, 1783–1858. He was MP for Berkshire, 1812–25, and succeeded by Robert Palmer, who opposed the construction of the Great Western in 1834. Lord Braybrooke was later praised in the *Eastern Counties Railway Guide*, 1851, for opening Audley End to the public every day except Sunday and welcoming picnic parties. This was subsequently quoted in A.D. Bayne, *A Royal Illustrated History of Eastern England* (Great Yarmouth: James Macdonald, 1873): 99.
72. See Hepple, thesis: 140. HLRO Min. of Evidence, HC 1836, Vol. 18, Northern and Eastern Railway (20 April): 119.
73. N.W. Cundy, *Observations on Railways, Addressed to the Nobility, Gentry, Clergy, Agriculturalists, etc. in Connection with the Great Northern and Eastern Railway* (Great Yarmouth: J. Palmer, 1834).
74. See J.C. Francis, *A History of English Railways, 1820–45* (London, Longman Brown, 1857): 256-63, for an account of the tortuous negotiations between Braybrooke and the Eastern Counties directors.
75. Parliamentary Act for Construction of Eastern Counties Railway at Newport by Cambridge to Ely, HL/PO/PB/1/ 1844, 7 & 8 Vict. 1c1 XII. See also 'Audley End Tunnel', *British Railways Eastern Region Magazine* Vol. 7 (July 1956): 131; also Bayne, *A Royal History*: 99.
76. Gordon Biddle, *Britain's Historical Railway Buildings* (Oxford, 2003): 198.
77. www.yeoldsussexpages.com/history (accessed Oct. 2016).
78. Churton, *Rail Road Book*: 160.
79. Leleux, *Regional History:* 110. See also: Marilyn Palmer and Peter Neaverson, *Industry in the Landscape, 1700–1900* (London: Routledge, 2002): 9; F.S. Williams, *The Midland Railway: its Rise and Progress* (Derby: Strahan & Co.): 1874.
80. RAIL 1149/49: Parliamentary Committee of the House of Commons (25 March 1835): 160.
81. See Tim Brydon, *Brunel, the Great Engineer* (Shepperton: Ian Allan, 1999): 68.
82. RAIL 1149/49 (23 March 1835): 40.
83. Ibid.: 40.
84. *Times*, 4 July 1836: 2.
85. Brunel University Broad-Gauge Trilogy; http://dev.brunel.ac.uk (accessed Oct 2016).
86. See Adrian Vaughan, *Brunel, An Engineering Biography* (Shepperton: Ian Allan 2006): 35.
87. RAIL 1149/49: 112.
88. RAIL 250/82 Brunel's Reports (8 Oct. 1835).
89. *Times*, 2 June 1838: 6.
90. RAIL 1149/2 Brunel's Letters (8 and 10 March 1836).

91. RAIL 1149/2 Brunel's Letters (21 April 1837); see also Adrian Vaughan, *The Intemperate Engineer* (Shepperton: Ian Allan, 2010): 101-02.
92. RAIL 250/82 report (20 Nov. 1837).
93. Shockerwick was built in the 1740s and attributed to Bath architect John Wood the Elder. It was owned by the Wiltshire family from 1745 until 1889. It is now a hotel.
94. See HL/PO/PB/5/1/1, minutes of evidence (6 July 1835): 392.
95. *Railway Magazine* No. XIX (Sept. 1837): 279. For an excellent survey of the architecture of Bath see Walter Ison *The Georgian Buildings of Bath* (London: Faber & Faber, 1948).
96. RAIL 1149/49: House of Commons Committee (23 March 1837): 73. See Ordnance Survey *Historical Map and Guide, Georgian Bath* (Bath Archaeological Trust, 1989) for 1:2500 scale record of route of railway through Sydney Gardens and Bath peninsular.
97. RAIL 1149/49 House of Commons Committee (25 March 1835): 86-7.
98. Ibid.: 87.
99. Ibid.: 86.
100. RAIL 1149/3 (14 Dec. 1837): 175-76.
101. RAIL 1149/5 (23 Jan. 1839): 53; RAIL 1149/5 (6 Jan. 1840): 310.
102. RAIL 1149/5 (23 Jan. 1839): 53.
103. RAIL 1149/5 (6 Jan. 1840): 310.
104. *The Civil Engineer and Architect's Journal* (Jan. 1840): 38.
105. RAIL 250/100 (21 Aug. 1840).
106. Brunel Archive, Sketchbook 8, fol. 29 (1839).
107. *Bristol Mercury*, 14 Dec. 1839: 2.
108. RAIL 250/82: Brunel Reports 1835-42 (14 Sept. 1835).
109. Ibid.: (14 Nov. 1836).
110. *John Bull* (31 March 1839): 156. It seems that the name of the house 'Tiverton' was used by Brunel for a preliminary sketch for one of his tunnel portals that subsequently became Twerton (long) Tunnel.
111. V.C.H. *Cambridgeshire* Vol. 10 (1989): 84; Cecil J. Allen, *The Great Eastern Railway* (Shepperton: Ian Allan 1967): 45. Between 1885–1945 Warren Hill Station stood just north of the tunnel, specially to serve the needs of race-goers.
112. See James Stephen Curl. *Kensal Green Cemetery, 1824–2001* (Chichester: Phillimore, 2001).
113. Ibid.: 47.
114. Ibid.: 69.
115. Ibid.: 69.
116. Ibid.: 69.
117. See Jack Simmons. 'The Power of the Railway,' in *The Victorian City*, ed. H.J. Dyos and Michael Wolf, Vol. 1 (London: Routledge, 1973): 304.
118. *Imperial Gazetteer of England and Wales*, (London: A. Fullarton, 1869): 167.
119. Jeaffreson, *Stephenson*: 269-70.
120. See W.E. Aytoun, 'Champions of the Rail,' *Blackwood's Magazine* Vol. 70, No. 434 (Dec. 1851): 739-50.

121. Francis, *English Railways*: 256.
122. Barbara Kerr, *Country Professions in the Victorian Countryside,* Vol. 1 (London: Routledge, 1981): 294.
123. Ibid.: 295. Kerr cites *Kingsbridge Gazette,* 25 March 1870.
124. See S.G. Checkland, *The Rise of Industrial Society in England* (London: Longman, 1964): 14-15.
125. HL/PO/HC/1876, Vol. 42, Westerham Valley Railway (22 March 1876): 104-106; see Hepple, thesis: 324-26.
126. See Francis, *English Railways*: 184.
127. Ibid.: 186-89.
128. See Hepple, thesis: 53-72.
129. O.F. Christie, *Transition from the Aristocracy 1832–1867* (London: Seeley Services & Co., 1927): 222; cited in Hepple, thesis.: 107.
130. See McDermot, *Great Western Railway,* Vol. 1: 60.
131. Simmons, *The Railways of Britain*: 52-53.
132. See D.M. Palliser, *The Staffordshire Landscape* (London: Hodder, 1976): 134-36 for reference to the landscaping of the estate park; for background history on project see, Robin Mathams and Dave Barrett, 'The Trent Valley Railway,' *Back Track* Vol. 28, No. 1 (Jan. 2014).
133. *Caledonian Mercury,* 26 Dec. 1839.
134. *Morning Chronicle,* 24 April 1841: 5.
135. *Morning Chronicle,* 9 Aug. 1841: 5.
136. STAFF. R.O. Q/RU m73. Hidcot Hall Estate.
137. STAFF. RO. Anson Family. D1798. (28 Dec. 1831.)
138. Ibid.
139. Curzon Street Station was replaced by the through New Street Station in 1854.
140. *Morning Chronicle,* 9 Aug. 1842: 6.
141. *Morning Post,* 30 July 1842: 6.
142. *Dictionary of National Biography* Vol. 34 (Oxford: Oxford University Press): 230.
143. STAFF R.O. P240/M/E/430/25 (11 March 1844): Report of Joseph Lock, Chief Engineer for the Trent Valley Railway Company on proposed route of track.
144. N.W. Webster, *Britain's First Trunk Line, The Grand Junction Railway* (Bath: Adam & Dart, 1972): 157; Wilfred L. Steel, 'The History of the London and North Western Railway,' *Rail and Travel Monthly* (1914).
145. STAFF R.O. D260/M/C/430/25: Trent Valley Railway. Directors' correspondence with Lord Hatherton, Earl of Lichfield's representative.
146. STAFF R.O. P260/M/E/260/25 (22 March 1844): Trent Valley Railway, Directors' correspondence with Lord Hatherton.
147. STAFF. R.O. P260/M/E/430/25 (29 March 1844): letter from Lord Anglesey to Directors of Trent Valley Railway Company.
148. STAFF R.O. D615/E(A) 17 (18 April 1844): letter from Earl of Lichfield to his Land Agent, Harvey Wyatt.

149. STAFF. R.O. D615/E(A)17 (11 Nov. 1844): Letter from Earl of Lichfield to brother, Col. George Anson.
150. STAFF R.O. D615/E(A)17 (12 Nov 1844): Letter from Col. Anson to Trent Valley Railway Company.
151. STAFF R.O. D615/E/A/17 (12 Nov.1844).
152. STAFF R.O.D615/E/A/17 (19 Nov.1844).
153. STAFF R.O. D615/E/A/17 (15 Dec.1844).
154. STAFF R.O. D615/E/A/17 (16 Dec.1844).
155. RAIL699/1 Trent Valley Minute Book.
156. Trent Valley Railway Bill, House of Commons Select Committee 1845 XXX1 (29 April 1845): 34.
157. STAFF. RO. D615/E/(2)14/2. Agreement between Trent Valley Company and Earl of Lichfield.
158. STAFF RO. D615/E(A)17 (June 1845). Request by Col. Anson for ornamentation of Shugborough Estate.
159. Ibid.
160. STAFF. RO. D 615/E/14/2; see Tim Warner, 'Country House Railway Stations', *Back Track,* vol. 11, No.6 (June 1997): 299.
161. STAFF RO. D 615/E/14/2: 7; agreement for policeman to patrol tracks to prevent trespass or damage to estate.
162. STAFF R.O. D615/E(2)14/2 (1 May 1845).
163. STAFF R.O. D615/E(A)17 (2 June 1845); RAIL 699/4; map of track and land between Rugby & Stafford.
164. STAFF R.O. D615/E/14/2; see Warner, *Back Track* (June 1997): 299; see also Clement E. Stretton, *A History of the Trent Valley Railway*, a paper given at Tamworth (21 June 1897) NMR Archive, LID 65.
165. RAIL 699/1: Trent Valley Minute Book.
166. *Railway Times* (15 Nov. 1845): 22.
167. *Aberdeen Journal,* 28 April 1847.
168. *Morning Post,* 18 Nov. 1846: 2.
169. RAIL 699/1: Trent Valley Minute Book.
170. *The Standard* (28 June 1847). See also Michael Hitchins, *Trent Valley Railway* (Stroud: Sutton, 2003): 8. He cites the London & Birmingham Railway as paying some landowners three times the true value of land.
171. Rail 699/1: Trent Valley Minute Book (11 Feb. 1847): 99.
172. *Staffordshire Chronicle,* 19 June 1848.
173. RAIL 699/4 section of tunnel on route map, 1846.
174. RAIL 699/2 Trent Valley Minute Book (8 July 1847) ; *Railway Times* (17 July 1847): 932. See also Brook, *The Railway Navvy*: 60.
175. Williams, *Our Iron Rails:* 154.
176. NMR Archive 140263: Board of Trade Map of projected Lines through the Trent and Churnet Valley, referred to in a report ordered by House of Commons, 13 March 1845.
177. See Mark Bowden, *Unravelling the Landscape* (Stroud: Tempus, 1999): 160.

178. See, Mike Chrimes 'The Influence of Landowners on Route selection', *Studies in the History of Civil Engineering*, Aldershot, Ashgate, 1997: 240.
179. Quoted in Charles E. Lee, 'Railway Engineering and its Impact on Civilisation,' *Transactions of Newcomen Society* Vol. 36 (1963): 113.

CHAPTER 4
1. Charles Harper, *The Brighton Road, London* (London: C. Palmer, 1922): 223.
2. Subterranea Britannica is the best: www.subrit.org.uk.
3. *Tim Warner,* 'Monstrous Cavities,' *Back Track*, Vol. 3, No. 5 (Nov–Dec 1989): 226-29. Recent books on tunnel exploration include Antony Clayton, *Subterranean City: Beneath the Streets of London* (London: Historical Publications, 2010); Bradley L. Garrett, *Subterranean London: Cracking the Capital* (London: Prestel Publishing, 2015).
4. See David E. Nye, *American Technological Sublime* (Cambridge, US, MIT, 1994): 45-76.
5. Ibid.: 47.
6. Nye, *American Technological Sublime:* 54.
7. Ibid.: 58.
8. Ibid.: 76.
9. John Dixon Hunt, 'Gardens and the Picturesque,' in *Studies in the History of Landscape Architecture,* (Cambridge US: MIT, 1997): 179. See also Malcolm Andrews, *The Search for the Picturesque* (Aldershot, Scholar Press 1989).
10. Leonardo da Vinci, Codex Arundel, British Library; see Liana Bartolon, *The Life and Times of Leonardo* (London: Paul Hamlyn, 1967).
11. Edward Bradbury, *Midland Railway Sketches*, May 1879 (reprinted Sheffield: Midland Railway Society, 1999): 36.
12. Edmund Burke, *A Philosophical Enquiry into the Origin of our Ideas of the Sublime and the Beautiful,* 1757 (edited by James Boulton, Oxford: Blackwell's, 1958).
13. Horace Walpole, *The Castle of Otranto, a Gothic Story,* 1764 (London: William Bath, 1811): 17.
14. Naomi Miller, *Heavenly Caves, Reflections on the Garden Grotto* (London: George Allen & Unwin, 1982): 51.
15. Anthony Beckles-Wilson, *Alexander Pope's Grotto at Twickenham* (Twickenham Museum & Garden History Society, 1998).
16. Yale Centre for British Art and Derby Museum. The view is from within the grotto looking to the entrance.
17. Charles Philip Moritz, *Travels in England,* 1782 (London: Humphrey Milford Oxford University Press, 1926): 85.
18. Bradbury, *Midland Railway Sketches:* 48.
19. George Woodward and Isaac Cruickshank, *Eccentric Excursions or Literary and Practical Sketches … in England and Wales* (London: Allen & West, 1797): 201.
20. B.C.L. Spencer Stanhope MS 2246/65. *Journal of Transport History,* 3rd series, Vol. 4, No. 2 (Sept. 1983): 53.

21. Abraham Rees, *The Cyclopaedia,* Vol. VIII (London: Longman, Hunt, Rees, Orme & Brown,1819), article on coal. This description was originally published in *The Picture of Newcastle-upon Tyne,* Newcastle, 1807; and published in full in M.J.T. Lewis, *Early Wooden Railways* (London: Routledge & Kegan Paul, 1970): 324-26.
22. Ibid.
23. Warner, 'Monstrous Cavities' *Back Track,* (1989): 229.
24. See Claire Moorhead, 'The Labrynth at Edge Hill,' *Institute of Historic Buildings Conservation Journal* (May 2009): 23-25.
25. RAIL 250/115; GWR Traffic Committee Minutes (20 Aug. 1840).
26. RAIL 1014/30.
27. *Peter Parley's Annual* (Boston, US: S.G. Goodrich, 1840): 129.
28. Henry Booth, *Eight Views Illustrating the Liverpool and Manchester Railway* (Liverpool: Wales & Barnes: 1830).
29. *Times,* 3 Aug. 1829: 4.
30. *Times,* 3 Aug. 1829: 4.
31. W.O. Skeat, *Stephenson the Engineer* (London: ICE 1973): 123.
32. See Rudolf Elvers, *Felix Mendelssohn, a Life in Letters* (New York: Fromm, 1986): 92-93.
33. Skeat, *Stephenson the Engineer*: 123.
34. *Times,* 18 June 1830: 3.
35. Ibid.
36. Frances Ann Kemble, *Record of a Childhood* Vol. 1 (London: R. Bentley & Son, 1878): 199-201. This autobiography by Kemble ought to be better known as she paints a picture of many other aspects of Regency and Victorian life and events both in Britain and America, where she lived for some years. Her first experience of tunnelling was in 1827 when she visited the workings of Marc Brunel's Thames Tunnel.
37. Kemble, *Record of Childhood* Vol. 2: 154.
38. Ibid.: 156. Because of the novelty of the railway she even described the basic nature of a rail road, and how the 'wheels were placed upon two iron bands (rails) which formed the road … The carriages were set in motion by a mere push'.
39. Ibid.: 159.
40. Ibid.
41. Ibid.: 160.
42. See *Lady Dorchester, Recollections of a Long Life, the Letters and Diaries of 1st Lord Broughton, 1786–1869,* Vol. V (London: John Murray, 1910): .3.
43. *Frazer's Magazine* (April 1838): 430-31.
44. Nathaniel Hawthorne, *Passages from the English Notebooks* Vol. 1 (Boston, US: Mifflin & Co., 1870: 172.
45. *Fraser's Magazine*: 67.
46. *Leicester Journal,* 20 July 1832.
47. C. R. Clinker, 'The Leicester and Swannington Railway', *Leicestershire Archaeological Society Transactions,* vol. XXX (1954): 68.

48. See Francis Whishaw, *Analysis of Railways* (London: John Weale, 1837): 290.
49. *Times,* 16 Jan. 1836: 5.
50. Sir George Head, *A Home Tour through the Manufacturing Districts of England* (London: John Murray, 1835): 201.
51. For the impact of railway guides as an aid to travel see Alan Everitt, 'The Railway and Rural Tradition, 1840–1940,' Chapter 14 in *The Impact of the Railway on Society in Britain,* ed. A.K.B. Evans and J.V. Gough (Aldershot: Ashgate, 2003).
52. George Measom, *Guide to the North Eastern and North British Railway* (London: Griffin, Bohn, 1861): 160. See also G.H. Martin, 'Sir George Measom 1818–1901, and his Railway Guides,' Chapter 17 in *The Impact of the Railway on Society in Britain,* ed. A.K.B. Evans and G.V. Gough (London: Routledge, 2003).
53. *Bury's Views on the London and Birmingham Railway* (London: Ackermann, 18 Sept. 1837). Bury was an architect by profession, articled to Augustus Charles Pugin who also produced prints for Ackermann.
54. J.C. Bourne, *The London and Birmingham Railway* (London: J.C. Bourne, 1838). The book contained thirty-two views.
55. *Freeling's Companion for the London, Birmingham and Liverpool and Manchester Railway* (London: Whittaker & Co., 1838): 33.
56. Roscoe, *The London and Birmingham Railway*: 1.
57. See letters in *The Civil Engineer and Architect's Journal* (Feb. 1841): 65; (March 1841): 95. Lecount was from a naval background and was later employed as sub-engineer on the London and Birmingham Railway. It may be questioned as to how far he had a flair for historical or topographical writing.
58. James Drake, *Drake's Road Book of the Grand Junction and London and Birmingham Railway* (London: Hayward & Moore, 1838): 28.
59. Francis Coghlan, *Coghlan's Iron Road; London and Birmingham and Liverpool Companion* (London,: A.H. Bailey & Co., 1838): 5. If one includes the cut-and-cover tunnel beneath a corner of Kensal Green cemetery the number of tunnels is eight.
60. See Samuel Sidney, *Rides on the Railways* (London: W.S. Orr & Co., 1851; repub. Chichester: Phillimore, 1973).
61. *Times,* 18 Sept. 1838: 3.
62. *Caledonian Mercury,* 29 Aug. 1850.
63. Freeling, *Companion*: 33.
64. See Henry Noel Humphrey, 'Fragments of a Provincial Tour,' *The Architectural Magazine and Journal* in *Architecture, Building and Furnishing,* Vol. 5 (1838): 677-82.
65. Drake, *Road Boo*: 15. The length of the tunnel is 1,220 yards.
66. Roscoe, *Guide*: 45.
67. J.W.W. Wyld, *The London and Birmingham Railway Guide and Companion* (London: James Wyld, 1838).
68. G.E. Osborne, *Guide to the London and Birmingham Railway* (Birmingham: E.C. & W. Osborne, 1838): 121-22.

69. Roscoe, *London and Birmingham Railway*: 65.
70. J.W.W. Wyld, *The Railways of Great Britain and Ireland* (London: James Wyld, 1842): 43.
71. *Times* 24 Aug. 1839: 6.
72. See P.S. Richards, 'The Railway's influence on Leighton Buzzard,' *Bedfordshire Magazine*, vol. 15, 1975.
73. Roscoe, *London and Birmingham Railway:* 72-73.
74. Wyld, *Railway Guide:* 52.
75. Samuel Sidney, *Rides on the Railway* (London: William Orr & Son, 1851); reprinted with introduction by Barrie Trinder (Chichester: Phillimore & Co., 1973): 28
76. *Civil Engineer and Architect's Journal*, 1837–38: 326.
77. *Times*, 3 Nov. 1838: 6.
78. Henry Cole, *Railway Chronicle Travelling Charts No. 1, London-Wolverton-Birmingham* (London: Railway Chronicle, 1846).
79. Sidney, *Rides on Railways*: 64.
80. Drake, *Road Book*: 75. It is not clear how a person could look down one of these shafts since they are many feet above ground level.
81. Wyld, *The London and Birmingham Railway Companion:* 150.
82. Francis, *A History of English Railway*: 213.
83. George Measom, *Illustrated Guide to the Great Western Railway* (London: Richard Griffin, 1852): 48.
84. *Times*, 18 April 1842: 7
85. *Daily Telegraph*, 12 April 1859.
86. Ibid.
87. See Martin Barnes, 'Maths throws light on Brunel Legend,' *New Civil Engineer* (4 April 1985): 29-31; Martin Barnes, 'A not so modern myth, the Box Tunnel on the Great Western and the Legend that the Sun shines right through it on Brunel's Birthday,' *British Sundial Society* No. 94 (June 1994): 15-17; see also C.P. Atkins, 'Box Tunnel and I.K. Brunel's Birthday, a Theoretical Investigation,' *Journal of British Astronomical Association* Vol. 95, No. 6 (Oct. 1985): 260-62; *The Great Western Railway Magazine* (Sept. 1928): 356-58. See also *Track Topics, a Book of Engineering for Boys of all Ages* (London: GWR Paddington, 1935).
88. *Girls' Own Paper*, 24 July 1886: 687.
89. *Young Folks' Paper*, 7 Dec. 1889: 363.
90. Charles Read, *The Box Tunnel* (Boston, USA: Tiden & Field, 1857): 93-108. Box appears in a recent children's fictional story, *IS* by Derek Webb, in which the heroine IS is reincarnated as I.K. Brunel; www.IKbrunel.org.uk.index.php (accessed Oct. 2016).
91. James Stephen Curl, *Victorian Architecture* (Reading: Spire Books, 2007): 78.
92. Churton, *The Rail Road Book*: 94.
93. *Bath Chronicle*, 1840, quoted in Andrew Swift, *The Ringing Grooves* (Bath: Akemann Press, 2006): 111.
94. At 1 mile 1,125 yards it was longer than Kilsby at 1 mile 666 yards; it was to be exceeded in 1841 by the opening of Box at 1 mile 1,452 yards. See length tables in Blower, *British Railway Tunnels*, 1964.

95. *Parliamentary Gazetteer of England and Wales*, 1851, Vol. 3: 19-20.
96. A.F. Tate, *Introduction to Views on the Leeds and Manchester Railway* (Liverpool: A.F. Tate, 1845): 16. See Michael Freeman, *Railways and the Victorian Imagination* (Yale: London, 1999): 232-33.
97. W.N. Webster, *Joseph Locke, Railway Revolutionary* (London: Allen & Unwin, 197): 113.
98. See Malcolm Timperly, 'Light at the End of the Tunnel,' *Back Track* Vol. 29, No. 3 (March 2015): 178-83.
99. C.R.F., 'The North Midland Railway,' in *Derby Mercury*, 9 Dec. 1840: 1.
100. See Edward Bradbury, *Midland Railway Sketches by Strephon* (Derby: Midland Railway, May 1879); republished (Sheffield: Midland Railway Society, 1999).
101. Ibid.: 48.
102. Ibid.: 52.
103. Ibid.: 53.
104. Ibid.: 54.
105. Ibid.: 54.
106. *Bradshaw's Handbook,* section IV: (London: John Bradshaw, 1863; reprinted Oxford: Old House, Botley, 2012): 12. See *Railway Wonders of the World*, Vol. 2, ed. Clarence Winchester (London: Amalgamated Press, 1935–36): 1232 for reference to numerous long tunnels on the former Midland Railway. Between Chesterfield and Manchester there are over 9 miles of tunnelling in 30 miles.
107. Joseph Devey, *Life of Joseph Locke, Civil Engineer* (London: Richard Bentley 1862): 134.
108. Norman W. Webster, *The Grand Junction Railway* (Bath: Adam & Dart, 1972): 79.
109. George Measom, *Illustrated Guide to the London and South Eastern Railway* (London: W.H. Smith & Son, 1853): 54-55.
110. *Railway Magazine and Annals of Science* (March 1838): 198. The references to *Railway Magazine* are to the journal founded and edited by John Herapath and not the present journal of the same name founded in July 1897.
111. *Railway Magazine* (April 1838): 298.
112. Whishaw, *Railways of Great Britain*: 408.
113. *Times*, 1 Nov. 1839: 6.
114. *Railway Times* (5 Oct. 1839): 779.
115. *Kentish Gazette*, 7 Nov. 1843: 3. See Roger St Clair, 'Earlier Tunnelling on the Kent Coast,' in *Back Track* Vol. 8, No.2 (March/April 1994): 80. See also http:// Dover-kent.co.uk/Wellington.http (accessed Oct. 2016).
116. *Gentleman's Magazine,* Vol. 176 (1844): 414.
117. *The Builder* (2 March 1844): 100.
118. Ibid.
119. *The Builder* (3 Feb. 1844): 58.
120. Churton, *Road Book*: 177.
121. See *Railway Times* (19 Oct. 1839): 827.
122. *Official Guide to the London, Brighton and South Coast Railway* (London Bridge: 1893): 108.

123. Henry Cole, *Railway Chronicle Travelling Charts or Iron Road Book for Perusal on the Journey, London to Dover Route* (London: Railway Chronicle, 1846).
124. *Jobbin's London and Brighton Railway Guide,* Jobbins, London, 1841, 40.
125. Harper, *Brighton Road:* 233.
126. *Brighton Herald,* 16 May 1840.
127. *Brighton Herald,* 25 Sept. 1841.
128. Michael Mansfield, *Memoirs of a Lawyer* (London: Bloomsbury Publishing, 2009): 8.
129. Coghlan, *Iron Road Book*: 34.
130. Ibid.
131. Ibid.
132. Charles Dickens, 'The Signal-Man,' *All the Year Round,* Dec. 1866: 21.
133. See Simon Bradley, *The Railways, Nation, Network and People* (London: Profile Books, 2015: 159).
134. R.L. Stephenson, *Edinburgh Picturesque Notes* (London: Seeley & Co. 1878): 111. The literary reference was to William Harrison Ainsworth, a now largely forgotten Victorian historical novelist. See also David Mclean, 'Lost Edinburgh, the Scotland Street Tunnel,' *Scotsman,* 12 August 2013.
135. See Ian Kennedy and Julian Treherz, *The Railway in the Age of Steam,* London: Yale, & Walker Art Gallery Liverpool, 2008. For a comprehensive survey of early railway art see also 'The Artists' Eye', Chapter 5 in Jack Simmons, *The Victorian Railway* (London: Thames & Hudson, 1995): 120-54.
136. See Wosk, *Breaking Frame*: 35.
137. Jack Simmons, *The Image of the Train* (Bradford: National Museum of Photography, Film and Television, 1993): 7.
138. Ibid: 8.
139. See Michael Freeman, *Railways and the Victorian Imagination* (London: Yale, 1999): 196-98.
140. Palmer and Neaverson, *Industry in the Landscape*: 187. See also Whyte, *Landscape and History*: 123-25.
141. See Whyte, *Landscape and History*: 124 & 187. See also Gareth Rees, *Early Railway Prints, a Social History of the Railways from 1825 to 1850* (London: Phaidon, 1980).
142. See Rees, *Early Railway Prints*: 20.
143. Ibid.
144. A.F. Seeley and D. Walters, 'The First Railway Architecture,' *Architectural Review,* Vol. 135 (March 1963): 364-66.
145. See C.F. Dendy Marshall, 'The Liverpool and Manchester Railway,' *Transactions of the Newcomen Society,* Vol. 2 (1921): 12-44 for a complete catalogue of prints.
146. John Blackmore, *Views on the Newcastle and Carlisle Railway* (Newcastle upon Tyne: Currie & Bowman, and London: C. Tilt, 1836).
147. NRM, c2. 1. 1977. 7732. 77/21/632.
148. Michael Freeman, *Transport in Victorian Britain* (Manchester: Manchester University Press,1988): 6.
149. Ibid.

150. See www.sciencemuseum.org.uk/onlinestuff/stories/john_cooke_bourne for brief biography of Bourne including his later achievements (accessed Oct.2016).
151. Camden Archives, Heal Coll. A X11. 69 includes drawing by R.B. Schnebbelie of short Kensal Green Tunnel, dated 13 September 1837.
152. Simmons, *Victorian Railway*: 14.
153. Ibid: 120-29. See, Simmons, Chapter 5, *The Artist's Eye*.
154. Head, *Stokers and Pokers*: 8.
155. N.R.M. 1906 – 18/4 D257.
156. *The Gentleman's Magazine*, Vol. 167 (1840): 187.
157. Elton Collection, Coalbrookdale Museum of Iron, Ironbridge, AE 1978. 17.
158. *Illustrated London News* (4 Dec. 1847): 367.
159. NRM archive, 1977 -7671 77/21/565.
160. *Illustrated London News* (4 Dec.1847): 367.
161. Francis D. Klingender, *Art and the Industrial Revolution*, rev. and ed. Arthur Elton (London: Routledge and Paul, 1971): 158.
162. *Railway Wonders*, ed. Winchester (1935–36).
163. Bath, BATVG, P /1917.5.
164. Ibid.
165. BATVG. Hunt Coll. Vol. 50: 150.
166. See illustration in A.T. Brooks and A.E. Peace, *Bath Stone, a Quarry History* (Cardiff: Univ. Cardiff Dept of Extramural Studies, and Bath: Kingsmead Press, 1979); also James Phimester and Jerome Tait, 'Corsham's Hidden Landscape,' *Landscapes,* Vol. 15, No. 1 (June 2014) for a study of the recent history of the underground quarry workings at Box and how they impinged on the railway tunnel.
167. The Eastern Entrance to Abbotscliffe Tunnel, lithograph published by Clerk & Co. 202 High Holborn. NRM. 77/121/661 1977-7758 0245.
168. Great Western Railway Museum, Swindon.
169. A.F. Tait, Summit Tunnel; lithograph, published by Day & Haig, Lithographer to the Queen, 1845, NRM.77/21/7 1977 – 7196.
170. See Freeman, *Railways and the Victorian Imagination* (London: Yale): 232.
171. *Illustrated London News* (2 Aug. 1845).
172. Illustrated in Brooke, *The Railway Navvy*, fig. 6: 58.
173. See Greg Norden, *Landscapes under the Luggage Rack* (Northampton: GNRP, 1999) for a survey of railway art in the twentieth century, including depictions of tunnels.
174. See Reginald Silvester, *Official Railway Postcards of the British Isles,* pt. 1 (London: BPH Publications, 1978).
175. *Times*, 27 July, 1928:17; letter, 'Ever Changing Rhythms'.

CHAPTER 5

1. See Wosk, *Breaking Frame*: 30-66.
2. *The Railway Magazine* Vol. 1 (March 1836): 4. The carriages were of course rope-hauled through the tunnel.

3. See Ralph Harrington, 'The Neuroses of the Railways,' *History Today* (July 1994): 16. He expands this theme in 'The Railway Accident: Trains, Trauma and Technological crisis in nineteenth century Britain' York: University of York, 1999; www.york.ac.uk/inst/irs/irshome/papers/rtyacc.
4. Harrington, *Neuroses*: 15.
5. *Quarterly Review* Vol. 63 (1839): 22.
6. Schivelbusch, *The Railway Journey*: 129.
7. Ibid. 75; *Zeitung fur Eisenbahnen, Dampfschiffahrt und Maschinenkunde*, Vol. 1 (Berlin, 1845): 114-15.
8. Dickens, *Household Words*, vol. XI (1855): 415.
9. *House of Commons Journal* (20 March 1842); see also Ralph Harrington,' The Railway Journey & the Neuroses of Modernity', in *Pathologies of Travel*, ed. Richard Wigley and George Revill (Amsterdam: Ridolphi, 1999): 236-37. For additional fear of attack by criminals see also Wolfgang Schivelbusch, *Railway Journey*, Chapter 7 'The Pathology of the Railway Journey'.
10. J.D. Kohl, *The King of Saxony's Journey through England and Scotland in the Year 1844* (reprinted London: Map Collectors' Circle, 1968): 267. See also Robin Barnes, 'A Royal Progress, King Frederick II of Saxony in 1844,' *Back Track* Vol. 16 Nos. 6-7 (June & July, 2002): 343-50 & 406-13.
11. Peter Lecount, *A Practical Treatise on Railways* (Edinburgh: A. & C. Black, 1839): 196.
12. Ibid: 219.
13. Lieut. Peter Lecount wrote his *Treatise on Railways* initially for Encyclopaedia Britannica. He served under Admiral Sir Richard Moorson, whose son, Captain Constantine Moorson, served as joint secretary to the London and Birmingham Railway. Probably Lecount owed his position as sub-engineer on the London and Birmingham Railway to Moorson.
14. Roscoe, *London and Birmingham Railway*: 68.
15. Biddle, *The Railway Heritage of Britain*, 1983: XX.
16. Catherine Hickie, 'The Fatal Form of Contentment,' Vol. 13 No. 2 *The Permanente Journal* (Spring 2009): 88-91.
17. See Charles E. Lee *Passengers of Distinction* (Westminster: Railway Gazette 1946).
18. Roscoe, *London and Birmingham Railway*: 67.
19. See Freeman, *Railways and the Victorian Imagination*: 114.
20. See Jill L. Matus, 'Trauma, Memory, and the Railway Disaster, the Dickensian Connection,' *Victorian Studies*, Vol. 43 No. 3 (Spring 2001): 413-37.
21. Stuart Hylton, *The Grand Experiment: the Birth of the Railway Age, 1825–45* (Shepperton: Ian Allan, 2007): 134.
22. House of Lords: enquiry on proposed London and Brighton Railway, 27 July 1836. Carlisle was also an early exponent of the Gothick novel with the *Horrors of Oakendale Abbey*, published under the pseudonym of 'Mrs Carver'. See, R.J. Cole, '*Sir Anthony Carlisle*,' (Annals of Science, 3 Sept. 1952): 225-70.
23. *Times*, 1 Aug. 1836: 1.
24. Ibid.

ENDNOTES • 269

25. Francis, *History of English Railways, 1830–45*, Vol. 1: 90.
26. *Times*, 19 Feb. 1839: 7.
27. Ibid.
28. See http://en.wikipedia.org./list_of_rail_accidents_in_United_Kingdom. (accessed Oct. 2016).
29. Smiles, *Life of George Stephenson*: 339.
30. Harrington, *Neuroses*: 17.
31. Ibid: 21.
32. See *Gentleman's Magazine* Vol. 148 (1844): 449.
33. *Brighton Patriot*, 20 Nov. 1835: 1; *Railway Magazine* (December, 1835): 263. Nicholas Cundy 1778–1837, was an architect and engineer who was involved in several abortive railway proposals. See entry in A.W. Skempson's *Engineers of Great Britain and Ireland*. See also *The Times*, 16 Aug. 1836.
34. *Railway Magazine* (April 1836): 58.
35. See *Civil Engineer and Architect's Journal*, V ol.1 (1838): 77.
36. RAIL 634. SEBL&NR. Provisional committee meetings 1836–37.
37. See Pat Milward, 'The Building of the Balcombe Tunnel, 1838–41,' *Sussex Industrial History* No. 30 (2000): 2-25. The fifth tunnel was the short one at Preston Park near Brighton.
38. *Railway Magazine* No. X (December 1836): 446.
39. *Hampshire Advertiser and Salisbury Guardian*, 19 May 1837. Actually there is a short tunnel on the approach to Southampton.
40. *Railway Magazine* Vol. 1 No. 2 (April 1836): 137.
41. *Railway Magazine* No.1 (November 1835): 217.
42. *Times*, 20 April 1836: 7.
43. *Brighton Patriot*, 20 Nov. 1835: 1.
44. George Measom, *Great Western Railway*: 61.
45. Ibid: 48.
46. *Railway Magazine* Vol. 1, No. 2, April 1836: 54.
47. Ibid:. 55.
48. *Civil Engineer and Architect's Journal* (1837–38): 324.
49. *Penny Satirist* (11 Sept. 1841): 2.
50. *The Builder* (17 Jan. 1846): 33.
51. GWR 4th Half yearly meeting held at Bristol, 31 Aug. 1837.
52. *Railway Magazine* (Dec. 1837): 412.
53. John Herapath, 'Of Smoke 'Noise' etc. in Tunnels,' *Mechanics' Magazine* Vol. 23 (11 July 1835):2 77. The paper also discussed lighting and temperature in tunnels.
54. J. Walker and G. Smith, 'On Ventilation and Lighting Tunnels particularly by Reference to the One on the Leeds and Selby Railway.' Institution of Civil Engineering, *Transactions* Vol. 1 (1836): 95-98; and see report by G. West 'On Ventilation,' *Transactions* Vol. 1 (1838): 32.
55. Osborne, *London and Birmingham Railway*: 111.
56. Coghlan, *Iron Road*: 34.
57. *Civil Engineer and Architect's Journal* (1837–38): 354.

58. Kohl, *The King of Saxony's Journey*: 156.
59. Coghlan, *Iron Road Book*: 34.
60. Dionysius Lardner 1793–1859, was born in Ireland and educated at Trinity College, Dublin. He turned to science and wrote numerous papers on algebraic geometry, natural philosophy and astronomy, as well as editing the 133-volume *Cabinet Cyclopedia*. He was a founder member of University College, London, and its first Professor of Natural Philosophy, 1828–31. He wrote on railway matters for the British Association, 1838–41 and had disagreements with Brunel over the speed and power of locomotive *North Star* and what would happen if its brakes failed in the Box Tunnel. His last years were spent in France as a result of a scandal, although he lectured in America on railway matters. He died in Naples and is buried there.
61. *Times*, 16 Jan., 1836: 5.
62. Ibid.
63. Ibid.
64. See Reginald B. Fellows, *History of the Canterbury and Whitstable Railway* (Canterbury: J. Jennings, 1930): 32. The rope-hauled passage took about three and half minutes. Steam haulage was introduced only in 1846.
65. *Railway Magazine* Vol. 1, No. 2 (April 1836): 54-58.
66. Ibid.: 55.
67. Ibid.: 58.
68. *Railway Magazine* (May 1836): 137.
69. *Railway Magazine* (April 1837): 257-59.
70. *Fraser's Magazine* (April 1838): 427.
71. *Railway Magazine* (April 1837): 257.
72. Ibid.: 259.
73. Ibid.: 260.
74. Ibid.: 262.
75. Dr Neil Arnott, *Warming and Ventilation* (London: J. & A. Churchill): 1838.
76. *Bristol Mercury*, 24 March 1838.
77. Coghlan, *Iron Road Book*: 6.
78. Ibid.
79. Bourne, *London and Birmingham Railway*: 17.
80. *The Builder* Vol. 1 (24 June 1843): 241; 'the tunnelling upon the Great Western Railway for the first 20 miles out of Bristol amounts to nearly 4 miles in length'.
81. *The Builder* (5 June 1847): 269.
82. Ibid.
83. See Sir Cusack P. Roney, *Rambles on Railways* (London: Effingham Wilson, 1868): 412-15.
84. See John C. Hughes, 'Fourteen Tunnels to Lime Street,' *Back Track* Vol. 4, No. 4 (July-Aug. 1990): 160-64.
85. C. Nixon, 'Description of the Tunnels between Bristol and Bath'. Institution of Civil Engineers, Proceedings 3 May 1842: 138-41.
86. *Times*, 8 June 1842: 8

87. MT 6/1/122: 12 Aug.1842.
88. *Times,* 29 March 1845: 5. The tunnel had to be closed for a month in 1916 for substantial relining due to falls of rock. See *Times,* 15 Nov. 1916.
89. This was not the end of the Box Tunnel safety saga. On 23 February 1895 there was a fall of 700 tons of rock, closing the tunnel. Traffic was diverted via Bradford-on-Avon. On 5 July 1906, there was a fall of 600 tons of blue clay. A further section of tunnel was then lined in brick. See Colin Maggs: *The GWR Swindon to Bath* (Stroud: Sutton Publications, 2001).
90. *Times,* 21 Sept. 1854: 6; *Bradford Observer,* 21 Sept. 1854; See Board of Trade report on Bramhope Tunnel incident, 2 Oct. 1854: 31-32.
91. *Times,* 1 Jan. 1855: 5.
92. *Times,* 9 July 1849: 7.
93. 'Burying Alive in Railway Tunnels,' *Bradford Observer,* 5 Oct. 1854: 6. The anonymous correspondent considered the future possibility of tunnels wholly on the surface!
94. *The Builder,* 24 Aug. 1844. In the late 1990s the tunnel had to be closed and lined with concrete due to falls of rock.
95. *Morning Chronicle,* 22 July 1837: 3.
96. Osborne, *London and Birmingham Railway*: 82.
97. Wyld, *London and Birmingham Railway Companion*: 33.
98. Ibid.: 86.
99. *Morning Chronicle,* 22 July 1837: 3.
100. Measom, *London and Brighton Railway*: 62.
101. Barman, *Early British Railways:* 22.
102. *Railway Magazine,* Vol. 1 No. 2 (April 1836): 55.
103. *Railway Magazine* (October 1838): 384.
104. Wylde, *London and Birmingham Railway*: 56.
105. Ibid.
106. *Times,* 6 July 1837: 6.
107. Thomas, *The Liverpool and Manchester Railway*, 1980: 41. See also Jeffrey Wells, 'In Search of Light', *Back Track* Jan. 2011: 14-20.
108. *Autobiography of George Osbaldeston 1786–1866* (London: The Bodley Head, 1926): 136-37.
109. *Times,* 22 Sept. 1841: 7.
110. J.B. Jobbins, *The London and Brighton Railway Guide* (London: J.B. Jobbins, 1841): 20.
111. *Times,* 8 July 1841: 6.
112. Jobbins, *London and Brighton Railway*: 20.
113. *Times,* 22 Feb. 1842: 6.
114. David Joy, *Regional History of the Railways of Great Britain* vol. VIII (Newton Abbot: David & Charles, 1975): 35.
115. *Railway Magazine* (Jan. 1837): 16.
116. *Times,* 17 Sept. 1838: 7.
117. *Standard,* 13 Nov. 1844. See Bradley, *The Railways* (2015): 33-40 for early lighting in carriages.

118. RAIL 1149/49 Parliamentary Committee of House of Commons on GWR, 23 March 1835: 69.
119. *Times*, 15 July 1841: 3.
120. *Penny Satirist*, 11 Sept. 1841: 2.
121. Jeffrey Wells, 'In Search of Light' *Back Track* Vol. 25 No. 1 (Jan. 2011): 14.
122. *Bristol Mercury*, 27 March 1842: 4.
123. *Times*, 28 Oct. 1842: 3.
124. *Times*, 27 Sept. 1859: 10.
125. *Times*, 19 Oct. 1859: 11.
126. RAIL 250/116, Directors' Minute Book, 12 July 1860. The Rev. Lord Charles Thynne, 1813–94, was the son of the 2nd Marquess of Bath, a Canon of Canterbury, and Rector of Longbridge Peveril, Wilts.
127. *John Bull* (19 Sept. 1868): 638.
128. Wells, 'In Search of Light'.: 20.
129. *Times*, 9 May 1872: 12.
130. *Times*, 2 May 1851: 8; 8 May: 8; 9 May: 8; 12 May: 8; 14 May:5. See John C. Hughes, 'The Sutton Tunnel Disaster,' *Back Track* Vol. 15, No. 5 (May 2001): 288-90.
131. Board of Trade Report, 22 May 1851.
132. H. Stevens *Sunday Traffic on the London and Brighton Railway* (Brighton: Reference Library 1861). See Jack Simmons, *The Railway in Town and Country 1830–1914* (Newton Abbot: David & Charles, 1986): 237. For detail of the accident, see Board of Trade Report 5 Oct. 1861: 87-90 and Adrian Gray, 'The Clayton Tunnel Disaster' *Back Track,* Vol. 23 No. 10 (Oct. 2009).
133. *Times*, 17 Dec. 1864: 9.
134. *Times*, 19 Dec. 1864: 5.
135. *Times*, 11 June 1866: 9. See also L.T.C. Rolt, *Red for Danger* (Newton Abbot: David & Charles, 1966): 51.
136. Probably the greatest loss of life in a tunnel was in Armi Tunnel, Italy, on 2–3 March 1944, when a train stalled and killed 426 passengers by carbon monoxide poisoning.
137. Barnes, *Midland Railway*: 51-52.
138. Warner, 'Monstrous Cavities': 226-29.
139. *Times*, 7 Oct. 1841: 5.
140. *Illustrated London News* (1 July 1843): 3. Summit Tunnel was the scene of the worst tunnel fire in Britain when on 20 December 1984 a train of petrol tankers derailed and ignited, resulting in a fire that lasted for some days. Flames poured out of several shafts above the moor. It was feared the fabric of the tunnel might have been irrevocably damaged but this was found subsequently not to be the case. See *Times,* 21 Dec. 1984: 28.
141. *Times*, 21 Jan. 1842: 6.
142. *Times*, 30 Jan. 1850: 7.
143. *Times*, 2 July 1850: 8.
144. *Times*, 1 Nov. 1855: 5.
145. *Times*, 5 June 1858: 9 and 7 June: 9.

146. RAIL 250/115, 22 Oct. 1841.
147. *Times*, 6 Aug. 1842: 4.
148. William Peters, *Railway Dangers* (London: Effingham Wilson, 1853): 15.
149. Ibid.: 21.
150. Ibid.: 24.
151. RAIL 250/115, 8 Jan. 1841.
152. *Liverpool Mercury*, 9 Sept. 1836 and *Railway Magazine* (Oct. 1836).
153. Regulations printed in full in Head, *Stokers and Pokers*: 199-200.
154. Ibid.: 201-202.
155. *The Lady Newspaper*, 14 Aug. 1847: 151.
156. Alfred Ogan, *Rail Collisions Prevented* (London: G.T. Pope 1855): 11.
157. Board of Trade, Railway Accident Reports, 17 and 23 March 1854; www.railarchive.co.uk
158. See Harrington, 'The Railway Journey': 229-59 for fear of travelling in tunnels.
159. 'Railroads, their Past History, Present Conditions and Future Prospects,' *Fraser's Magazine for Town and Country* Vol. XVII (April 1838): 431.
160. *The Railway Traveller's Handbook* (London: Lockwood & Co., 1862): 94.
161. Schivelbusch, *The Railway Journey*: 79.
162. Ibid.: 80.
163. *Times*, 7 Jan. 1853: 5.
164. Ibid.
165. *Times*, 14 July 1864: 10.
166. *Times*, 21 April.1862: 10.
167. *Times*, 13 Sept. 1865: 11. Perhaps this inspired the 1899 film, *The Kiss in the Dark*. See Lee Grieveson and Peter Kramer, 'The Kiss in the Tunnel,' Chapter 3 *The Silent Cinema Reader* (London: Routledge): 2004.
168. See *Times*, 24 July 1881: 5; Nov. 7: 11; Nov. 9: 9 for the subsequent trial, which was reported at great length.
169. *Birmingham Daily Post*, 29 Nov. 1866: 8.
170. *Punch*, 16 Jan. 1864.
171. Warner. 'Monstrous Cavities': 228.
172. Quoted by Richard Pike in *Railway Adventures and Anecdotes* (London, Hamilton Adams, 1884, reprinted Nabu Press, USA, 2009): 120.
173. Nicholas Daly, 'Blood on the Tracks, Sensation Drama, the Railway and the Dark Face of Modernity,' *Victorian Studies* vol. 42, no.1 (Autumn, 1998–99): 50.
174. Ibid.
175. Performed at the Princess's Theatre in Oxford Street.
176. Dion Boucicault was the reputed son of Dionysius Lardner, and was apprenticed to Lardner as a civil engineer before taking up acting. Boucicault's eldest son, Willie, was killed in a rail accident at Abbots Ripton near Huntingdon in 1876.
177. Daly, 'Blood on the Tracks': 57.
178. *Times*, 30 Nov. 1861: 5.
179. University of Kent Theatre Collection UKC/CALB/AFT/LET: 190645.
180. *Times*, 17 Aug. 1868: 4.

181. See Martin Meisel et.al., *Scattered Chiaroscuro, in Melodrama, Stage Picture, Screen,* (London: BFI, 1994): 68-69.
182. Daly, 'Blood on the Tracks'.: 69.
183. Wosk, *Breaking Frame:* 56-60.
184. The collision in a tunnel recorded by Dickens in his 1850 record remains a mystery. While, as we have seen earlier in the chapter, two trains broke down in Blackheath Tunnel in 1850, they did not cause a collision. There is no record of a collision or incident in a tunnel in the 1850 monthly editions of *Household Words*. See Ewald Mengel, *The Railway through Dickens's World* (Frankfurt- am-Main: Peter Lang, 1989).
185. *Household Words,* 29 Nov. 1851: 217-20.
186. Norman Gash, *Robert Surtees and Early Victorian Society* (Oxford: Oxford University Press, 1993): 352-53.
187. F.S. Williams, *Our Iron Road* (1852): 369.
188. In 1867, W.F. Mills analysing Board of Trade figures for 1841 to 1865 quotes this figure; see Simon Bradley, *The Railways* (London: Profile Books, 2015): 143.
189. Wikipedia.org. List of railway accidents in the United Kingdom. It is also worth recording that on the evening of 3 September 1878 more than 650 passengers were drowned when the pleasure steamer *Princess Alice* collided with a collier, *Byward Castle,* in the Thames off North Woolwich.
190. Rolt, *Red for Danger*: 50.
191. Schivelbusch, *The Railway Journey*: 130.
192. Charles Dickens, 'Poetry on the Railways,' *Household Words,* Vol. XI (1855): 414-18.
193. Birmingham City Art Gallery and Museum.
194. Words first used on a memorial in Ely Cathedral south transept to William Pickering and Reginald Edgar, two workers killed constructing the Ely–Norwich Railway in 1845, and subsequently published as a ballad 'The Spiritual Railway' in a hand bill by James Lindsay of Glasgow in 1852.
195. See Denault and Landis, 'Motion and Means', www.holyoke.edu/courses/vschwart/incl_rev/rs/denault.htm.
196. Godwin, *An Appeal to the Public on the Subject of Railways* (London: J. Weale, 1837): 41.
197. Ibid.: 30.
198. Ibid.: 32.
199. Ibid.: 8.
200. Kemble, *Record of a Childhood*: 160-61.
201. Smiles, *George Stephenson*: 334.
202. *Letters of Queen Victoria 1837–61* Vol. 1, 1837–43 (London: John Murray, 1908): 404.
203. Schivelbusch, *The Railway Journey*: 130.

CHAPTER 6

1. Schivelbusch, *The Railway Journey*: 175.
2. Simms, *Practical Tunnelling*, 1844: 133-41.
3. Ibid: 134.

ENDNOTES • 275

4. Gordon Biddle and O.S. Nock, *The Railway Heritage of Britain, 150 Years of Railway Architecture and Engineering* (London: Michael Joseph, 1983): XX.
5. Bristol Univ. Brunel Archive. small sketchbook drawings, DM162/8//1/4, 1835. (Brunel Archive hereafter referred to as DM.) His designs for the pumping stations on the South Devon Railway were inspired by Venetian campanile such as those of St Mark's Basilica and the Church of the Friars.
6. See Michael M. Chrimes, 'Robert Stephenson and Planning the construction of the London and Birmingham Railway.' Proceedings of the 1st International Construction Congress, Madrid, 2003, *Construction History* (2003): 599-606.
7. Gordon Biddle, *The Railway Surveyors* (London: Ian Allan and Railway Property Board, 1990): 65.
8. See C.R. Clinker, 'Leicester and Swannington Railway,' *Transactions of Leicestershire Archaeological Society* Vol. XXX (1954): 64-66.
9. Ibid.
10. Several websites credit Linslade Tunnel as the earliest to have castellated portals, however Grosmont is plainly earlier if one includes rope haulage.
11. Francis Whishaw, *Analysis of Railways and Projected Railways of England and Wales* (London: John Weale): 290.
12. *The National Gazetteer of Great Britain and Ireland* (London: A. Fullarton, 1838).
13. Unspecified journal (Aug 1834) London Borough of Camden Archive, Heal Coll. A1X 140.
14. John Carey, *New Map of London and its Environs* (1836) Guildhall Museum Map coll. No. 279.
15. Act 7, George IV c25, 1827.
16. Act 5 & 6, Victoria c78.
17. See Edward Walton, *Old and New London* Vol. 5 (London: Cassell, 1878): 287-300 'Primrose Hill and Chalk Farm'.
18. London and Birmingham Railway Bill 1832, parchment Bill f. 34. With the proposed High Speed Two (HS2) from London to Birmingham in 2010, due for completion in 2035, concern has been expressed by residents of Primrose Hill over the proposed tunnel beneath Chalcot Square in the proposed route, *Times*, 9 June 2010: 37.
19. *The Civil Engineer and Architect's Journal* (Oct 1837–Dec. 1838): 125.
20. *The Architecture Magazine* (1839): 681.
21. Whishaw, *Analysis of Railways*: 227.
22. *Times*, 14 July 1837: 6; *John Bull* (17 July 1837): 339.
23. *Peter Parley's Annual*: 129.
24. Brian Morgan, *Civil Engineering, Railways* (London: Longman, 1971): 43.
25. Osborne, *London and Birmingham Railway*: 81.
26. *Times*, 15 Nov. 1852: 2 and 16 Feb. 1854: 10.
27. On the map it will be seen to run beneath King Henry Road.
28. Roscoe, *London and Birmingham Railway*: 56.
29. Ibid.: 98.
30. RAIL 384/328 c.1835–37.
31. RAIL 384/336. c.1835.

32. See Henry Noel Humphreys, 'Provincial Tour,' *Architectural Journal*, Vol. 5 (1838): 681-82. The Cloaca Maxima is the great sewer of Rome cut in *c.*600 BC.
33. Thomas Roscoe, *Home and Country Scenes on each Side of the Line of the London and Birmingham Railway* (London: Charles Tilt, 1840): 108.
34. See *Architecture Magazine* (1838): 683; described as Egyptian and praised for the use of fine bluish grey stone for string courses set into a face of red sandstone.
35. See Hepple, thesis: 148.
36. See Biddle, *British Historic Railway Buildings:* 247.
37. See Cliff Williams, *Driving the Clay Cross Tunnel: Navvies on the Derby–Leeds Railway* (Cromford: Scarthan Books, 1984).
38. RAIL 530/29.
39. Ibid.
40. *Times*, 18 Feb. 1837: 7.
41. *Civil Engineer and Architect's Journal* (Oct 1837–Dec. 1838): 236.
42. Biddle: *British Historic Railway Buildings:* 259.
43. RO D615/m/10.
44. E.W. Twining, 'The Original Tunnels of the Great Western Railway' *Railway Magazine*, Vol. 25 (Oct. 1909): 297-301.
45. Brunel-Noble, *The Brunels, Father and Son*: 107.
46. RAIL 1149/5, letter, 2 April 1839.
47. See John Binding, *Bristol Temple Meads* (Oxford: OPC 2001): 41.
48. Bristol University Social Sciences Library, Special Collections.
49. George Henry Gibbs, *Correspondence*, ed. Jack Simmons (Bath: Adam & Dart, 1971): 69.
50. Brunel Archive DM 162/10/2, folio 31-34, 13 June 1836.
51. DM 162/8/1/3 GWR sketchbook 11/folio 42.
52. www.networkrail.co.uk/VirtualArchive/box-tunnel.
53. DM 162/8/1/3/GWR Sketchbook 11 folio 41.
54. DM162/8/1/2/Small Sketchbook 27 folio 33.
55. DM162/8/1/3/GWR Sketchbook 11 folio 42.
56. NRCA1 10031.
57. NRCA1 10034 and NRCA1 10032.
58. DM162/8/1/4, misc. sketchbook 1 folio 55, DM 162/8/1/4, misc. sketchbook 1/folio 56.
59. RAIL 1149/5 20 March 1839: 98.
60. DM162/8/1/4, 1835 Misc. Sketchbook, folio 56.
61. DM162/8/1/41, Misc. Sketchbook folio 56, dated 9 March 1838.
62. NRCA1 10034. See www.networkrail;.co.uk/VirtualArchive/box-tunnel (accessed Oct. 2016).
63. NRCA1 10032.
64. DM162/8/1/4/ GWR Sketchbook, folio 6, 1838, index xyz.
65. *Penny Satirist*, 4 Sept. 1841.
66. *Punch* (31 Aug. 1844).
67. Angus Buchannan, *Brunel* (London: Hambledon & Lowden, 2002): 73.

68. RAIL 250/82: 44. In the Box tithe map of December 1838, five members of the Wiltshire family are listed as owning land in the vicinity of the proposed railway track. The family mansion of Shockerwick was, however, across the Box Brook in Somerset.
69. RAIL 250/82 (20 Nov. 1837): 94.
70. Wiltshire County Archives, Tithe map of Parish of Box, December 1838. See also HL/PO/PB/5//1/1 (6 July 1835): 392.
71. DM 162/8/1/3 GWR Sketchbook 5 (1838): 34 & 35.
72. RAIL 1149/1839: Brunel Letter Book (23 March 1839).
73. RAIL 250/107: GWR Sub–Committee on Progress of Work (20 Sept. & 18 Oct. 1839).
74. RAIL 250/107 (3 Jan. 1840).
75. RAIL 250/107 (12 Feb. 1840).
76. RAIL 250/114.
77. E.T. MacDermot, *History of the Great Western Railway,* Vol. 1, 1833–63 (London: GWR, 1927): 66.
78. ICE, HEW 381.
79. Adrian Vaughan, 'Brunel as a Creator of Environment,' in *Conserving the Railway Heritage,* ed. P. Burman and M. Stratton (London: E. & F. Spon, 1997): 83.
80. Adrian Vaughan, *Brunel, Engineering Knight Errant* (London: John Murray, 1992): 31.
81. DM162/8/1/4/ (1835) Sketchbook folio 10.
82. *Bristol Mercury,* 17 Dec. 1836.
83. The estate was later bought by the Carr family and the adjacent woodland is known as Carr's Wood. The house was demolished in 1960.
84. DM162/8/1/4/ (1836) Sketchbook 1, folio 18.
85. DM162/8/1/3/ GWR Sketchbook 5 (1838) folio 19.
86. RAIL 1149/49: 40 (23 March 1835).
87. *Railway Magazine* (Dec. 1838): 449.
88. RAIL 1149/3 (letter 18 Dec. 1837).
89. Network Rail Archive. York and DM162/8/1/3/GWR Sketchbook 5 (1838) folio 19, two pencil drawings.
90. David Brooke, 'The Equity Suit of McIntosh versus the Great Western Railway,' *Journal of Transport History,* 3rd Series (Sept. 1996): 141-42.
91. RAIL 1149/4 (letter, 2 Oct. 1838).
92. According to George Measom, *The Illustrated Guide to the Great Western Railway* (London: Griffin, Bohn, 1852): 56 this was 'the most disagreeable part of the whole journey'.
93. Brooke, The Equity Suit: 141.
94. DM162/8/1/4/ Sketchbook (1836) drawing, folio 7.
95. DM162/8/1/4/ Sketchbook (1836) drawing folio 6; see also Brooke, The Equity Suit: 141-42.
96. DM142/8/1/4/ Sketchbook (1836) folio 5.
97. RAIL 1149/2. (Letter 24 April 1837).
98. *Railway Magazine* (Dec. 1838): 445.

99. DM162/8/1/4/ Sketchbook (1835) folio 81; DM162/8/1/3/Sketchbook 6 (1835) folio 72.
100. DM162/8/1/3/ Sketchbook (1835) folio 72.
101. DM162/8/1/3/Sketchbook 6, folio 20.
102. DM162/8/1/3/GWR Sketchbook 7 (1839) folios 17-18.
103. DM162/8/1/3/GWR Sketchbook 8 (1839) folio 30.
104. Ibid.: folio 34.
105. Ibid.: folio 34.
106. DM162/8/1/3/GWR Sketchbook 5 (19 Sept. 1838): folio 8.
107. Isambard Brunel, *Life of Isambard Kingdom Brunel* (London: Longman Green, 1870): 83.
108. Whishaw: 148.
109. Churton: 194.
110. *Railway Magazine* (Dec.1838): 445.
111. Whishaw: 148.
112. DM162/8/1/3/Sketchbook (13 Dec.1835) folio.76.
113. DM162/8/1/3/Sketchbook 7 (undated) folio. 39.
114. RAIL 1149/5 (letters, 11 Feb.1840).
115. See Neil Mattingley and Gareth Slater, *Bradford's Railways*, Bradford-on-Avon Preservation Trust, (2007) and Tim Mowl, *A Trumpeter at a Distant Gate* (London: Yale, 1988).
116. On the former London and Birmingham Railway, Blisworth to Peterborough branch, and Lancashire and Yorkshire Railway respectively; see Leslie James, *A Chronology of the Construction of Britain's Railways*, 1778–1855 (Shepperton: Ian Allan, 1983).
117. *The Builder* (3 Aug. 1844): 388.
118. Christopher Awdry, *Brunel's Broad Gauge Railway* (Oxford: OPC, 1992): 71.
119. *Bradford Observer*, 12 July 1849.
120. Robin Leleux, *Regional History of the Railways: the East Midlands* (Newton Abbot: David & Charles, 1976): 47.
121. See *The Nottingham and Derby Railway Companion* (London: Hamilton Adams & Co., 1839): 23.
122. See Tim Warner, 'Leicestershire Landowners and the Railway: Resistance and Co-operation,' *Leicestershire Archaeological & Historical Society Transactions* Vol. LXI (1987): 51-60; see also Frederick Williams, *The Midland Railway, its Rise and Progress.* (London: Strachan & Co., 1876): 291.
123. E.G. Barnes, *The Rise of the Midland Railway 1844–1874* (London: George Allen & Unwin, 1966): 32.
124. Jobbins, *London and Brighton Railway*: 20.
125. He was High Sheriff of Sussex in 1820. There is no evidence in surviving Campion letters in the National Archives.
126. David Cole, 'Mocatta's Stations for the Brighton Railway,' *Journal of Transport History*, Vol. 3, No. 3 (1957–58): 154-55.
127. University of London Library, Rastrick Papers, MS242 111 (2) Diary 1840.
128. Univ. Lond., Rastrick Papers, MS242 111 (3) Diary 1842.

129. RAIL 386/41. For William Hoof, 1788–1855, see *Biographical Dictionary of Civil Engineers of Great Britain & Ireland,* Vol. 1, ed. A.W. Skempton, (London: ICE: 2008).
130. Elton Collection. Coalbrookdale Museums of Iron, Ironbridge, AE. 1978: 59.
131. RAIL 386/71 and RAIL 386/15.
132. Measom, *Guide to the Brighton Railway*: 46. See also Diana Gaye, 'My Ideal Cottage,' *Ideal Home* (June 1976): 52-53.
133. RAIL 386/91/ (34).
134. Barbara Jones, *Follies and Grottoes* (London: Batsford, 1953: 142).
135. See Malcolm Dawes, 'Clayton Tunnel Cottage,' *Sussex Archaeological Society Newsletter* (Jan. 2010): 6.
136. *Civil Engineer and Architect's Journal* (Oct. 1837–Dec. 1838): 46.
137. *Times*, 18 June 1841: 7.
138. RAIL 386/91/ (2).
139. I am grateful to David Porter, the present resident of Tunnel Cottage, for showing me his photographs of surviving gas brackets within tunnel wall recesses.
140. The relevant Pevsner volume, under Kirton-in-Lindsay, attributes it to John Weighton and Matthew Hadfield, who designed stations on the line. N. Pevsner, John Harris and Nicholas Antram, *Buildings of England, Lincolnshire* (London: Yale, 1989): 42.3.
141. Biddle and Nock, *Railway Heritage of Britain:* 43; *The Survey of London,* Vol. 26, London County Council, (1956) Lambeth, southern area, ill. 39b.
142. See Biddle, *Britain's Historic Railway Buildings*: 708. Joseph Mitchell was also responsible for the nearby crenellated Killiecrankie viaduct; National Archives of Scotland, RHP 129704-129705, sectional drawings, elevation, detail of tunnel and viaduct at Killiecrankie.
143. G. Drysdale Dempsey, *The Practical Railway Engineer* (London, John Weale, 1855): 236.
144. RAIL 357/30, Leeds and Thirsk Railway, Bramhope contract from commencement to 12 Oct. 1849.
145. RAIL 357/30, Leeds and Thirsk Railway Bramhope Tunnel, contract No. 18.
146. RAIL 357/30, item 853.
147. RAIL 357/30, items 670-73.
148. See Appendix 4.

CHAPTER 7
1. See Williams, *Notes*: 95-96.